POLITICAL

ANALYSIS

Series Editors: B. Guy Peters, Jon Pierre and Gerry Stoker

Political science today is a dynamic discipline. Its substance, theory and methods have all changed radically in recent decades. It is much expanded in range and scope and in the variety of new perspectives – and new variants of old ones – that it encompasses. The sheer volume of work being published, and the increasing degree of its specialization, however, make it difficult for political scientists to maintain a clear grasp of the state of debate beyond their own particular subdisciplines.

The *Political Analysis* series is intended to provide a channel for different parts of the discipline to talk to one another and to new generations of students. Our aim is to publish books that provide introductions to, and exemplars of, the best work in various areas of the discipline. Written in an accessible style, they will provide a 'launching pad' for students and others seeking a clear grasp of the key methodological, theoretical and empirical issues, and the main areas of debate, in the complex and fragmented world of political science.

A particular priority will be to facilitate intellectual exchange between academic communities in different parts of the world. Although frequently addressing the same intellectual issues, research agendas and literatures in North America, Europe and elsewhere have often tended to develop in relative isolation from one another. This series is designed to provide a framework for dialogue and debate which, rather than advocacy of one regional approach or another, is the key to progress.

The series will reflect our view that the core values of political science should be coherent and logically constructed theory, matched by carefully constructed and exhaustive empirical investigation. The key challenge is to ensure quality and integrity in what is produced rather than to constrain diversity in methods and approaches. The series will provide a showcase for the best of political science in all its variety, and demonstrate how nurturing that variety can further improve the discipline.

POLITICAL
 ANALYSIS

Series Editors: B. Guy Peters, Jon Pierre and Gerry Stoker

Political Analysis Series
Series Standing Order
ISBN 978-0-333-78694-9 hardback
ISBN 978-0-333-94506-3 paperback
(outside North America only)

You can receive future titles in this series as they are published by placing a standing order. Please contact your bookseller or, in the case of difficulty, write to us at the address below with your name and address, the title of the series and the ISBN quoted above.

Customer Services Department, Macmillan Distribution Ltd
Houndmills, Basingstoke, Hampshire RG21 6XS, England

The State

Theories and Issues

Edited by
Colin Hay
Michael Lister
and
David Marsh

First published 2006 by
PALGRAVE MACMILLAN
Houndmills, Basingstoke, Hampshire RG21 6XS and
175 Fifth Avenue, New York, N.Y. 10010
Companies and representatives throughout the world

PALGRAVE MACMILLAN is the global academic imprint of the Palgrave Macmillan division of St. Martin's Press, LLC and of Palgrave Macmillan Ltd. Macmillan® is a registered trademark in the United States, United Kingdom and other countries. Palgrave is a registered trademark in the European Union and other countries.

ISBN 978-1-4039-3425-3 hardback

ISBN 978-1-4039-3426-0   ISBN 978-0-230-80227-8 (eBook)
DOI 10.1007/978-0-230-80227-8

This book is printed on paper suitable for recycling and made from fully managed and sustained forest sources.

A catalogue record for this book is available from the British Library.

A catalog record for this book is available from the Library of Congress.

10   9   8   7   6   5   4   3   2   1
15   14   13   12   11   10   09   08   07   06

To Ailsa, Elspeth, Holly, Suzy, Mary, David and Emily

Contents

List of Figures and Tables

Figures

Tables

Slavic Scholastic Culture

Preface and Acknowledgements

This book arises, as many do, out of a sense of dissatisfaction. Our particular frustration, as editors of this volume, arises from our growing dismay at the now very limited range of introductions to the theory of the state available to students of politics, international relations, sociology and cognate disciplines. More frustrating still, those introductions that do exist tend, almost without exception, to focus rather narrowly on what we shall term the 'traditional triumvirate' of pluralism, elite theory and Marxism. They do so, moreover, in a manner that simply assumes that the state we study today is not recognizably different from the state that has formed the subject of the traditional triumvirate's analytical concerns for over a century.

To be fair, virtually no one would now accept that theories of the state come in only one of three varieties, nor that the object of the state theorist's analytical attentions has remained essentially unaltered since the development of pluralism, elite theory and Marxism as approaches to the study of the state. Yet this only makes more glaring the disparity between, on the one hand, a now widely accepted understanding that things have moved on and, on the other, the picture presented of the theory of the state in the standard works used to introduce the concept to students.

Of course, as editors we are by no means totally innocent of the sins we now seek to correct. The text from which the present volume has developed, the first edition of David Marsh and Gerry Stoker's *Theory and Methods in Political Science* (Palgrave, 1995), does contain a section on theories of the state. And, yes, that section is comprised of chapters on . . . pluralism, elite theory, Marxism and the degree of convergence between these perspectives. Whilst we could defend such a focus, we will not seek to do so. If this preface reads like a case for the prosecution, then Part III of the first edition of Marsh and Stoker is exhibit A. That section was dropped from the revised second edition not, as it happens, as an act of contrition, but to make way for a fuller, richer and deeper consideration of the ontological, epistemological and methodological disputes which divide contemporary political analysts. And, serendipitously, that has provided the opportunity for the present volume – a volume dedicated to a consideration of the diversity of theoretical and analytical traditions that have something to say about the nature and development of the contemporary state, a volume committed to identifying the tendencies and counter-tendencies to which the contemporary state is subject, and a volume, above all, which seeks to explore the range of conceptual and theoretical resources on which we can now draw in making sense of the development of the state today.

No project such as this is possible without the dedicated support of one's publisher and the forbearance, understanding and good-will of the chapter authors. We have been exceptionally fortunate in both respects. We would like to thank Steven Kennedy, our exemplary, dedicated and seemingly tireless publisher. At times he has served almost as a fourth editor and there is no chapter that has not benefited from his considerable analytical insight and his editorial acumen. We would also like to thank the individual chapter authors for the efficiency and resourcefulness with which they have responded to our collective editorial requests, however whimsical at times they might have seemed (and may still seem). Thanks are also due to Laura Jenkins for editorial assistance. The editing of the project has proved a remarkably pleasurable experience – would that one could always say the same.

Finally, and as ever, the project would not have been possible without the love and support of our families. It is, appropriately, to them that we dedicate this volume. It is testimony to how grateful we are to them that, unlike our students, they will not be obliged to read it.

Birmingham

COLIN HAY
MICHAEL LISTER
DAVID MARSH

Notes on the Contributors

John Barry is Acting Director of the Institute of Governance and Co-Director of the Centre for Sustainability and Environmental Governance, both at Queen's University Belfast. His main areas of interest are the normative dimensions of green politics, theories of green political economy, and environmental/sustainability governance. He previous works include, *Rethinking Green Politics* (1999), *Environment and Social Theory* (1999), *Citizenship, Sustainability and Environmental Research* (2000), and various edited volumes: *International Encyclopaedia of Environmental Politics* (2001); *Sustaining Liberal Democracy* (2001) and *The Nation-State and the Global Ecological Crisis* (2005). He is also co-leader of the Green Party in Northern Ireland.

Peter Doran is a Visiting Research Fellow at the Institute of Governance at the Queen's University, Belfast, and a Researcher at the Northern Ireland Assembly. He works at the interface of environmental policy and academic writing on critical global environmental politics. He is a contributor to the forthcoming volume on the World Summit on Sustainable Development in Johannesburg, *Furthering Consensus: Meeting the Challenges of Sustainable Development* (2005). Peter is also a senior writer and editor for the International Institute for Sustainable Development's *Earth Negotiations Bulletin* at United Nations conferences on the environment and development.

Mark Evans is Professor of Political Science and Head of the Department of Politics and Provost of Halifax College at the University of York in the United Kingdom. His books include, amongst others: *Charter 88: A Successful Challenge to the British Political Tradition?* (1995); *Constitution-making and the Labour Party* (2003); *Policy Analysis and Process* (2003), with Graeme Wilson; and, *Policy Transfer in Global Perspective* (2004). He is editor of the journal *Policy Studies*, co-ordinator of the *Worldwide Universities Public Policy Network* and has also published a range of articles on different aspects of policy analysis and British politics in the *British Journal of Politics and International Relations, Political Studies, Public Administration* and *Public Policy and Administration*.

Alan Finlayson is Senior Lecturer in the Department of Politics and International Relations, University of Wales Swansea, UK. A political theorist interested in analysing real politics, he is the author of *Making Sense of New Labour* (2003), editor of *Contemporary Political Thought: A Reader* *and Guide* (2004) and co-editor (with Jeremy Valentine) of *Politics and Poststructuralism* (2002). He has also published numerous articles concerned with Northern Irish politics, British politics, media politics and theories of rhetoric.

Matthew Flinders is Senior Lecturer in Politics at the University of Sheffield. He is the author or editor of several books on the inter-relationship between the evolution of the state and models of democracy (most recently, with Ian Bache, *Multi-level Governance*, 2004).

Colin Hay is Professor of Political Analysis and Head of the Department of Political Science and International Studies at the University of Birmingham. He is the author of a number of books, including *Political Analysis* (2002), *The Political Economy of New Labour* (1999) and *Re-Stating Social and Political Change* (1996). He is co-editor of the journals *British Politics* and *Comparative European Politics*, and was recently awarded the UKPAC prize for 2004 for an article published in *Public Administration*.

Andrew Hindmoor is a Senior Lecturer in the School of Political Science and International Studies at the University of Queensland. He lectures and writes about various aspects of British politics, public policy and rational choice theory. He has recently published *New Labour at the Centre: Constructing Political Space* (2004) and is currently working on a detailed text on rational choice theory to be published by Palgrave Macmillan in the series *Political Analysis*.

Nicola Hothi is currently working as an Executive Consultant in Public Policy in the UK. Nicola was awarded the UK Consultant of the Year Prize 2004 (awarded annually to the best consultant in Public Policy who has made a tangible difference in social, political and ethical fabric and harmony across the international arena). She is the author of *Globalization and Manufacturing Decline: Aspects of British Industry* (2005) and is currently working on a monograph entitled *UK Plc* (to be published 2006).

Johanna Kantola obtained her PhD from the University of Bristol, where she is currently working as a post-doctoral researcher. She has published articles about gender and the state in the *International Feminist Journal of Politics*, *European Journal of Women's Studies* and *European Political Science* and contributed chapters to various edited volumes. She is also affiliated to the Political Science Department at the University of Helsinki (Finland), where she published a monograph titled *The Mute, the Deaf and the Lost: Gender Equality at the University of Helsinki Political Science Department* (2005). She is the co-editor of the *Finnish Women's Studies Journal*.

Michael Lister is Lecturer in Politics at the University of Surrey, and was previously an ESRC/Office of the Deputy Prime Minister Post-doctoral Research Fellow at the University of Birmingham. He has published articles on citizenship and political participation in *Government and Opposition* and *Contemporary Politics*, contributed to various edited collections, and is currently researching the impact of local governance institutions upon citizenship participation.

David Marsh is Professor of Political Sociology and Head of Department of the Department of Sociology at the University of Birmingham. He is the author/co-author or editor/co-editor of ten books, including *Theory and Methods in Political Science* (2002), *Policy Networks in Comparative Perspective* (1998), *Marxism and Social Science* (1999) *and Post-war British Politics in Perspective* (1999).

James Martin is Senior Lecturer in the Politics Department at Goldsmiths College, University of London, UK. He has published on Italian political theory of the interwar period, particularly the work of Antonio Gramsci, and contemporary poststructuralist and post-Marxist theory. He is author of Gramsci's *Political Analysis* (1998), editor of *Antonio Gramsci: Critical Assessments* (2002) and co-author, with Steve Bastow, of *Third Way Discourse* (2003). He has recently co-edited, with Terrell Carver, the series entitled Palgrave Advances in Continental Political Thought.

Matthew Paterson is Associate Professor of Political Science at the University of Ottawa, Canada. He has published widely on the politics of climate change, in particular in *Global Warming and Global Politics* (1996), and more generally on critical approaches to global environmental politics, including *Understanding Global Environmental Politics* (2000). He is currently working on a book on cars.

B. Guy Peters is Maurice Falk Professor of American Government at the University of Pittsburgh. He is also Professor II at Hogskolan i Bodo in Norway and at the City University of Hong Kong. Among his recent publications are the *Handbook of Public Administration*, co-edited with Jon Pierre, 2003. *The Quest for Control: Politicization in the Civil Service*, co-edited with Jon Pierre, 2004 and the second edition of *Institutional Theory in Political Science* (1999).

Jon Pierre is Professor of Political Science at the University of Gothenburg and adjunct professor at the University of Pittsburgh. He previously held a chair in Politics at the University of Strathclyde. He is co-author, with Guy Peters, of *Governance, Politics and the State* (2000) and *Governing Complex*

Societies (2005), co-editor, with Guy Peters, of *Handbook of Public Administration* (2003) and editor of *Debating Governance* (2000).

Vivien A. Schmidt is Professor of International Relations and Jean Monnet Professor of European Integration at Boston University. She has published widely in the areas of European political economy, institutions, and public policy as well as on the philosophy of the social sciences. Her books include *Policy Change and Discourse in Europe*, co-edited with Claudio Radaelli, (2005); *The Futures of European Capitalism* (2002); *Welfare and Work in the Open Economy*, co-edited with F. W. Scharpf (2 vols, 2000); *From State to Market? The Transformation of French Business and Government* (1996); and *Democratizing France* (1990), as well as over seventy articles and chapters in books. Her forthcoming book: *Democracy in Europe: The EU and National Polities* (2006) explores the impact of the European integration on national democracies.

Martin Smith is Professor of Politics at the University of Sheffield. He has published widely on public policy and British politics. He is currently directing an ESRC project on policy delivery in the Home Office. He is editor of the journal *Political Studies*.

Nicola Smith is a Research Fellow at the Department of Political Science and International Studies at the University of Birmingham. She is the author of *Showcasing Globalization? The Political Economy of the Irish Republic* (2005). Nicola is currently undertaking, with Colin Hay, an ESRC-funded cross-country survey of policy-makers' attitudes to globalization and European integration.

Georg Sørensen is Professor of Political Science at the University of Aarhus, Denmark. His recent books include: *The Transformation of the State: Beyond the Myth of Retreat* (2004); *Changes in Statehood* (2001); with Robert Jackson, *Introduction to International Relations: Theories and Approaches* (2003); *Democracy and Democratization: Processes and Prospects in a Changing World*, second edition (1998).

Introduction: Theories of the State

COLIN HAY AND MICHAEL LISTER

No concept is more central to political discourse and political analysis than that of the state. Yet, whilst we all tend to think we know what we're talking about when we refer to the state, it is a notoriously difficult concept to define. Since the seventeenth century, when the term was first widely deployed, the concept of the state has been heavily contested (Skinner 1989; Viroli 1992). It remains so today. The state has meant, and continues to mean, a great variety of different things to a great variety of authors from a great variety of perspectives. Part of the aim of this volume is to look at family resemblances in those understandings of the state, in the hope that we might begin to piece together a more coherent picture of *what this state is* and, indeed, *how it is developing*. Yet that is no easy task, for whatever family resemblances we might discern are unlikely to hide the very considerable variations between contending accounts both of what the state is and of the trajectory of its development. We should then, from the outset, expect diversity.

Yet whether depicted as an overbearing apparatus of patriarchal oppression or as the very condition of social and political freedom, as an 'ideal collective capitalist' or a fetter on the self-regulating capacity of the market, few commentators would disagree that the concept of the state is fundamental to social, political and economic analysis. The state, for better or worse: mobilizes populations in defence of its realm; regulates, monitors and polices conduct within civil society; intervenes (whether we think we like it or not) within the economy; and regulates (and in some instances controls) the flow of information within the public sphere, to detail merely some of its more obvious activities. Few then would deny the ubiquity or pervasiveness of the influence of the state within modern societies.

Or so we might imagine. For in recent years the very relevance of the concept of the state has come under increasing dispute. In an era of globalization and of complex interdependence among nations it is often argued that the influence of the state (certainly in its incarnation as a nation-state) is waning, its very form and function under challenge. A second aim of the present volume is to review this influential if arguably rather blunt and

1

premature proposition. Indeed, stated most simply, our ambition is to survey the range and diversity of theoretical and conceptual resources within the pantheon of state theory for the analysis of the developmental paths and trajectories of the contemporary state. It is important, before so doing, however, that we put to one side a few contagious myths and popular fictions.

Though the state almost certainly accounts for a higher aggregate share of global GDP than ever before in its history, it attracts considerably less attention than 20 or even 40 years ago when that share was considerably smaller. And although it is frequently suggested that the share of GDP devoted to state-like activities in OECD countries has fallen somewhat since the early 1990s, that fall has proved far less pronounced than many commentators suggested. Rather more accurate, it would seem, is that the rate of increase of state revenue and/or expenditure has lessened somewhat. Moreover, at the time of writing, state expenditure is clearly on the rise once more (see Figures I.1 and I.2). As this suggests, whilst intellectual interest in the state has waxed and waned, the state has remained a constant (arguably even a growing) presence at the heart of contemporary politics. This makes its seeming disappearance from the political analyst's radar in the last two decades somewhat difficult to explain. The result is that the theory of the state, once a raging torrent, is now little more than a trickle, an intellectual backwater traversed only by hardened theorists. A 'return to the state', by no means the first (see, for instance, Evans *et al.* 1985), is now long overdue; and, as many of the chapters in this volume

Figure I.1 *State revenue as a percentage of GDP: OECD, EU15, USA, Australia, 1965–2000*

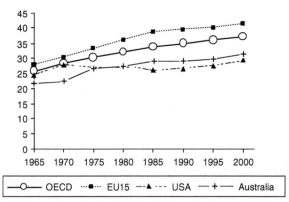

Source: OECD *Revenue Statistics, 1965–2001* (2003); authors' own calculations.

Figure I.2   *State expenditure as a share of GDP: selected OECD countries*

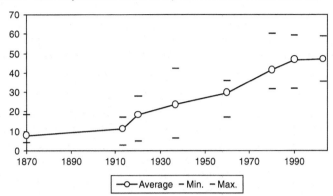

Sources: OECD, *Economic Outlook*; Tanzi and Schuknecht (2000). The data for France, Germany, Italy, Japan, Netherlands, Norway, Sweden, UK and US (the only OECD countries with an uninterrupted series of data) have been calculated by the authors.

make clear, the beginnings of such a return might just about be discerned in a number of contemporary developments from a diverse range of theoretical perspectives.

It would be presumptuous to think that a volume such as this might contribute in all but the most meagre of ways to such a 'return to the state'. What it can hope to offer, however, is something of a stock-taking exercise. If the continued centrality of the state to contemporary political life is to be acknowledged and reflected in the accounts of political dynamics offered by contemporary political analysts (as we think it should), then it is crucial that we interrogate the range and diversity of theoretical resources at our disposal to interrogate the state. That is the more modest aim of this volume.

In this relatively brief introductory chapter we examine first the emergence and development of the distinctive concept of the modern state in European political thought. We then turn to the still considerable influence of the Weberian approach to, and definition of, the state in more contemporary state theory. We show how the Weberian understanding of the state continues to exert a powerful influence on the traditional triumvirate of state theories – pluralism, elite theory and Marxism. We turn next to the challenge to the ascendancy of this mainstream conception of the state posed by Foucauldian, discourse-analytical and, above all, feminist perspectives. We conclude by considering the prospects for the state, and for the theory of the state, in an era of supposed globalization and neoliberal retrenchment.

Defining the state

Introductions to the state tend, unremarkably, to begin by addressing the question of definition. All too frequently, however, they fall short of providing an answer. The importance of defining the state is all the greater given that, as Dunleavy and O'Leary note, the state is not a material object; it is a conceptual abstraction (1987: 1). As such its utility as a concept cannot and should not be taken for granted since it does not have a self-evident material object of reference. Its utility must be demonstrated; and in order to demonstrate that utility we must first be clear about what we are referring to.

That may sound fine in principle, yet the question of definition raises particular problems for a theoretically pluralistic volume such as this. Indeed, it is sorely tempting, in a text which makes something of a virtue of the diversity of theoretical resources we have on offer to interrogate the role of the state, to suggest that this is a question for each distinct approach to the state – and to leave it at that. And as already indicated and at the risk of sounding trite, the state does indeed mean a variety of different things in a variety of different perspectives. Yet we cannot quite leave it at that. For whilst the state may, and indeed does, mean different things to different authors, the commonality between seemingly diverse definitions should not be overlooked – and cannot be allowed to provide an excuse for a failure to consider the ontology of the state – what the state *is*. In order to help us achieve this, and to offer some historical context for the chapters which follow, we consider first the genealogy of the concept of the state before turning to by far the most influential definition of the modern state – that offered by Weber.

Before doing so, however, it is first important to say something about the development of the modern state itself – or, at least, the development of the political institutions now generally held to characterize the modern state (for a far more extensive treatment see Gill 2003). For, unremarkably, our conception of the state has not developed in isolation from the development of the institutions we associate with the state. We cannot consider one without the other.

The development of the modern state

As John A. Hall and G. John Ikenberry note in their useful introduction to the term, 'most of human history has not been graced by the presence of states' (1989: 16). This is undoubtedly the case. Moreover, whilst the term has been used retrospectively to refer to mechanisms and processes of political governance arising in Mesopotamia as early as 3000 BC, it is only since the seventeenth century that human history has been graced by the concept of the state. According to most conventional accounts, the origins of the state lie in the transition from the nomadic subsistence of hunter-gatherers to more agrarian societies characterized, increasingly, by organized agriculture (Hall 1986; Mann 1988; Sahlins 1974). Indeed, it was the relative geographical immobility of agricultural production that led to the development of the institutions and infrastructure capable of governing and projecting power, albeit at first in a rather diffuse way, over a specific and delineated territory. As Hall and Ikenberry again note, 'irrigation works – and date and olive trees – tie agricultural producers very firmly to the land, and thus make them better fodder for the state' (1989: 18). In this way the institutional capacity to project power over a territory which we now associate with the state owes its origins to the historical accident of the replacement, first in Mesopotamia, Meso-America, the Indus river valley, China and Peru and then more generally, of hunting and gathering by agriculture.

In these initial stages of its development, the state was largely despotic and coercive in the manner in which it exercized power over a population. And it is in this context that a second key factor becomes important – religion. Hunter-gatherer communities tended to be tribal – based on kinship ties – whereas the agrarian states which replaced them were not. This made them both rather more reliant upon coercion and, in the absence of strong kinship relations amongst their members, rather more fragile politically when that coercion was challenged. In this context, as Patricia Crone (1989) demonstrates, it was the capacity of religion to lend legitimacy to the organized and increasingly centralized use of coercive power (through the appeal to divine authority) that made possible, where otherwise it might not have been, the consolidation of state power. This, in turn, facilitated the further development of the institutional capacity to govern and regulate a geographical territory and, with it, the capacity to mobilize militarily. The association between the state and military might was, then, established early on and arguably persists to the present day. Conquest rapidly became the primary mechanism through which the institutional form of the state became diffused, since the organizational capacity which the state developed conferred upon it a competitive advantage when it confronted pre-state-like societies.

If the origins of the state itself lie in Mesopotamia, then it is to Western Europe that we must turn if we are to establish the origins of the modern state. What is invariably taken to characterize the modern state is the simultaneous combination of, on the one hand, its claim to act as a public power responsible for the governance of a tightly delineated geographical territory and, on the other, its separation from those in whose name it claims to govern. The modern state is, then, an institutional complex claiming sovereignty for itself as the supreme political authority within a defined territory for whose governance it is responsible.

The factors that made possible the development of such an institutional form in Western Europe were, again, both complex and bound up with the role of religious authority. And once again the process was a highly contingent one. It was the church, in particular, that challenged the authority of Imperial Rome. The result was a previously unprecedented degree of cultural homogeneity, as an initially unlikely synthesis of Christian doctrine and the strong legal residue which carried over from the Roman Empire facilitated both the development of consensual trading relations throughout the European economy and the diffusion of the institutional template of the modern state. The result was the birth of the so-called absolutist state in the sixteenth and seventeenth century in Bourbon France, Habsburg Spain and Tudor England. These were the precursors for the institutional complex we now recognize as the state – having a centralized bureaucracy and tax-raising capacity, a standing army, a system of diplomatic relations with other states and, for the most part, clearly delineated and commonly accepted territorial borders.

It is, once again, to Western Europe that the origins of the most recent phase of significant state re-structuring and expansion can be traced. This bout of institutional dynamism, largely confined to the most developed economies and occurring in many cases in the immediate wake of the Second World War, is associated with the rise of the welfare state. It has seen the creation of the most extensive state regimes that the world has ever seen. As we saw in Figures 1a and 1b, these welfare states account, in many cases, for in excess of 50 per cent of GDP and 15 per cent of the total work-force. They represent, at least to date, the highest point in the development of the institutional capacity of the state. Whether they are increasingly anachronistic and a burden on economic growth and prosperity in an ever more closed integrated world economy is a source of very significant debate and a key theme of this volume. Suffice if for now to note that, despite the now customary hyperbole, there would seem to be little evidence to date of their ongoing or imminent demise.

The genealogy of the concept of the state

Having considered the institutional origins and development of the state, we are now better placed to consider and contextualize the development of the concept of the state. Etymologically, the notion of the state is derived from the Latin *status*, meaning literally social status, stature or standing, specifically of an individual within a community. By the fourteenth century the use of the term to refer to the standing or status (indeed to the 'stateliness') of rulers, distinguishing and setting them apart from those subject to their rule, was commonplace. In the idea that the state resides in the body of the ruler, indeed that the state and the 'sovereign' are synonymous, this was a characteristically pre-modern formulation (Shennan 1974; Skinner 1989).

The development of a distinctively modern conception of the state would take a further three centuries – and its development would parallel the emergence of the institutional complex described above as the absolutist state. A first step was taken by the authors of the so-called 'mirror-for-princes' writings, most famously Machiavelli in his *Il Principe* (The Prince; 1532). In this literature, the state (*lo stato*) now became synonymous not only with the prince himself, but with the character of the political regime, the geographical area over which sovereign authority was claimed and maintained, and the very institutions of government required to preserve such authority.

A second development came with the republican political theory of the Renaissance (see Skinner 1978; Viroli 1992). This movement championed the cause of a self-governing republican regime that might inaugurate a 'state' or condition of civic liberty – in Dante's terms *lo stato franco*. Here, at last, we see the emergence of a conception of an autonomous civil and political authority regulating the public affairs of an independent community or 'commonwealth'. The state is here presented as claiming and enjoying a monopoly over the legitimate use of violence, and as deriving the authority for this claim not from the power or stature of its ruler(s), but from the people themselves. The state is referred to for the first time as a distinct apparatus of government which rulers have a duty to maintain and which will outlast their rule, as opposed to an extension of the latter's innate authority.

The final step came with the rise of the absolutist state in Europe in the seventeenth century. Here, in particular in the writings of Bodin and Hobbes, the state is eventually conceptualized as truly separate from the powers of the ruler and the ruled. Three aspects of this formulation set it apart as a distinctively modern conception of the state: (i) individuals within society are presented as subjects of the state, owing duties and their allegiance not to a ruler but to the state itself; (ii) the authority of the state is singular and absolute; and (iii) the state is regarded as the highest form of authority in all matters of civil government (Skinner 1989: 90). Hobbes' *Leviathan* (1651 [1968]), and the rise of the absolutist state which this work reflects, marks the end of the pre-modern concept of the state in which political power is understood in personal and charismatic terms. The state now comes to be seen as a distinct form of authority independent of those who give effect to its power.

The Weberian definition of the modern state

It is this modern conception of the state that still dominates contemporary state theory. Indeed, the definition of the state most often accorded the status of *the* definition the state – the Weberian one – displays considerable similarities with that of Hobbes. Weber, as is often noted, defined the state not in terms of its function but in terms of its *modus operandi*. More specifically, he saw the state in terms of its organization and deployment of the means of coercion and physical force. As he explained, 'a compulsory political organization with continuous operations will be called a "state" insofar as its administrative staff successfully upholds the claim to the monopoly of the legitimate use of physical force in the enforcement of its order' (Weber 1921/1978: 54).

Two aspects of this definition are particularly noteworthy, providing as they do the basis, and/or point of departure, for much contemporary reflection on the state. First, the state for Weber is a set of institutions with a dedicated personnel. This observation has been taken up and developed by a diverse group of neo-Weberians, neo-statists and institutionalists working in particular in the USA (see Chapter 4). They argue that the differentiation of the state from civil society allows state managers to develop an array of distinct interests, preferences and capacities which cannot be explained by reference merely to societal factors.

In their efforts to 'bring the state back in' as both an actor and an independent force in social causation, the neo-statists have emphasized both the autonomy of the state from society and the power of 'state-centred' explanations of political outcomes. More specifically they have concentrated on: the ability of state managers to exercise power independently and autonomously of non-state forces; the 'infrastructural power' of the state to infiltrate, control, supervise, police and regulate modern societies; and the ways in which the specific institutional structures of particular states at particular moments in time may enhance or undermine such general capacities. Such an idea has also proved increasingly influential in neo-Marxist state theory (see, for instance, Block 1990 and, more generally, the discussion in Chapter 5), in neo-pluralism (see Chapter 1) and, albeit in a rather different form, in public choice theory (see Chapter 3).

Second, Weber regards the modern state as wielding a monopoly of authoritative rule-making within a bounded territory. This is in turn backed by a monopoly of the means of physical violence within this same territorial space. Institutionalists and neo-statists, whose indebtedness to Weber is perhaps clearest, have concentrated on the mechanisms by which the state preserves (or at least seeks to preserve) its monopoly of authoritiative rule-making. They have focused in particular on the question of political legitimacy, on the often democratic and/or nationalist strategies and mechanisms through which it is constructed and sustained, on the processes leading to its withdrawal, on the consequences for the always fragile balance between coercion and consent in modern societies, and on the mechanisms through which legitimacy might be re-established (through changes of regime and, in some instances, revolution). Yet, these too have increasingly become concerns for neo-Marxists (particularly those keen to develop the insights of Gramsci) and neo-pluralists. Other neo-statists, the so-called war-centred state theorists, have focused on the state's supposed monopoly of the means of violence and in particular on the military dimension of state power. Stimulated perhaps by the intuitive appeal of Charles Tilly's remark that 'wars make states and states make war' (1975), such theorists have considered the war-making capacity of the state, the extent to which the internal organization of the state apparatus reflects military imperatives, and the consequences of war-making and of mobilization for war on the evolution and transformation of the state itself — in short, on the relationship between war-making and state-shaping. Such themes have also been taken up more recently by feminist scholars, most notably perhaps Cynthia Enloe (1990), in interrogating the complex relationship between the state, organized violence, militarism and masculinity (see Chapter 6).

As the above discussion would seem to indicate, a substantial and rather disparate literature can trace some lineage from the Weberian conception of the state. Yet despite this seeming diversity, neo-Weberian perspectives do tend to display certain shared characteristics – and indeed weaknesses. First, such theories have tended to concentrate rather one-sidedly on political factors internal to the state. As a consequence they have often relegated political forces outside and beyond the state, such as social movements and pressure groups, to a marginal role. Second, much neo-Weberian theory rests on the rather tenuous distinction between state and societal variables and an explanatory emphasis on the former at the expense the latter. In the context of the attempt to 'bring the state back into' American social science in the 1970s and 1980s this tilting of the stick towards the side of the state was entirely appropriate. Yet now that 'state-centred' approaches have become as, if not more, dominant than their 'society-centred' counterparts ever were, it is crucial that we acknowledge that the casualty of both perspectives has been the attempt to develop an understanding of the complex and ever changing relationship *between* the state and society, the public and the private. This is the challenge to which contemporary theories of the state must now respond (see Chapter 12).

The concept of the state

It is all very well to have a clear and consistently articulated conception of the state and all the better if that is framed in a clearly articulated definition of the state. Yet, given that the state is not an immediately transparent or self-evident material object, this is merely one step in defending a view of politics which places the state at centre stage.

To develop a concept (and, by extension, a theory) of the state is to look at politics in a particular way. It is a choice which can and should be defended. This is an important point with clear implications. Political analysis can – and often does – proceed in the absence of a concept of the state (see, for instance, Easton 1967; Allen 1990). If we are, then, to justify a 'return to the state', we must first provide an answer to the question 'What conceptual work does this concept (or theoretical abstraction) do'? Stated more starkly still, 'What analytical purchase does the concept of the state offer the political analyst?

However good, and however obvious, a question this might seem, it is not one to which theorists of the state, with a few notable exceptions, have rushed to provide answers. Even Dunleavy and O'Leary (1987: 1–6), who, as we have seen, perhaps get closest to tabling this as the relevant question, fail to provide an answer, contenting themselves with noting that the state is an analytical abstraction and then pointing to certain family resemblances in the definitions of the state offered by theorists of the state. In so doing they identify the kinds of theoretical abstraction that state theorists are appealing to in invoking the state as a category, differentiating in so doing between organizational and functional definitions. Yet what they don't do is to assess and defend the analytical purchase on political reality offered by such abstractions. To be fair, some of this is implicit in what they say. But, for present purposes it is important that we are perhaps a little more explicit. Two elements, in particular, of the analytical utility offered by the concept of the state might usefully be identified. Both are concerned with the ability to contextualize political behaviour: the first relates to the structural and/or institutional contextualization of political actors, the second to the historical contextualization of political behaviour and dynamics. Consider each in turn.

The state as institutional contextualization

As later chapters will testify, theories of the state vary significantly in terms of the assumptions about the state that they reflect. Yet, almost without exception the state is seen, by those who deploy it as a concept, in structural and/or institutional terms. Thus, whether the state is seen functionally or organizationally – as a set of functions necessitating (in so far as they are performed) a certain institutional ensemble, or as an institutional ensemble itself – it provides a context within which political actors are seen to be embedded and with respect to which they must be situated analytically. The state, in such a conception, provides (a significant part of) the institutional landscape which political actors must negotiate. This landscape is, in Bob Jessop's terms, 'strategically selective' – it is more conducive to certain strategies, and by extension, the preferences of certain actors, than others (Jessop 1990: 9–10; see also Hay 2002: 127–31). It provides the unevenly contoured backdrop to political conflict, contestation and change – a strategic terrain with respect to which actors must orient themselves if they are to realize their intentions.

As this perhaps serves to suggest, the appeal to the concept of the state tends to draw the political analyst's attention to – and to sharpen the analyst's purchase on – the opportunities and, more often than not, the *constraints* that political actors face in realizing their intentions. A political analysis informed by a theory of the state is less likely to see political actors in voluntarist terms – as free-willed subjects in almost complete control of their destiny, able to shape political realities in the image of their preferences and volitions. For, in contrast to voluntarism and more agent-centred accounts, theorists of the state tend to see the ability of actors to realize their intentions as conditional upon often complex strategic choices made in densely structured institutional contexts which impose their own strategic selectivity (the pattern of opportunities and constraints they present).

Such considerations are important and have the potential to provide a valuable and much-needed corrective to the tendency of an at times behaviouralist-dominated political science mainstream to see actors' preferences alone as the key to explaining political outcomes. State theory reminds us that the access to political power associated with a landslide electoral triumph does not necessarily bring with it the institutional and/or strategic capacity to translate such a mandate into lasting social, political and economic change. If political will and the access to positions of power and influence were all that were required (as, for instance, in some pluralist and elitist conceptions), wholesale political change would be endemic. That this is not the case suggests the value of institutionally contextualizing abstractions like the state. And these, in turn, encourage a rather more sanguine and realistic assessment of 'political opportunity structures' (Tarrow 1998).

Yet such valuable insights do not come without their own dangers. State theory, as many of the chapters in this volume demonstrate, has at times been characterized by a tendency to structuralism. Indeed, this would seem to be the pathology to which it is most prone. In at least some of their many variants, Marxism, institutionalism, green theory, feminism and even public choice theory, have all legitimately been accused of structuralism. For each has, at times and in certain forms, appealed to essential and non-negotiable characteristics of the state (its capitalism, its patriarchy, its complicity in the destruction of the natural environment, and so forth) reproduced independently of political actors. Such essentialism is both fatalistic and apolitical; it does nothing to enhance the analyst's purchase on political reality. Indeed, in a sense it denies that there is a *political* reality to be interrogated (on politics as the antithesis of fate, see also Gamble 2000).

Yet whilst structuralism has proved an almost perennial target for critics of state theory, contemporary theories of the state would seem more acutely aware of its dangers today than at any point in the past. Indeed, the recent development of state theory can at least in part be read as a retreat from structuralism.

The state as historical contextualization

If the appeal to the concept or abstraction of the state serves to sensitize political analysts to the need to *contextualize political agency and agents institutionally*, then no less significant is its role in sensitising political analysts to the need to *contextualize the present historically*. Indeed, the two are intimately connected.

The characteristic concern of the political scientist with government and the holders of high office tends to be associated with an analytical focus on the present. Within this conventional framework, the determinants of political outcomes are invariably seen to lie in factors specific to a particular context at a particular point in time – typically, the motivations and intentions of the actors immediately involved and their access to positions of power and influence. This somewhat ahistorical approach is immediately problematized by appeal to the concept of the state. For whilst governments come and go, the state, as an institutional ensemble, persists as it evolves over time. That evolution is shaped by the intended and unintended consequences of governing strategies and policies. Yet this is a reciprocal relationship. For, at any given point in time, the strategic context in which governments find themselves is in turn a reflection of the strategic capacities and competences of the institutions of the state and the constraints and opportunities these impose. To understand the capacity for governmental autonomy is, then, to assess the extent of the institutional, structural and strategic legacy inherited from the past. It is, in short, to understand the dynamic relationship between state and governmental power over time.

An example may serve to reinforce the point. If the institutions of the British state in 1997 (when a New Labour administration was elected for the first time) looked different from those in 1979 (when the first Thatcher government was elected), then this is likely to have exerted a significant influence on the autonomy of an incoming Labour administration, regardless of the size of its majority. Yet, as this example perhaps already serves to indicate, there is a certain danger of structuralism here too. The newly incumbent Blair administration certainly had to grapple with the institutional, political and cultural legacy of Thatcherism in 1997. Yet, in our desire to contextualize historically we may come to overemphasize the burden the past places on the present. In so doing we may inadvertently absolve contemporary political actors of all responsibility for the consequences of their conduct – attributing, say, the lack of radicalism of the first Blair administration to the legacy of Thatcherism when it might more plausibly be attributed to the lack of an animating political conviction. State theory, especially in its neo-institutionalist form (see Chapter 5), is perhaps rather too predisposed to see continuity, inertia and, at best, incremental evolution over time. States, like governments, change and, under certain conditions, despite their path-dependent nature, they may change surprisingly rapidly. It is important, then, that the historical contextualization of the present that the abstraction of the state encourages does not lead us to an historically undifferentiated account of the endless reproduction of the status quo ante. As this suggests, whilst the appeal to the concept of the state can certainly heighten our sensitivity to historical dynamics, it need not necessarily do so. An overly structuralist and overly historicized account may dull rather than sharpen our analytical purchase on questions of change over time. Yet, as already noted, contemporary theories of the state are perhaps rather more acutely aware of this danger than their predecessors. Recent developments in the theory of the state are characterized, as much as by anything else, by their emphasis upon the uneven pace of the state's development over time.

Recent developments in state theory

In recent years the ascendancy of the neo-Weberian perspective that came to dominate the revival of interest in the state in the 1970s has been challenged. Two theoretical currents are here particularly noteworthy: the development of a distinctly feminist theory of the state, and the rejection of the very notion of the state by poststructuralists (in particular Foucauldians and discourse-analysts).

Feminism, or so it is often argued, lacks a theory of the state. Yet where once Judith Allen's comment that 'where feminists have been interested in the state their ideas on its nature and form have often been imported from outside' (1990: 21) was certainly warranted, things are now somewhat more complicated. Some argue that feminism has no (independent) theory of the state and needs one urgently; others, that feminism has no theory of the state and has no need for one; while yet others suggest that feminism not only needs but has at last begun to develop precisely such a theory. The evidence of recent scholarship would seem to support this latter view: that in recent years feminists have indeed begun to establish the basis for very adequate and distinctively feminist theor*ies* of the state (see Chapter 6). Indeed many of the most exciting and original developments in contemporary state theory have come from feminist scholars. Such insights include a number of key observations: (i) if the state can in some instances be seen to act as if an 'ideal collective capitalist' it may also be seen as a 'patriarch general', a key site in the reproduction of relations of patriarchal domination within society; (ii) with the growing feminization of poverty, ever-increasing numbers of women are becoming dependent upon the state for their very survival, giving the state a historically unparalleled prominence in the lives of women; (iii) paradoxically, at the same time the state is ever more dependent upon the unpaid domestic labour of women in an era of welfare retrenchment; (iv) as this demonstrates, the reproduction of capitalist social relations is integrally bound up with the reproduction of patriarchal relations – an adequate theory of either must deal with their mutual articulation.

If in recent years feminists have increasingly turned to a theory of the state then the rise of Foucauldian and discourse-analytical perspectives marks something of a counter move – a move *from* the state (see Chapter 8). Such approaches present a fundamental challenge to conventional theorists of the state, suggesting as they do that the notion of the state is itself something of a mystifying illusion. Following the work of Michel Foucault they argue that the concept and discourse of the state is but one part of a broader process governing and shaping our very conduct and bringing it in line with various 'governing strategies'. From this perspective state effects exist precisely because people act as if the state existed, orienting themselves to the image constructed of it. Thus insofar as the state exists, it exists in the ideas we hold about it. This has led many theorists to reject the notion of the state altogether (see, for instance, Abrams 1988). Yet the idea that discourses of the state are partly constitutive of its power, authority and essence is hardly as devastating for the theory of the state as some might contend. It does however demonstrate that if theorists of the state are not to reproduce its mythology, they must give rather more attention to the processes through which the state is conceived of on the one hand, and the relationship between such conceptions and the institutions, processes and practices of the state on the other.

Beyond the state?

A final challenge to the theory of the state has come from a rather unexpected source – the challenge to the state itself. In recent years the value of state theory has come under attack from those who reject neither its sophistication nor the significance of the insights it has generated. What they do reject, however, is its contemporary relevance. The state, they argue, in an era of globalization and internationalization, financial integration and capital mobility is rapidly becoming obsolete. It is becoming (if it has not already become) an anachronism: too small to deal with the big problems which are now increasingly projected on an international or global stage and too clumsy to deal with the small problems which are increasingly displaced to the local level. It is difficult to deny the appeal of such an argument. Yet it is important to treat some of the often heroic claims made about the contemporary crisis of the nation-state with a degree of caution and some scepticism. First, globalization is not a particularly novel phenomenon. Indeed it can be traced at least as far back as the imperial age. The mode of globalization has certainly changed with time, but the mere presence of globalizing forces need not herald the demise of the state form. It is certainly true that financial integration, heightened capital mobility, the emergence of regional trading blocs and the proliferation of supra-national regulatory bodies significantly alter the context (economic and political) within which states operate, and may indeed be reflected in the changing form and function of the state. Yet this is in no sense to pronounce the death of the state. In all likelihood people will continue to live, as they do now, in territorially-bounded communities governed primarily by state institutions on which they continue to confer legitimacy, and which they continue to regard as responsible in the first instance for the social and economic context in which they find themselves. As this suggests, globalization may well pose a challenge to the nation-state, but it is a challenge that it has not thus far proved incapable of responding to. The nature of that response, not as yet associated with any significant scaling back or retrenchment of its activities, defines the contemporary agenda for state theorists. On all the available evidence, then, rumours of the death of the state and of the demise of state theory would, thankfully, seem greatly exaggerated.

Structure of the book

The volume begins with reappraisals of the classical triumvirate of pluralism, elitism and Marxism. In his chapter on pluralism, Martin Smith emphasizes that pluralism has been and in many ways continues to be a massively influential perspective in political analysis generally, and state theory in particular. In identifying the developments in pluralist thought, from the growing dominance of American pluralism, through neo-pluralist reformulations to the contemporary reinvigoration of pluralist thought through radical democracy and multiculturalism, the chapter points to both contemporary developments in pluralist thought and the stable core at the heart of such pluralist approaches. That core is characterized by the continued emphasis upon the centrality of groups, a belief in limiting the power of the state and the understanding of power as diffuse. The chapter also highlights a continuing and persistent weaknesses of the theory, namely its failure to problematize the state and its associated tendency to see it in rather neutral terms. Paraxodically, then, whilst invariably seen to provide the central reference point in the theory of the state and a point of departure for all others, pluralism's conception of the state is itself curiously under-theorized. Mark Evans, in his chapter on elitism, similarly seeks to explore how the core of elite theory has developed. He identifies a series of core propositions – that rulers form a cohesive group, selected on the basis of their access to economic, political or ideological resources, are based within a territory, and are closed off from those who are ruled. Partly in response to theoretical and empirical criticism, and partly due to contemporary changes in global political and economic structures, Evans suggests that these propositions have altered. Contemporary political elites are engaged – or seen, by elite theorists, to be engaged – in competition with one another, on the basis of a broader range of resources. Whilst such elites may well be territorially based, invariably they form linkages with other global elites. Again emphasizing contemporary developments, the chapter concludes by examining theories which seek to analyse the form and function of elites at different levels of governance.

Colin Hay's chapter on Marxist theories of the state builds upon the oft-cited truism that Marx did not develop a coherent and systematic theory of the state himself. He traces the development of Marxist state theory from the fragments of Marx's reflections on the state, through the move away from economism initiated by Gramsci, via the structuralism *vs* intentionalism debate, to the contemporary expressions of Block and Jessop. The chapter, developing the theme of variation within as well as between paradigmatic approaches to the state, concludes by arguing that despite claims that both the state and Marxism are in decline, the Marxist approach still has much to offer.

The following two chapters on public choice theory and institutionalism represent some of the major debates within the contemporary political science mainstream. As Andrew Hindmoor suggests, public choice theory sees the state in terms of failure. Utilizing economic methods and building primarily from the assumption that individuals are self-interested utility maximizers, public choice theorists argue that the notion of the state acting as the guardian of the public interest is a myth, as state actors (as all individuals) rationally pursue their self-interest. The chapter outlines a number of examples of the ways in which public choice theorists have suggested that such self-interested actions from state actors leads to state failure. The new institutionalism can perhaps be seen as a reaction both to the assumptions of public choice theory and to the behaviouralist revolution of the 1960s. It has sought to rehabilitate the state, being in some sense a continuation of the attempt in the 1980s to 'bring the state back into' political analysis. As Vivien Schmidt argues, rather than reducing political action to its individual parts, it has sought to analyse the collective element of political action. There are, of course, a diverse range of new institutionalisms to which the chapter attends: rational choice institutionalism, historical institutionalism, sociological institutionalism and discursive institutionalism. These vary in quite how they approach this insight, but all share a concern with how institutions modify individual action – be that through incentive structures, historical legacies, or cultural and/or discursive norms. Curiously, though, as Schmidt points out, the state as a concept is quiet or absent from much new institutionalist scholarship – the ghost at the feast. Thus whilst what new institutionalists most frequently mean by an institution is a state institutions, it is in the rather more generic language of institutions, rather than the state, that their analyses are framed. This perhaps reflects the 'success' of public choice theorists' accounts of the failure of the state.

The book then moves on to consider some perspectives on the state which (currently) lie outside of the mainstream. These present a significant series of challenges to more conventional approaches whilst providing new tools with which to examine the state. In her chapter on feminism, Johanna Kantola points out that feminism has long been marked by an ambiguous position towards the state. Echoing other chapters, the diversity of feminist perspectives on the state is emphasized. The chapter points to the 'in' and 'out' dichotomy, where the emancipatory potential of the state is debated, primarily between those who view the state as essentially neutral and those who see it as essentially patriarchal. Yet a range of feminist authors have sought to transcend this rather stark distinction including those in the Nordic countries. Such authors see differences between state processes and outcomes for women, primarily in terms of differences in social rights. Poststructuralist feminists have rejected totalizing narratives on the state and seek instead to point to its differentiated nature. As this suggests, as feminist state theory has developed it has increasingly moved from questioning what the state *is* to a focus on what the state *does*.

Green theorists, like their feminist counterparts, have had a somewhat ambiguous position on the state. Yet Matthew Paterson, Peter Doran and John Barry argue that this has altered as green theorists have sought to engage with the underlying assumptions and practices associated with unsustainable development. They go on to outline a range of green criticisms of the state, which focus on why and how the modern state produces, reproduces and reinforces ecologically unsustainable dynamics. Yet the authors reject the eco-anarchistic view that the state is always and everywhere unreformable. The chapter goes on to consider how theorists have sought to 'green' the state, placing the emphasis for real change upon civil society, and, echoing developments in other theories, upon a move from totalising narratives of the state.

The final chapter in this section of the book presents the most significant challenge to traditional theorizing on the state. The aim of poststructuralism, Alan Finlayson and James Martin argue, is to investigate political language and discourse, to garner something of its structure, rules and how they have been institutionalized, in order to open up what has been excluded and, in so doing, to make possible alternatives. In terms of the state, the chapter emphasizes how poststructuralism questions the state itself, arguing that the fixing or definition of the state is an inherently political activity. The state is therefore an *outcome* of politics rather than something with which to explain politics. The work of Foucault on governmentality and his analysis of how power is dispersed throughout society emphasizes that the state and government are not contained in one locus but, rather, range across power/knowledge networks.

Many of the chapters mapping and analysing existing theories of the state make reference to how such perspectives have evolved in light of, and in response to, contemporary social, political and particularly economic changes. The second section of the book examines some of these changes and how they have and might impact upon the study of the state. In particular, it seems that the Weberian, or neo-Weberian view of the state as exerting a monopoly of authority through dedicated state actors, is increasingly challenged. However, all the chapters caution against simple arguments of the decline of the state; indeed, each argues for its continuing centrality.

Nicola Hothi, David Marsh and Nicola Smith examine how globalization has impacted upon the state. Globalization, it is widely claimed, has served to undermine the nation state. In an increasingly interconnected world, what the state can do has become more and more circumscribed, it is often claimed. However, after reviewing some more critical strands of the literature on globalization, it is noted that whilst there may be changes taking place in the global economy, the impact of these is mediated by the economic and political–institutional structure that pertains in particular contexts. The outcomes of the process of globalization are, then, very uneven. This, in turn, entails a rejection of the kind of totalizing narratives about globalization's inevitable consequences that have tended to dominate discussion.

The impact of globalization upon the capacities of the nation state receives further analysis in Georg Sørensen's chapter on the transformation of the state. His chapter reviews debates between those who see the state as in retreat, those who see the state remaining strong, and a third, synthesizing position, which suggests that states have changed and lost some influence and autonomy, yet simultaneously have been strengthened in other respects. Sørensen then goes on to consider the transformation of the state in the key areas of the economy and polity and with respect to the key concepts of community and sovereignty, suggesting that we are witnessing a change from what he terms the modern to the postmodern state. He also usefully reminds us that positions on the transformation of the state are heavily influenced by the different theories of the state which inform them.

The transformation of the state is widely held to have reduced the role of state actors, and simultaneously, to have enhanced the role of societal actors. This change is often captured in terms of the shift from *government* to *governance*. B. Guy Peters and Jon Pierre in their chapter on governance, government and the state, however, suggest that what is happening is a shift in the centrality of government in governance and how government operates within this new arrangement. They argue for the analytic priority of the state and its continued importance, before analysing the role of state institutions in governance. They go on to argue that the state has adapted and altered to a different mode of governance, one of blended, or dual sovereignty, utilizing different policy implementation tools and decentralization. Rather than reducing the role of the state in governance, these changes may represent a reassertion of its influence; the state exercising power in different ways.

The increasing prominence of private actors within the operation of the state provides the key focus for Matthew Flinder's chapter on the boundaries of the state. He suggests that fragmentation and disaggregation mark the state and points to the potential dangers of viewing the state as a homogenous entity. The chapter goes on to examine the broader sphere of delegated or distributed public governance, the 'grey zone' of which public–private partnerships are an important aspect. Yet these debates clearly raise important issues concerning the role of private sector and the state and particularly, the potential limits to private sector involvement.

In the conclusion, we attempt to identify some of the common themes and concerns which arise in the preceding chapters. We return to the theme of convergence amongst theories of the state discussed in the first edition of Marsh and Stoker's *Theory and Methods* (1995). In the conclusion, we revisit the issue, to examine if such a trend can be observed when considering a broader range of perspectives on the state. We suggest that whilst strong claims about convergence may be unwarranted, the disparate theories of the state reviewed in this volume do exhibit a series of common themes and concerns. Notable amongst these is the question of the continuing relevance of the state itself, both conceptually and substantively. In the conclusion, we review such arguments and discussions, and in keeping with the argument of other chapters, suggest that whilst the state may be subject to a range of pressures which may have altered its position and role, it remains a central focus for political analysis.

Further reading

Evans, P. B. *et al* (eds) (1985) *Bringing the State Back In* (Cambridge: Cambridge University Press).

Hay, C. (1996) *Re-Stating Social and Political Change* (Buckingham: Open University Press).

Mann, M. (1988) *States, War and Capitalism* (Oxford: Blackwell).

Pierson, C. (1996) *The Modern State* (London: Routledge).

Skinner, Q. (1989) 'The State'; in T. Ball *et al.* (eds), *Political Innovation and Conceptual Change* (Cambridge: Cambridge University Press).

Chapter 1

Pluralism

MARTIN SMITH

Pluralism has been one of the most dominant frameworks for understanding politics in mainstream political science. It has influenced much of the thinking on the nature of the relationship between the government and civil society from the late nineteenth century until the present day. Modes of pluralist thinking have influenced many subfields of political science, including pressure groups, political theory, multiculturalism, public administration and discourse theory. In addition pluralist analysis has been used for analysing a range of types of political systems from liberal democracies to authoritarian regimes. Many political scientists often work with an implicit pluralist framework.

Despite it influential position, there are a number of issues that arise when attempting to outline the pluralist theory of the state. First, there is no agreement on what constitutes pluralism. Pluralism is conceptualized in numerous ways across the fields of political science, international relations and political theory. As Nichols (1975:1) points out:

> The principal causes of confusion has been the fact that the term has been used by separate groups of thinkers who have rarely attempted to relate their particular use of the term to its other usages.

In addition, pluralism can be linked to a range of ideological thought including that of anarchists, socialists, Whigs and Conservatives (see Laborde 2000; Hirst 1994).

Second, pluralism pays little attention to the nature of the state and even less to state theory. Because of its roots in English empiricism and American pragmatism, pluralism is curiously non-theoretical. Jordan (1990: 286) points out that 'pluralism has been an under explicit theory'. Ironically, the basis of pluralist theory is a critique of the state. However, pluralism, in most manifestations, has a benign view of both the existing state in democratic society and the future potential of the state as a mechanism for political organization. Finally, the epistemological foundation of pluralism is an opposition to monism and the view that there can be a single unified and universal body of knowledge. Yet the dominant methodology of pluralists in the second half of the twentieth century is a behaviourism based on

21

an assumption of absolute truth and that social facts can be discovered through investigation (as well as a methodological individualism which opposes the notion of group identities). Because of its diversity and theoretical naivety, there is a consequent lack of clarity or consistency in pluralist state theory. In addition, as in many theories, there is a continual elision between normative and explanatory theory.

The chapter begins by examining the historical roots of pluralism and then examines the bifurcation of pluralisms into the American and English schools. It will examine the growing dominance of US pluralism and discuss how the focus on the US shaped the pluralist understanding of the state and how the normative element of pluralism prevented any conception of the state in the West as other than a liberal and representative institution. The chapter will then outline the growing criticisms of pluralist theory and the attempts by a range of political scientists to defend a pluralist tradition, despite empirical and conceptual challenges. Finally, the chapter discusses the reinvigoration of pluralist thought from the unlikely sources of postmodernism, radical democracy, governance and multiculturalism, and highlights how thinkers from different epistemological positions have developed some of the themes of traditional pluralism such as diversity, the limits of the political and the need to constrain the role of the state. The chapter will illustrate that whilst the state is a core feature of pluralists concerns, they actually pay little attention to the nature of the state. The state is problematic for pluralists because they fail to see it as an independent source of political power.

The roots of pluralism

In Europe pluralism began as a reaction to the notion of monism and the idea of an absolutist state. In the United States pluralism developed as a more practical response to the desire to limit state power in the new constitution. There is, in the early pluralism, a conscious rejection of Hegelian idealism (see Follet 1918; Wahl 1925). For the original English pluralists such as G. D. H. Cole, J. N. Figgis and H. Laski, pluralism was a normative theory concerned with how society should be organized in order to achieve a just and liberal, socialist society (see Hirst 1989; Nichols 1994). Fundamental to all pluralists and pluralist thought is the notion that diversity is a social good that prevents the dominance of one particular idea. Power should be dispersed and not allowed to accumulate in the state. Nichols (1975: 5) sees the three main principles of English pluralism as being:

(a) that liberty is the most important political value, and that it is best preserved by power being dispersed,
(b) that groups should be regarded as 'persons', and
(c) that ideas of state sovereignty should be rejected.

The central tenet of pluralism derived from liberal thought; the importance of liberty and a distrust of the state which means that state power needs to be limited. However, the early English pluralists opposed the individualism of liberalism, seeing groups as the main constitutive element of society. For certain pluralists, individuals have no independent existence other than through groups. For all pluralists group identities and representation are an important element of the political structure. For Laski groups had a personality and we personalize them because 'we must':

> We do it because we feel in these things the red blood of a living personality. Here are no mere abstractions of an over-exuberant imagination. The need is so apparent to make plain the reality beneath. (Laski 1989: 165)

For the English pluralists, and for the later American pluralists, groups are the building block of politics and the state. However, much pluralist thought is shaped by a failure to problematize either the state or state/civil society relations. Laborde (2000: 177) illustrates how for English pluralism the distinction between state and civil society is one of the fundamental principles of pluralism but points out that: 'such a distinction was hardly couched in antagonistic terms. The state was seen as an unproblematic instrumental requirement and the border between public and private was confused in pluralist writings'. The English pluralists were concerned with two elements in their understanding of the state. One is the notion of sovereignty and the second is the role/relationship of groups.

In keeping with their opposition to monism, pluralist theorists rejected the notion of a single and indivisible sovereignty embodied in the state. Figgis, Cole and Laski embodied the pluralist suspicion of the state, rejecting its claims to universality and contesting notions of sovereignty (Laborde 2000: 70 and 74). Like liberals, they believed that the state should be constrained. The mechanism for constraint was the distribution of social organization through a myriad of groups and associations. The conception of public/private organization was not far from the way the British state and civil society was organized up until the First World War. Public goods were provided by a combination of public, private and voluntary groups and the state played a minimal role.

In the United States, pluralism also developed out of a reaction to monism – and more directly in opposition to a powerful imperial state – and in many ways shared similar concerns with the British pluralist movement. It developed in particular through the work of Dewey and Follet (Stears 2002). Like the English pluralists, they were concerned with the power accrued by the state as a consequence of industrialization and the First World War. Follet was strongly opposed to the impact of individualism and to the notion of an overbearing state. Follet, like Laski, saw individuals as existing only through groups and that individual identity was an expression of group membership (Follet 1918: 77). Follet and Dewey believed that modern life inevitably led to a pluralistic and complex society, and that it was necessary to ensure that the powers of the state were limited to avoid groups being crushed. Stears (2002: 147) highlights their view that: 'The centralized state had to be replaced by a new institutional order that placed multiple groups at the center of its organization.' The early English and American pluralists share similar concerns and notions of politics. However, political circumstances led to very divergent paths after the First World War.

The development of pluralism has to be understood within the context of particular political circumstance. In Britain the development of pluralism in the early twentieth century reflected concerns about an increasingly strong state and was built of the notion of a strong civil society – through voluntary organizations and trade unions – delivering public goods. However the period between 1914 and 1945 effectively destroyed the liberal state form that existed in Britain. The British state nationalized the pluralistic delivery of public goods so that the services delivered by the voluntary sector, private business and local government were taken over by the central government (for example supplies of gas or the creation of the NHS). In addition, the primacy of parliamentary sovereignty and the Haldane conception of the civil service – which saw decisions being made within a symbiotic relationship between ministers and officials – meant that power was monopolized within a closed and elitist state. Whilst Middlemas (1979) emphasizes a corporate bias in the British state – the role of groups was always mediated through a sovereign core executive and was highly limited in the influence on policy. Whilst pluralist conceptions existed within British political discourse, particularly in the high Toryism of people like Quentin Hogg and Harold Macmillan, the reality of British government was an increasingly centralized, sovereign state. The British state is based on the notion of indirect, individual representation, a decision-making elite isolated from civil society and unresponsive to group interests, combined with an indivisible notion of internal and external sovereignty. The epitome of anti-pluralism was the Thatcherite conception of state with its suspicion of groups and intermediate institutions and emphasizing the direct relationship between a sovereign government and the individual. As a consequence of these developments, pluralism had little purchase in Britain and the work of Cole, Figgis and Laski effectively disappeared from both political and academic debate until the 1980s.

In the United States the state form was not so suffocating of pluralist thought. There, despite the very considerable expansion of state activity during the New Deal in the 1930s, the state was never sought or developed the capabilities to draw all areas of activity into its domain. A comprehensive welfare state failed to develop, local and state government retained considerable autonomy, the private sector remained strong – there was no attempted beyond specific sectors in planning or nationalization – and the central state was institutionally fragmented as a consequence of the separation of power entrenched within the constitution. Consequently, there was sufficient plurality in the political system to ensure that pluralism continued to reflect some elements of the reality of American politics. The period between the First World War and the end of the 1960s saw pluralism becoming the dominant conception of the American state.

The rise of American pluralism

In the post-war period pluralism (what some call interest group pluralism) became the dominant paradigm in US political science and had a considerable impact on the analysis of politics in the rest of the world. It developed as both an empirical and normative political theory; a mechanism for understanding US politics and a framework of what politics should be. There is an assumption in the literature on pluralism of a break between the pluralism of the early twentieth century theorists and the post-war empirical political pluralism. In fact, many of its concerns and conceptions of post-war pluralism are indebted to the more radical pluralism of the early twentieth century. And through the founder of modern American pluralism, Arthur Bentley, there is a direct link to John Dewey (Ratner and Altman 1964). From Bentley, modern pluralists have adapted the classical pluralist emphasis on the role of groups in politics and the need to contain the power and competence of the state. For Bentley groups are no different to individual (Bentley 1967: 211–12). The themes of Bentley's work were developed by David Truman (1951) and empirically in the analysis by the work of Dahl, Lindblom and 'the Yale school' (see Merelman 2003).

As pluralist theory developed, however, it transformed from a normative theory – this is how things should be – to an empirical theory – analysing how power is distributed. It then became, in the words of Merelman (2003: 18), a legitimizing discourse: 'That is, they support the claims American political leaders typically make to justify their power'. Pluralist theorist in post-war America confused normative claims with empirical reality. Pluralists desired a state limited by multiple power centres and the influence of groups and this was their perception of politics in post-war America. Consequently, the US pluralist theory of the state was actually a model of how they believed American politics operated and, in a manner similar to the way in which the works of Walter Bagehot and Sir Ivor Jennings legitimized executive sovereignty in Britain, the pluralists legitimized the US political system.

The key elements of pluralist state theory are well summarized by Dahl (1963: 325):

> Important government policies would be arrived at through negotiation, bargaining, persuasion and pressure at a considerable number of different sites in the political system – the Whitehouse, the bureaucracies, the labyrinth of committees in Congress, the federal and state courts, the state legislatures and the executives, the local governments. No single organized political interest, party, class, region or ethnic groups would control all of these sites.

For pluralists the state was fragmented into multiple power centres and check points. According to Dahl (1963: 327), 'Neither the executive, the House nor the Senate is monolithic.' It is impossible for any single actor to control all of these centres and any over-powerful interest will be constrained by other elements of the system. For Dahl, it is rare 'for any coalition to carry out its policies without having to bargain, negotiate and compromise with its opponents; often, indeed, it wins a victory in one institution only to suffer defeat in another'. Powerful groups are likely to be constained by countervailing powers (Galbraith 1963). If there are no countervailing groups, they will be checked by 'potential groups' (Truman 1951a).

Underpinning the modern democratic system then are three core principles: first, is the centrality of groups to the political process; second, is the way in which power is dispersed between different power centres and third, is the degree of consensus underlying the political process. Consensus, which was a core concept in the work of the early American pluralist Mary Follet, plays a key role in post-war pluralism. For pluralists the fundamental features of US politics are agreed. Political conflicts are not about the boundaries of the system, they are usually about the distribution of resources within the system (Dahl 1963: 329–40). In addition, consensus is a sign of agreement. Or more critically, the lack of political opposition is seen as a sign of agreement. If groups do not organize and lobby, they are assumed not to have a grievance of sufficient strength to warrant concern. There is within this conception of political behaviour an implicit rational choice ontology. If I am suffering enough I will bear the cost of political activity and do something about it. If the grievance is minor it is outweighed by the cost of activity and so I will stay at home. The assumption is that grievance leads to activity leads to political action. The state is open to justifiable demands. Groups are never a threat because people have multiple memberships and there are numerous countervailing powers within the political system. This is where the post-war pluralists differ greatly from the early pluralists. For the early English and American pluralists human community was the site of politics but for the postwar pluralists, politics was a secondary concern only really acted upon when grievances were threatened.

The American pluralists constructed a benign notion of the state. Like Ivor Jennings in Britain, they confuse the constitution with the actual practice of politics. Institutional fragmentation means that the state is open to a wide array of interests. Perhaps most importantly power is not only fragmented but non-cumulative. Success in one area does not lead to success in other areas.

However the dominance and complacency of American pluralism was short-lived. Whilst the ink was still drying on Dahl's claim (1963: 24) that, 'The theory and practice of American pluralism tend to assume that the existence of multiple centers of power, none of which is wholly sovereign will help (may indeed be necessary) to tame power, to secure the consent of all, and to settle conflicts peacefully', blacks in the South were being killed for demanding their political and civil rights. The point where the Yale school thought pluralism was firmly established in the US was the point when its limitations were becoming apparent. During the 1960s and 1970s pluralism was subject to both an empirical and academic critique.

Empirically many of the assumptions concerning pluralism were challenged by the civil rights movement and the anti-Vietnam war movements of the 1960s. The civil rights movement illustrated that a group with a forceful grievance was excluded from the political protest. Despite the apparent pluralism of the American system, there were considerable barriers to political participation. Robert Putnam's response to the assassination of Martin Luther King, and the riots that followed, captures the pluralist impasse: 'What that glow in the sky on that evening of the Martin Luther King assassination conveyed was a sense that there was something happening in American politics that was not encompassed by the conceptual framework that we were all working with' (Merelman 2003: 211–12). In many ways the Vietnam War was a greater challenge to pluralism. It undermined any claim that American politics was based on consensus. The anti-war protest refuted the idea of a shared sense of US politics and society-wide agreement over the form of the political system.

The collapse of the consensus fed into a number of academic critiques of pluralism. First, rather than there being a consensus, what pluralism was presenting was a Cold War inspired view of the American system. The picture of a perfect functioning democracy, differentiating power and open to all interests was hiding a process of manipulation, exclusion and elite dominance. This was Merelman's legitimizing discourse, intent on demonstrating the superiority of the American system. Second, the Vietnam War and civil rights movement, and the more radical women's and gay movements that followed, undermined the notion there was a general acceptance of values in society (see Lockwood 1964). Indeed, the period since the 1960s has seen a considerable bifurcation of beliefs in the US between say those who support notion of gay marriage and the fundamentalist Christian Right.

Third, Bachrach and Baratz (1962) and Lukes (1974) highlighted the way in which notion of consensus can be manipulated in the political process. Lukes and Bachrach and Baratz were also critical of the pluralist dependence in behavioural methodology derived from Bentley. Pluralism was based on observable power not the way hidden structures and ideas shape the political agenda (Polsby 1980: 4; Polsby 1960: 477). The work of Lukes highlighted the structural mechanisms that meant that consensus often covered forms of coercion. As Merelman (2003: 99) boldly states, a combination of social change and theoretical critique meant that: 'By the early 1970s, pluralism had been dethroned at Yale.'

The reformulation of pluralism

Pluralist theorists did respond to the events of the 1960s and the 1970s and there was some considerable rethinking. The reformulation took different forms in the United States and in Britain. In the United States there was the development of a distinct notion of neo-pluralism which grew out of some critiques of American democracy in the work of Lowi (1969) and McConnell (1953, 1966) and the rethinking of the nature of pluralism in the work of Dahl and Lindblom. Neo-pluralism continues the pluralist concern with the role of groups in the policy process but accepts that particular groups, especially business, will often come to dominate within policy areas and are at a clear advantage compared to groups like consumers (Dunleavy and O'Leary 1987; Kelso 1978). McConnell (1967) saw business as exercising great power in the US polity and, for Lowi (1969), interest groups did not result in pluralism but in structures of privilege that excluded the public from policy-making arenas.

Lindblom was firmly in the Yale school of pluralists but recognized that business enjoyed extra resources in the political sphere. First, government is dependent on economic growth for its own success and therefore it is likely to meet business demands for favourable tax and economic policies. As a consequence business is in 'a privileged position in government'. Second, in a market system many decisions that have a major impact on the lives of people are taken without any democratic control (Lindblom 1977: 175). Businesses can close factories or pollute environments without any accountability. This leads Lindblom to a non-behavioural conclusion. He sees business as not just having power through its lobbying ability but having structural power (see Chapter 3).

Lindblom's remarkable *volte-face* places him more closely with Marxists such as Claus Offe and David Coates than with the classical pluralists of post-war America (see McLennan 1989 on convergence). However, unlike Marxists, Lindblom maintains the pluralist focus on groups and actually pays little attention to the nature of the state. He accepts the pluralist conception of the state as fragmented but then argues that business has a privileged position in that fragmented state. Manley maintains that the neo-pluralists still see the state as neutral but considering their suggestion that it has to respond to business this is not convincing. What they do is fail to problematize the state in the way that the pluralists of the past failed. Lindblom (1982) recognized the many flaws in the conventional pluralist conception of the state and argued for the mainstream to at least consider the hypothesis of radical and Marxist conceptions of the state. For instance, Lindblom examines the notion of socialization which in US social science was used in a benign sense of transmitting social values and rules and asks whether the Marxist notion that it is a form of indoctrination allowing the advantaged to retain control should at least be tested (1982: 19–20). In what is a strong critique of pluralism Lindblom (1982: 19) argues:

> We fall into a bad habit of simply taking for granted that people in society will think alike, as though agreement was a natural phenomena that requires no explanation. Even natural phenomena require explanation...Agreement on political fundamentals cries for an explanation.

Lindblom is questioning the fundamental pluralist notion that consensus is necessarily an indication of political contentment. He concludes by calling for conventional theory to bring in the radical thought 'from the cold' (Lindblom 1982: 20). Neo-pluralists escape from the pluralist position as seeing policy making as *a priori* pluralistic and the Marxist position as seeing it as *a priori* dominated by a ruling class. For Lindblom this is a question that has to be tested.

Developments in British pluralism

Perhaps one of the great ironies of the intellectual history of British political science is that a time when major figures in American pluralism were rejecting the pluralist framework, and a government was elected in Britain that was explicitly opposed to group intervention in politics, attempts were being to revive the pluralist tradition in British politics. During the 1950s and 1960s pluralism did not develop the dominance in Britain that it had in the United States. It was difficult to map the American pluralist model on to an elitist and insular system based explicitly on a unified conception of sovereignty. Nevertheless pressure groups studies developed in Britain during the 1960s with a number of writers making the case for analysing the role of groups in British politics and adopting an explicitly pluralist framework (Finer 1966; see Smith 1990: 304–5). Finer's work was followed by a long line of case studies emphasizing the impact of groups on the policy process.

However, it was the work of Richardson and Jordan that did the most to inject a pluralist conception of decision-making into contemporary British political science (see Richardson and Jordan 1979; Jordan and Richardson 1987a; Jordan and Richardson 1987b; Jordan 1981). Their work drew explicitly on the work of American political scientists in the pluralist tradition such as Bentley. They argued 'the interplay of interest groups is the dominating feature of the policy process in Western Europe' (Richardson and Jordan 1979: 3) and that the adoption of policies is 'the reflection of the strength of particular groups at any one time' (Richardson and Jordan 1979: 6). Both of these were hyperbolic claims considering the strength of state traditions in many West European countries, including Britain. However, Richardson and Jordan did try to develop the pluralist tradition by drawing on the work of later American group theorists, such as Heclo (1978), Ripley and Franklin (1980) and Gais, Peterson and Walker (1984), who saw the political system as fragmented into distinct policy domains. Within some of these domains it was possible that there were barriers to entry and that particular groups dominated. Consequently, Richardson and Jordan used the term policy community to describe the way that the British state had fragmented into a number of segmented policy domains within which particular interests may predominate.

Despite their modifications of American pluralism, Richardson and Jordan maintained most of the presumptions of the pluralist position. First, they saw groups as crucial to the policy process and in fact saw state–group relations as undermining the parliamentary system. Second, they maintained that power was dispersed and fragmented across a range of policy areas with no single interest dominating across a range of policy communities. Third, they presented the dominant policy style in Britain (if there can be such a thing) as one of negotiations. They suggested that civil servants were driven by the imperative of consensus to consult widely and to take account of the views of different groups. Policy-making was characterized by co-operation and consensus (Jordan and Richardson 1982). Fourth, they believed that access to policy-making was relatively open with most reasonable groups being able to gain access to the consultation lists of Whitehall departments.

Richardson and Jordan's framework was undermined by the fact that the Thatcher government was anything but consensual in terms of most pressure groups and by their failure to recognize that many groups were excluded from the policy domains that they saw as relatively open. They made three fundamental errors. One was the common error of pluralists: to mistake, as Marsh (2002) argues, plurality for pluralism. The existence of many groups and policy domains does not mean that power is dispersed and that access is open. Second, they assumed that the existence of groups on consultation lists and involved in discussion with officials meant they had influence.

Third, they saw networks as essentially agency-based, in other words dependent on personal relationships, and, so like other pluralists, they ignored the structural and institutional barriers to inclusion.

Developments in contemporary pluralism

Despite almost a century of empirical and theoretical critiques of pluralism, the pluralist tradition remains strong. It has reinvigorated itself over the past decade in a range of fields, each drawing on different parts of the pluralist tradition. Pluralism's strength derives from its normative appeal and the fact that much of it accords with our intuitive sense of liberal democracy. In addition, the critics of pluralism, in particular Marxism and elitism, have in the case of the former been discredited, or the latter have either not developed or become incorporated into different elements of pluralist thought (see Chapters 2 and 3).

There are four main ways that pluralism has developed in contemporary political science. Notions of governance have developed out of post-war American pluralism. Interests in social capital and civil society have drawn on themes highlighted by the early American pluralists. Similarly notions of associational democracy and radical democracy have explicitly borrowed from the early English pluralists and the anarchist strands found in French pluralism (Laborde 2000). Finally, the development of multiculturalism can be linked back to what Nichols (1974) calls the plural society literature. We will now examine each of these developments.

Governance

Governance is a term used to describe the making of public policy and the delivery of public goods in modern states following the rise of the new right, the development of new public management, public sector reform and globalization. For the theorists of governance, it describes a new way of understanding the state and its relationship with civil society. However, much of what comes within the framework of governance could be derived from mainstream American pluralism. The term governance, like pluralism, covers a wide spectrum of views and a range of different sub-disciplines within political science. The fundamental premise of the governance position is that the central state is no longer the dominant force in determining public policy. For some, such as Rosenau (1992), we now live in a centreless society. The main contention of governance can be traced directly from the American pluralists of the early 1960s. It is that there is not a single centre of government but many, which link together a whole variety of actors, be they at the local, national or supranational level. For Pierre (2000: 2),

The overarching question is what significance or meaning remains of the liberal democratic notion of the state as the undisputed centre of political power and its self-evident monopoly of articulating and pursuing the collective interest in the era of 'economic' globalization, a hollowing out of the state, decreasing legitimacy for collective solutions, and a marketisation of the state itself.

For the proponents of governance, public sector reform and privatization have hollowed the state from within, whilst developments within civil society and the globalization of economies have constrained the state from without. It appears that we are seeing the pluralist dream of the state competing as one power centre among many. For Rhodes (1997) it is governing without government and hence the development of a differentiated polity where no single interests is able to dominate the policy process.

Where the governance school differs from the American pluralists is in the way it emphasizes the international context within which decisions are made and so moves away from much of the insularity of both British and American pluralists. One of the most important developments has been the notion of multi-level governance (MLG) (see Bache and Flinders 2004). Developing out of analysis of the European Union, the multi-level governance literature suggests that there is an increasingly complex process of governance with decision-making operating between different levels. The levels interact to produce new forms of policy-making. The key premise of multi-level governance, like the rest of the governance school, is that authority has dispersed away from centralized nation states, and that there are multiple sites of decision-making each involving different actors and interests. MLG again adopts pluralist assumptions about the way power is dispersed and the limits on the state. It effectively by-passes the issue of how actors with different levels may exercise power on each other. Jessop (2002: 67) makes the point that what appear to be self-regulating networks are in fact organized by political authorities that

> provide the group rules for governance, ensure the compatibility of different governance mechanisms and regimes, deploy a relative monopoly of organizational intelligence and information.

The problem with governance accounts of state reform and development is that they fall back on the simplistic assumptions of traditional pluralism. They again confuse plurality with pluralisms and ignore the asymmetries of power that potentially exist even in network relations (Marsh, Richards and Smith 2003). Perhaps the main problem is the way in which the governance assumes that the central state has lost power when there is a raft of empirical evidence to demonstrate the high level of resource and authority that remains within the central state. The governance literature solves part of the pluralist problem by theorizing the state and in particular theorizing the type of state that exist in a new global context. However, they continue the pluralist error of not problematizing the state. It is seen again as a benign force that has weakened significantly and is now challenge by multiple power centres. What this conception really indicates is how modern political science continues to be influenced by US conceptions of the state as a fragmented and weak organization.

Civil society and social capital

One of the themes of early pluralists in both the United States and Britain is that a strong civil society, community organization and citizen activism are important both as bulwarks against the state and as mechanisms for deliverying public goods. The early American pluralists, Dewey and Follet, emphasized that individual identity did not exist outside of groups and that group identity was essential both to protect individual freedom and to limit the power of the state. For Follet (1918) the group was the building block of a healthy and democratic polity. In a sense groups provided an alternative mode of collective organization to the state and also, then, a mechanism for delivering public goods and political interaction. Follet believed that groups were a mechanism for self-government. For authoritarian and social democratic thinkers the resolution to collective action problems lies in the state. For pluralists the dependence on the state for collective provision of goods results in an overbearing state and the loss of individual liberty. Consequently, many pluralists looked to the community or the group for collective provision.

This is precisely the sort of argument that Putnam is making in his work on social capital. Putnam sees the decline in membership of local associations of whatever type as a major cause of social and economic ills in the United States and elsewhere. For Putnam membership of associations builds trust and this social capital is essential for economic development: 'Social capital is coming to be seen as a crucial ingredient in economic development around the world' (Putnam 1993: 37). Putnam, like the early English and American pluralists, sees membership of associations as essential for both personal and community development. For Putnam, the strengthening of civil society is a necessary mechanism for restoring democracy and economic development throughout the world. Putnam is a graduate of Yale and locates himself firmly within the tradition of American pluralism (Merelman 2003: 196).

He makes errors similar to those of traditional and American pluralism. The poor of the inner cities are not poor because of structured inequality, economic reorganization or racial prejudice but because of their failures to join groups and build social capital (see DeFilippis 2001). Putnam examines Tuscany and Sicily and suggests that Sicily's lack of economic development and democracy is because of the absence of social capital not because of patterns of land ownership or it position on the periphery of Europe. He is insistent on the causal relation being one of lack of social capital leading to the absence of economic development rather than the other way around. Like other pluralists he sees a simple, voluntarist solution to deep-seated structural problems and ignores the constraints that may exist on group organization. What this perspective leads to is a limited role for the state. The state has to develop social linkages rather develop large-scale welfare and economic programmes to tackle social inequality and economic development.

Radical democracy and associationalism

Modernized notions of pluralism, which have resonance with social capital, are the concepts of radical democracy and associationalism. Ironically whilst pluralism appears foundationalist in its epistemology and positivist in its methodology, pluralist concerns can be discerned in postmodernist writings. Like pluralists, postmodernists reject monism and in particular the Marxist belief in a single truth and explanation. Postmodernists and radical democrats pick up on many of the traditional concerns of democracy. According to McClure (1992: 15),

> [they] have been articulated in crucial opposition to unitary, monolithic or totalizing conceptions of the political domain, particularly in so far as these presume some singularly sovereign or unique agency overseeing or determining political processes and/or social relations

This leads to a pluralist conception of knowledge. No organization can have a monopoly of knowledge. Wainwright (1993) highlights knowledge as socially constructed; it is impossible for a single person, group or party to know everything. Ideally knowledge should be demystified into a range of social movements. Thus central to radical democrats, like Putnam, is a strong belief in the richness of civil society and the importance of social movements as a mechanism for controlling and circumventing the monopolizing tendencies of the state. Like traditional pluralists radical democrats see social movements as crucial elements in society. Civil society is complex and pluralist, with individuals belonging to an array of social groups. These groups do not have a preordained existence or identity but develop as a consequence of struggle and social interaction (McClure 1992: 115).

Radical democrats offer their pluralism as a critique, rather than legitimization, of liberal democracy and in their extreme relativism take a very different epistemology to classical pluralism. Nevertheless, some of the criticisms of traditional pluralism can also be made of radical democracy. Like most of the forms of pluralism discussed in this chapter they fail to develop a convincing theory of the state. State power is almost bracketed off into a separate sphere from the world of social movements and self organization. Where radical democrats do conceptualize the relationship between the state and civil society, they tend to offer an almost benign notion of the state (see Dryzek 1996). Consequently, they do not offer effective strategies for overcoming state power. Like traditional pluralists and Putnam, hope for political transformation is vested in social groups. However, the relativism of postmodernists means that they can make no moral claims regarding the status of various groups and thus cannot deal with groups that do not subscribe to the goals of radical democracy. Their approach is to politicize the whole of society (which is very different to traditional pluralism). The problem then arises of how the interests of minorities are protected if the state is weak and political interests are highly salient?

Multiculturalism and the plural society

Multiculturalism attempts to deal with some of the problems radical pluralism raise in a more grounded and normative approach. Multiculturalism can be rooted in pluralist thought because it is based on the idea that no single set or norms or values should dominate a society and that the role of the state should be about reconciling different interests rather than ensuring the dominance of a particular group. It can be traced back to the notions of the plural society which develop as a way of analyzing colonial societies where different groups were forced together. Consequently, within a colonial system there could be a number of ethnic groups living side by side with little interaction and each maintaining their traditional patterns of social life, norms and values (see Nichols 1974). However, unlike notions of multiculturalism which is seen as normatively good, plural societies were held together merely by the existence of a shared economic system and force.

Multiculturalism has become one of the central debates in political theory. Whilst in many ways it differs from the sorts of pressure group pluralism we have discussed earlier in the chapter, and unlike the notion of a plural society, it does not see a multicultural society as being based on force but as being normatively good. It reflects some of the themes that reoccur in plural society. First, multiculturalism is based on the notion of group identities. What is important for multiculturalists is group rights. Second, multiculturalists are opposed to the notion that a single group (and in particular the majority group) can dominate other groups. The basis of multiculturalism is the equal treatment of groups and so the role of the state is to balance conflicting group interests. There is a presumption amongst some multiculturalists such as Walzer that the state 'stands above all the various ethnic and nationalist groups in the country' (Kymlicka 2001: 16). Walzer in particular, like the mainstream American pluralists, takes a benign view of the US state seeing it as 'neutral among the various thick cultures sustained by different groups of immigrants' (Walzer 2001: 151). However, the multiculturalist debate has been moved on to examine how the state should develop a positive role in developing and protecting the rights of minority groups. This view is based again on a benign view that the state is the force able, and possibly willing, to protect the rights of minorities. Of course, whilst in some liberal states, policy will make rhetorical concessions to minority rights, the impact on groups in terms of employment, housing and education may be limited. Other liberal states, such as France, are still concerned with protecting the rights of majorities from a multiculturalist frame.

Multiculturalists also draw on the pluralist tradition of seeing rights as group based rather than individually based. It may be a good thing to protect the rights of Muslims to sustain their culture and religion in Britain. However, there may be some Muslim women who want to have their rights protected as individuals rather than as Muslims. Why should our rights be linked to groups that are essentially arbitrary? This, of course, is the dilemma of multiculturalism: how do group rights impact on individual rights and is their a tension between the two sets of rights?

Conclusion

Pluralism is in many ways a remarkable perspective. At one level it is not a coherent theory but contains a variety of approaches, methods, and epistemologies. Despite the myriad forms of pluralism, most pluralists share a number of assumptions. The primary assumption is that groups rather than individuals are crucial to understanding of politics. Second, the role of the state needs to be limited. Third, groups can be an alternative to the state as a mechanism of collective organization and the production of collective goods. Fourth, in opposition to Marxists and elitists, in liberal societies there is a dispersal of power and there is some separation between economic and political power, and between different spheres of government.

A common problem that pluralists fall prey to is that they fail to problematize the state. This is ironic as pluralism is derived from a fear of an over-powerful state and the belief that strong associations are necessary to limit the power of the state. Nevertheless, many pluralists from the early

English pluralists through the American pluralists to the multiculturalists, see the state as a benign organization. Because of their focus on groups, and the often implicit assumption that the state is a neutral arena for groups, they fail to take the state seriously and to examine how it contains considerable power that often is not used for benign ends or distributed evenly between groups. Whilst some of the neo-pluralist work began to think seriously about state power, the work on social capital, radical democracy, and multiculturalism fails to tackle the issue of state power. Governance focuses specifically on the nature of the contemporary state but elides the issue of state power.

Nevertheless, despite a century of criticism, pluralism has remarkable resilience and is perhaps in a stronger position the other classical state theories. There are two explanations of pluralism continuing strength. First, as a normative theory it is tremendously appealing to liberals and radicals, and to conservatives. Who would oppose diversity, the protection of groups rights and the distribution of power? It does accord with our sense of what a liberal democracy should be like; tolerant, diverse and responsive to the demands of a range of groups. What better solution to social ills than building networks of trust? Second, pluralism has been willing and able to respond to its critics and to changing realities. Consequently, we have seen continual adaptation in pluralist thought. Pluralism as an approach shares much with its analysis. There has been no attempt to define a single pluralist theory and as we have seen in this chapter there are numerous theories that can be loosely placed within the category of pluralism. Consequently, pluralism has been able to respond rapidly to criticism, changing realities and new debates in social science. It is an interesting commentary on pluralism that it continues to influence many of the current debates in political science, whilst at the same time drawing on many of the themes raised by the English and American pluralists of the early twentieth century.

Acknowledgements

I would like to thank Jean Grugel and Dave Richards for their comments on this chapter.

Further reading

Hirst, P. (1994) *Associative Democracy* (Cambridge: Polity Press).
Kymlicka, W. (2001) 'Western Political Theory and Ethnic Relations in Eastern Europe', in W. Kymlicka and M. Opalski (eds), *Can Liberal Pluralism be Exported?* (Oxford: Oxford University Press).

Laborde, C. (2000) *Pluralist Thought and the State in Britain and France, 1900–25* (Basingstoke and New York: Palgrave Macmillan).

McFarland, A. (2004) *Neopluralism: The Evolution of Political Process Theory* (Kansas: University Press of Kansas).

Merelman, R. (2003) *Pluralism at Yale* (Wisconsin: University of Wisconsin Press).

Stears, M. (2002) *Progressives, Pluralists and the Problems of the State* (Oxford: Oxford University Press).

Chapter 2

Elitism

MARK EVANS

Classical elite theorists such as Gaetano Mosca (1939: 50), argue that the history of politics has been characterized by elite domination:

> In all societies...two classes of people appear – a class that rules and a class that is ruled. The first class, always the less numerous, performs all political functions, monopolizes power and enjoys the advantages that power brings, whereas the second, the more numerous class, is directed and controlled by the first.

Classical elite theory therefore challenges the key premises of most western liberal assumptions about politics, the organization of government and the relationship between the state and civil society. For elitists', the nature of any society – whether it is consensual or authoritarian, pacifist or totalitarian – is determined by the nature of its elite. Four key propositions underpin the classical elitist perspective on the character of political systems:

(a) the rulers of society constitute a socially cohesive group;
(b) this group is territorially based within a nation state;
(c) the ruling elite is 'closed-off' from the ruled; and,
(d) its members are selected by virtue of their economic, political or ideological resources.

Hence, in its classical formulation, elite theory had a clear, if problematic, set of propositions about the distribution of power in society. The elitists' conception of a governing elite has much in common with Karl Marx's conception of a ruling class, as both concepts highlight socio-economic and political inequalities between rulers and the masses. However, these inequalities are understood in different ways. For Marx (1847 [1971]: 3), 'the history of all hitherto existing society is the history of class struggle'. Thus class conflict is the commanding facet of all societies after primitive communism. Hence religious, ethnic and national divisions and conflicts are, for Marx, secondary to those of class and the conflict between classes is the catalyst to social change. In contrast, classical elitists' view the relationship between the governing elite and the masses as a passive one and by

39

implication present a narrower understanding of the rise and decline of elites and the determinants of social change. The governing elite in the classical elitist formulation, is also assumed to be a cohesive group – a claim that is difficult to sustain empirically. As Tom Bottomore (1973: 274) illustrates, C. Wright Mills, in his seminal study of 'power elites' (1956), makes an attempt

> to explain the power position of three principal elites...business executives... military chiefs...and that of the national political leaders – but the unity of the power elite as a single group, and the basis of its power, are not explained. Why is there one power elite and not three?

More recent elitist approaches have, however, become more flexible in their treatment of these issues and this has allowed for some modifications to the core propositions underpinning elite theory:

(a) the rulers of society are engaged in an ongoing process of competitive elitism;
(b) while this group remains territorially based within a nation state, due to global imperatives it will have linkages and/or membership of global elite networks in order to maintain its power base in society;
(c) the ruling elite remains 'closed-off' from the ruled; and,
(d) the power bases of its members are selected by virtue of a broader range of resources –economic, political, ideological or technical.

These conceptual modifications represent a source of partial convergence with the Marxist conception of the ruling class as the outcome of class struggle and the emphasis within neo-pluralisms on the uniquely privileged role of sectional interests in contemporary policy-making. Furthermore, as the world of public policy has become increasingly small due to dramatic changes in global political and economic institutional structures and to nation states themselves, the territorial claim underpinning classical elite theory has been challenged too. A process of external 'hollowing-out' has occurred to different degrees in different states as a consequence of the differential impact of processes of globalization on domestic policy formation such as changes in the nature of geopolitics, political integration, the internationalization of financial markets and global communications. These processes have created the space for the emergence of new elites at the transnational (e.g. multi-national corporations), supranational (e.g. the European Union bureaucratic elite), and international (e.g. international policy-making elites associated with global financial institutions such as the International Monetary Fund and the World Bank) levels.

Coterminously, a process of internal 'hollowing-out' of the state has occurred to different degrees in different countries as a consequence of the differential impact of processes of privatization, the marketization of public services, and, decentralization on both the institutional architecture of the state and domestic policy formation. This shift from traditional government to collaborative governance has increased the range of non-state actors involved in delivering public goods, transforming the character of governing elites and facilitating an opportunity structure for cross-sectoral and international policy learning. The policy agenda in many, but not all, nation states has thus become increasingly internationalized, particularly with regard to issues such as: stable economic management and economic prudence; public management based upon economy, efficiency and effectiveness; a change in the emphasis of government intervention so that it deals with education, training and infrastructure and not industrial intervention; public–private partnerships in economic development; reform of the welfare state through managed welfarism; and, reinventing government through decentralization and the opening-up of government.

This chapter provides a critical review of the content and nature of elite theory from its classical origins and assesses its contribution to our understanding of contemporary societies. The argument is organized into three parts. Part one discusses the emergence of classical elitism and its core propositions. In part two we examine the contribution of a range of modern elitist perspectives, which seek to understand the operational bases of modern governing elites. Part three focuses on four contemporary elitist approaches – the epistemic community approach, the statecraft approach, policy network analysis and urban regime theory. Each of these approaches offer an elitist perspective on the form and function of governing elites at different levels of governance: epistemic community theory at the international level; the statecraft approach at the macro level; the policy network approach at the sub-sectoral level; and, urban regime theory at the city level.

Classical elitism

Although the origins of the ideas informing elite theory can be extrapolated from the political thought of Plato, Machiavelli and others, elitism as a theory of social power is most associated in its earliest form with the work of Robert Michels (1911 [1962]), Vilfredo Pareto (1935), and Gaetano Mosca (1896 [1939]). Their common thesis was that the concentration of social power in a small set of controlling elites was inevitable in all societies and they disagreed with Karl Marx's vision of evolutionary change towards a classless society. Each of these thinkers engage in a critique of Marxism and Pluralism which emphasizes the rejection of both the concepts of class domination and the diffusion of power on pluralist lines.

Michels (1911 [1962]: 364) argued that the practical ideal of democracy consisted in the self-government of the masses in conformity with the decision-making of popular assemblies. However, while this system placed limits upon the extension of the principle of delegation, it fails, 'to provide any guarantee against the formation of an oligarchic camarilla'. In short, for Michels, direct government by the masses was impossible. He also applied a similar argument to political parties. In his view, the technical and administrative functions of political parties make first bureaucracy and then oligarchy inevitable. Hence, for Michels (1911 [1962]: 364) '[w]ho says organization, says oligarchy'. This maxim clearly determined his conception of the nature of elites. His much quoted notion of the 'iron law of oligarchy' provides the key to Michels thoughts on the nature of elite structures, as it emphasizes the dominance of the leadership over the rank and file membership. Elite circulation is maintained by the inability of the masses to mobilize against the leadership view. This ensures their subjugation to the whim of the elite. In essence, it is the very existence of this system of leadership, which is incompatible with the tenets of liberal democracy and pluralism.

Pareto argued that historical experience provides testimony to the perpetual circulation of elites and oligarchy and that every field of human enterprise has its own elite. He borrowed two categories of elites from Machiavelli, 'Foxes' and 'Lions' (1935 [1961]: 99 and 110), in order to illustrate the nature of governing elite structures. The two categories stand at opposite ends of a continuum of government. 'Foxes' govern by attempting to gain consent and are not prepared to use force; they are intelligent and cunning, enterprising, artistic and innovative. However, in times of crisis their misplaced humanitarianism leads them towards compromise and pacifism. Hence, for Pareto, when final attempts to reach a political solution have failed the regime is fatally weakened. 'Lions' are situated at the opposite end of the continuum. They are depicted as men of strength, stability and integrity. Cold and unimaginative, they are self-serving and are prepared to use force to achieve or maintain their position. 'Lions' are defenders of the status quo in both the state and civil society and they are likely to be committed to public order, religion and political orthodoxy. For Pareto, the qualities of 'Fox' and 'Lion' are generally mutually exclusive and history is a process of circulation between these two types of elites. This ongoing process of elite renewal, circulation and replacement help to illuminate his thesis that an elite rules in all organized societies. Pareto's ideal system of governance would reflect a balance of forces, which exhibits characteristics of both 'Fox' and 'Lion'.

Pareto's identification of the concentration of power in the hands of a narrow political elite represented a rejection of both vulgar economistic Marxism and political liberalism. It rejected the Marxist conception of the state as a mere tool of the ruling class and the notion of class conflict. At the same time, Pareto's elitist perspective is at odds with the claims of political liberalism that state acts as a co-ordinator of the national interest in a plural society.

In a similar vein, Mosca argued that elites were inevitable as all societies are characterized by the dictatorship of the majority by the minority. He identified the existence of a ruling, but not necessarily economically dominant, class from which key office holders were drawn. Within Mosca's formulation each ruling class develops a political formula, which maintains and legitimates its rule to the rest of the population. Elite circulation will usually occur through inheritance but, from time to time, power will pass into the hands of another class due to the failure and collapse of the political formula. Mosca's conceptualization of the political formula has much in common with the concept of hegemony, which was derived from the views of Marx and Engels in *The German Ideology*; that the ideas of the ruling class are in every historical stage the ruling ideas. Hence, the ruling class, which is the dominant economic group in society, is, at the same time, its ruling intellectual force. In other words, a Marxist would say that those people owning the means of production also control the process of government and can use this source of domination to impose their views on society. This results in a false consciousness among the proletariat, whereby they accept their subordinate position in capitalist society and do not question the existing social and political structure. Mosca failed to develop the concept of political formula in any systematic way unlike his Marxist contemporary, Antonio Gramsci. Nevertheless, the centrality of the ideological dimension to an understanding of the dialectic of power domination and control is an important consideration which Mosca's research clearly overlooked.

The classical elitists in perspective

Michels, Pareto and Mosca generally assume the integration of elites without any rigorous empirical investigation. Michels argued that Western European political parties were characterized by elite domination, but his fondness for selecting convenient empirical evidence to support his arguments is vulnerable to counter critique. Moreover, Pareto failed to demonstrate a theory of elite domination in his native Italy and while Mosca showed that governments in the past were often characterized by a self-serving elite, he did not establish that this was always the case. Perhaps not surprisingly then given this classical legacy, subsequent elite theorists have strongly disagreed about the nature, causes and consequences of elite rule in western industrialized societies.

Modern elitist perspectives – from radical elitism to the statists

This section reviews a selective number of modern elitist perspectives. It concentrates on two key areas of consideration within the history of elitist thought: national elite power studies and state-centred 'governing elite' perspectives.

National elite power studies

The study of national elite power networks has long been a focus of study in the United States and Britain. The key concern of this literature has been to identify the degree to which national elite structures are unified or diversified. The origins of these studies lie in the pluralist–radical elitist debates of the 1940s and 1950s in the United States. These had two chief protagonists: C. Wright Mills (1956) who in *The Power Elite* provided an account of the role of power elites within the US executive; and James Burnham who argued in *The Managerial Revolution* (1943) that a new managerial elite was in the process of establishing control across all capitalist states.

It was the work of the radical elitist C. Wright Mills, however, which had the most impact on future studies. His theory involved a three-level gradation of the distribution of power. At the top level were those in command of the major institutional hierarchies of modern society – the executive branch of the national government, the large business corporations, and the military establishment. The pluralist model of competing interests, Mills argued, applied only to the 'middle levels', the semi-organized stalemate of interest group and legislative politics, which pluralists mistook for the entire power structure of the capitalist state. A politically fragmented 'society of the masses' occupied the bottom level.

Mills (1956: 167–9) work suggested a close relationship between economic elites and governmental elites – the 'corporate rich' and the 'political directorate'. He maintained that the growing centralization of power in the federal executive branch of government had been accompanied by a declining role for professional politicians and a growing role for 'political outsiders' from the corporate world (*ibid.*: 235). However (*ibid.*: 170), he believed that it would be a mistake 'to believe that the political apparatus is merely an extension of the corporate world, or that it had been taken over by the representatives of the corporate rich.' Here Mills wanted to distinguish his position from what he termed the 'simple Marxian view', which held that economic elites were the real holders of power. For this reason, he used the term 'power elite' rather than 'ruling class', a term, which for him implied too much economic determinism (*ibid.*: 276–7). Crucially, Mills argued that political, military, and economic elites all exercised a considerable degree of autonomy, were often in conflict, and rarely acted in concert. *The Power Elite* provided the most important critique of pluralism written from an elitist perspective. It emphasized that, far from being an independent arbiter of the national interest, the state was actually dominated by a power elite comprised of politicians, military and corporate bosses who moulded public policy to suit their own ends:

> The conception of the power elite and of its unity rests upon the corresponding developments and the coincidence of interests among economic, political, and military organizations. It also rests upon the similarity of origins and outlook, and the social and personal intermingling of the top circles from each of these dominant hierarchies. (Mills 1956: 292)

The existence of a broad, inclusive network of powerful persons with similar social origins, in different institutions, is an important feature of this view of the power structure. However, the power-elite literature identifies three key dimensions of political elite integration: social homogeneity which emphasizes shared class and status origins; value consensus which focuses on agreement among elites on the 'rules of the game', and, personal interaction among elites both informally through social and personal interaction and formally through membership of common organizations. This third dimension is reflected in the interlocking directorates of major US corporations. These ties are seen to foster integration, cohesiveness and consensus within the business community. Many social scientists, particularly in the US, have examined these sociometric ties among elites in individual communities (see Kadushin 1974; Laumann and Pappi 1973, 1976; Laumann *et al.* 1977) but few have turned their attention to the national level.

The pluralist critique of elite studies rests on the view that these elites are not cohesive; that is that they fail to act in concert. Each elite group is distinct and narrowly based, with its influence confined to the issues most relevant to its membership (see Dahl 1961a; and Polsby 1963). Thus, elites are seen as fragmented rather than integrated since each is involved primarily with its own relatively narrow concerns and constituencies. In a critique of elitism, Dahl (1958) argued that elite theorists frequently make the mistake of equating a capacity for control with facilitative power. The formation of a ruling elite requires not only control over important resources but also the establishment of unity and cohesiveness among its members. Clearly, the Marxist account of ruling class theory would place less emphasis upon the importance of social origins among members of the political elite in a society with a capitalist economy. The Marxist approach would argue that bias in favour of capitalist interests is built into the policy-making process, guaranteeing that those interests are protected by occupants in key positions within the state apparatus, whatever their origins (see Miliband, 1969).

In the UK, power elite studies have rarely reached any degree of sophistication. Several historians have considered the fate of the English aristocracy dwelling on the changing nature of the relationship between landed and mercantile interests or the declining role of the landed aristocracy in the government of rural England. William Gutsman (1963), for example, studied the decline of the upper class and the rise of the middle class as a principal source of elite renewal. While Anthony Sampson (1962, 1965, 1971, 1982) in his exhaustive accounts of the anatomy of Britain argued that the aristocracy no longer rules and, indeed, that there is no longer a real social elite at all. Further, Sampson contends that the various hierarchies of British society have become gradually more open in their recruitment and the diversity of these hierarchies is such that there is no single centre of power. Sampson's analyses remain limited, however, in the sense that they fail to place political power in its broader socio-economic context.

John Scott (1991), remains the most imaginative of contemporary British social scientists working within the power elite tradition. Scott (1991: 1) argues that there is a widely held view in Britain that, 'there is a small minority, which holds a ruling position in its economy, society, and political system'. This minority has been described in numerous varying ways: 'The establishment', 'the powers that be', 'the ruling few', the 'elite', or more prosaically, 'them'. His work is structured by an interest in two key issues which characterize modern elitist thought: is the elite a nominal category of office holders or a real, cohesive active and self-perpetuating social group?; and, do members of the elite use their power for sectional or public purposes? Scott (1991: 119) identified two central forms of power elite, *exclusive* and *inclusive*. The former exists, 'where the power bloc is drawn from a restricted and highly uniform social background and so is able to achieve a high level of solidarity'; the latter where 'a solidaristic power bloc is not dominated by any particular class'.

Scott's analysis (1991: 4–5) epitomizes the convergence between elitist and Marxist theories of the state drawing on the work of both Weber and Marx, '[s]pecifically, I use Weber's analytical distinctions between class, status, and party as ways of clarifying the Marxian concepts of the capitalist state and the ruling class'. Indeed, for Scott, the concepts of 'capitalist class', 'upper circle' and 'state elite' are interchangeable terms for describing privileged groups, which exercise power deriving from class, status, and politics. His conclusion (1991: 151–2) to the question 'Who rules Britain?' reflects the balance of these concerns: 'Britain is ruled by a capitalist class whose economic dominance is sustained by the operations of the state and whose members are disproportionately represented in the power elite which rules the state apparatus. That is to say, Britain does have a ruling class.'

The statists and the governing elite

By the mid-1980s virtually every significant current of theoretical work in political science was united in a renewed interest in the state itself as the fundamental unit of analysis. As Peter Evans, Dietrich Rueschemeyer and Theda Skocpol (1985: 3) acknowledge, 'the state as an actor or institution has been highlighted'. The two leading exponents of the statist position are Theda Skocpol (1979) and Michael Mann (1988).

Skocpol advances what she terms an organizational realist approach, which rejects the dominant assumption of both Liberal and Marxist variants of social theory that political structures and struggles can be reduced (at least 'in the last instance') to socio-economic forces and conflicts. In this view, the state is nothing more than an arena in which social and economic conflict takes place – the crucial difference between these theories rests on whether the arena is legitimate and consensually constructed or a vehicle for coercive domination. For Skocpol, in contrast, the state as a system of organized coercion needs to be treated as an autonomous structure and actor. Skocpol (1979: 26) argues that 'within the terms of these theories, it is consequently virtually impossible even to raise the possibility that fundamental conflicts of interest might arise between the existing dominant class or set of groups, on the one hand, and the state rulers on the other.' However, she does concede that developments in the Marxist theory of the state are cognizant with this problem and, through the debate on the relative autonomy of the state (Miliband 1970, 1973), have identified the potential for independent agency by the state from direct control by the dominant class.

Within this literature much attention has been devoted to the range of structural constraints, which an existing regime of accumulation places upon the options for state structure and agency. The argument has developed that state elites may at times need to be free from a specific dominant class group in order to forward the long-term interest of an entire dominant class. However, Marxists have stopped short of asserting that states are potentially autonomous from dominant classes, class structures or modes of production. Skocpol attempts to move beyond the Marxist assumption that state forms and activities vary in accordance with modes of production and that state rulers cannot possibly act against the basic interests of a dominant class. She thus explicitly treats the state as autonomous and thus implies that state and civil society co-exist as two separate entities; a clear methodological flaw. Only in this limited sense does Skocpol move beyond the argument of how states vary with, and function for, modes of production and dominant classes.

Skocpol develops six key propositions which characterize the statist position:

1. the class upheavals and socio-economic transformations which have characterized social revolutions have been closely intertwined with the collapse of the state organizations of the old regimes and with the consolidation and functioning of the state organizations of the new regimes, hence, we can make sense of socio-revolutionary transformations only if we take the state seriously as a macro-structure;
2. the administrative and coercive organizations are the basis of state power;
3. these state organizations are potentially autonomous from direct-dominant class control;
4. state organizations necessarily compete to some extent with the dominant class(es) in appropriating resources from economy and society;
5. although a state usually functions to preserve existing economic and class structures it nonetheless has its own distinct interests vis-à-vis the dominant class(es); and
6. states exist in determinant geopolitical environments in interaction with other actual or potential states/ geopolitical environments as well as economic and class structures condition and influence a state structure and the activities of its elite.

This formulation is significant in the sense that it stresses both the role of a powerful governing elite and the importance of treating the question of the legitimacy of governing elites as a key explanatory concept.

Mann's (1988: 4) principal interest lies in what he terms, 'the centralized institutional ensembles called states and the powers of the personnel who staff them'; hence, the 'governing or state elite'. His work confronts the question: what is the nature of the power possessed by states and state elites? He contrasts the power of state elites with power groupings in civil society such as: ideological movements; economic classes; and military elites. Mann emphasizes two meanings of state power, which correspond to the rise in the size, and complexity of the state and the decision-making process in advanced industrial societies. He recognizes these two meanings as analytically distinct and autonomous dimensions of power. The first, 'despotic power', relates to the range of actions which the elite is empowered to take without traditional negotiation with civil society and the second, 'infrastructural power', refers to the capacity of the state to actually penetrate civil society and to implement political decisions. Mann (1988: 5) observes that, '[t]he state penetrates everyday life more than did any historical state. Its infrastructural power has increased enormously.'

However, he also argues that although the capitalist state has a strong infrastructure it is also despotically weak. Capitalist states with strong infrastructures are powerful in relation to individuals and to the weaker groups in civil society, but feeble in relation to dominant groups, at least in comparison to most historical states. From these two independent dimensions of state power Mann derives the four ideal types of state formation: feudal, bureaucratic, imperial, and authoritarian. The first two he characterizes as low in despotic power but high in infrastructural co-ordination, the latter two as high in despotic power but low in infrastructural co-ordination. His typology stresses two major historical tendencies: a developmental tendency in the growth of the infrastructural power of the state; and, no general developmental tendency in the despotic powers of the state. Hence, although Mann (1988: 31) is in agreement with reductionist theorists that the state is essentially a contested arena, he locates this as precisely the origin and mechanism of its autonomous powers:

> Such state power resources, and the autonomy to which they lead, may not amount to much. If, however, the state's use of the conferred resources generates further power resources – as was, indeed, intended by the civil society groups themselves – these will normally flow through the state's hands, and thus lead to a significant degree of power autonomy. Therefore, autonomous state power is the product of the usefulness of enhanced territorial centralization to social life in general.

In Mann's view this has varied considerably through the history of societies, as has the power of states and governing elites.

The modern elitists in perspective

It would be wrong to exaggerate the novelty of the revival of interest in the state, for as Bob Jessop (1990: 283) has observed, 'the statists have simply rediscovered themes well known to traditional state theorists and not unknown in more recent pluralist, neo-Marxist and structural–functionalist work'. Moreover, as Domhoff (1987: 160) notes, the statists simply revisited the work of the radical elitists, who were well aware of the potentially autonomous power of the state. There is thus considerable disagreement amongst commentators as to whether there is a distinctive elitist approach (see, for example, Birch 1993: Ch. 11; and, Dunleavy and O'Leary 1987: Ch. 4). Certainly there has been a great deal of convergence with the distinction between the pluralist, Marxist and elitist positions becoming more blurred as the capitalist state has matured. Nonetheless it is important to note that elitism has always been a broad church. Indeed many theorists have treated Marxist theory as an elitist theory due to its its emphasis upon the state as an instrument for securing ruling class domination (see Birch, 1993: 186).

Contemporary elitist approaches

This final section of the chapter presents an analysis of the utility of four contemporary elitist perspectives which have been used for understanding policy-making processes at four different levels of governance: the international level; the macro-state level; the sub-sectoral level; and, the city level.

Elite governance at the international level – the epistemic community approach

In an attempt to reduce uncertainty in an interdependent world, co-operation between nation states through international regimes, such as the European Union (EU), has become inevitable (Keohane and Nye 1977). Epistemic communities play a key role in processing policy ideas through international regimes and diffusing such ideas to member states (see Table 2.1). An epistemic community may be viewed as a policy-making elite, which is comprised of natural, and/or social scientists or individuals from any discipline or profession with authoritative claims to policy relevant knowledge (Haas 1990). Epistemic communities have close relations with international regimes and attempt to use their knowledge resources to promote global awareness of certain policy problems and policy options. The membership of these communities share a set of causal and principled beliefs (analytic and normative) about policy-making that act as a filter mechanism for precluding certain unacceptable policy inputs and circumscribing membership of the community. A continuous process of bargaining and negotiation takes place within and between epistemic communities in a war of ideas. It has been argued by Adler and Haas (1992), and others, that policy-makers have become increasingly dependent on the intelligence-gathering skills and knowledge resources of epistemic communities. Indeed, a significant degree of international policy convergence can be identified with regard to food aid, financial regulation and environmental issues as a consequence of the influence of epistemic communities in regime politics in, for example, the EU. Regimes are the practical functional application of elite governance in international relations; for it is regimes that privilege certain elite actors above others (such as epistemic communities) and help to establish international policy agendas (see Higgott 1996: 21).

Regime theory and the concept of the epistemic community have been criticized in three main ways. First, regime theory underestimates the role of domestic actors and politics in shaping international policy agendas, for the views of state policy-makers ultimately determine the influence of an epistemic community. Secondly, regimes often act as a site of struggle between member states which may well lead to policy divergence rather

Table 2.1 *The characteristics of epistemic communities and policy communities*

Dimension	An epistemic community (Adler and Haas)	A policy community (Marsh and Rhodes)
Membership		
number of participants	Limited, a shared set of causal and principled beliefs (analytic and normative) act as a filter mechanism to preclude certain inputs.	Limited, a shared set of causal and principled beliefs (analytic and normative) act as a filter mechanism to preclude certain inputs.
type of interest	Includes natural and social scientists from any discipline or profession with authoritative claims to policy relevant knowledge which reside in international regimes.	Normally includes representatives of governmental interests, economic groups, and/or professional interests in tight-knit decision structure.
Integration		
frequency of interaction	An ongoing process of bargaining within and between epistemic communities.	Frequent, high-quality, interactions on all matters related to the policy arena.
continuity	Membership and values persist over time as long as reputation survives.	Membership, values and outcomes persist over time.
consensus	All participants share a consensual knowledge base and a common policy enterprise.	All participants share basic values and accept the legitimacy of the outcome.
Resources		
distribution of resources (within network)	All participants have knowledge resources in an exchange relationship.	All participants have resources in an exchange relationship.
distribution of resources (within participating organizations)	Policy-makers are dependent on the intelligence gathering skills and knowledge resources of the epistemic community.	Hierarchical; leaders can deliver members.
Power	The view of policy-makers ultimately determines the influence of an epistemic community and its status of acceptance.	A balance of power exists among members – although one group may dominate, it must be a positive-sum game if the community is to persist.

Sources: Adapted from Marsh and Rhodes (1992) and Adler and Haas (1992).

than convergence. Thirdly, epistemic communities tend to have influence in areas of policy-making with a high level of technical content such as environmental policy, but have much less influence in most other areas of policy-making. This third criticism illustrates the limited scope of the epistemic community approach as an elite theory of policy-making with general application.

Elite governance at the macro level: the statecraft approach

A more recent statist perspective is worthy of consideration here – the statecraft approach. Although this approach remains underdeveloped and in certain aspects lacking in conceptual clarity, it does provide a useful conceptual approach for understanding the approach of state elites to public policy-making. So what does the statecraft approach involve? The approach was originally developed by the British political scientist Jim Bulpitt in 1986 and has subsequently been applied by writers such as Jim Buller (2000). It emerged in response to a number of authors who stressed the importance of the New Right ideological project as an understanding of the emergence and development of Thatcherism in the UK (see Hall and Jacques 1983). Bulpitt disagreed with writers such as Stuart Hall and Martin Jacques that the New Right project provided the grand design of the Thatcher project and shaped the nature of the policy agenda. He argued that ideas themselves were never that important. Instead he emphasized the importance of what he termed statecraft or the 'politics of governing'.

The statecraft approach centres on the study of a political elite, which Bulpitt (1986 a and b; 1995) refers to as 'the Centre' or 'the Court', composed of party leaders and top civil servants and policy advisers. Bulpitt argues that this group has its own interests, which are distinct from the rest of society and can often successfully pursue these interests, even in the face of opposition from other actors. In other words, the statecraft approach is an elite theory of public policy-making. According to Bulpitt, there are three conditions of successful statecraft. Firstly, the Centre/Court needs to establish a set of governing objectives with the aim of winning elections and retaining office by achieving an image of governing competence. Secondly, in order to achieve these objectives it has to develop a governing code: a semi-secret set of principles, beliefs and practices. This involves the preservation and promotion of domestic autonomy over what Bulpitt calls 'High Politics' and the devolution of responsibility to 'Low Politics'. In practical terms, High Politics referred to all those policy issues, which the Centre considers to be vital to its chances of winning elections and achieving an image of governing competence. For Bulpitt, autonomy over High Politics was crucial to the achievement of governing competence.

Low Politics was a residual category. It refers to all the other matters perceived by the Centre to be too mundane, difficult or time-consuming to handle. Thirdly, in trying to win elections and achieve some semblance of governing competence, the Centre/Court will employ a set of 'political support mechanisms' to assist the governing code. These mechanisms refer to the functions of party management and the achievement of political argument hegemony. As Bulpitt (1986: 22) puts it, this refers to 'a winning rhetoric in a variety of locations, winning because either the framework of the party's arguments becomes generally acceptable, or because its solutions to a particularly important political problem seem more plausible than its opponents'. In other words, it is about winning the war of political ideas.

In short then, statecraft is about the politics of governing. It involves short-term tactical manoeuvring – qualities which are essential to every successful electoral strategy. It is also concerned with longer-term strategic calculation and action. For Bulpitt, governments can think strategically – alter institutions and structures to help them achieve their political goals more easily. The most high-profile illustration of the application of the statecraft approach to state governance was Thatcherism in the UK (1979–90). It represented an elite strategy which achieved domestic autonomy and governing competence and with it, electoral dominance throughout the 1980s.

Although the statecraft approach remains theoretically underdeveloped, it does provide the contours for an elite theory of domestic statecraft that emphasizes the relatively autonomous role of the party political elite in forwarding a strategy for winning the war of political ideas and maintaining electoral success. However, a comprehensive theory would involve a detailed operational exposition of the concepts of political argument hegemony, governing competence, polity management and strategy (see Buller 1999 for a full critique).

Elite governance at the sub-sectoral level: the case of policy networks

Policy network analysis has become the dominant paradigm for studying policy-making in European Political Science and has been applied at every level of governance (Rhodes 1997). Jack Walker (1989), for instance, analyses national elite policy networks which he argues exist in the transnational policy domain, while others use policy network analysis to understand sub-sectoral policy making within European Union, central, intergovernmental and local governance (see Marsh and Rhodes 1992). Policy network analysis is even employed as a method of comparative enquiry (see Marsh (ed.) 1998).

Network analysis proceeds from three simple, if contestable, assumptions about the nature of policy-making in liberal democracies. First, policy-making is the outcome of the interaction between policy networks, hierarchies (i.e. governmental structures) and markets. Secondly, it is an empirical regularity that policy communities are the most common form of network found in liberal democracies. These are tight-knit decision-making structures characterized by a limited number of privileged participants in a resource dependent relationship. Thirdly, policy communities constitute an elite system of governance.

In a seminal article, J. K. Benson (1982: 148) defines policy networks as a, 'cluster or complex of organizations connected to each other by resource dependencies and distinguished from other clusters or complexes by breaks in the structure of resource dependencies'. The concept of a policy network is thus employed as a generic term to categorize the relationship between groups, third sector organizations and government/ government agencies. Within the general categorization there are different types of policy network. These can be situated along a continuum with policy communities at one end of the spectrum and issue networks at the other. In a policy community there is a limited number of participants who share values on policy outcomes with a limited number of decision-making centres (see Table 2.1). All participants have resources that are integral to successful policy development. Hence the basic relationship between actors is an exchange relationship based upon resource dependency. Decisions are made with the exclusion of the public and legislatures. If a policy community exists it is possible to depoliticize a policy arena by excluding groups from the policy-making process who are likely to disagree with the established policy agenda. This process of gate-keeping maintains the status quo and establishes insiders and outsiders in the policy process. In contrast, in an issue network there exists a broad range of policy actors moving in and out of the policy arena with different conceptions of the public good engaged in a war of ideas. Hence, policy-making is more likely to be pluralistic.

Most network analysts tend to emphasize the dominance of sectional interests within the policy-making process, particularly in liberal democracies with centralized systems of governance such as Greece or the UK (Chondroleou 2002). This is reflected in the identification of closed elite-driven policy communities in which elite circulation is dependent on the bargaining resources of the sectional interests involved. In the edited volume *Policy Networks in British Government* (1992), David Marsh and Rod Rhodes, together with a team of research students and junior lecturers at the University of Essex, provided an empirical test of what has become the dominant approach to the study of policy networks – the Rhodes model (see Table 2.1). Rhodes's meso-level typology was combined with a limited macro-level analysis with the aim of assessing policy network effects on policy outcomes and, by implication, policy change. However, Marsh and Rhodes (1992: 260) conclude that: 'networks are but one component of an explanation of policy change – there is no agreed definition of, or criterion for measuring, the degree of change in policy networks'. Hence, for Marsh and Rhodes, while networks matter, policy network analysis itself was not equipped to provide an explanation of policy change.

The notion of a policy network does appear to capture some of the key features of contemporary governance – collaboration between state and non-state actors in the delivery of public goods at the sub-sectoral level; the importance of resource dependency; the increasing influence of privileged groups in policy-making at the sub-sectoral level; and, the multi-level character of contemporary governance. However, policy network analysis itself has self-evident shortcomings as an explanatory theory of policy-making (see Dowding 2001 and Evans 2001). Minimally, an explanatory theory involves a systematically related set of statements, including some law-like generalizations that are empirically testable. Policy network analysis does not meet this definition. At best it may be viewed as a metaphor that likens policy formation to the outcome of interactions between governmental and non-governmental actors within a network setting but does not explain how and why they change over time. This argument does not negate the importance of the policy network approach. A sound model is not necessarily one that purely explains or predicts with precision. It can be one rich with implications. Novel hypotheses may be extracted from the policy network approach which must themselves be articulated in a systematic fashion and subject to empirical test.

Elite governance at the city level: the case of urban regimes

Urban regime theory (URT) has its roots in Charles Lindblom's neo-pluralism (Lindblom 1977: 175). In coming to terms with obvious flaws in the classical pluralist approach, he recognized that governments in capitalist countries need the economy to be successful and that in a market system, decisions are taken by business in which government plays no role:

> Any government official who understands the requirements of his position and the responsibilities that market orientated systems throw on businessmen will therefore grant them a privileged position. He does not have to be bribed, duped or pressured to do so...He simply understands...that public affairs in market orientated systems are in the hands of two group leaders, government and business, who must collaborate and that to make the system work government leadership must often defer to business leadership.

This passage reflects the assumptions upon which Stephen Elkin (1986) draws in his discussion of the city regime. The emergence of growth machine and urban regime theories may also be interpreted as a revival of the community power debate of the 1950s and 1960s around the question of: who runs cities?

Elkin (1986) develops the concept of the city regime from his identification of systematic bias towards business in US city government. The systematic bias, which he identifies, does not arise as a consequence of immutable economic determinants, but rather through political and institutional structures, which privilege the economic domain. For Elkin (1986: 18), City politicians, administrators and political institutions are systematically biased in favour of business interests. The dispersal of political power is a consequence of the 'division of labour between state and market that is manifest in cities'. There are two interdependent structural considerations to take into account here – the notion of representative government and the private ownership of productive assets by the business community. Public officials cannot control economic performance at the local level. The city government can, indeed must, 'induce' but not 'command' economic behaviour. The objective of Elkin's research is to demonstrate that the system is skewed against the emergence of policies which are concerned with broader social issues and that the city government is required to labour on behalf of the business community. This represents a structural failure of popular control. Business domination is facilitated by three principal factors. First, the relationships between city government and the business community are defined by the need for cities to raise credit in private markets. Credit is linked directly to the perceived economic prospects of the city. Hence antipathy towards business would be an immediate invitation to 'fiscal trouble'. Secondly, the balance of forces is weighed towards business interests by virtue of the non-dependence of capital in the locality. Thirdly, local politicians are also dependent upon privately backed electoral coalitions, which must maintain a 'sufficient flow of benefactions'. While Elkin (1986: 30–88) does not detect systematic bias among bureaucrats, he argues that parochialism and self-interest among those concerned with economic development leads them to favour business in that area. The key policy arena around which growth alliances of this type form is that of land use. This is based upon the assumption that land and property values are the key indicator of the ability of the city government to obtain credit. The overall conclusion to be drawn from Elkin's work is not that elected officials are dominated by business, but rather that they have a mutual interest in economic growth.

The public policy literature adopts diverse conclusions in assessing the comparative utility of URT. There is a broad spectrum of opinion, from those who argue that if properly adapted it represents a suitable framework

(Stoker and Mossberger 1994), to those who consider that the concept may highlight the need for a focus on the phenomenon of partnership, but that it does not adequately explain this in the UK or European context (see Davies 2001). The dependence of city governments upon business interests and hence the issue of whether there is a need for an urban regime, ultimately rests on the degree of the city's reliance on local capital in order to discharge its responsibilities. In political systems characterized by strong party discipline and centralized systems of local government finance such as the UK, the need for urban regimes only emerges in city's featured by brute scarcity or the need to fund large scale projects such as Manchester's successful bid to host the Commonwealth Games.

In summary

The relative value of elite theory must be assessed by its ability to resolve important questions about the nature of contemporary political systems. Do the rulers of society constitute a social group? Is it cohesive or divided? Is it territorially based? How are its members selected? What is the basis of their power? Is this power constrained by other groups in society? Are there differences between societies in these respects, and if so, how can we explain them. It is clear from this survey that many of the core propositions underpinning classical elite theory are no longer tenable. There is insufficient evidence to suggest that governing elites act as cohesive, active and self-perpetuating social groups. Moreover, while the power of governing elites remains territorially based, success rests on the ability to gain competitive advantages within global market places through international networks of governance. Furthermore, when contrasted with other theories of the state, contemporary elite theory tends to be preoccupied with the nature and role of privileged elites in decision-making centres and pays less attention to developing a broader understanding of the relationship between the state and civil society or the relationship between elite circulation and the nature of state crisis and legitimation. This is because elite theory as a grand narrative remains difficult to sustain in an empirical sense.

Nonetheless, elitism still provides an important focus for the work of political scientists because both the ownership and control of wealth and the monopoly of political power still resides in the hands of the few. As Domhoff (cited in Olsen and Marger (eds) 1993: 180) puts it, with regard to the United States:

we should continue to remind ourselves that members of an upper class making up less than 1 per cent of the population own 20 to 25 per cent of all privately held wealth and 45 to 50 per cent of all privately held corporate stock; they are over represented in seats of formal power from the corporation to the federal government; and they win much more often than they lose on issues ranging from the tax structure to labor law to foreign policy.

Moreover, as Pierce (2004: 1) notes of the United Kingdom:

> seven hundred aristocratic landowners continue to own a tenth of the total land area of England. Whilst this acreage may appear small, it is larger than the combined estates in England of the Forestry Commission, the Ministry of Defence, the National Trust and the Crown Estate.

In sum, elitism continues to present a compelling critique of the Liberal democratic model in theory but has proved limited in providing the methodological tools necessary to demonstrate that all societies must be elitist in practice.

Further reading

Bottomore, T. (1993) *Elites and Society* (London: Routledge).

Domhoff, G. (1987) *Who Rules America?* (Engiewood Cliffs, NJ: Prentice-Hall).

Keohane, R. and Nye, J. (1977) *Power and Interdependence* (Boston: Little, Brown).

Krasner, S. D. (ed.) (1983) *International Regimes* (Ithaca, NY: Cornell University Press).

Michels, R. (1911 [1962]) *Political Parties* (New York: Free Press).

Mills, C. W. (1956) *The Power Elite* (New York: Oxford University Press).

Mosca, G. (1896 [1939]) *The Ruling Class* (New York: McGraw-Hill).

Pareto, V. (1935) *The Mind and Society* (London: Cape).

Scott, J. (1991) *Who Rules Britain?* (Cambridge: Polity Press).

Chapter 3

(What's Marxist about) Marxist State Theory?

COLIN HAY*

> Like Henry Higgins who, through his work changed the object of his studies into something other than what it was, the purpose of the Marxist theory of the state is not just to understand the capitalist state but to aid in its destruction. (Wolfe 1974: 131)

If Marxism, like feminism, is seen as 'engaged theory' (Bryson 1992: 1), not content merely to interpret the world but motivated by an overriding ambition to change it, then it is something of an understatement to say that the Marxist theory of the state cannot be judged a complete success. Indeed, a decade and half after the disintegration of 'actually existing socialism' it is surely tempting to dismiss the Marxist theory of the state as of purely historical interest. Yet the argument of this chapter is that, partly by virtue of its attempts to explain capitalism's (for its) surprising longevity, Marxist theories of the state offer a series of powerful and probing insights into the complex and dynamic relationship between state, economy and society in capitalist democracies, from which other theorists of the state can learn much.

Consequently, this chapter aims to provide an assessment of the contribution of Marxism to our understanding of the state whilst charting, albeit in a stylized way, the development of Marxist and neo-Marxist approaches to the study and analysis of the state from Marx and Engels, via Lenin and Gramsci, Miliband and Poulantzas to a range of contemporary authors, notably Block and Jessop. The argument unfolds in three sections. In the first we consider why it is that Marxists require a theory of the state and how Marxists have conceptualized this focus of their attention. The second section traces the development of the Marxist theory of the state through the work of the founding fathers, its reformulation by Lenin and Gramsci,

---

* An earlier version of this chapter appeared under the title 'Marxism and the State' in Andrew Gamble, David Marsh and Tony Tant (eds), *Marxism and Social Science* (1999), and sections taken from that source are reproduced here by permission of Palgrave Macmillan and the University of Illinois Press.

and the revival of interest in Marxist state theory in the post-war period. The final section considers the contemporary development of Marxist/ neo-Marxist state theory asking whether such theories have become ever more sophisticated by becoming ever less Marxist and asking whether we need a Marxist theory of the state today.

Marxism and the state

> The modern state is ... an amorphous complex of agencies with ill-defined boundaries performing a variety of not very distinctive functions.
> (Schmitter 1985: 33)

It might seem somewhat strange, if not downright defeatist, to begin a chapter on the Marxist theory of the state with this comment. Yet in one sense it provides a particularly appropriate starting point. For, as I have remarked elsewhere, 'there is no more arduous task in the theory of the state than defining this notoriously elusive and rapidly moving target' (Hay 1996a: 2). We begin then with perhaps the second most neglected question in the study of the state – what is it? – before moving on to the first – why do we need a theory of it anyway? In fact, as we shall see, although the definitions offered by Marxists are often implicit rather than explicit, and although their justifications for a concern with the state are often somewhat cryptic, it is to their credit that theorists within this tradition have not been short of answers.

What is the state?

A moment's foray into the now substantial annals of Marxist state theory will reveal that whilst Marxists may well rely *implicitly* upon certain conceptions and understandings of the state, they are notoriously bad at consigning these to the page. This makes it somewhat difficult to identify any analytically precise Marxist definition of the state as an object of inquiry, let alone one that is commonly agreed upon. Family resemblances in the assumptions which inform Marxist conceptions of the state can nonetheless be identified – indeed, these can be crystallized into four rather different conceptions of the state.

The state as the repressive arm of the bourgeoisie

According to Martin Carnoy: 'it is the notion of the [capitalist] state as the repressive apparatus of the bourgeoisie that is the distinctly Marxist characteristic of the state' (Carnoy 1984: 50). This somewhat one-dimensional conception of state power (the state as the expression of the repressive might of the ruling class) is most closely associated with Lenin's *The State and Revolution* (1917 [1968]), but is also appealed to in the work of Engels (see, for instance, 1844 [1975]: 205–7; 1884 [1978]: 340; cf. van den Berg 1988: 30–1). Its functionalism – the attempt to explain something by appeal to its consequences – is well captured by Hal Draper:

> The state...comes into existence insofar as the institutions needed to carry out the common functions of society require, for their continued maintenance, the separation of the power of forcible coercion from the general body of society. (Draper 1977: 50)

The state as an instrument of the ruling class

The 'instrumentalist' position as it has become known (see below) provides perhaps the most prevalent conception of the state within Marxist theory. It is most often accorded the status of *the* Marxist theory of the state, despite the fact that instrumentalism itself spans a wide diversity of positions expressing rather divergent *theories* of the state. In its most crudely stated form it implies that the state is 'an instrument in the hands of the ruling class for enforcing and guaranteeing the stability of the class structure itself' (Sweezy 1942: 243). Within this distinctive school, 'the functioning of the state is...understood in terms of the instrumental exercise of power by people in strategic positions, either directly through the manipulation of state policies or indirectly through the exercise of pressure on the state' (Gold *et al.* 1975a: 34). Instrumentalists or 'influence theorists', as Offe terms them (1974: 32), have concerned themselves with the analyses of: (i) the patterns and networks of personal and social ties between individuals occupying positions of economic power in so-called 'power structure research' studies (Domhoff 1967, 1970, 1980; Mintz and Schwartz 1985; for a review see Barrow 1993: 13–24); (ii) the social connections between those holding positions of economic power and the state elite (Domhoff 1979, 1990; Miliband 1969; for a review see Barrow 1993: 24–41); and (iii) the social processes moulding the ideological commitments of the state and social elite (Miliband 1969).

The state as an ideal collective capitalist

The conception of the state as an ideal collective capitalist has its origins in Engels' frequently cited (though incidental) remark in *Anti-Dühring*, that 'the modern state, no matter what its form, is essentially a capitalist machine, the state of the capitalists, the ideal personification of the total national capital' (1878 [1947]: 338). Advocates of this conception of the state point to the fact that capital is neither self-reproducing nor capable on its own of securing the conditions of its own reproduction. For the very continuity of the capitalist social formation is dependent upon certain interventions being made which, though in the general interest of capital collectively, are not in the individual interest of any particular capital (Hirsch 1978: 66). In rational choice theoretical terms, this is a 'collective action problem' (see, for instance, Dunleavy 1991: 30–6). An external, and at least *relatively* autonomous body or institutional ensemble is thus called upon to intervene on behalf of capital in its long-term general interests (as opposed to the conflicting short-term interests of individual capitals). This body is the state – the 'ideal collective capitalist' (Altvater 1973). As Offe explains, 'it is not without good reason that Engels...calls the state the "ideal" collective capitalist; for the state as a "real" collective capitalist would clearly be a logical impossibility... firstly because the state apparatus is not itself a "capitalist"... and secondly because the concept of the collective capitalist is itself nonsensical in that competition...is essential for the movement of capital' (1974: 31).

The state as a factor of cohesion within the social formation

Though most clearly associated with the work of Nicos Poulantzas whose phrase it is, the notion of the state as a 'factor of cohesion' can be traced (as indeed it is by Poulantzas) to another incidental and (characteristically) underdeveloped comment by Engels in *The Origin of the Family, Private Property and the State*:

> [I]n order that...classes with conflicting economic interests, shall not consume themselves and society in fruitless struggle, it became necessary to have a power seemingly standing above society that would moderate the conflict and keep it within the bounds of 'order'; and this power, arisen out of society but placing itself above it and alienating itself more and more from it, is the state. (Engels 1884 [1978]: 205–6; see also Bukharin 1921 [1926])

Within this conception, the state is understood in terms of its effects and is defined in terms of its role in maintaining 'the unity and cohesion of a social formation by concentrating and sanctioning class domination' (Poulantzas 1978: 24–5; see also 1973: 44–56, esp. 44, 304; Gramsci 1971: 244; Jessop 1985: 61, 177). We return to the problems of this conception below.

As the above discussion demonstrates, the state has meant (and continues to mean) many things to many Marxists.

Why do Marxists need a theory of the state?

Given Alan Wolfe's comments with which this chapter opened, it would not seem unreasonable to expect of those who advance such a theory an answer to the question 'how precisely does a Marxist theory of the state advance the cause of progressive social transformation'? Yet, unlike, say, their feminist counterparts (Brown 1992; Connell 1990; MacKinnon 1982, 1983, 1985; see also Chapter 6), Marxists have rarely been called upon to offer any such justification for their theoretical endeavours and choices. Explicit answers to the question 'Why do Marxists need a theory of the state?' (far less, 'Why does anyone else need a *Marxist* theory of the state?') are difficult to find. Yet they are not, perhaps, so difficult to derive from what Marxist theorists have said about the state's form and function.

Here we can usefully follow the so-called German 'state-derivationists'. For although their work is in many respects deeply problematic (see Barrow 1993: 94–5; Jessop 1982: 78–101), it certainly served to highlight the centrality of the state to the process of capitalist reproduction. The derivationists, as the label would imply, sought to *derive* the form and function of the capitalist state from the requirements of the capitalist mode of production. For our purposes we are not concerned to demonstrate, as were they, that the state must by some inexorable inner logic necessarily satisfy such functional requirements, but merely that it is indeed implicated in processes crucial to the reproduction of capitalist relations. Thus, although their perspective can never *explain* the form and/or (dys)function of the capitalist state, as its advocates believed, it can nonetheless provide us with an exceedingly useful heuristic. For insofar as capitalist social relations *are* reproduced (and it doesn't take much insight to see that in the societies we inhabit they are), such functions must indeed be performed by some institution, apparatus, or combination thereof. It is not a particularly large step to suggest that many (if not all) of these institutions are either state apparatuses themselves or are heavily regulated by the state. The state thus emerges as a nodal point in the network of power relations that characterizes contemporary capitalist societies and, hence, a key focus of Marxist attention. It is not surprising then that Ralph Miliband is led to conclude that: 'in the politics of Marxism there is no institution which is nearly as important as the state' (1977: 66).

So how, precisely, is the capitalist state implicated in the expanded reproduction of capital? Or, to put it another way, what are the functions that must be performed by the state *if* capitalist social relations are to be reproduced? Numerous aspects of this role can be identified. Taken together they provide ample justification for a distinctively Marxist theory of the state within Marxist theory more generally.

Firstly we might point to the fact that capital is fragmented into a large number of competitive units, yet crucially relies on certain generic conditions being satisfied if surplus value is to be extracted from labour and profit secured (Altvater 1973). The state is, in short, a response to capitalism's collective action problem. Picture a hypothetical capitalist economy unregulated by the state (the archetypal free market) and comprised inevitably of a multitude of competing capitals. Such an economy is inherently crisis-prone. For no individual capital competing for its very survival will sacrifice its own interest in the general interest. Contradictions or 'steering problems' inevitably arise within such an unregulated economy yet can never be resolved. Accordingly they will accumulate until they eventually threaten the very stability of capitalism itself – precipitating a fully-fledged crisis of the mode of production. A capitalist economy without regulation, despite the now pervasive rhetoric of the free-marketeers, is inherently unstable (Aglietta 1979; Habermas 1975; 24–31; Jänicke 1990: 8; Offe 1975; cf. the discussion of 'market-failure' in Chapter 5).

Now enter the state – as a more-or-less 'ideal collective capitalist'. Altvater argues that this state must necessarily intervene within the capitalist economy to secure conditions conducive to continuing capitalist accumulation, thereby performing what he calls a 'general maintenance function' (1973; Jessop 1982: 90–1). This comprises: (i) the provision of general infrastructure – 'the material conditions that are necessary to all business activities but that cannot be produced directly [*and profitably*] by individual private businesses' (Barrow 1993: 80); (ii) the capacity to defend militarily a national economic space regulated by the state and to preserve an administrative boundary within which the state is sovereign; (iii) the provision of a legal system that establishes and enforces the right to possession of private property and which outlaws practices (such as insider-dealing) potentially damaging to the accumulation of capital within the national economy; and (iv) the intervention of the state to regulate and/or ameliorate class struggle and the inevitable conflict between capital and labour.

Such interventions establish what Jürgen Habermas terms the 'logic of crisis displacement'. By this he means that fundamental crises originating (as 'steering problems') within the economy (and which might otherwise have rung the death-knell of capitalism itself) now become the responsibility of the state as the supreme regulator of the economy. Crises are thus *displaced* from the economy (which does *not* have the internal capacity to resolve them) to the state (which *may*, or *may not*). If the state as currently constituted cannot resolve such a crisis, then in the first instance it is the particular form of the capitalist state that is called into question, not the very stability of the capitalist mode of production itself. Consider, for instance, the widely-identified crisis of the late 1970s in Britain. Though precipitated to some extent by economic factors (such as the exhaustion of the post-war 'Fordist' mode of economic growth), as the subsequent Thatcherite restructuring demonstrates, this was a crisis of the British state, not of British capitalism *per se* (see Hay 1996a: Chs 5 and 6). The implications of this for a Marxist theory of the state are profound. For the state is revealed, once again, as playing a crucial role in safeguarding the circuit of capital. If we want to understand the operation of the capitalist mode of production we cannot afford to dispense with a theory of the state. Moreover, Habermas' argument suggests that if we wish to develop a theory of capitalist crisis (an understandably high priority within Marxist theory), then it is to the state that we must turn initially. For economic crises, at least within contemporary capitalism, are likely to become manifest as crises of economic regulation and hence crises of the state. In summary, if we wish to develop insights into the 'normal' functioning of the capitalist mode of production, and to the transformation of capitalism in and through moments of crisis, we require a dynamic theory of the capitalist state. It is to the resources we have at our disposal in developing such a theory that we turn in the next section.

A genealogy of the state in Marxist theory

No aspect of Marxist theory has been so greatly blurred, distorted or befogged as this. (Lefebvre 1972: 123)

Marx and Engels

In 1977, in the first (and probably still the best) systematic and comprehensive review of Marxist theories of the state, Bob Jessop noted that it was a 'truism' that Marx and Engels developed no consistent, single or unified theory of the state (1977: 353). By 1982 (in his book *The Capitalist State*) this truism had become a 'commonplace' and it is now so oft-remarked upon that it is perhaps one of the few truly undisputed 'social scientific facts' (see for instance van den Berg 1988: 14; Bertramsen *et al.* 1990: 38; Carnoy 1984: 45; Dunleavy and O'Leary 1987: 203; Finegold and Skocpol 1995: 175; Miliband 1965; Poulantzas 1978: 20; Wolfe 1974: 131; cf. Draper 1977). *There is no (single) Marxian, far less Marxist, theory of the state.* This might be considered something of a devastating blow for a chapter on the Marxist theory of the state. Indeed, reviewing Marxist state theory might be considered not merely an exercise in flogging a dead horse, but one that first required the altogether more macabre practice of exhuming and assembling a dismembered corpse limb by limb. Moreover, given the great variety of concerns that animated Marx and Engels' work (to say nothing of Marxism more generally), it is not at all clear that all the limbs belong to the same corpse. For, as Jessop notes, 'Marx and Engels adopted different approaches and arguments according to the problems with which they were concerned' (1982: 28). Nonetheless, a clear development of Marx and Engels' ideas on the state can be traced.

The early Marx

The *Critique of Hegel's Doctrine of the State* (1843a [1975]) contains Marx's first extended reflections on the state. Though a sustained and at times polemical critique of Hegel, it is still couched within a fundamentally Hegelian framework. In Hegel's almost mystical idealism the separation between the state and civil society – between the universal and the particular – finds its resolution in the state. The latter is understood, not as an ideal collective capitalist but as an *ideal collective citizen* capable of expressing the general and communal interest of all its subjects. Marx regards this as pure mystification. Thus although he accepts Hegel's distinction between state and civil society, sharing his understanding of the latter as 'the sphere of economic life in which the individual's relations with others are governed by selfish needs and individual interests' (59), Marx denies that the state can indeed act in the universal interest. For insofar as state power is thoroughly implicated in the protection of property rights, the state actually functions to reproduce 'the war of each against all' in civil society. The solution lies in what Marx terms 'true democracy', 'the first true unity of the particular and the universal' (88). The interpretation of this concept in the early Marx is highly contentious. The Althusserian structuralists wish to dismiss these early formulations as unredeemably Hegelian, and as separated by a radical 'epistemological break' from his 'mature' and 'scientific' later writings (Althusser 1969: 32–4, 62–4, 249). In complete contrast, Shlomo Avineri detects in the concept of 'true democracy' what would later be termed 'communism'. Accordingly, he argues:

> the decisive transition in Marx's intellectual development was not from radical democracy to communism, any more than it was from idealism to materialism ... The *Critique* contains ample material to show that Marx envisages in 1843 a society based on the abolition of private property and on the disappearance of the state. Briefly, the *Communist Manifesto* is immanent in the *Critique*. (Avineri 1968: 34; see also Colletti 1975: 41–2)

This latter reading is perhaps reinforced by Marx's essay *On the Jewish Question* (1843b [1975]). Here he distinguishes between political emancipation – associated with formal (and constitutionally-codified) democracy – and real human emancipation (or 'true democracy'). Whilst the former represents a significant advance it is but one step on the road to full human emancipation.

The latter can only be realised by the transcending of bourgeois society to usher in a qualitatively new social order (Miliband 1965: 281–2). In his 'Introduction' (1844 [1975]) to the *Critique*, Marx eventually identifies the proletariat as the agents of this transformation, laying the basis for a class theory of the state in his later writings.

Marx mark two: The 'mature' works

In the *German Ideology*, Marx and Engels come closest to formulating a systematic theory of the state as a class state. They assert famously that the state is 'nothing more than the form of organization which the bourgeoisie necessarily adopt both for internal and external purposes, for the mutual guarantee of their property and interest' (1845/6 [1964]: 59), a conception echoed in the *Communist Manifesto* (1848 [1975]: 82). This broadly instrumentalist framework (which conceives of the state as an instrument in the hands of the ruling class) is identified by Miliband as Marx and Engels' 'primary' view of the state (1965: 283; see also Sanderson 1963). Yet it is not their only formulation, nor does it remain unqualified. Indeed as Marx notes in *The Class Struggles in France* (1850 [1978]) and *The Eighteenth Brumaire of Louis Bonaparte* (1852 [1979]) it is often not the ruling class so much as fractions of the ruling class which control the state apparatus. This is particularly so in the case of the most advanced capitalist societies of the time, England and France. Furthermore, the personnel of the state often belong to an entirely different class to that of the ruling class. Such comments are a reflection of a modified and qualified, but nonetheless still essentially instrumentalist, conception of the state. The state is granted a certain degree of autonomy from the ruling class, but it remains *their* instrument — ultimately those who pay the piper call the tune.

At times however, and particularly in their more historical writings, Marx and Engels' qualified instrumentalism gives way to a more structuralist position. Thus in *The Eighteenth Brumaire* and again in *The Civil War in France* (1871 [1986]), Marx grants the state a far more independent role than that previously assigned to it in, say, *The German Ideology*. This 'secondary' view of the state as Miliband describes it (1977: 284–5), is restated by Engels in *The Origin of the Family*. Thus although Louis Bonaparte is seen by Marx as 'representing' (or at least claiming to represent) the smallholding peasants, neither he nor the state is a genuine expression of their interests. As Miliband explains, 'for Marx, the Bonapartist State, however independent it may have been *politically* from any given class remains, and cannot in a class society but remain, the protector of an economically and socially dominant class' (*ibid*.: 285, original emphasis). The very structure and function of the (capitalist) state would appear to guarantee (or at least powerfully select for) the reproduction of capitalist social relations. This impression is confirmed in *The Civil War in France*. Here Marx categorically states that the apparatus of the capitalist state cannot be appropriated for progressive ends and that the revolutionary project of the proletariat must be to smash this repressive bourgeois institution. In so doing:

> Marx implies that the state is a system of political domination whose effectiveness is to be found in its institutional structure as much as in the social categories, fractions or classes that control it... [T]he analysis of the inherent bias of the system of political representation and state intervention is logically prior to an examination of the social forces that manage to wield state power. (Jessop 1978: 62; see also 1982: 27)

Given the sheer scope and diversity of the positions briefly outlined above, it is not surprising that Alan Wolfe is led to conclude, 'to study the state from a Marxist perspective means not the application of an already developed theory to existing circumstances, but the creation of that very theory, based on some all too cryptic beginnings in Marx himself. Hence the excitement of the project, but hence also its ambiguity' (1974: 131). In the next section we embark on a roller-coaster ride through this exciting yet ambiguous world.

'The ambiguity and the excitement': Marxism and the state after Marx

Lenin and Gramsci

Lenin's writings on the state can trace a strong lineage to the Marx of *The Civil War in France*. In *The State and Revolution* (1917 [1968]), regarded by Lucio Colletti as 'by far and away his greatest contribution to political theory' (1972: 224), Lenin draws out the implications of Marx's writings on the Paris Commune for revolutionary strategy. The state, he argues, is 'an organ of class *rule*, an organ for the *oppression* of one class by another'. Since the state is simply and unequivocally the repressive apparatus of the bourgeoisie, it cannot be used to advance the cause of socialist transformation. Moreover, as a coercive institution it must be confronted by force. Hence, 'the liberation of the oppressed class is impossible not only without a violent revolution, but also without the destruction of the apparatus of state power' (1917 [1968]: 266, original emphasis.). As Colletti again observes:

> The basic theme of *The State and Revolution* – the one that indelibly inscribes itself on the memory, and immediately comes to mind when one thinks of the work – is the theme of revolution as a *destructive* and *violent* act... The essential point of the revolution, the *destruction* it

cannot forgo is...the destruction of the bourgeois state as a power *separate* from and *counterposed* to the masses, and its replacement by a power of a new type. (1972: 219–20, original emphasis)

Lenin's narrow definition of the state as an essentially coercive apparatus is reflected in his vision of revolution as a violent act in which the repressive might of the state is pitched against the massed ranks of the proletariat. Its consequences, of historical proportions, are all too apparent. Thankfully they may now be viewed with the benefit of some degree of hindsight. In contrast, Gramsci's more inclusive definition of the state leads him in a somewhat different direction.

Gramsci's distinctiveness and enduring significance lies in his attempt to incorporate human subjectivity as a dynamic agent within the Marxist philosophy of history (Femia 1981: 1). His work thus marks a clear break with the economism and crude reductionism that had come to characterize the Marxist tradition since the death of Marx. The central question that he poses, and with which contemporary Marxist theorists continue to grapple, is this – what gives capital the capacity to reproduce and reassert its dominance over time despite its inherent contradictions? His search for an answer leads him to define a new concept (or, more accurately, to redefine an old concept) – that of *hegemony*; and to extend the Marxist definition of the state to include all those institutions and practices through which the ruling class succeeds in maintaining the consensual subordination of those over whom it rules (Gramsci 1971: 244, 262). The key to Gramsci's theoretical toolbox is the concept of hegemony. With this he demonstrated that a dominant class, in order to maintain its supremacy, must succeed in presenting its own moral, political and cultural values as societal norms; thereby constructing an ideologically-engendered *common sense*. Yet, as Miliband (1994: 11) observes, hegemony is not merely about instilling the values of the ruling class within civil society. Increasingly,

> it must also be taken to mean the capacity of the ruling classes to persuade subordinate ones that, whatever they may think of the social order, and however much they may be alienated from it, there is no alternative to it. Hegemony depends not so much on consent as on resignation.

For Gramsci then the obstacles to class consciousness are far greater than Lenin envisaged (and, it might well be argued, have become far greater since the time of Gramsci). Whilst there is football on TV, the revolution is likely to be postponed indefinitely. As Gramsci's biographer, Giuseppe Fiori (1970: 238), comments:

> the [capitalist] system's real strength does not lie in the violence of the ruling class or the coercive power of its state, but in the acceptance by the ruled of a 'conception of the world' which belongs to the rulers. The philosophy

of the ruling class passes through a whole tissue of complex vulgarizations to emerge as 'common sense': that is, the philosophy of the masses, who accept the morality, the customs, the institutionalized behaviour of the society they live in.

Gramsci's central contribution is to insist that the power of the capitalist class resides not so much in the repressive apparatus of the state as an instrument of the bourgeoisie – however ruthless and efficient that might be – but in its ability to influence and shape the perceptions of the subordinate classes, convincing them either of the legitimacy of the system itself or of the futility of resistance. Given that Gramsci was, at the time, languishing in a cell in one of Mussolini's prisons and thus, presumably, only too well aware of the ruthless efficiency of the state's coercive arm, this insight was all the more impressive. It led him to a highly significant observation and one for which he is rightly famous:

> In the East the state was everything, civil society was primordial and gelatinous; in the West, there was a proper relation between state and civil society, and when the state trembled a sturdy structure of civil society was at once revealed. The state was only an outer ditch, behind which there stood a powerful system of fortresses and earthworks. (Gramsci 1971: 238)

The implications of this for socialist strategy are highly significant, and Gramsci was not slow to point them out. Whereas in the East (Russia) where civil society was 'primordial and gelatinous' a *war of manoeuvre* – a 'frontal assault' on the state – was indeed appropriate, in the West such a strategy was doomed to failure. For in societies like his own the strength of the bourgeoisie lay not in the coercive resources that it could muster, but in its ability to legitimate its domination within civil society, thereby securing passive acquiescence. Thus before the proletariat could challenge the state it would first have to wage a successful *war of position* – a 'battle for the hearts and minds' within civil society. As Carnoy notes: '*consciousness itself* becomes the source of power for the proletariat in laying siege to the state and the means of production, just as lack of proletarian consciousness is the principal reason that the bourgeoisie remains in the dominant position' (1984: 88). Gramsci had indeed succeeded in reinserting human subjectivity as a dynamic agent within the Marxist philosophy of history.

Structuralism versus instrumentalism in the 'Miliband–Poulantzas debate'

If the historical significance (however unfortunate) of Lenin's writings on the state, and the theoretical and strategic prescience of Gramsci's work, should guarantee them both a place in any discussion of the Marxist theory of the state, then the same cannot be said of the (in)famous Miliband–Poulantzas debate (Poulantzas 1969, 1976; Miliband 1969, 1970, 1973; Laclau 1975). Indeed its importance lies neither in the quality of the theoretical exchange, nor in its historical significance, but rather in the problems it reveals in Marxist conceptions of the state and in its symbolic status as a point of departure for many contemporary developments. The debate sees neither protagonist at his brilliant theoretical best. Yet it does well display the extremes to which Marxist state theorists seem, on occasions, inexorably drawn.

It takes the form of a dense theoretical exchange, initially polite but increasingly ill-tempered, about the source of power within contemporary capitalist societies and the relationship between the ruling class and the state apparatus in the determination of the content of state policy. Is the modern state a state in capitalist society or a capitalist state, and what difference does it make anyway?

Poulantzas' opening salvo (1969) takes the form of a detailed textual critique of Miliband's path-breaking *The State in Capitalist Society* (1969). Poulantzas notes the absence (excepting the work of Gramsci) of a systematic attempt to formulate a Marxist theory of the state and praises Miliband for his attempts to fill this theoretical vacuum as well as his devastating critique of the bourgeois mythology of the state. However, after the spoonful of sugar comes the medicine. In seeking to expose the dominant bourgeois ideology of the neutrality and independence of the state, Miliband is unwittingly drawn onto the terrain of his adversaries (1969: 241–2). His reflections thus remains tarnished by the residue of bourgeois assumptions about the state – principally that power resides not in the state apparatus itself but in the *personnel* of the state. He thereby fails to grasp what Poulantzas sees as the objective structural reality of social classes and the state. Instead Miliband entertains the bourgeois mythology of the free-willed active agent. Accordingly, he focuses on *class* in terms of inter-subjective relationships instead of objective structural locations within the relations of production, and on the *state* in terms of the inter-personal alliances, connections and networks of the state 'elite' (242) instead of the structure, form and function of this (capitalist) institution.

This point lies at the heart of the debate. Yet from here on it degenerates into a somewhat crude and polarized struggle between *instrumentalism* (Poulantzas' caricature of Miliband's position) and *structuralism* (Miliband's caricature of Poulantzas' position). Ironically, in the debate itself (though not in their more thoughtful work), both protagonists come close to living up to the crude parodies they present of one another.

Instrumentalism, as we have seen, tends to view the state as a neutral instrument to be manipulated and steered in the interests of the dominant class or ruling 'elite' (the term Miliband deploys). Its basic thesis is that the modern state serves the interests of the bourgeoisie in a capitalist society because it is dominated by that class. Such a perspective asserts the causal primacy of *agency* (the conscious actions of individuals or social forces) over *structure*. In the determination of state policy, the personnel of the state are thus accorded primacy over the state's form and function (as a capitalist apparatus). As Kenneth Finegold and Theda Skocpol (1995: 176) note:

> An instrument has no will of its own and thus is capable of action only as the extension of the will of some conscious actor. To understand the state as an instrument of the capitalist class is to say that state action originates in the conscious and purposive efforts of capitalists as a class.

Instrumentalism (as expressed in the work of Domhoff and the early Miliband) may thus be regarded as *agency-* or *personnel*-centred, and as expressing a simple view of the relationship between the state apparatus and the ruling-class – the latter is an instrument of the former (see Table 4.1). The instrumentalist thesis can be summarized in terms of its answers to three questions:

Q: *What is the nature of the class that rules?*
A: The capitalist class rules and is defined by its ownership and control of the means of production
Q: *What are the mechanisms that tie this class to the state?*
A: Socialization, interpersonal connections, and networks. The capitalist class uses the state as an instrument to dominate the rest of society
Q: *What is the concrete relationship between state policies and ruling class interests?*
A: State policies further the general interests of the capitalist class in maintaining their domination of society

(Questions from Gold et al. 1975a: 32; answers
adapted from Barrow 1993: 16)

An instrumentalist theory of the state is thus a theory of *the state in capitalist society* (the title of Miliband's book) as opposed to a theory of the capitalist state. For if the state in a capitalist society is indeed capitalist it is only contingently so. That the state is engaged in the reproduction of capitalist social and economic relations is not in any sense guaranteed. Rather, such a situation can arise only by virtue of the dominance of a capitalist 'ruling elite' within capitalist society and its personal ties to the members of the state apparatus.

In marked contrast, a structuralist position (such as that outlined by the state derivationists and by the Poulantzas of 'the debate') asserts the causal priority of structures over agents and their intentions. Agents are conceived of as the 'bearers' (or *träger*) of objective structures over which they can exercise minimal influence. Within such a framework, the capitalist state is viewed as a structural system with form and function determined largely independently of the aspirations, motivations and intentions of political actors or members of the dominant class. It is a theory of the *capitalist state*. A structuralist account, as the term would imply, is *structure-* or *state-* centred. It also expresses a simple view of the relationship between the state apparatus and the ruling-class – the former acts in the long-term collective interest of the latter (see Table 3.1).

The Miliband–Poulantzas debate did not advance the cause of Marxist theory very far. However, in pointing to the limitations of both structure-centred and agency-centred accounts, it has provided a point of departure for many recent developments in state theory. It is to the two most fruitful attempts to exorcise the ghost of the Miliband–Poulantzas debate that we now briefly turn.

Table 3.1 *Beyond structuralism vs instrumentalism*

	Personnel-centred (Agency-centred)	*State-centred (Structure-centred)*
Simple view of the relationship between the state apparatus and the ruling class	Instrumentalism (Domhoff, early Miliband)	Structuralism (early Poulantzas, state derivationists)
Dialectical view of the relationship between the state apparatus and the ruling class	*The state as custodian of capital* (later Miliband, Block)	Strategic-relational approach (Jessop, later Poulantzas)

Beyond structuralism versus instrumentalism: Block and Jessop

Before considering the 'state of the art' in the Marxist theory of the state, it is important first to note that Miliband and Poulantzas were not to remain resolute and intractable in defence of the positions to which they were drawn in the heat of the theoretical exchange. Indeed both moved towards more dialectical conceptions of the relationship between structure and agency in their later work, locating political actors as strategic subjects within complex and densely-structured state apparatuses. Thus Miliband, in an exercise of apparent contrition, concedes, 'the notion of the state as an "instrument"... tends to obscure what has come to be seen as a crucial property of the state, namely its *relative autonomy* from the "ruling class" and from civil society at large' (1977: 74). He emphasizes the need for a consideration of 'the character of [the state's] leading personnel, the pressures exercised by the economically dominant class, *and* the structural constraints imposed by the mode of production' (73–4; see also 1994: 17–18). Such observations are more systematically developed in the work of Fred Block (1987a, 1987b).

Block's concern is to demonstrate how, despite the division of labour between 'state managers' and the capitalist class, the state tends to act in the long-term collective interest of capital. He begins by noting that the capitalist class, far from actively sponsoring major reforms in its long-term interest, often provides the most vociferous opposition to such measures. The capitalist class must then be regarded as simply incapable of acting in its own long-term collective interest. Yet at the same time

> ruling class members who devote substantial energy to policy formation become atypical of their class, since they are forced to look at the world from the perspective of state-managers. They are quite likely to diverge ideologically from politically unengaged ruling-class opinion. (Block 1987a: 57)

This provides the basis for an answer to Block's conundrum. State managers may in fact have interests far closer to the long-term collective interest of capital than capital itself (see also Marsh 1995: 275). Here Block points to the relationship of 'dependency' between state managers on the one hand, and the performance of the capitalist economy on the other. As Carnoy (1984: 218) explains, such dependency exists since

> economic activity produces state revenues and because public support for a regime will decline unless accumulation continues to take place. State managers willingly do what they know they must to facilitate capital accumulation. Given that the level of economic activity is largely determined by private investment decisions, such managers are particularly sensitive to overall 'business confidence'.

The state becomes the *custodian* of the general interest of capital. Block manages to reconcile within a single account a sensitivity to the intentions, interests and strategies of state personnel (and their relative independence from the ruling class) with an analysis of the structural context within these strategies are operationalized and played out. His work displays a complex and *dialectical* view of the relationship between the state apparatus and the ruling class which escapes both the intentionalism and indeterminacy of instrumentalist accounts and the functionalism and determinism of structuralist formulations. In its overarching concern with state managers as utility-maximizing rational subject, it is nonetheless *personnel-* or *agency*-centred (see Table 3.1).

Though it represents a considerable advance on its more instrumentalist forebears, Block's work is still ultimately somewhat frustrating. For as Finegold and Skocpol (1995: 198) point out, he remains ambiguous as to whether capitalist reforms initiated by state managers – and the subject of political pressure from both working and ruling classes alike – will *always* prove functional for capital in the last instance (for evidence of this ambiguity compare Block 1987a: 62, with 1987a: 66). If so, then Block's gestural nod to the independent interests of state managers in promoting economic growth is scarcely sufficient to account for such an exact (and convenient) functional fit. If not, then how precisely is it that dysfunctional outcomes that might prove threatening to capitalist stability are avoided whilst those less damaging of the system (and, one might have thought, easier to avoid) are allowed to develop? Either way, Block seems to fall back on a residual functionalism which is not so very different from that associated with the notion of the state as an 'ideal collective capitalist'. His achievement should not, however, be under-emphasized. Yet it surely lies more in his *recognition* of the need to specify the mechanisms ensuring that the actions of state personnel do not, by and large, jeopardize continued capital accumulation, than in the particular mechanisms that he proceeds to specify!

If Block's conception of the state as *custodian of capital* is the dialectical heir to the legacy of instrumentalism, then Bob Jessop's *strategic–relational approach* is the dialectical heir to the structuralist inheritance (see in particular Jessop 1990, 2002; for commentaries see Barrow 1993: 153–6; Bonefeld 1993; Hay 1994, 2004; Mahon 1991). More convincingly than any other Marxist theorist past or present, he succeeds in transcending the artificial dualism of structure and agency by moving towards a truly dialectical understanding of their inter-relationship. Structure and agency logically entail one another, hence there can be no analysis of action which is not itself also an analysis of structure. All social and political change occurs through strategic interaction as strategies collide with and impinge upon the structured terrain of the strategic context within which they are formulated. Their effects (however unintentional, however unanticipated) are to transform (however partially) the context within which future strategies are formulated and deployed.

Such a formulation has highly significant implications for the theory of the (capitalist) state. Jessop follows the later Poulantzas in conceiving of the state as a strategic site traversed by class struggles and as 'a specific institutional ensemble with multiple boundaries, no institutional fixity and no pre-given formal or substantive unity' (Jessop 1990: 267; Poulantzas 1978). The state is a dynamic and constantly unfolding system. Its specific form at a given moment in time in a particular national setting represents a 'crystallization of past strategies' which privileges certain strategies and actors over others. As such, 'the state is located within a complex *dialectic of structures and strategies*' (129, emphasis added). This introduces the important notion that the state, and the institutions which comprise it, are *strategically selective*. The structures and *modus operandi* of the state 'are more open to some types of political strategy than others' (260). The state presents an uneven playing field whose complex contours favour certain strategies (and hence certain actors) over others.

Within such a perspective there can be no guarantee that the state (and governments wielding state power) will act in the general interest of capital (whatever that might be). Indeed, insofar as the function of the capitalist state can be regarded as the expanded reproduction of capital, the specific form of the capitalist state at a particular stage in its historical development is always likely to problematize and eventually compromise this function. The state thus evolves through a series of political and economic crises as the pre-existing mode of intervention of the state within civil society and the economy proves increasingly dysfunctional. The outcome of such crises, however, and the struggles that they engender cannot be predicted in advance. For if we are to apply the strategic–relational approach, they are contingent upon the balance of class (and other) forces, the nature of the crisis itself, and (we might add) popular *perceptions* of the nature of the crisis (Hay 1996b) – in short, on the strategically-selective context and the strategies mobilized within this context.

Jessop's approach then, despite its concern with state structures and their strategic-selectivity (see Table 3.1), and despite its structuralist pedigree, eschews all forms of functionalism, reductionism and determinism. The strategic–relational approach offers no guarantees – either of the ongoing reproduction of the capitalist system or of its impending demise (though, given the strategic selectivity of the current context, the odds on the latter would appear remote). It is, in short, a statement of the contingency and indeterminacy of social and political change (1990: 12–13). The casualty in all of this is the *definitive* (and very elusive) Marxist theory of the state. As Jessop himself notes, there can be no general or fully determinate theory of the capitalist state, only theoretically-informed accounts of capitalist states in their institutional, historical and strategic specificity (1982: 211–13, 258–9; 1990: 44; though cf. 2002).

We would appear to have come full circle. We end where we began, with a paradox: there is no Marxist theory of the state – there couldn't be.

Conclusions

Why do *we* need a *Marxist* approach to the state *today*? For in a world which is seemingly either globalized or globalizing and in which Marxism as a political project is defunct, it is tempting to dismiss Marxist attempts to theorize the state as anachronistic and of purely historical interest – if that. With the nation-state on the wane do we really need a theory of the state anyway? And even if we think we do, with Marxism in retreat why a *Marxist* theory of the state?

The first objection can be dealt with fairly swiftly. Yes, the current phase of capitalist accumulation is qualitatively different from all previous stages – in terms of the international mobility of capital and in the truly global nature of the social, political and environmental crises with which it is associated. Yet it would be dangerous to conclude either: (i) that this threatens to precipitate the end of the nation-state; or (ii) that even if it did we could afford to dispense with the theory of the state. For whilst national communities, states and governments still provide the primary focus of political socialization, mobilization, identification, and representation, the nation-state is firmly here to stay. Moreover, while this remains so, the sort of concerted inter-state response necessary to deal with global ecological crisis is likely to be thwarted and hijacked by more parochial national interests and considerations. Hence the very form of the state itself (its national character) may militate against a genuinely global response to a genuinely global crisis. The *national* form of the state may problematize its *global* function. Environmentalism may concern itself with global problems, but environmentalists require a theory of the state (see Chapter 8). Furthermore, as Jessop notes, the internationalization of capital has rendered (more) porous the boundaries of formerly closed national economies, but it has not lessened the significance of national differences or indeed national *states* in the regulation of capitalist accumulation. The form of the state may have changed, and it may have been subject to a 'tendential hollowing-out' as many of its previous functions and responsibilities have been displaced upwards, downwards and outwards, but its distinctively national character remains (Jessop 2002). Thus the process of globalization (more accurately, the processes that may *interact* to sustain any tendency to globalization) merely demonstrate the continuing centrality of the state to the dynamics of capitalist accumulation.

It is one thing to demonstrate the continuing need for a theory of the state; it is another thing altogether to claim this as justification for a distinctively *Marxist* approach to the state. The proof of any pudding must be in the eating and it should be remembered that this particular pudding comes in a great variety of different flavours. Nonetheless two general arguments for a sophisticated Marxist conception of the state (such as that formulated by Jessop) can be offered: one substantive, the other analytical.

For the first we can return to the above example. Environmental crisis has its origins in an industrial growth imperative. This might suggest the relevance of a theory of *the state in industrial society* to the political economy of ecology. Yet a moment's further reflection reveals that the growth imperative that characterizes contemporary societies – and is thus responsible for the environmental degradation we witness – is a *capitalist* growth imperative, sustained and regulated by the capitalist state. Environmentalists then need not merely a theory of the state, but a theory of the *capitalist* state. As such a theory, Marxism clearly has much to offer.

The second reason is somewhat more esoteric, and relates to the analytical sophistication of contemporary Marxist approaches to the state. Though characterized for much of its history by the seemingly intractable dispute between structural functionalism on the one hand and instrumentalism on the other, considerable analytical advances have been made in Marxist state theory in recent years. In this respect contemporary Marxist state theory has much to offer to Marxists and non-Marxists alike. For as authors like Anthony Giddens (1984) and Nicos Mouzelis (1991; 1995) have noted, the dualism of structure and agency (of which the structuralism–instrumentalism battle is merely a reflection) is not only a problem within Marxism but has characterized social and political science since its inception. In the strategic–relational approach it has eventually been transcended in a simple yet sophisticated manner. Though not all will share the analytical, critical and political concerns that animate contemporary Marxist theory, few can help but benefit from the analytical insights it offers.

Jessop's central achievement has been to take Marxist state theory beyond the fatuous question: *is the modern state a capitalist state or a state in capitalist society?* If his work receives the attention it deserves, feminists need not duplicate the errors and deviations of Marxist theory by asking themselves: *is the contemporary state essentially patriarchal or merely a state in a patriarchal society?* Contemporary Marxist theory will probably never get the chance to follow Henry Higgins in transforming the object of its study. But those who might can surely learn a thing or two from its deviations.

Further reading

Barrow, C. W. (1993) *Critical Theories of the State: Marxist, Neo-Marxist, Post-Marxist* (Madiscon: University of Wisconsin Press).

Finegold, K. and Skocpol, T. (1995) 'Marxist Approaches to Politics and the State', in *idem, State and Party in America's New Deal* (Madison: University of Wisconsin Press).

Gramsci, A. (1971) *Selections from Prison Notebooks* (London: Lawrence & Wishart).

Jessop, B. (2002) *The Future of the Capitalist State* (Cambridge: Polity Press).

Miliband, R. (1969) *The State in Capitalist Society: An Analysis of the Western System of Power* (London: Weidenfeld & Nicolson).

Poulantzas, N. (1978) *State, Power, Socialism* (London: New Left Books).

Chapter 4

Public Choice

ANDREW HINDMOOR

During his inaugural address as the fortieth president of the United States of America in January 1980, Ronald Reagan spoke of the 'economic ills we [Americans] suffer that have come upon us over several decades'. In a line that was to become emblematic of his presidency he went on to suggest that 'in the present crisis, government is not the solution to our problem; government is the problem'. Over the following decade, elected politicians and unelected officials in an ever-greater number of countries attempted, in Margaret Thatcher's (1993: 745) preferred terminology, 'to roll back the frontiers of the state'. In this task they were assisted by an intellectual revolution in the study of politics the full effects of which were, at this time, only just beginning to be fully appreciated.

Rational or public choice theory, I will use the terms interchangeably here, was developed by a number of American economists in the 1960s. At first mainstream political scientists simply ignored this new approach to the study of politics. By the early 1980s it had however acquired a growing influence in American political science departments and some British and European outposts. In 1967 around 5 per cent of the articles published in America's most prestigious political science journal, the *American Political Science Review*, used public choice theory (Green and Shapiro 1994: 3). By 1982 this figure had risen to around 20 per cent. By 1992 it stood at nearly 40 per cent.

Public choice theorists do not have a particularly well thought-out account of what the state is. Practitioners constantly slip between talking about the state, the government and the public sector without ever indicating whether these are meant to refer to different entities. What they do however possess is a distinctive and distinctively hostile account of what the state does and why it does it. Stated simply, public choice theorists regard the state as a source of inefficiency. Indeed James Buchanan (1988: 3), who in 1986 was awarded the Nobel Prize for his work in developing the theory, defines public choice as 'the science of political failure'.

Once public choice theory had begun to establish its academic credentials, right-wing think-tanks like the Cato Institute in America and the Institute for Economic Affairs in Britain (Cockett 1995) began to popularize and publicise its arguments. At a time when the post-war social democratic consensus was beginning to crumble, public choice theory, together with the monetarism of Milton Friedman (1963), the economic liberalism of Friedrich Hayek (1978) and the social conservatism of writers like Irving Kristol (1983), provided intellectual ammunition and a burgeoning policy agenda for New Right politicians like Reagan and Thatcher (Dunleavy and O'Leary 1987; King 1987; Self 1993; Stretton and Orchard 1994). At this point, James Buchanan (1984: 21) is, once again, worth quoting:

> The rapidly accumulating developments in the theory of public choice... have all been influential in modifying the way that modern man views government and political processes...at all levels...limiting the expansion of government power.

As I will be at pains to emphasize throughout this chapter, public choice remains a controversial way of studying politics. Elitism, pluralism, and other state theories have of course attracted their critics. But with the possible exception of its polar political opposite, Marxism, no theory has attracted as much criticism as public choice. As the fortunes of the New Right waned in the 1990s with the election of New Democrats and New Labour, public choice theory came under increasingly heavy fire. In America this culminated, in January 2001, with the launch of a petition berating public choice theory's influence within political science (Jacobsen 2001). No doubt many of the readers of this chapter will also regard public choice theory's arguments about the state as a one-dimensional caricature of a messy political reality. But even those who want, instinctively, to dismiss public choice theory out of hand need first to understand it. For whilst the heyday of public choice theory may now have passed, this still remains a intellectually and politically influential approach whose analysis and prescriptions deserve to be taken seriously whether or not they are thought valid.

I proceed as follows. In the following section I define public choice as involving the application of the methods of economics to the study of politics and, in particular, as requiring the assumption of self-interested behaviour. I then place the development of public choice theory within the broader context of post-war economic theory and, in particular, of the theory of market failure used by many economists to justify state intervention in the 1950s and early 1960s. In these first two sections the argument is pitched at a very general level. To compensate for this I go on to introduce some specific accounts of state failure as they relate to the behaviour of politicians, firms and public servants. I close the chapter by rehearsing one obvious but nevertheless still powerful criticism of public choice theory: that people do not behave, or at least do not always behave, in a purely self-interested way. I show how public choice theory can actually, albeit unexpectedly, be used to reach the same conclusion about people's motives and how an alternative public choice research agenda might be extracted from this insight.

Public choice

Public choice involves the application of the methods of economics to the study of politics (Mueller 2003: 1). By this I mean two things. First, that public choice theorists, like economists, assume that people, all people, are rational, self-interested utility-maximizers. Second, that public choice theorists, like economists, use this assumption to construct models from which can be deduced explanations and predictions of actors' behaviour. Before going on to discuss each of these in turn I will clarify one point. I have, so far, referred to public choice theory as being both a method and a theory. It is a method because it requires practitioners to study politics in a particular way using particular assumptions and techniques. It is a theory because the application of that method has resulted in the development of an intellectually coherent set of arguments about the state. As a method, public choice might be compared and contrasted with methods like interpretivism and institutionalism. As a theory, public choice might be compared and contrasted with pluralism, elitism and Marxism.

As it is interpreted by public choice theorists, rationality requires people to have (i) complete, and (ii) transitive preferences which (iii) they act upon. If there are just three available options, A, B and C, a person's preferences are complete if they either prefer one option to another or are indifferent between them. A person's preferences are transitive if they are ordered in such a way that if, for example, they prefer A to B and B to C that they also prefer A to C. A person can be said to have acted upon their preferences if, when given a choice, they choose the option they most prefer. Because the satisfaction of preferences is a source of personal welfare or utility, a person who consistently chooses the option they most prefer can be described as a utility-maximizer. Although I will not pursue the argument here, the assumption of utility-maximization is a contentious one. Amartya Sen (2002: 2–15) argues that whether out of a sense of duty, solidarity or love, people frequently do things they do not 'really' want to do. They visit elderly relatives when they would rather go to the pub, and cook themselves healthy meals when they would rather eat junk food. The real sticking-point for public choice's critics is however the assumption of self-interest. In itself there is nothing in the assumption of utility maximization which implies that actors must be self-interested. A person who prefers giving money to charity to spending it upon themselves is maximizing their utility if, when given the choice, they donate money to charity. But public choice theorists routinely assert that the preferences people have are nearly always reflective of and derived from their self-interest. Gordon Tullock (1976: 5), whose work on 'rent-seeking' is examined shortly, is typical in claiming that 95 per cent of all behaviour is self-interested. As we will soon see, it is the assumption of self-interest which underpins public choice theory's hostility toward the state.

Turning now to the second part of the definition, public choice theorists, like economists, use the assumption of self-interested behaviour to construct stripped-down models of political processes from which they deduce predictions and explanations about behaviour and outcomes. These explanations are, I now want to emphasize, of a very general sort. They relate to the behaviour of a particular class or 'type' of actor rather than named individuals. Consider the decision of Labour's incoming Chancellor, Gordon Brown, to give the Bank of England operational independence in May 1997. A political biographer or historian might try to explain this decision in terms of particular features of Gordon Brown's background and personality such as his determination to assert authority over domestic policy-making or his political friendship with American economists and politicians who had previously extolled to him the virtues of the independent American Federal Reserve (Rawnsley 1998: 31–49; Routledge 1998: 292–6). Alternatively, they might focus upon particular features of the situation in which Gordon Brown found himself, such as the need to reassure financial markets of New Labour's fiscal prudence after eighteen years in opposition. It is possible that a series of such studies into the decision to give different central banks their independence in a number of different countries might reveal a consistent pattern. It might, for example, turn out that political parties are more likely to give central banks independence after a long period in opposition. But such comparative explanations would have to be build inductively from the 'ground up'. What then of public choice theory? Its basic explanation for central bank independence runs as follows (Rogoff 1985). Financial markets consider promises made by central bankers about inflation to be more credible than those of elected politicians. They therefore 'reward' countries that have independent banks with lower interest rates. Vote-maximizing politicians know that voters prefer lower interest rates and therefore have an incentive to give central banks independence. From this general argument we can of course then derive an explanation of why Gordon Brown gave the Bank of England independence. Public choice is not the only political science theory to attempt such 'top-down' deductive explanations. The combination of this approach with the assumption of self-interested behaviour is however distinctive to public choice.

Public choice, market failure and state failure

In order to understand why public choice theorists display such a hostile attitude towards the state, its development needs to be placed in the broader context of the history of economic theory. One obvious starting-point here is perhaps the single most famous and influential work in economic theory, Adam Smith's *Wealth of Nations*. Smith (1776 [1983] Vol. 1: 12) argued that the 'propensity to truck, barter and exchange' are inherent features in human nature and the ultimate source of economic prosperity. When trading with each other, individuals will rigorously guard their self-interest. In doing so they will however be led, as if by an 'invisible hand', to promote the common good. This is because so long as there is sufficient competition, it will be in the interest of producers to try and maximize their profits by lowering prices and improving quality. However well-intentioned, state intervention, Smith argued, would usually threaten the operation of the invisible hand and undermine prosperity. Although other economists had previously extolled the virtues of competitive markets (see Rima 1996: 68–86), *The Wealth of Nations* was a landmark publication credited with destroying the intellectual foundations of mercantilism, the economic theory which held that a state's prosperity requires the mainten- ance of a positive trade balance and so the erection of import barriers and the state-led encouragement of exports.

Over the next few hundred years, the academic discipline of economics was transformed. Smith's 'classical' economics with its emphasis upon the wealth of nations gave way to a 'neo-classical' focus upon the satisfaction of preferences. Political economy gave way to micro-economics and, at the same time, verbal reasoning gave way to mathematical formulae. Yet Smith's defence of *laissez-faire* economics nevertheless remained (Ingaro and Israel 1990). In the immediate post-war years, economists like Kenneth Arrow and Gerald Debreu (Arrow and Debreu 1954) were feted for their demonstration that, in conditions of perfect competition, markets would 'clear' allowing profit-maximizing firms and utility-maximizing consumers to achieve a welfare-maximizing equilibrium. Yet, however technically impressive and rigorous, general equilibrium theorists like Arrow and Debreu were in many ways simply restating Smith's 200-year-old argument about the invisible hand.

With the general parameters of general equilibrium theory having been set, a new generation of economists began to question the free-market orthodoxy in the late 1950s and early 1960s. As we will presently see, they were far from being the first to do so. But the willingness of these welfare economists to use the same basic methods as their rivals helped ensure their success. Arrow and Debreu had shown that perfect competition would lead to perfect results. Welfare economists argued that competition is rarely perfect and that markets frequently fail. I do not want to get sucked too far into the details of economic theory here. But the argument in subsequent sections will benefit from the discussion of three particular causes of market failure: monopoly, externalities and public goods (for an account of other forms of market failure see Sandler 2001: 20–6; and Stiglitz 1997: 27–64).

(i) Monopoly

For competition to be perfect there must be a large number of buyers and sellers who are individually unable to influence the price of their product. But many industries are very obviously dominated by, at most, a handful of firms who individually have a great deal of influence over prices. Firms with such monopoly power will be able to increase their profits by raising prices and restricting output. This will however reduce consumer welfare as those buying their product have to pay an inflated price.

(ii) Externalities

For competition to be perfect, the costs and benefits of producing and consuming a good must be borne exclusively by the person or persons producing and paying for it. But in many cases the costs or benefits of production or consumption fall on third parties. In some cases these 'external effects' are positive. A well-tended garden benefits not only the person who planted it but those passing-by. At other times, external effects are negative. The costs of maintaining a factory fall not only on the owner who must pay for labour and raw materials but on neighbouring residents who must endure the resulting pollution and noise. Because producers and consumers have no reason to take account of these effects, too much will be produced of goods which generate negative externalities and too little of those goods which generate positive externalities.

(iii) Public goods

For competition to be perfect, goods must be private in the sense of being both excludable and rival. A good is excludable if its owner can control access to it. A good is rivalrous if its consumption by one person reduces the amount available to be consumed by others. Some goods are however public goods. Consider the beam emitted by a lighthouse. It is non-excludable because ships sailing by cannot be prevented from seeing it. It is non-rival because the benefit one ship derives from the light does not reduce the amount of light available for others. Where consumers have preferences for public goods the market will fail because individuals will not contribute toward the cost of goods they cannot be excluded from using.

When competition is perfect, there is, as Smith, Arrow and Debreu demonstrated no need for state intervention. But when competition is imperfect there would seem to be an obvious *prima facie* case for state intervention to either prevent or correct market failures. When there are monopolies there would seem to be a strong case for using the state to either break up that monopoly or to regulate its prices. When there are externalities there would seem to be a strong case for using the state to either subsidize or tax production. When there are public goods there would seem to be a strong case for state provision. This is the political pay-off of welfare economics.

Public choice theory emerged in a handful of North American universities in the 1960s (Grofman 1995). One way of understanding it is as a reaction to and critique of the theory of market failure. Public choice theorists argued that whilst welfare economists had shown how and why the market might sometimes fail they had simply asserted rather than demonstrated the ability and willingness of the state to correct those failures. In comparing the virtues of the state with those of the market, welfare economists had made a misleading comparison between the reality of imperfect markets and the fiction of a perfect state. In actual fact, public choice theorists maintained, the state would fail for many of the same reasons as the market. They concluded that the comparison ought therefore to be between imperfect markets and an equally imperfect state; a comparison which would undermine much of the case for state intervention.

Why will the state so frequently fail? In the following section I want to show how monopolies, externalities and public goods can also afflict state provision. In the final part of this section I however want to tie the argument about state failure to the core assumption of self-interested behaviour. Monopolies, externalities and public goods do not, in themselves, cause markets to fail. People cause markets to fail. It is because entrepreneurs are self-interested profit-maximizers that they exploit monopoly positions by raising prices and reducing output. It is because factory owners are self-interested profit-maximizers that they take no account of the effects of their actions upon neighbouring residents. It is because individuals are self-interested utility-maximizers that they 'free ride' upon the provision of public goods (Olson 1971). But welfare economists apparently assumed that self-interest had its limits. For in extolling the possibilities of state intervention to correct for market failures, they assumed that those working for the state would act as benevolent guardians of the public interest. Politicians, it was tacitly assumed, would set the right taxes to correct for negative externalities. Regulators, it was assumed, would set the right prices to control for the effects of monopoly and so on. It was upon this inconsistency that public choice theorists seized. Practical experience required, they argued, the extension of the assumption of self-interested behaviour to *all* actors. In itself, this does not mean that the state will fail. For it may well be possible to design institutions and policies in such a way that actors are led, in the pursuit of their self-interest, to further the common good. But the assumption of self-interest means that proponents of state intervention cannot simply take it for granted that the state will act in the required, welfare-maximizing, way. Just as self-interest can lead to market failure so too can it lead to state failure.

Forms of state failure

Up until this point the argument has been sustained at the most general of levels. I now want to look at four specific accounts of state failure developed by public choice theorists over the last forty or so years. These four accounts, it should be emphasized, look at vary different areas of the state's activities. The first, rent-seeking, examines the interaction between pressure groups and the state. The second, political business cycles, looks at the way in which competitive elections encourage incumbent politicians to manipulate the economy to their own electoral advantage. The third, on vote-swapping or trading, shows, in a more abstract way, how politicians might make deals with each other that benefit their constituents but harm the country. The fourth, on budget-maximizing, shows why public sector workers, or bureaucrats, often have an incentive to try and extract more and more money from their political masters.

This list of state failures is far from constituting an exhaustive review of public choice theory. Theorists have identified dozens of reasons why the state might fail. The examples considered here may however be considered representative. They all assume the existence of a 'Western' liberal democracy in which there are regular elections and a mixed economy. They all assume state actors rigorously pursue and protect their individual self-interest and that this generates *economic* inefficiencies. As I will also go on to show, they argue that these inefficiencies can be related to the existence of monopoly, public goods and externalities within the state as well as market sectors.

Rent-seeking

State interventions in the economy – whether they come in the form of tariffs, quotas, subsidies, price supports, import licences, export credits, health and safety directives, planning requirements, regulatory pricing agreements or any one of a hundred other forms – create both economic winners and losers. Consider the subsidies paid to farmers through the Common Agricultural Policy. These benefit European farmers with large, high-intensity, farms. They harm European consumers who must, on average, pay around twelve pounds more a week for their food. They also harm Third-World farmers on whose domestic markets European surpluses are 'dumped'. How can we explain the decision of the state to intervene in some areas of the economy but not others? The answer public choice theorists would like to see themselves as debunking is that the state acts on the basis of judgements about the public interest to correct market failures. The very different public choice answer is that the state intervenes to create special economic privileges, or rents, benefiting its political supporters and campaign contributors and harming its political opponents (Tullock 1976 and 1989; Tollison 1997). Farming is not subsidized because it is in the public interest to do so. It is subsidized because farmers are a powerful political lobby whose criticisms politicians must seek to avoid and whose money they must try to attract.

Rent-seeking, the investment of resources by firms and pressure groups in the expectation of securing economic privileges, is, public choice theorists maintain, economically crippling. Indeed 'for those concerned with advancing the nation's wealth, the elimination of rent-seeking... is on a par (almost) with support of the flag, motherhood and apple pie' (Rowley and Tullock 1988: 3). Rent-seeking is damaging for two reasons. Firstly, because state intervention, any state intervention, distorts competition and impedes the operation of the invisible hand. Consider the 'clear-cut' (Tullock 1989: 55) example of a struggling American steel firm which, in an effort to revive its profits, invests resources in an effort to secure a ban on the imports of a rival Korean firm's goods on the 'grounds that [they are] environmentally dangerous'. Tullock's example is an entirely hypothetical one although it might be noted that George W. Bush imposed a set of tariffs on the import of steel in March 2002. Much of the American steel industry was located in the key 'swing' states of Ohio, Pennsylvania and West Virginia. The tariffs were eventually lifted in December 2003 after the World Trade Organization had ruled the American tariffs illegal and the European Union had threatened to impose sanctions on imports from America.

What are we to make of such behaviour? Tullock argues that competition will be reduced and price increased if the firm successfully secures the ban. At a first glance, rent-seeking theorists would, at this point, seem to be in danger of overstating their case. For as we have already seen markets do sometimes fail. Surely this means that state intervention cannot *always* be damaging? But one of the reasons why markets fail is because of the presence of monopoly. What public choice theorists are arguing here is that government intervention routinely takes the form of creating and supporting monopolies by rewarding some firms with subsidies and export credits and punishing others with pricing agreements and draconian health and safety rulings. Monopolies do not, in other words, simply appear. They are created. State intervention is damaging *because* it leads to market failure. Rent-seeking is also damaging because resources invested in the pursuit of state-supported privileges cannot then be productively invested in ways that will benefit the consumer. Whether or not its lobbying is successful, resources invested by the American firm in trying to secure a ban on Korean imports cannot be used to buy new machinery which will lower production costs and prices.

Deficits, elections and the politics of economics

At the start of the previous section I showed how, in the 1950s and early 1960s, welfare economists developed the theory of market failure as a challenge to the orthodoxy of laissez-faire economics. Theirs was not however the first such challenge. In the 1930s John Maynard Keynes (1936) had famously argued that capitalist markets were inherently unstable and easily pulled into recessions from which no invisible hand could rescue them (see Skidelsky 1992: 537–71 for an overview). Writing at a time when laissez-faire economics had very obviously failed to pull Britain or America out of the great depression, Keynes argued that the state could and should act as the guarantor of economic growth and stability. The basic logic of what came to be known as Keynesian economics is not difficult to relate. When threatened with recession, the state ought to increase expenditure and cut taxation in order to boost consumer demand, even if that means creating a temporary public sector borrowing deficit. Conversely, when an economy is overheating and inflation is rising, the state ought to cut expenditure and increase taxation in order to dampen consumer demand so eliminate past deficits.

To this argument, Buchanan and Wagner's (1977, 1978) public choice riposte runs as follows. Keynes was an economist who saw his role as being one of acquiring knowledge and offering advice to a small group of enlightened politicians who could be trusted to do the 'right thing'. Keynes did not stop to consider the application of his policy prescriptions to a democratic society in which parties fight to gain and retain elected office. At times of impending recession, vote-maximizing politicians will increase expenditure and cut taxation because it will be in their self-interest to do so. Politicians know that voters prefer high public expenditure to low public expenditure and low taxation to high taxation and that raising the former and reducing the latter will therefore increase their chances of being re-elected. But they have no corresponding incentive to cut expenditure and increase tax during periods of economic boom. To put the matter crudely, politicians are no more likely to raise taxes in the run-up to an election than turkeys are to vote for Christmas. This asymmetry in incentives means that, over time, public expenditure, taxes and borrowing deficits will all rise. This will, eventually, result in either slower economic growth or recession and higher unemployment. As politicians then start, quite literally, to print money in order to maintain public expenditure whilst meeting deficit repayments, inflation will also increase:

> The grafting of Keynesian economics onto the fabric of a political democracy has wrought a significant revision in the underlying fiscal constitution. The result has been a tendency toward budget deficits and, consequently, once the workings of democratic political institutions are taken into account, inflation. (Buchanan and Wagner 1978: 23)

Between 1951 and 1955 only one of what was to become the G7 countries – the United States, Canada, Japan, France, Germany, Italy and Britain – ran a government budget deficit. Between 1961 and 1965 every single one did so (Mueller 2003: 464–5). Such was the difference made by Keynesianism. As the economic recession in the 1970s was eventually to prove, the economic costs of vote-maximizing Keynesianism were severe. For politicians seeking re-election in the 1960s these costs were, however, beyond their political horizon. Self-interested politicians have reason to care about what happens in the next election and, perhaps, the one after that. They have no self-interested reason to weigh the short-term benefits of more votes against the long-term costs of eventual recession.

The politics of pork

It is one of the limitations of the principle of 'one-man-one-vote' that it makes no allowance for the expression of intense preferences. Vote-trading can, in principle, be used to ameliorate this problem. A person might, for example, agree to vote the way someone else wants in a local election about which they do not have strong views in return for that person then voting the way they want in a subsequent general election. In practice, the secret ballot makes such arrangements extremely difficult to enforce. In legislatures where voting is in public and the numbers involved are relatively small, vote-trading is however possible. In the United States, where party discipline is relatively weak, and where, according to public choice theorists (Weingest and Marshall 1988), Congressional committees serve to enforce such deals, vote-trading is, as political scientists have always recognized (Schattschneider 1935), extremely common. The question public choice theorists want to ask is whether it increases efficiency and leads to better legislation? Because vote-trading allows individuals to express the intensity of their preferences and because it results in mutually beneficial exchange it might be concluded that it does (Buchanan and Tullock 1965). But it can also be shown that vote-trading facilitates one of the least attractive and most inefficient features of American politics, the pork barrel.

Pork barrel politics arise when a group of politicians agree to support an amendment to a piece of legislation specifically designed to benefit voters in the constituency of the person proposing the amendment in return for that representative's subsequent support for amendments designed to benefit their own constituents. Such deals allow the politicians involved to demonstrate their ability to further the interest of their constituents. Vote-trading of this sort does however result in the imposition of negative external costs upon the constituents of politicians not involved in the deal and the passage of inefficient legislation. Consider a simple situation in which there are just three legislators (1, 2 and 3) and three expenditure proposals (A, B and C) the fate of which are to be decided by simple majority voting. Table 4.1 shows by how much, on average, the constituents of each legislator will benefit if the proposal is approved. Notice that the benefits of proposals A and C are relatively concentrated in the constituencies of the first and third legislators respectively. Assume that each proposal costs £30 and that this cost is to be divided equally between the constituencies. Economic efficiency would, at a minimum, seem to require the approval of those proposals and only those proposals for which total benefits are greater than total costs. In this case the only proposal which meets this criterion is B. In the case of proposals A and C total benefits are less than £30.

With simple majority voting and no vote-trading, efficiency will be secured. Vote-maximizing legislators will vote for those proposals whose benefits for *their* constituents are greater than their £10 share of the total cost. All three will therefore vote for B. The second and third legislators will however vote against A and the first and second legislators will vote against C. But if vote-trading is possible, the first and third legislators will find it in their interests to come to a deal whereby the third legislator supports A in return for the first legislator's support for C. Such a deal would be mutually beneficial. The first legislator will lose £4 from the passage of C but gain £10 from the approval of A. The third legislator will lose £6 from the passage of A but gain £7 from the approval of C. The loser in all this is the second legislator. The passage of A costs them £8 and that

Table 4.1   *Vote trading*

Legislator	Expenditure proposal		
	A	B	C
1	£20	£15	£6
2	£2	£16	£6
3	£4	£11	£17
Total	£26	£38	£29

of C £4. Notice that this negative externality is greater than the total gains of the first and third legislators.

Bureaucracy and budget-maximizing

Over the last century, in both developed and developing countries, state expenditure has consistently grown as a proportion of overall gross domestic product. In the United Kingdom, state expenditure as a share of gross domestic product has risen from 12.7 per cent in 1913 to 43 per cent in 1996. In the United States it rose from 7.5 to 45 per cent over the same period. In Germany and Italy, state expenditure had, by the early 1990s, risen to over 50 per cent of gross domestic product (Tanzi and Schuknecht 2000). Why has this growth occurred? It is not difficult to think of an explanation couched in terms of the public interest. As personal income has grown and more basic needs have been satisfied, voters' demand for goods and services like health and education traditionally provided by and through the state has grown (Mueller and Murrell 1986). Far from constituting evidence of its failure, expenditure growth therefore provides, on this reading, evidence of the state's responsiveness to changes in its citizen's preferences. Buchanan and Wagner's critique of Keynesianism offers one public choice alternative to this explanation. State expenditure has grown because vote-maximizing politicians have powerful incentives to raise expenditure, cut taxation and increase deficits. An alternative public choice explanation is provided by William Niskanen (1971, 1994).

Within neo-classical economic theory it is usually assumed that firms try to maximize their profits. But state bureaucracies funded through public grant do not operate in a profit and loss environment. They are funded by government and usually provide their services free at the point of delivery. For Niskanen, this raised the following question. What is it that self-interested state bureaucrats will attempt to maximize? His answer is that they will attempt to maximize the size of their budget because increases in budget will be positively related to salary, power, patronage, public reputation, prerequisites of office and output (Niskanen 1971: 38). Bureaucrats, all bureaucrats, are budget-maximizers who, whatever the particular area of state policy in which they are engaged, will seek to increase the budget of their department, division or particular sub-section.

This is, however, only the first part of Niskanen's argument. He goes on to suggest that bureaucrats will be relatively successful in their efforts to increase their budgets. This is because state bureaucracies are organized in ways that give bureaucrats considerable monopoly power. At both national and sub-national levels, bureaucrats are organized into departments defined by their responsibility for particular policy areas, be they health or foreign affairs. Judged intuitively, this would seem to make a great deal of sense. Why have two education departments inevitably duplicating much of each other's work? But from the public choice perspective, this functional division of labour makes no more sense than giving one firm a monopoly over car production on the grounds that it would be wasteful to build two assembly lines. The division of the state into monolithic departments gives bureaucrats a monopoly over the formulation, costing and implementation of policies. Monopoly is a source of market failure. It is, as Niskanen argues, also a source of state failure. Bureaucrats will use their monopoly position to extract larger budgets from their sponsors, so providing an 'output up to twice that of a competitive industry faced by the same demand and cost conditions' (Niskanen 1994: 64).

The critique of public choice

Within economics departments, the use of deductive models grounded upon the assumption of self-interested behaviour is now largely unchallenged (Lawson 1997). Undergraduates taking economics degrees are simply no longer exposed to methodological alternatives. In the 1980s practitioners confidently predicted that public choice would soon acquire a similar status within political science (Mueller 1993). This does not now seem particularly likely. Public choice will continue to attract support and provide a trenchant alternative to pluralist and other theories of the state. But it seems no more likely than any of these other theories to completely dominate political science. Indeed, far from becoming an unquestioned orthodoxy, public choice has if anything recently attracted growing criticism. Much of this continues, perhaps inevitably, to focus upon the assumption of self-interested behaviour (Mansbridge 1990; Paul *et al.* 1997). One standard argument here runs as follows. In deciding how to act people are usually guided by norms telling them how they *ought* to behave (Elster 1989). The existence and motivational force of such norms does *not* mean that people are always and everywhere cuddly altruists. For in many cases norms support and encourage self-interested behaviour. Entrepreneurs negotiating contracts with their suppliers are not considered to have done anything socially reprehensible if they drive a hard bargain in their attempt to maximize profits. But in every society norms proscribe self-interested behaviour in, for example, dealings with friends, family and the elderly and infirm.

How does this relate to the theory of the state? In many countries a set of norms best described as constituting a 'public service ethos' require politicians, bureaucrats and others working for the state to be guided in their decision-making by considerations of the public interest and to avoid using their positions to further their self-interest. Of course such norms are not always adhered to. In the 1990s, to take just one example, a number of Conservative MPs in the UK started to ask parliamentary questions in return for cash payments (Leigh and Vulliamy 1997). But this does not mean that public service norms do not exist. Indeed the efforts of these MPs to conceal the real motives for their behaviour and the force of the scandal which eventually broke over them in some ways confirm their existence. At one level the existence of such norms poses no explanatory problem for public choice. Because once a norm has been established, it will often be in a person's self-interest to adhere to it. In this way public choice theorists can argue that it is politicians' self-interest which leads them to be guided by consider-ations of the public interest. But this is precisely what public choice theorists do not argue. Instead, and as we have seen, they set about trying to debunk the 'romantic' (Buchanan 1984) myth that those working for the state are guided by considerations of the public interest.

This critique of the assumption of self-interested behaviour has one further and important element to it. Practitioners routinely describe public choice as offering a 'scientific' approach to the study of politics (Lustick 1997). It is not difficult to see why. Because the natural sciences carry a great deal of explanatory authority, the scientific label is one worth investing in. But one way in which social sciences like politics differ from natural sciences like physics is in terms of the differences their arguments and explanations make to the world. Theories about black holes do not and obviously cannot change the behaviour of black holes. Theories about why, for example, states concede independence to their central banks can make a difference to political behaviour and outcomes. Indeed over the last few decades the argument that financial markets reward countries that have independent banks with lower interest rates has become one of the key arguments wielded by those favouring independence (Bell 2004). One possible lesson to draw from this 'reflexivity' is that the social sciences ought to be self-consciously 'critical'. They ought not simply to try and explain the world but change it.

In many ways this is of course precisely what public choice theorists have done. Public choice has modified the way 'modern man views government' (Buchanan 1984: 21). In America, the critique of Keynesianism has fuelled demands for legislation requiring governments to pass balanced budgets whilst rent-seeking has been used to justify demands for reforms to campaign finance law. In Britain and America, Niskanen's theory of the budget-maximizing bureaucrat has encouraged the development of internal competitive tendering and privatization (Dowding 1995: 63–78). Yet from a self-consciously critical perspective, the problem with public choice is that the assumption of self-interest legitimates and promotes such behaviour in the 'real world'. It does so by making purely self-interested actions seem a perfectly normal, unobjectionable and unavoidable part of our nature

(Stephens 1991). So whilst self-interested behaviour may once have been a very inaccurate assumption to make about the behaviour of most people, the academic success of public choice theory may have contributed to making it more truthful. Public choice theorists may, in other words, have recreated the world in their own, rather unattractive, image. Given their motivational starting-point, public choice theorists see their normative task as being one of 'constructing a political order that will channel the self-serving behaviour of participants toward the common good' (Buchanan and Wagner 1978: 18). The possibility that maximizing the common good requires public spiritedness and that the role of the social sciences is to say so loudly and clearly simply passes public choice theorists by.

Public choice without prejudice

The debate between the proponents and opponents of public choice has tended to polarize political science opinion. In this final section I want to show how the basic terms of this increasingly contentious debate might nevertheless be changed. The starting-point here is the relationship between the state and the market. Economists seeking to explain market behaviour present consumers as choosing between products on the basis of their self-interested preferences. Public choice theorists have, traditionally, sought to explain voting behaviour in analogous fashion (Downs 1957: 295). Voters are like consumers who choose between candidates and parties in the same self-interested way that consumers choose between different brands of soap powder.

As two public choice theorists, Geoffrey Brennan and Loren Lomasky (1993), have however recognized, the analogy between market and electoral decision-making is that, in one crucial respect, misleading. In a market environment consumers are decisive over their choices. When a utility-maximizing consumer who prefers apples to oranges chooses oranges they get oranges. Voters are in a very different position. In anything other than the smallest of electorates, the chances of any one individual's vote making any difference to the outcome of an election are miniscule. A voter may want candidate X and may choose X in the polling booth but nevertheless get Y. The inference public choice theorists have traditionally drawn from this is that it is irrational to vote (Downs 1957: 265–70; Riker and Ordeshook 1968). Even if measured solely in terms of the shoe leather expended whilst walking to the polling booth, the costs of voting will always be greater than the benefits of voting discounted by the probability of being decisive. For this reason, rational, self-interested, utility-maximizing individuals should not vote. An alternative inference to draw is however that those who do vote have no reason to do so on the basis of their self-interest.

Voting gives voters an opportunity to 'express' beliefs and values about themselves and the world.

There is a link to be drawn here with the earlier argument. For one form expressive voting might take is the extension of support to politicians who, in their words and deeds, have committed themselves to the pursuit of the public interest and, conversely, the withdrawal of support from those believed to have, for example, manipulated the economy or sold policy favours for their own gain. In so far as voters are prepared to express themselves in this way, self-interested politicians intent upon achieving their re-election will have an incentive to commit themselves to the pursuit of the public interest. There is nothing new here. I have already suggested that the existence of norms gives people a self-interested reason to abide by those norms. For public choice theory the implications are nevertheless stark. Public choice theorists want to argue that there is no real difference between the market and the state. Both are prone to efficiency failures. Both are populated by self-interested actors. Both are prone to problems caused by monopolies, externalities and public goods. Yet if Brennan and Lomasky are right, there is an enduring and important difference between the market and the state. Actors in the former have stronger incentives to act in self-interested way and for this reason it cannot *necessarily* be assumed that markets and the state will always fail for the same reasons and in the same way. Public choice involves the application of the methods of economics to the study of politics and, in particular, the assumption of self-interested behaviour. The extension of this assumption to the political arena may however be totally inappropriate.

How might 'traditionalist' public choice theorists react to this argument? If we accept the basic logic of the argument about expressive voting, public choice theorists might nevertheless say that all that has been established is the incentive self-interested politicians have to provide a public interest 'cover' for their actions (see Tullock 1990). Expressive voting makes no real difference. Self-interested state actors will still pursue their self-interest but will simply do so in slightly more subtle ways. Parties may subsidize farming because farmers provide the largest campaign cheques but they will justify and explain their actions with reference to the need to preserve a rural way of life. Politicians may cut income tax in the run-up to an election in order to gain votes but they will need to justify and explain their actions by pointing to the need to stimulate consumer demand. Bureaucrats may want larger budgets in order to expand their empires but they will need to justify and explain their demands with reference to the need to maintain front-line services and meet government targets.

The need to provide a public interest 'cover' does nevertheless make a difference. Politics is not simply about the expression of self-interest. It is also about argument and persuasion. In pursuing their self-interest, politicians and other state actors must try and persuade sceptical voters, journalists and opponents that their actions are consistent with the public interest. It is not difficult to imagine the basic terms of an alternative research agenda in which this interaction between self-interest and the public interest is brought to the explanatory fore (Hindmoor 2004). The methodological victim in such an approach would not be the assumption of self-interest upon which so much attention has been lavished in this chapter. It would instead by the attempt to provide 'top-down', deductive, explanations. Conceptions of what the public interest consists of vary from country to country and from period to period. The rhetorical efforts of politicians and other state actors to persuade their audiences of the public interest justification for their actions will therefore be similarly varied. Whilst we might, at the most general of levels, say that politicians' and other actors will seek to provide a public interest 'cover' for their actions we cannot say what form this cover will take. We cannot, that is, construct 'top-down', all-purpose general explanations of actors' behaviour.

Conclusion

> Philosophers have only interpreted the world in various ways; the point is, however, to change it. (Karl Marx, Theses on Feuerbach, *The German Ideology*)

The use of 'top-down', deductive, models based upon the assumption of self-interested behaviour is generally held to have transformed the academic study of economics and given it an intellectual status approaching those of the natural sciences (but see Lawson 1997). It is therefore not surprising that economists have attempted to export their methods to the study of politics. Anthony Downs is, for example, quite explicit in his desire to emulate economics. *An Economic Theory of Democracy* opens with the following observation:

> Little progress has been made toward a generalized yet realistic behaviour rule for a rational government similar to the rules traditionally used for rational consumers and producers. As a result, government has not been successfully integrated with private decision-makers in a general equilibrium theory. This thesis is an attempt to provide such a behaviour rule for democratic government and to trace its implications. (Downs 1957: 3)

Yet public choice theorists have not simply interpreted the world. They have also sought to and succeeded in changing it. In the 1960s and 70s public choice theorists challenged what they saw as a post-war orthodoxy about the need for and benefits of an 'active' state. They succeeded in drawing academics' and politicians' attention to the failings of the state.

The extent of public choice theory's influence should not be exaggerated. 'New Right' politicians like Ronald Reagan and Margaret Thatcher would have been elected and would have sought to curtail the state whether or not public choice theory had been developed. Theirs was not a conversion on the road to Damascus prompted by a reading of James Buchanan or Gordon Tullock. But public choice theory did provide the New Right with a particular language in which the failings of the state could be dissected and a set of policy recommendations to deal with them. Whether or not it is a better place, the world is certainly a different place for the presence of public choice theory.

Further reading

Buchanan, J. (1984) 'Politics Without Romance', in J. Buchanan and R. Tollison, (eds), *The Theory of Public Choice II* (Ann Arbor: University of Michigan Press).
Dunleavy, P. and O'Leary, B. (1987) *Theories of the State* (Basingstoke: Macmillan).
Elster, J. (1986) 'Introduction', in J. Elster (ed.), *Rational Choice* (Oxford: Blackwell).
Laver, M. (1997) *Private Desires, Political Action* (London: Sage).
Mueller, D. (2003) *Public Choice III* (Cambridge: Cambridge University Press).
Rosenberg, A. (1995) *The Philosophy of Social Science* (Colorado: Westview Press).
Stretton, H. and Orchard, L. (1994) *Public Goods, Public Enterprise, Public Choice* (Basingstoke and New York: Palgrave: Macmillan).

Chapter 5

Institutionalism

VIVIEN SCHMIDT

The so-called 'new institutionalism' is a relatively recent addition to the pantheon of theories of the state and, like some of the other perspectives considered in this volume, it is by no means *only* a theory of the state. Nonetheless, and as explained in the introductory essay, its origins lie in the attempt to 'bring the state back into' mainstream political science by a range of theorists critical of the dominant agent-centred and behaviouralist approaches of the time (see, for instance, Evans *et al.* 1985). Such authors argued for the need to contextualize politics institutionally – in other words, to see the conditions of political opportunity as being, to a significant extent, set institutionally. In so doing, they developed a corrective to the dominance, as they saw it, of input-oriented theories of politics, which emphasized the pressures and influences brought to bear upon the state, rather than the capacity of the institutions of the state to respond to such pressures. This institutional contextualization of politics was initially confined to the attempt to bring the state back into political analysis but was later generalized, as neo-statism gave way to a more overarching new institutionalism. Yet, whilst the exclusive focus on the state has softened in the development of the new institutionalism out of neo-statism, the state still lies at the heart of new institutionalist scholarship – even if it not always labelled as such.

Institutionalism is characterized, unremarkably perhaps, by its emphasis upon the institutional context in which political events occur and for the outcomes and effects they generate. In contrast to the then prevailing behaviouralist and rational choice orthodoxies it emphasizes the extent to which political conduct is shaped by the institutional landscape in which it occurs, the importance of the historical legacies bequeathed from the past to the present and the range of diversity of actors' strategic orientation to the institutional contexts in which they find themselves (Hay 2002: 14–15). Each contributes to its distinctive view of the state.

In recent years, 'new institutionalism,' which involves 'bringing institutions back in' to the explanation of politics and society, has gained increasing currency in political science. What political scientists mean by new institutionalism, however, depends upon their preferred methodological approach to political science, and its particular epistemological and ontological presuppositions. And this in turn has significant implications for the study of the state. There are three main new institutionalisms – rational choice, historical, and sociological institutionalism – plus a fourth newer 'new' institutionalism–discursive institutionalism. Each has different objects, goals, and standards of explanation with regard to the state, and each has different advantages and disadvantages with regard to analyses of the state.

Rational choice institutionalism portrays the state either as itself a rational actor pursuing the 'logic of interest' or as a structure of incentives within which rational actors follow their preferences. Historical institutionalism concentrates instead on the origins and development of the state and its constituent parts, which it explains by the (often unintended) outcomes of purposeful choices and historically unique initial conditions in a 'logic of path-dependence'. Sociological institutionalism sees the state as socially constituted and culturally framed, with political agents acting according to the 'logic of appropriateness' that follows from culturally-specific rules and norms. Finally, the newest of the 'new' institutionalisms, 'discursive' institutionalism, considers the state in terms of the ideas and discourse that actors use to explain, deliberate, and/or legitimize political action in institutional context according to the 'logic of communication.'

This chapter begins with a discussion of the 'old institutionalism' that provided a largely descriptive view of the state's institutional arrangements, of the 'holistic' approaches that looked instead to political systems, of the behaviourism that rejected both in favour of a focus on individual human behaviour, and of the 'new institutionalism' that proposed to supersede all the previous approaches. It follows this with a closer analysis of each of the three main 'new institutionalisms', providing definitional accounts of their main characteristics, their epistemological and ontological differences, their benefits and their drawbacks, and how they interrelate and intersect. It concludes with a consideration of the fourth and newest new institutionalism, as a remedy for some of the problems of the older new institutionalisms.

From the 'old institutionalism' to the 'new institutionalism'

No account of the new institutionalisms would be complete without first mentioning the 'old' institutionalism. The original institutionalism studied the formal institutions of government and defined the state in terms of its political, administrative, and legal arrangements – as epitomized in the work of Woodrow Wilson. It used a largely descriptive methodology to explain the relations among levels and branches of government, with concepts of the state drawn from traditional political philosophy and understood in terms of sovereignty, justice, power, citizenship, and legal status in international law. Where the old institutionalism was comparative, it mainly juxtaposed different state configurations to demonstrate similarities or differences in how governments worked. It remained largely atheoretical, although some political theories did develop, such as pluralist theory of interest groups (e.g., Bentley), while there were some methodological dissenters in favour of 'scientism,' like Charles Merriam (see Somit and Tanenhaus 1982).

By the 1950s and 1960s, systemic approaches to political science had largely superseded the old institutionalism, whether structural-functionalist or other 'holistic' approaches, such as Marxian analysis, which had its heyday in the 1960s and 1970s. In structural-functionalism, the concept of the state was replaced by the political system and explained in terms of the equilibrium-seeking functioning of its structural parts – through interest articulation and aggregation (Almond and Powell 1966; Easton 1957). This had an essentially conservative bias in favour of the status quo. Embedded in the approach was the uncritical normative assumption that the system would go on so long as its structures functioned in such a way as to achieve its goal – self-maintenance – and that 'societies which fulfil the functions more completely are *pro tanto* better' (Taylor 1967: 156). Moreover, the system was static in the sense that revolutions were anomalies, unexplainable within the system, and change was absorbed by the system as an instance of 'homeostatic equilibrium'. Where the approach was linked to a political theory of the state, it picked up on traditional interest group theory, and assumed that the state's role was to arbitrate among competing interests, with the outcome the public interest (Dahl 1961a; see also Chapter 1). The counter-theory was Marxian analysis which, although equally systemic, cast the state as a superstructure in the service of one interest, the bourgeoisie, and saw the system as a whole functioning via class conflict rather than interest competition, with the expected outcome not self-maintenance but self-destruction through revolution (Dahrendorf 1959; see also Chapter 3)]. This approach was clearly also normative in its assumptions, but critical of the status quo as well as socially determinist.

By the 1960s and 1970s, behaviourism, also begun in the 1950s, had for the most part submerged the old institutionalism as well as political systems approaches as the predominant approach in political science with a focus on individuals and their behaviour (Somit and Tanenhaus 1982). The state as a term disappeared altogether, as did the political system. 'Methodological individualism' replaced the 'methodological holism' of structural-functionalist and Marxian approaches, while the old institutionalism was dismissed as mere description. The behavioural 'revolution' sought to explain the 'phenomena of government in terms of the observed and observable behavior of men' (Truman 1951, cited in Dahl 1961b) and rejected the normative biases of both structural-functional and Marxian approaches in favour of 'objective' empirical observation – since the political scientist was concerned with 'what *is*, as he says, not what *ought* to be' (Dahl 1969). In addition, most behaviourists assumed that 'human and social behavior can be explained in terms of general laws established by observation' (Przeworksi and Teune 1970: 4) and sought to develop precise techniques by which to measure data and to demonstrate the validity of law-like theories (Kirkpatrick 1971: 71–3). Naturally, that which could be most readily quantified, such as voting and public opinion via electoral studies, survey research, and opinion polling, became the focus. Where this was more difficult, rational choice (or public choice) approaches were pioneered using mathematical models drawn from economics – most notably with the work of Anthony Downs (1957; see Chapter 4).

'New institutionalism' began in the late 1970s and early 1980s with the desire by a wide range of scholars to bring the institutions of the state back into the explanation of political action. It was less focused on rejecting the 'old institutionalism', most of the concepts and information of which it treated as background knowledge, than on providing a counter to behaviourism. Behaviourism itself was by now under attack from the inside as well as from the outside because it was perceived as plagued by overquantification and undertheorizing, without much cumulation of knowledge into a coherent body of theory (see, e.g., Ostrom 1982; Wahlke 1979).

'New institutionalism' was a response to the absence of institutional analysis, of considering collective action *qua* collective – through composite or institutional actors – rather than reducing political action to its methodological individualist parts. The theoretical core uniting the very disparate kinds of institutionalisms that emerged rejected the proposition that observable behaviour was the basic datum of political analysis and argued instead that behaviour cannot be understood without reference to the 'institutions' within which such behaviour occurs (Immergut 1998: 6–8).

But while the new institutionalists have been united on the importance of institutions and in the rejection of behaviourism, they have been divided along a number of other dimensions. These include first and foremost the way in which they define the state – understood now as the whole range of governing structures in and/or through which political actors, governmental as well as non-governmental, interact – and the logic of political action. But new institutionalists have also been divided along continua ranging from universalistic to particularistic generalizations, from positivism to constructivism, and from static to more dynamic explanations of political action.

Rational choice institutionalism

Rational choice institutionalism in political science has its roots in the problems encountered by rational choice analysts, in particular those interested in American congressional behaviour. Because conventional rational choice analyses predicted instability in congressional decision-making due to uncertainties resulting from the multiplicity of individual preferences and issues (e.g., Riker 1980), how could it explain the unexpected stability of outcomes? The answer was found in the institutions of the state, in particular in the rules of procedure in Congress that lowered the transaction costs of making deals, thereby solving seemingly insoluble collective action problems (Shepsle 1986).

In short, rational choice institutionalists brought the state back in as a way of explaining outcomes that could not be explained by universal theories of rational action without reference to institutional context. But rather than asking about the context itself, meaning the state, they generally took the institutions as given and asked about the nature of rational action within such institutions. Thus, they posit rational actors with fixed preferences who calculate strategically to maximize those preferences and who, in the absence of institutions that promote complementary behaviour through co-ordination, confront collective action problems such as the 'prisoners' dilemma' and the 'tragedy of the commons', where individual actors' choice can only lead to sub-optimal solutions (Elster and Hylland 1986; Ostrom 1990).

In American politics, rational choice institutionalist analyses are found in principal-agent theories of how 'principals' – e.g., congress, the executive, or political parties – maintain control or gain compliance from the 'agents' to which they delegate power – e.g., bureaucracies, regulatory agencies, or courts (e.g., McCubbins and Sullivan 1987). In comparative politics, rational choice institutionalists consider delegation between European Union institutional actors (Moravcsik 1998; Pollack 1997), the European Parliament as agenda setter (Tsebelis 2002), and the collective decision-making traps in Europe (Scharpf 1999), while in international relations they examine delegation in international organizations (Martin 2000) or use a game-theoretic approach to democratic transitions (Przeworski 1991).

Rational choice institutionalism works best at identifying the interests and motivations behind rational actors' behaviour within given institutional settings. The deductive nature of its approach to explanation means that it is tremendously helpful at capturing the range of reasons actors would normally have for any action within a given institutional incentive structure as well as at predicting likely outcomes, even if future-oriented predictions are rarely offered. It is also good at bringing out anomalies or actions that are unexpected given the general theory. However, for the most part it cannot explain these anomalies if they depart radically from interest-motivated action, and therefore might better be explained in sociological, historical, or discursive institutional terms (Scharpf 1997). Moreover, where the push is toward universalistic generalizations, problems with overgeneralization abound. One approach that consciously seeks to avoid this problem is the 'actor-centred institutionalism' of Fritz Scharpf (1991), which develops 'bounded generalizations' about the outcomes of actors' institutionally-constituted strategic interactions through the identification of subsets of cases in which variance in policy outcomes can be explained by variances in the same set of factor constellations (i.e., problems, policy legacies, actors' attributes, and institutional interactions).

But however 'bounded' the generalizations, because of rational choice institutionalism's very deductiveness, along with a theoretical generality that starts from universal claims about rationality, rational choice institutionalism has difficulty explaining any one individual's reasons for action within a given context or any particular set of real political events (Green and Shapiro 1994). The recent attempt to 'contextualize' analyses through 'analytic narratives' in which individual events are subsumed under more general theories represents something of a corrective to this problem (Bates *et al.*, 1998). But even so, individuals *qua* individuals are not present here, and the high level of abstraction with which rational choice institutionalist explanation works offers a very 'thin' definition of rationality indeed, with a somewhat simplistic understanding of human motivation that misses out on the subtleties of human reasons for action (see Mansbridge 1990).

The rational choice institutionalist approach is also often highly functionalist because it tends to explain the origins of an institution largely in terms of its effects; highly intentionalist because it assumes that rational actors not only perceive the effects of the institutions that affect them but can also create and control them; and highly voluntarist because they see institutional creation as a quasi-contractual process rather than affected by asymmetries of power (see Bates 1987; Hall and Taylor 1996: 952).

In addition, rational choice institutionalist explanation is static (see Blyth 1997; Green and Shapiro 1994). Because it assumes fixed preferences and is focused on equilibrium conditions, it has difficulty accounting for why institutions change over time other than in purely functionalist terms. Moreover, rational choice institutionalists' emphasis on the self-interested nature of human motivation, especially where it is assumed to be economic self-interest, is value-laden, and can appear economically deterministic. The normative assumptions lie in positing political action as motivated by instrumental rationality alone, and thereby risks making the utilitarian calculus within established institutions the universal arbiter of justice (e.g., Elster and Hylland 1986: 22 – see the critique by Immergut 1998: 14). What is more, despite the fact that rational choice institutionalists could question the institutional rules within which rational actors seek to maximize their utility, either in terms of the justness of the institutional rules or of the exercise of institutional power, they generally do not (see Immergut 1998: 13). They don't even question them in terms of efficiency (e.g., North 1990)! Instead, as Terry Moe complains, they tend to see institutions 'as good things, and it is their goodness that ultimately explains them: they exist and take the forms they do because they make people better off' (2003: 3, cited in Thelen 2004). A notable exception is Margaret Levi's Marxian rationalist analysis of the 'predatory' state with regard to tax collection (1989). But mostly, institutions – and with them the state – are assumed to be good things that create greater stability for rational actors' utility-maximization.

Historical institutionalism

Historical institutionalism is arguably the institutionalism most influenced by the old institutionalism as well as by political systems approaches, both structural-functional and Marxian approaches. From the old institutionalists came the continuing interest in the state and the formal institutions of government; from the structural-functionalists, the emphasis on structures (but not functions); and from the Marxists, the focus on power, with the state seen 'no longer as a neutral broker among competing interests but as a complex of institutions capable of structuring the character and outcomes of group conflict' (Hall and Taylor 1996: 938). Thus, historical institutionalism, unlike rational choice institutionalism, focuses most explicitly on the state and its institutional development – with the state just as problematic as the action within it. Historical institutionalists have explored not just state structures but all the structures through which governing occurs: in political economy not just state actors but also labour organizations, business associations, and financial institutions; in public policy not just state legislators but also organized interests, the electorate and the judiciary (Hall and Taylor 1996; see also Steinmo *et al.* 1992).

Historical institutionalism began in the late 1970s with the works of comparativists like Theda Skocpol (1979) and Peter Katzenstein (1978), international relations scholars like Stephen Krasner (1980), and Americanists like Stephen Skowronek (1982), all of whom were intent on 'bringing the state back in' (Evans *et al.* 1985). These scholars argued that political action could not be reduced to individual behaviour alone or even to group activity because of the importance of how the state structured action and of how state capacity and policy legacies structured outcomes. Their work formed the basis for the subsequent, more self-consciously historical institutionalist body of literature. Among these, Peter Hall (1986) explained the different trajectories of British and French political economic development as the result of the structural constraints implicit in their socio-economic organization; Peter Katzenstein (1985) demonstrated that the economic openness of small states combined with strong welfare states could be explained by historically-developed, corporatist institutional structures; while Paul Pierson (1994) showed how past welfare state policies set the conditions for future policies in a comparison of the US and Britain.

Historical institutionalism works best at delineating the origins and development of institutional structures and processes over time. It tends to focus on sequences in development, timing of events, and phases of political change. It emphasizes not just the asymmetries of power related to the operation and development of institutions but also the path-dependencies and unintended consequences that result from such historical development (Hall and Taylor 1996: 938; Steinmo *et al.* 1992; Thelen 1999). Path-dependency ensures that rationality in the strict rational choice sense is present only insofar as institutions are the intended consequences of actors' choices. But this is often not the case, given the unintended consequences of intentional action and the unpredictability of intervening events.

Interests, moreover, rather than being universally defined, are contextual (Thelen 1999; Zysman 1994). Compared to rational choice institutionalism, historical institutionalism tends to be less universalistic in its generalizations and more 'mid-range' in its theory-building, by focusing on changes in a limited number of countries unified in space and/or time or on a specific kind of phenomenon that occurs in or affects a range of countries at one time or across time (Thelen 1999). But although more particular in its generalizations, the 'new' historical institutionalism rarely stays at the level of the 'mere story-telling' of which it is sometimes accused by rational choice institutionalists. Noticeably absent is the focus on 'great men' or 'great moments' characteristic of more traditional historical approaches in the old institutionalism. In fact, the macro-historical approach prevalent in most accounts tends to emphasize structures and processes much more than the events out of which they are constructed, let alone the individuals whose actions and interests spurred those events. Here too, then, there are no individual actors as such. What is more, any 'micro-foundational logic,' as rationalists put it, is generally missing from this macro-historical work. Instead, it follows the logic of path-dependency. Rather than appearing economically deterministic, therefore, historical institutionalism can appear historically deterministic or even mechanistic where it focuses exclusively on continuities and path-dependencies. The 'critical junctures' literature that looks at 'configurative' moments (e.g., Collier and Collier 1991; Gourevitch 1986) or 'punctuated equilibrium' (Krasner 1988) is something of a corrective to this problem; but it still has difficulty explaining what brings about the crisis that spurs change. Moreover, it assumes that change comes only in bursts, with stasis in between, and cannot account for incremental change. Instead, as Kathleen Thelen (2003; 2004) argues, institutional evolution can be explained by way of certain mechanisms of change such as the layering of new elements onto otherwise stable institutional frameworks and the conversion of institutions through the adoption of new goals or the incorporation of new groups. But even here, how change is instigated – either through layering or conversion – remains unclear without adding elements from other analytic approaches.

The main problem for the historical institutionalists, given their emphasis on structures, is how to explain human agency. For this, historical institutionalists mostly turn to analyses that add what Peter Hall and Rosemary Taylor (1996: 940–1) term either a 'calculus' approach–which puts the historical institutionalists closer to the rational choice institutionalists, albeit still with a primacy to historical structures that shape actors' interests – or a 'culture' approach – which puts them closer to the sociological institutionalists, although here historical structures add to norms to give meaning to actors' interests and worldview. There is, however, an alternative ontology to both culture and calculus, as Colin Hay and Dan Wincott argue (1998), which situates agency within the historical institutionalist approach itself. But this will be considered below, because it flows into the discussion below of ideas and discourse. Examples abound on the combination of historical institutionalism with rational calculus. Ellen Immergut's (1992) comparative study of healthcare reform explains cross-national differences in physicians' calculations of their interests in terms of the way in which governing structures – as veto-points – affect their expectations of future success in limiting (or not) reform efforts. Thelen's (2004) study of institutional change in skills regimes in Britain, Germany, Japan and the United States turns to rationalist accounts of ongoing political negotiation focusing on political coalitions and political conflicts to explain change through layering and conversion. Peter Hall in a collaborative project with David Soskice (2001) embedded a rationalist analysis of firm-centred co-ordination in a historical institutionalist analysis of the binary division of capitalism into liberal market economies (e.g., Britain) and co-ordinated market economies (e.g. Germany), in seeking microfoundations for historical institutionalism. Building on a combination of historical institutionalism and rationalist calculus but bringing the state back into a comparison of the evolving political economies of Britain, France, and Germany, I argue that there are at least three varieties of market economy, with France representing the third, state-enhanced variety (Schmidt 2002, Part II). Paul Pierson (2004), finally, in his study of the dimension of time in political analysis has tipped to the other side in an attempt to provide a temporal dimension to rational choice institutionalism (2004).

Sociological institutionalism

Sociological institutionalism, much like historical institutionalism, had its beginnings in the late 1970s, mainly in the sociological sub-field of organizational theory. Sociological institutionalists also rejected the older methodological approaches, including behaviourism, systems approaches, as well as rational choice analyses. Against Weberian assumptions about the rationality and efficiency of organizations in particular, sociological institutionalists turned to the forms and procedures of organizational life stemming from culturally-specific practices. Sociological institutionalists' institutions are cast as the norms, cognitive frames, and meaning systems that guide human action as well as the cultural scripts and schema diffused through organizational environments, serving symbolic and ceremonial purposes rather than just utilitarian ones. Here too, then, much like rational choice institutionalism, the state is the taken for granted environment in which action occurs – but the sociological institutionalist's state looks very different from the rationalists' state, as cultural practices rather rational action infuse it with meaning.

Rationality for sociological institutionalists is socially constructed and culturally and historically contingent. It is defined by cultural institutions which set the limits of the imagination, establishing basic preferences and identity and setting the context within which purposive, goal-oriented action is deemed acceptable according to a 'logic of appropriateness' (see DiMaggio and Powell 1983; DiMaggio and Powell 1991; March and Olsen 1989; Meyer and Rowan 1977; see also the discussions in Campbell 2004; Campbell and Pederson 2001: 7–8; Hall and Taylor 1996: 947–8). Sociological institutionalism is thus in direct contradiction to rationalists' views of human behaviour as following a 'logic of interest' which is prior to institutions, by which individuals may be affected but not defined.

Sociological institutionalist analyses that are particularly significant for political scientists include Frank Dobbin's (1994) study of nineteenth-century railways policy, where reasonably similar policies were 'concealed' as state actions in the United States but 'revealed' as state actions in France; Neil Fligstein's (1990) account of the transformation of corporate control as resulting from change not just in economic environments but also in corporate leaders' perceptual lenses; and Yasemin Soysal's (1994) contrast of immigration policy in Europe and America, which showed the importance of distinctive 'incorporation regimes' for absorbing immigrants based on differing models of citizenship. In political science itself, the seminal work is by James March and Johan Olsen (1989), who argued that cultural as well as historical structures matter, and who therefore have been claimed as one of their own by historical institutionalists as much as by sociological institutionalists. More recently, a number of political scientists have moved to sociological institutionalism (see Finnemore 1996a), in particular in international relations, where they often call themselves 'constructivists.' Most notable has been Peter Katzenstein's edited volume (1996a) that focuses on how interests develop from state identities, with norms acting as collective expectations about the proper behaviour for a given identity, and with state identities structuring national perceptions of defence and security issues.

Sociological institutionalism works best at delineating the shared understandings and norms that frame action, shape identities, influence interests, and affect what are perceived as problems and what are conceived as solutions. It stands in direct opposition to rational choice institutionalism in its assumption that norms, identities, and culture constitute interests, and are therefore *endogenous* because embedded in culture, as opposed to seeing interests as *exogenous* and culture, norms, and identity epiphenomena that follow from interests rather than preceding them (see Ruggie 1998; Wendt 1987).

But as a result, rather than being too general, it is sometimes accused of being too specific, and the 'cultural knowledge' it provides useful mainly as preliminary to rational choice universalization. However, when the objects of sociological institutionalism are subsumed under rational choice explanation, often the very essence of sociological institutionalism – the norms, rules, and reasons which are culturally unique or anomalous because they do not fit generally expected interest-motivations – get lost. Because such explanations are arrived at inductively rather than deductively, they can lend insight into individuals' reasons for action in ways that rational choice institutionalism cannot, whether they fit the norm or depart from it. Moreover, because such explanations account contextually for individuals' reasons for action, sociological institutionalism is better able to explain the events out of which historical institutional explanations are constructed. And because sociological institutional explanations emphasize the role that collective processes of interpretation and legitimacy play in the creation and development of institutions, they can account for the inefficiencies in institutions that rational choice institutionalism cannot (Meyer and Rowan 1977; see discussion in Hall and Taylor 1996: 953).

However, because sociological institutionalism makes no universalistic claims about rationality and is generally focused on explanation within rather than across cultures, it risks an implicit relativism which leads one to question whether sociological institutionalism allows for any cross-national generalizations at all. In fact, generalizations are possible here too, by invoking similarities as well as differences in cultural norms and identities, much in the way of historical institutionalism with country-specific institutional structures and processes. The resulting explanation, however, involves a lower level of generality and less parsimonious, 'thicker description' than in historical institutionalism, let alone rational choice institutionalism.

Finally, rather than appearing either economically or historically deterministic, sociological institutionalism can appear culturally deterministic where it emphasizes the cultural routines and rituals to the exclusion of individual action which breaks out of the cultural norm, i.e., rule-creating action as opposed to rule-following action. Moreover, its emphasis on macro-patterns may make it appear like 'action without agents' (Hall and Taylor 1996: 954) or, worse, structures without agents (see the critique by Checkel 1998: 335). And like the rational choice approach, it too can be too static or equilibrium-focused, and unable to account for change over time – although where it adds a historical perspective, it can also show how norms are institutionalized, as in the case of the police and military in postwar Japan and Germany (Katzenstein 1996b) or how state identities can change and pull interests along with them, as in the case of anti-militarism in Germany and Japan (Berger 1998).

Discursive institutionalism

Discursive institutionalism is the term I use for the fourth and newest of the 'new institutionalisms' (Schmidt 2002; see also Campbell 2001), although other terms such as ideational institutionalism (Hay 2001), constructivist institutionalism (Hay 2006), and economic constructivism (Abdelal, Blyth and Parson 2005) would also be appropriate. This approach has grown out of many new institutionalists' concern with the seeming inability of any of the three older new institutionalisms to explain change, given their often very static view of institutions. The problem with the other approaches was brought home as a result of real events, in particular as Communist states collapsed following the fall of the Berlin wall, giving the lie to the static presuppositions of all three approaches (see Blyth 2003), and as the rationalist presuppositions of neo-liberalism encountered problems with democratic transitions (Campbell and Pederson 2001: 7–8; Campbell 2004). The turn to the role of ideas and discourse was a natural next step for scholars immersed in all three of the new institutionalisms but concerned to explain changes within the state and to the state. And in so doing, most added the institutional context of their own preferred approaches. But while for some, turning to ideas meant staying within the initial constructs of their own institutionalist approach, others moved beyond, into discursive institutionalism, and a primary concern with ideas and how they are communicated through discourse.

Among rational choice institutionalists, the foray into the realm of ideas has been relatively short-lived. In international relations, an early move to ideas was made by Judith Goldstein (1993), who suggested that under conditions of uncertainty, ideas behave like switches (or 'road maps') that funnel interests down specific policy directions, serving as filters, focal points, or lenses that provide policy-makers with strategies (see also Bates *et al.* 1998; Goldstein and Keohane 1993; Weingast 1995). Here, ideas have not gone very far beyond interests, since they are little more than mechanisms for choosing among interests, or as focal points for switching among equilibria (see critique by Ruggie 1998: 866–7). Douglass North (1990) went farther, first by using ideas to overcome the problem of how to explain institutional construction, then by casting ideas as 'shared mental modes'. However, as Mark Blyth (2003: 696–7; 2002, Ch. 2) insightfully argues, the contradictions inherent in both such approaches may have been 'a bridge too far'. First, if ideas create institutions, then how can institutions make ideas 'actionable?' But second, if instead ideas are 'mental modes,' then what stops ideas from having an effect on the content of interests, and not just on the order of interests? And if ideas constitute interests rather than the other way around, then how can rationalists maintain their notion of the 'fixed' nature of preferences which is at the basis of their thin model of rationality? This helps explain why rational choice institutionalists quickly abandoned the pursuit of ideas.

In the historical institutionalist tradition, the move into ideas has been more lasting. Here, the question is really where the tipping point is between historical institutionalists who continue to see institutions as constitutive of ideas, determining which ideas are acceptable, and those who might better be called discursive institutionalists within a historical institutionalist tradition because they see ideas as constitutive of institutions even if shaped by them. Thus, Peter Hall, whose earliest work was squarely within historical institutionalism, focusing on the institutional stability of institutions over time (1986), and whose latest work combined historical institutional structures of capitalism with a rational choice institutionalist focus on strategic firm co-ordination (2001), in between focused on the role of economic ideas to explain change. However, whereas in his first ideational approach, on the adoption of Keynesianism ideas (Hall 1989), he remained largely historical institutionalist because historical structures come prior to ideas, influencing their adoptability, in the second, on the introduction of monetarist ideas in Thatcher's Britain (Hall 1993), he crossed the line to discursive institutionalism, since ideas are central to change and constitutive of new institutions. Interestingly enough, even in the book that gave historical institutionalism its name (Steinmo *et al.* 1992), the few chapters that were focused on ideas – those of Peter Hall, Desmond King, and Margaret Weir – take us beyond historical institutionalism. Desmond King (1999) in his book on illiberal social policy in Britain and the US makes this move quite explicit through the focus on the role of ideas and knowledge in the making of

policy, although King also retains a strong historical institutionalist component with his emphasis on how institutional context makes it easier for the
British government to take up ideas and impose reform than in the US.
Within the historical institutionalist tradition, in fact, much recent work
focused on ideas tips into what I call discursive institutionalism – although
the dividing line is admittedly fuzzy. What defines these is the focus on
ideas as explanatory of change, often with a demonstration that such ideas
do not fit predictable 'rationalist' interests, are underdetermined by structural factors, and/or represent a break with historical paths (see discussion
in Blyth 2003). Examples include Sheri Berman's (1998) historical contrast
between the German Social Democrats' capitulation before Nazism, in
large measure because they could not think beyond their long-held Marxist
ideas, and the Swedish Social Democrats' success in not only fighting
fascism but also in creating a social democratic state because they were free
of any such ideational legacy and able to reinvent socialism; Kate McNamara's
(1998) account of European monetary union which posited a three-step
learning process of, first, policy failure, second, the search for new ideas
that led to a neo-liberal consensus on monetarism and, third, the adoption
of the German exemplar; and finally Mark Blyth's (2002) analysis of the
role of foundational economic ideas at moments of economic crisis first in
'embedding' liberalism in the 1930s and then 'disembedding' it beginning
in the 1970s in Sweden and the United States. My own analysis of the political economies of Britain, France, and Germany highlights the differences
between historical institutionalist and discursive institutionalist approaches
by first presenting (in Schmidt 2002, Part II) a calculus-oriented, historical
institutionalist examination of the evolution in the three countries'
economic practices followed (in Part III) by a discursive institutionalist
discussion of the changing ideas and discourse in the politics of economic
adjustment.

It is interesting to note that most of the ideational approaches that follow
from the historical institutionalist tradition sit closer to the positivist end of
the positivist-constructivist continuum, and are found for the most part in
comparative politics. In these approaches, ideas are seen as representing the
necessary conditions for collective action within the state, by serving to
redefine economic interest and to reconfigure interest-based coalitions. The
focus tends to be on the cognitive aspects of ideas, that is, on how new
ideas get accepted, how to determine kinds and degrees or 'orders' of
change, generally following Kuhn (Hall 1993; Hay 2001; Schmidt 2002:
Ch. 5), and what criteria for success can be applied in terms of relevance,
applicability, and coherence or consistency (Schmidt 2002: Ch. 5).

Most ideational approaches that are within the sociological institutionalist
tradition, by contrast, sit closer to the constructivist end, and are mostly
found in international relations. In these approaches, ideas constitute the

norms, narratives, discourses, and frames of reference which serve to (re)construct actors' understandings of interests and redirect their actions within the institutions of the state. The focus here is on the normative aspects of discourse, that is, how and why new ideas 'resonate' with national values, and how they may 'revaluate' values, all within a logic of appropriateness (March and Olsen 1989; Rein and Schön 1991; Schmidt 2000).

In the sociological institutionalist tradition, one cannot talk about a move into ideas as such, since ideas have always been at the basis of the approach – as norms, cognitive frames, and meaning systems. However, there is also a tipping point here. On the one side are those scholars who see ideas more as static ideational structures, as norms and identities constituted by culture, and thus remain largely sociological institutionalists as per the earlier definition. These include 'constructivists' like Katzenstein and his colleagues (1996) who stay largely within sociological institutionalism because they 'cut into the problem of ideational causation at the level of "collective representations" of ideational social facts and then trace the impact of these representations on behavior' (Ruggie 1998: 884–5). On the other side are constructivists who more clearly fit under the rubric of discursive institutionalism because they present ideas as more dynamic, that is, as norms, frames, and narratives that not only establish how actors conceptualize the world but also enable them to reconceptualize the world, serving as a resource to promote change. These include Alexander Wendt, who sees social structures as having 'an inherently discursive dimension in the sense that they are inseparable from the reasons and self-understandings that agents bring to their actions' while agents and structures are 'mutually constitutive', with 'each in some sense an effect of the other' (1987: 359–60). Scholars who explore this more dynamic dimension empirically include Martha Finnemore (1996b), who examines the diffusion of international norms to developing countries, and Thomas Risse (2001), who considers the ways in which different European countries successively constructed and reconstructed their state identities and ideas about European integration.

Some scholars don't fit neatly into one or the other camp. In comparative politics in particular, those who focus on the role of economic ideas may look positivist because they consider the cognitive usages of those ideas in legitimizing policy change. But they are often also constructivists in their critique of the normative spin of those ideas. Colin Hay and Ben Rosamund in particular have been explicit in their investigation of the normative underpinnings of neo-liberal ideas and their social construction in the process of globalization (Hay and Rosamund 2002; Hay 2005; Rosamund 2005). But Schmidt (2000) and Blyth (2002), and to a lesser extent Schmidt (2002), could also be seen as constructivist in their combination of cognitive and normative analysis of ideas.

Most of the discursive institutionalists just discussed – whether in the historical or sociological institutionalist tradition or straddling the two – tend to deal mainly with ideas, leaving the interactive processes of discourse implicit as they discuss the ideas generated, accepted, and legitimized by the various actors. Some scholars, however, have gone farther to formalize the interactive processes of idea generation, acceptance, and legitimization, and to clarify how they are structured. They tend to see discourse not only as a set of ideas bringing new rules, values and practices but also as a resource used by entrepreneurial actors to produce and legitimate those ideas. Their approaches can be divided into those focused on the 'coordinative' discourse among policy actors and those more interested in the 'communicative' discourse between political actors and the public (see Schmidt 2002: Ch. 5)

In the co-ordinative sphere, discursive institutionalists tends to emphasize primarily the individuals and groups at the centre of policy construction who generate the ideas that form the bases for collective action and identity. Some of these scholars focus on the loosely connected individuals united by a common set of ideas in 'epistemic communities' in the international arena (Haas 1992). Others target more closely connected individuals united by the attempt to put those ideas into action through 'advocacy coalitions' in localized policy contexts (Sabatier and Jenkins-Smith 1993) or through 'advocacy networks' of activists in international politics (Keck and Sikkink 1998). Yet others single out the individuals who, as 'entrepreneurs' (Fligstein and Mara-Drita 1996; Finnemore and Sikkink 1998) or 'mediators' (Jobert 1992; Muller 1995) draw on and articulate the ideas of discursive communities and coalitions in particular policy domains in domestic or international arenas.

In the communicative sphere, discursive institutionalists emphasize the use of ideas in the mass process of public persuasion in the political sphere. Some of these scholars focus on electoral politics and mass opinion (Mutz, Sniderman and Brody 1996), when politicians translate the ideas developed by policy elites into the political platforms that are put to the test through voting and elections; others are more concerned with the 'communicative action' (Habermas 1996) that frames national political understandings; yet others, on the more specific deliberations in the 'policy forums' of informed publics (Rein and Schön 1991) about the on-going policy initiatives of governments.

Discursive institutionalism works best at explaining the dynamics of change (but also continuity) through its attention to ideas and discursive interactions, new or continuing. As such, it largely avoids the economic, historical, or cultural determinism of the other three 'new institutionalisms'. By the same token, however, it risks appearing highly voluntaristic unless the structural constraints derived from the three newer institutionalisms are included. This is not so much an issue for the discursive institutionalist scholars discussed above, given that their approaches already follow from one or a combination of institutionalist traditions – but where 'text' appears without context, as in postmodernist approaches, the risks are significant. There are other problems, however. In discursive approaches that follow in the sociological institutionalist tradition, there is always the danger that social construction goes too far, and that material interests *qua* material interests are ignored in favour of seeing everything as socially constructed within a given culture (see the critique of Sikkink 1991 by Jacobsen 1995). This leads one to question whether there is anything 'out there' at all, mutually recognizable across cultures. But while discursive approaches in the sociological institutionalist tradition may suffer from too much constructivism, those in the historical institutionalist tradition may suffer from too much positivism, with political action assumed to be motivated by instrumental rationality alone (even if contextualized by history and culture), such that cognitive ideas about interests overdetermine the choice of ideas, crowding out the normative values which also colour any conceptualization of interest.

Finally, establishing causality can be a problem. Discourse, just as any other factor, sometimes matters, sometimes does not in the explanation of change. The question is *when* does discourse matter, that is, when does it exert a causal influence on policy change, say, by redefining interests as opposed to merely reflecting them in rationalist calculations (see Schmidt 2002), and when are other factors more significant, say, where the creation of new institutional paths or cultural norms may be better captured by historical or sociological institutionalist analysis, because actors don't have any clear idea about what they are doing when they are doing it. Part of the reason many political scientists avoid explanations related to discourse is that it is difficult to separate it from other variables, to identify it as *the* independent variable. But instead of ignoring discourse because of the difficulties, because it cannot be *the* cause, it is much better to ask when is discourse *a* cause, that is, when does discourse serve to reconceptualize interests rather than just reflect them, to chart new institutional paths instead of simply following old ones, and to reframe cultural norms rather than only reify them.

Conclusion

The study of the state, as we have seen, is very different depending upon the kind of new institutionalism. Each has a different object of explanation – whether rational behaviour, historical structures, norms and culture, or ideas and discourse; a different logic of explanation – whether interests, path-dependency, appropriateness, or communication; a different emphasis on continuity or change – whether on continuity through fixed preferences, through path dependency, or through cultural norms, or on change through ideas and discursive interactions (see Table 5.1). The result is that there are very different kinds of institutionalist studies of the state, many of which focus little on the state itself but, rather, on different kinds of action within the state. To get a sense of how all of this fits together in a very general way, I conclude with a chart that situates the works cited above within each of the four institutionalisms while arraying the four institutionalisms along a horizontal continuum from positivism to constructivism – from interests to culture, with history in between – and along a vertical continuum from statics to dynamics, with interests, history, and culture at the static end, ideas and discourse at the dynamic end (see Figure 5.1). I put historical institutionalism between rational choice and sociological institutionalism, mainly because rational choice and sociological institutionalism are largely incompatible, whereas historical institutionalism can go either to the positivist or the constructivist side when it adds agency. I put discourse institutionalism underneath all three because, although it is distinctive, it

Table 5.1 *The four new institutionalisms*

	Rational choice institutionalism	Historical institutionalism	Sociological institutionalism	Discursive institutionalism
Object of explanation	Rational behaviour	Historical structures	Norms and culture	Ideas and discourse
Logic of explanation	Interest	Path-dependency	Appropriateness	Communication
Ability to explain change	Static: emphasis on continuity through fixed preferences	Static: emphasis on continuity through path dependency	Static: emphasis on continuity through cultural norms	Dynamic: emphasis on change and continuity through ideas and discursive interaction
Examples	Principle-agent theory; game theory	historical institutionalism process tracing varieties of capitalism	Constructivism; norms; cultural analysis	Ideas; discourse; constructivism; narratives; frames; advocacy coalitions; epistemic communities

Figure 5.1   *Scholars' use of the four new institutionalisms: rational choice (RI), historical (HI), sociological (SI) and discursive (DI)*

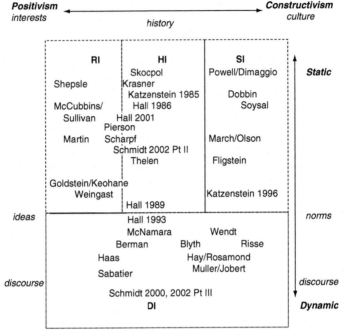

can rest upon the insights of any one of the three and because scholars often see themselves as continuing to fit in one or another of the traditions even as they fit best in discursive institutionalism. I have a darkened line under rational choice institutionalism to indicate its inability to handle ideas and discourse in a dynamic way

Among the questions that remain to be answered is one crucial one: can these four new institutionalisms fit together? Can empirical studies of any one issue mix approaches? Many of the most theory-driven of new institutionalists would answer in the negative, because their purpose is to demonstrate how their particular approach is the best way of explaining politics. More problem-oriented scholars mix approaches all the time, using whichever approaches seem the most appropriate to explaining their object of study. More recently, some scholars have also been addressing the question of how to use the insights of all four approaches in their empirical work. In policy analysis, to take just one example, David Marsh and Martin Smith (2000) have proposed a dialectical approach to understanding policy networks which uses methods from all four new institutionalisms to explaining the ways in which policy actors in given institutional contexts under certain constraints with particular learning experiences and ideas choose different courses of action over time. But while this may help answer the practical question of how to meld approaches in empirical investigation, it does not resolve the question of how they may fit together theoretically. Indeed, a look at the responses to Marsh and Smith demonstrates this well, as all come back to defend their own approaches (e.g., Dowding 2001; Raab 2001). For a theoretical answer to the question of how the various approaches fit together, new institutionalists need first to stop seeing their relations with rival approaches as methodological wars where the battles are fought over conceptual territory. They would do better to declare peace, and begin exploring areas of mutual compatibility along their borders. This would surely move all four new institutionalisms forward theoretically, while providing the greatest benefits for empirical research.

Further reading

Hall, Peter and Taylor, Rosemary (1996) 'Political Science and the Three New Institutionalisms', *Political Studies*, 952–73.

March, James G. and Olsen, Johan P. (1989) *Rediscovering Institutions: The Organizational Basis of Politics* (New York: Free Press).

Pierson, Paul (2004) *Politics in Time: History, Institutions, and Social Analysis* (Princeton, NJ: Princeton University Press).

Schmidt, Vivien A. (2002) *The Futures of European Capitalism* (Oxford: Oxford University Press).

Somit, Albert and Tanenhaus, Joseph (1982) *The Development of American Political Science from Burgess to Behavioralism* (New York: Irvington).

Thelen, Kathleen (1999) 'Historical Institutionalism in Comparative Politics', *The Annual Review of Political Science* (Palo Alto: Annual Reviews, Inc.).

Chapter 6

Feminism

JOHANNA KANTOLA

Introductory texts on feminism and politics frequently start by noting the difficult relationship between feminist approaches and political science (Phillips 1998; Randall 2002). The dilemmas that feminists face when studying the field are particularly clear regarding one of its key concepts: the state. Feminists have been ambivalent about the need to theorize the state. In the 1960s, the so-called second wave feminist movement searched for alternative channels of political influence mainly from the civil society. Later, the idea of a feminist state theory resulted in deep uneasiness among feminist scholars. Some claimed that such theory was non-existent and sorely needed (MacKinnon 1989), others that it was unnecessary (Allen 1990). Typically feminist engagements with the concept have ranged between the promise of significant gains in struggles for gender equality and fears of co-optation and compromise.

This has been the case particularly in the Anglo-American context, where feminist debates about the state were paralysed by an 'in' and 'out' dichotomy. In feminist state theories, liberal feminists represented the 'in' the state position. Here the aim was to reform the state from 'inside'. Critics of liberal feminism argued that they risked co-optation to the state's patriarchal structures. Radical feminists, in contrast, represented the 'out' of the state position. They steered away from the state, searched for alternative ways of working, and aimed to develop an extra-statist form of politics. This categorization reduced feminist strategies in dealing with the state into two: either integration (inside the state) or autonomy (outside the state). Since, many feminist scholars have directed their energies at deconstructing the dichotomy, which still continues to haunt feminist perspectives on the state.

This chapter will reach beyond the dominant Anglo-American strand in feminist state theory, epitomized by the 'in and out' dichotomy. The endeavour is underpinned by a desire to emphasize diversity within feminism and to focus on feminisms (Randall 2002). Feminist contributions to the debates about the state are diverse and at times approaches contradict one another. Despite such disagreements, however, feminism's main contribution has been to expose the gendered and patriarchal character of state institutions, practices and policies. In gendered processes, advantage and disadvantage, exploitation and control, meaning and identity, are patterned through a distinction between male and female, masculine and feminine (Acker 1992: 251–5). Feminists show that the state impacts on women in gender-specific ways and helps to construct gender relations, but at the same time, the activities of different women and women's movements impact on the state and are in turn impacted on by the state (Waylen 1998: 1).

The main goal of this chapter is to map out the diversity of feminist perspectives on the state. These include liberal, radical, Marxist and socialist, Nordic, and poststructural feminisms. These have theorised the state, respectively, as: (i) the neutral state, (ii) the patriarchal state, (iii) the capitalist state, (iv) the women-friendly welfare state, and (v) the poststructural state. The chapter begins by exploring the contributions of each of these perspectives. It then focuses on the criticisms directed at these ways of conceptualizing the state. Finally, the chapter considers current feminist debates about the state by analysing two opposing trends. On the one hand, some scholars question the utility of strategies of state reform for feminists and women's movement activists. On the other hand, feminists are increasingly engaging the state, both theoretically and in practice. The chapter argues that understanding the pitfalls and benefits of the two tendencies requires being explicit about the notion of the state underpinning our analyses.

Feminist contributions

The neutral state

Liberal feminists have conceptualized the state as a neutral arbiter between different interest groups in a way that comes close to pluralist state theories (see Chapter 1). They have recognized that state institutions have tended to be dominated by men, adopting policies reflecting masculine interests, but have argued that the state can be 'captured back' from the interests and influence of men. In this conception, the state is a reflection of the interest groups that control its institutions. To many liberal feminists, more women 'in' the state (as state personnel) would result in more women's policy, including initiatives and legislation to promote gender equality and to address women's concerns (Watson 1990; Waylen 1998). Liberal feminists stress the principle of formally equal treatment before the law. Differences between women and men ought to be non-pertinent in the public sphere – both should be, and can be, treated as equal citizens by the state.

Betty Friedan's *Feminine Mystique* (1962) illustrates some implications of the liberal feminist perspective. Friedan passionately critiqued women's position in 1960s America and argued that women must enter the public and governmental arena and fight for legislation. For her, the full participation of women in society was dependent on making the differences between the sexes irrelevant. She argued that emphasizing the differences between men and women worked against women's equality. For Friedan then, feminism signified first and foremost advancing and strengthening the formal rights of women.

Another liberal feminist, Susan Moller Okin, argued that the liberal models of justice had to be extended from the sphere of the benign state to the sphere of the family. Okin argued that the family was a major site of unequal relations and a source of unequal opportunities (1989: 170). She criticized the state's indirect role in the reproduction of inequalities in families. Notwithstanding the abstract commitment to the importance of a prohibition on state intervention in the private sphere, liberal states had in practice regulated and controlled the family (Squires 2004). For Okin, the solution to these problems lay with the liberal state: in its public policies and reforms of family law. She differed from mainstream liberals in accepting the extension of the state, as a means to achieve justice, to the family, which contradicted the liberal ideal of a minimal state.

Liberal feminist ideas have been influential in policy terms. The concepts of equality and universality – both the embodiment of liberal theories – remain central in public debates surrounding equal pay, quotas and citizenship in Western countries, and are powerful tools for demanding entry for women to the male dominated state institutions. In sum, liberal feminists have provided a series of important and influential ideas about justice that continue to be employed in feminist debates.

The patriarchal state

Radical, Marxist and socialist feminist analyses of the state presented a fundamental critique of the notion of state in general and of the liberal feminist notion of the neutral state in particular. These approaches reflected the rise of so-called second wave feminism in the 1960s. This challenged liberal feminism. The radical nature of second-wave feminism was symptomatic of the disillusionment with liberal feminist politics. The period was important in changing feminist understandings of the concepts of politics, state, patriarchy and gender.

Radical feminists defined the state in terms of its patriarchal nature. With Kate Millett, the concept of patriarchy acquired a new meaning (1970). Until her *Sexual Politics*, patriarchy had signified the rule of the father or the rule of the head of the household (Coole 1988: 71). Millett argued that what patriarchy actually was about was the rule of men – male supremacy. The concept of patriarchy captured the insight that the oppression of women was not haphazard or piecemeal but rather that the diverse forms of oppression women experienced were interconnected and mutually sustained. The radical nature of this feminist analysis stemmed from the claim that the state was not only contingently patriarchal, but was essentially so. Furthermore, patriarchy was global. The particular forms that states took were not particularly significant as all were patriarchal states (for discussions see Dahlerup 1987; Dale and Foster 1986; Elshtain 1981).

Whilst liberal feminists understood the state in terms of its political institutions, radical feminists extended their focus to the wider structures of the state and society. Their analyses revealed the patriarchal nature of the formal and informal practices followed in decision-making. The concept of patriarchy informed feminist strategies and political goals: the whole structure of male domination had to be dismantled if women's liberation was to be achieved (Acker 1989: 235). From the radical feminist point of view, the state, which was essentially patriarchal, its values and structures being established and dominated by men, could not help to solve the problems of patriarchy elsewhere. Therefore, there was no point in turning to the state. Civil society, rather than the state, was the sphere in which women should concentrate their energies in order to challenge patriarchy.

Catharine MacKinnon articulated a radical feminist stance on the state (1987, 1989). She argued:

> The state is male in the feminist sense: the law sees and treats women the way men see and treat women. The liberal state coercively and authoritatively constitutes the social order in the interest of men as a gender – through its legitimating norms, forms, relations to society, and substantive policies. (1989: 161–2)

Feminists could not expect the state to liberate women because it was impossible to separate state power from male power. MacKinnon directed her critique at the liberal state in particular and criticised its laws and policies. On the one hand, it had been men who made the laws from a masculine perspective and, on many occasions, these laws worked for men. On the other hand, even if laws on rape, abortion and pornography were formally present, they were never fully and effectively enforced (MacKinnon 1989).

Radical feminism employed the concepts of gender and sexuality. MacKinnon asserted: 'Sexuality is to feminism what work is to marxism: that which is most one's own, yet most taken away' (quoted in Smart 1989: 76). States enforced the equation of women with sexuality. However, via consciousness-raising it became possible to rediscover what it was to be truly female, restoring women's ability to speak politically with their own voice. Whereas liberal feminists understood differences between the sexes as non-pertinent, radical feminists celebrated and valued them. At best, this created new visions, for example, about alternative, anti-hierarchical ways of working (Ferguson 1984: 5).

In sum, the radical feminist contribution was to offer important tools for feminist theories of the state by stressing the patriarchal nature of the state. Their critical analyses helped to reveal the role of the state in perpetuating gender inequalities. Radical feminist theorising helpfully stressed women's different concerns and provided new, alternative visions for tackling them.

The capitalist state

The strong influence of Marxism on feminism in the 1970s was also reflected in feminist analyses of the state. Whereas, for radical feminists, the state was a patriarchal state, for Marxist feminists, the state was a capitalist state (McIntosh 1978: 259). The state was not just an institution but a form of social relations (Watson 1990: 4). Women's subordination played a role in sustaining capitalism through the reproduction of the labour force within the family. The influence of Marxist categories can be seen in the debates about the concepts of work and reproduction, the so-called 'domestic labour debate' (Barrett 1980; Delphy and Leonard 1992; Kuhn and Wolpe 1978; Molyneux 1979). Women were oppressed both in work and in being excluded from it and Marxist feminists argued that familial ideology was to blame. When criticizing welfare states, Marxist feminists argued that the state helped to reproduce and maintain the familial ideology primarily through welfare state policies. In contrast to radical feminism, Marxist feminists argued that women were important in the struggle against capitalism as workers, not as women (McIntosh 1978) and the category of women was employed in reproductional terms – women were the mothers who reproduced labour force (Sargent 1981: xxi).

Socialist feminists attempted to combine the insights of both Marxist and radical feminism. From radical feminists, socialist feminists derived the understanding of the system of oppression called patriarchy, and from Marxist feminists the importance of the class oppression defining the situation for all workers (Sargent 1981: xxi). The two approaches were combined in analyses of this 'dual system' of capitalism and patriarchy. For Zillah Eisenstein, the concept of capitalist patriarchy captured the 'mutually reinforcing dialectical relationship between capitalist class structure and hierarchal sexual structuring' (Eisenstein 1979: 17). Michèle Barrett, in turn, identified a number of ways in which the state promoted women's oppression: women were excluded from certain sorts of work by protective legislation, the state exercised control over the ways sexuality was represented through pornography laws, and the state's housing policy was resistant to the needs of non-nuclear families (Barrett 1980: 231–7).

The debates revolved around questions about the relative autonomy of the two systems. Some theorists argued that patriarchy was more autonomous than capitalism (Harding 1981; Hartmann 1981) and others that capitalism had the upper hand (Young 1981). For Eisenstein, the capitalist class did not rule the state or government directly but instead exercised hegemony. A large part of the mystificatory role of the state was in this seeming identification of male interests and bourgeois interests (Eisenstein 1984).

The Marxist and socialist feminist contribution was to conceptualize the state as a social relation and to stress the importance of understanding capitalist relations when theorizing the state. It focused upon women's unpaid labour in the family and added new dimensions to liberal and radical feminist perspectives on the state. The socialist feminists' emphasis on economic justice is increasingly important for some feminists (see Jaquette 2003).

The women-friendly welfare state

Towards the end of the 1980s, liberal, radical, Marxist and socialist feminist perspectives on the state were challenged from locations outside of the Anglo-American core. Nordic feminists, femocrats in Australia, and gender and development scholars highlighted differences between states. These scholars were united in arguing that there was a need to move beyond narrow Anglo-American understandings of the state outlined above.

The term 'femocrat' was coined in Australia to analyse feminists working within state bureaucracies to achieve positive social change (see H. Eisenstein 1991, 1996; Sawer 1990, 1991; Watson 1992). Development scholars, in turn, exposed the fundamentally different meaning of the state in non-Western countries (see Afshar 1996; Alvarez 1990; Dore and Molyneux 2000; Rai and Lievesley 1996; Visvanathan *et al.* 1997). Like Western debates, this literature was concerned to examine the processes and functions of state institutions in the exercise of power in various areas of the public and private lives of women and women's resistance to these intrusions (Rai and Lievesley 1996: 1). However, there were important differences. The focus on post-colonialism, nationalism, economic modernization and state capacity emerged as key themes in the Third World literature, whereas Western feminists often took these issues for granted, focusing instead on how best to engage with the state (Chappell 2000: 246).

Nordic feminist analyses of the state were markedly different to radical and Marxist feminist perspectives, which had less resonance in the Nordic context of social democratic welfare states than, for example, in the British top-down, elitist democracy dominated by a hierarchical class structure (Raaum 1995: 25). Nordic feminist experience was not one of pervasive

patriarchy (Borchorst and Siim 1987; Hernes 1987), and the analyses highlighted that different states meant different things for women. Unlike radical
and Marxist feminist theories, Nordic feminist understandings of the state
provided scope to work within existing state structures.

Helga Maria Hernes defined Nordic states as potentially women-friendly
societies (1987). A woman-friendly welfare state signified that women's
political and social empowerment happened through the state and with the
support of state social policy (Anttonen 1994). The social democratic
citizenship tradition resulted in more optimistic acceptance of the state as
an instrument for social change. Hernes argued:

> In no other part of the world has the state been used so consistently by
> all groups, including women and their organizations, to solve collectively
> felt problems. (1988: 208)

For Hernes, Nordic women acted in accordance with their own culture in
turning to the state, even in those instances where they wished to build
alternative institutions (1988: 210).

Studies of the Nordic women-friendly welfare states were concerned with
the roles of women as political actors. In Nordic feminism, it was argued that
women become empowered as political subjects through the institutionali-
sation of gender equality (Borchorst and Siim 2002: 91). An exclusive focus
on patriarchy, in contrast, risked reducing women to victims of patriarchal
structures, which meant that their contribution to maintain or change
gender relations became invisible (Siim 1988).

Nevertheless, Nordic feminism was more pessimistic and less simplistic
in its analysis of gender and the state than liberal feminism. The private
dependency of women on individual men was transformed to public dependency on the state in the women-friendly welfare states (Dahlerup 1987).
The expansion of the public sector, even if it benefited women, was planned
and executed by a male-dominated establishment. The parameters for distribution and redistribution policies were increasingly determined within the
framework of the corporate system, where women had an even more marginal
role to play than in the parliamentary system. Thus, women were the objects of
policies (Hernes 1988a: 83). This tendency was exacerbated by the
observation that women's lives were more dependent and determined by
state policies than men's (Hernes 1988a: 77).

This approach contributed to feminist debates on the state by demonstrating that context mattered in feminist state theory and that knowledge
was situated. It recognized the historical and spatial varieties of states and
avoided making *a priori* claims about gendered states. One of its analytical
contributions was to challenge universal theories and conclusions about
women's relation to the welfare state based upon Anglo-American theory
and research (Borchorst and Siim 2002: 91; see also Lister 1997: 174).

A further contribution was to sensitize analysts to the importance of women's agency when theorizing gender and the state (Bergqvist *et al.* 1999; Siim 2000). Recognition of the structural constraints on women's interaction with the state did not blind the analyses of the possibilities of women's action.

The poststructural state

Postructuralism has had a twofold impact on feminist theorizing of the state. Firstly, poststructuralism's deconstruction of the state resulted in the rejection of the very category of the state. Judith Allen argued:

> Feminism has not been guilty of oversight or failure in not developing a distinct theory of 'the state'. Instead feminist theorists' choices of theoretical agendas with priorities other than 'the state' have a sound rationale that deserves to be taken seriously. The 'state' is a category of abstraction that is too aggregate, too unitary and too unspecific to be of much use in addressing the disaggregated, diverse and specific sites that must be of most pressing concern to feminists. (Allen 1990: 22)

She argued for other priorities in political analysis in contrast to lavishing further attention on the problematic concept of the state.

Secondly, for those who did not dismiss it altogether, poststructuralism resulted in a more nuanced theorizing of the state. Poststructural feminist approaches highlighted differences amongst and within states. They challenged the unity of the state in previous feminist theorizing and argued that the state consisted of a set of arenas that lacked coherence (Pringle and Watson 1990: 229). In other words, the state was a differentiated set of institutions, agencies and discourses and had to be studied as such (Waylen 1998: 7). The approaches shifted the emphasis to state practices and discourses rather than to state institutions. The state was depicted as a discursive process, and politics and the state were conceptualized in broad terms (Waylen 1998: 6).

The state was not inherently patriarchal but was historically constructed as patriarchal in a political process whose outcome was open (Connell 1987: 129). The patriarchal state could be seen, then, not as the manifestation of patriarchal essence, but as the centre of a reverberating set of power relations and political processes in which patriarchy was both constructed and contested (Connell 1987: 129–30). Particular discourses and histories constructed state boundaries, identities and agency (Cooper 1995: 61; Pringle and Watson 1992: 54).

Feminists working with poststructural feminist methodologies focus on the micro-practices of states (Cooper 1998; Gwinnett 1998). For example,

Davina Cooper examines hunting, the arts, religious orthodoxy, sexuality, public space and secondary education to grasp the nature of governance in a liberal state (1998). Her analysis is motivated by a series of specific questions: Is the state going too far? Should it be rolled back? Where does the boundary between public and private lie? (Cooper 1998: 4) Others highlight the ways in which different policy fields present a different picture of the state. A collection edited by Linda Briskin and Mona Eliasson studies trade unions, immigration, violence against women, and sexuality to challenge stereotypical images of Canada and Sweden (Briskin and Eliasson 1999).

Poststructural approaches have contributed significantly to feminist debates about the state by highlighting the differentiated nature of the state and by questioning the unity of state responses. An important question for poststructural feminists was what the most effective strategies were for empowering women in their engagements with the state (Randall 1998: 200). In other words, the feminist aim became to make sense not only of the state's impact on gender, but also of the ways in which the state could be made use of and changed through feminist struggles. In this way, poststructural feminists destabilized the dichotomy between 'in' and 'out' of the state, arguing that the dichotomy failed to capture the multifaceted nature of the state. Their analyses allowed the complex, multidimensional and differentiated relations between the state and gender to be acknowledged. They recognized that the state could be a positive as well as a negative resource for feminists and sensitised feminists to gender diversity, the fluidity and the constructed nature of the category of women.

Criticisms of feminist perspectives on the state

Evidently feminists have approached the concept of the state from a number of different perspectives and have generated important insights into gendered states. Nevertheless, feminist perspectives on the state are problematic for a number of different reasons. The critiques discussed in this section stem mainly from within feminist debates themselves. As the mainstream state theory literature still fails to engage extensively with feminist approaches, feminist debates have been conducted primarily among feminists with little input from mainstream scholars.

Like pluralists, liberal feminists sometimes failed to distinguish between the normative, prescriptive and descriptive elements of their state theories (see Chapter 1). Problematically, it was at times unclear whether liberal feminists were analysing the abstract idea of the state or actual states. Furthermore, the liberal feminist notion of the state was very narrow and understood the state mainly in terms of institutions. Such a narrow conception of the state and politics was rejected by other feminists. Critics argued that liberal feminists, such as Friedan, failed to understand the structural relations in which women's lives were situated – the family, the sexual division of labour, sex-class oppression – as part of the political life of society (Eisenstein 1986: 181). As liberal feminism did not challenge the deep structures of male dominance, it could be argued to create space for a new form of patriarchy, one which was subtler, and potentially more stable and powerful than earlier forms (Pringle and Watson 1990: 231). Legislation provided formal equality but, at the same time, diverted attention away from powerful economic, social and psychological bases for inequality. Zillah Eisenstein argued:

> The major purpose of patriarchy, besides actualizing its system of power, is mystifying the basis of this power so that it cannot be recognized by the oppressed. (1986: 223)

Similarly, for Kathy Ferguson, liberal feminism had become a voice subservient to dominant patriarchal discourses (1984: 193). An exclusive focus on integrating women into state institutions produced a situation that perpetuated dominant patriarchal discourses and norms rather than challenging them. Important questions were not asked, critical arguments were not formulated, and alternatives were not envisioned (Ferguson 1984: 29).

Radical feminists, in contrast, tended to essentialize the state as patriarchal. For example, Wendy Brown saw MacKinnon's approach as flawed because she naturalized male dominance (1995: 178). Also, problematically, radical feminists sought to specify a single cause of women's oppression, namely the exploitative structure of patriarchy (Barrett and Phillips 1992: 3). In the model, the state became a key source of patriarchal power and power became men's power, authority or dominance over women (Dahlerup 1987: 94). For critics, neither the state nor masculinity had a single source or terrain of power (Brown 1995: 179). Carol Smart argued:

> Part of the power that law can exercise resides in the authority we accord to it. By stressing how powerless feminism is in the face of law and legal method, we simply add to its power. (1989: 25)

According to this line of argument, the radical feminist understanding of the state risked adding to the unequal power relations by not engaging the patriarchal state.

Radical feminism was insensitive to differences between women and risked claiming that states oppressed women everywhere in the same way (Acker 1989: 235). For example, MacKinnon posited the objects of pornographic representation so unambiguously in the position of victim that she denied the agency of the oppressed. Thus, she failed to recognize that lesbian and gay pornography did not simply replicate structures of victimization, but, in fact, had emancipatory implications for those whose sexuality was otherwise denied public expression (McNay 1999: 180).

The universalising tendencies were also strongly rejected by black feminists who pointed out that their solidarity was often with black men rather than white women. The black feminist criticism was directed both at radical and liberal feminists who failed to understand the different meanings that concepts such as work and family have for black women. Work never symbolized 'freedom' for black women but was a necessity, and the sphere of family was not a site of oppression as white feminists assumed (Amos and Pamar 1984; Barrett and McIntosh 1985; Palmer 1983). Also, American black women did not perceive themselves as the weak, idle, dependent gentlewoman as depicted in Western feminist theory (Coole 1988: 250). Moreover, such theory largely ignored the experience of Third World women under the post-colonial state. The assumptions made were West-centred but the theorizing took on a universalizing language (Rai 1996: 5).

Marxist and socialist feminist perspectives on the capitalist state were also critiqued. Sophie Watson argued that despite the Marxist and socialist feminist emphasis on the state as a form of social relation, the state still appeared to be an 'entity which limits and determines our lives, which acts in the interests of capital, which defines who we are and what we need, which deflects class conflict and which obscures class divisions' (Watson 1990: 4). More specifically, Marxist feminist accounts employed reductionist and functionalist arguments to explain the persistence of sexual divisions and the patriarchal family form, which ended up subsuming gender relations within the all-powerful system of something called the 'needs of capital' (Watson 1990: 6).

In other words, Marxist feminists were criticized for privileging Marxist categories of analysis at the expense of feminist ones. Heidi Hartmann argued:

> The 'marriage' of marxism and feminism has been like the marriage of husband and wife depicted in English common law: marxism and feminism are one, and that one is marxism. Recent attempts to integrate marxism and feminism are unsatisfactory to us as feminists because they subsume the feminist struggle into the larger' struggle against capital. To continue our simile further, either we need a healthier marriage or we need a divorce. (Hartmann 1981: 2)

Privileging Marxist categories meant that Marxist feminists continued to suffer from the problems faced by Marxists: structuralism, determinism and an over-emphasis on economics (see Chapter 3). Socialist feminists did provide more nuanced analyses of the two systems. However, at times the capitalist and patriarchal structures of the society remained so dominant that there was hardly any room for positive social change.

Critics have argued that Nordic feminist theory of the women-friendly welfare state is more a 'consensual political strategy' than an analytically coherent starting point for feminists to theorize the state (Kreisky 1995: 215). It could be argued that the Nordic feminist focus on actors and empowerment underestimated continuous patterns of gender hierarchies and segregation both in the state and in the society (Borchorst and Siim 2002: 92). Problematically, the values of the women-friendly welfare state were promoted normatively outside the Nordic context, for example in other European countries (Borchorst and Siim 2002a; Towns 2002).

Because the term women-friendly welfare state was premised on the idea of common and collective interests of women (Borchorst and Siim 2002: 91), the category of women was very homogenous. Hernes noted herself that the egalitarian values had their limitations when it came to introducing pluralism of any form (Hernes 1987: 17). The concerns of, for example, lesbians and ethnic minorities have yet to enter the agenda of Nordic feminism and there has been little analysis of the impact of the welfare state on ethnic minorities or, conversely, of the impact of the ethnic minorities on the welfare state (Christensen and Siim 2001). Gender equality signified, first and foremost, equality for the white heterosexual working mother in the Nordic context (Lindvert 2002). Diversity and fluidity within the category of women and women's identity were missing from Nordic feminist analyses of women-friendly welfare states.

Like liberal feminists, Nordic feminists tended to opt for the sameness route to equality, which signified the idea of gender equality as a condition where men's and women's lives were uniform (Lindvert 2002: 100). The normative foundation of the women-friendly welfare state rested on a dual-breadwinner model where both women and men were wage-workers. In other words, the feminist discourse about women-friendliness was based upon the premise that women's labour market participation was a key to gender equality (Borchorst and Siim 2002: 92). Measures associated with civil rights, rather than social rights, and their importance were neglected in the women-friendly welfare state literature (Lindvert 2002: 101). Julia O'Connor, Ann Shola Orloff and Sheila Shaver argued that liberal countries – the United States, Canada, Australia and Britain – offered a somewhat different set of gender-equality measures from those offered in the social democratic states (1999). These included reproductive or body rights, anti-discriminatory regulations and workplace policies. The measures were associated with civil rights rather than with social rights.

Nancy Fraser, in turn, argued that neither a politics of redistribution – remedying social inequalities – nor a politics of recognition – revaluing disrespected identities – were sufficient on their own (1995, 1997). Nordic feminists problematically showed partiality towards the politics of redistribution and, as a consequence, gender equality became separated from cultural politics (Siim 2000: 126, Borchorst and Siim 2002: 95–6). Such fundamental civil right issues as the right to bodily integrity (violated by violence against women) were notoriously slow to arrive on the Nordic agenda, partly as a result of the minor role played by the gender difference approach to gender theory.

Poststructural feminist understandings of the state were criticized for focusing on discursive processes. This shifted attention away from institutions and policies. Foucauldians, in particular, concentrated on relations and techniques of governance, treating institutions as an effect of processes and practices rather than as their origin (Cooper 1998: 10). Due to their lack of focus on institutions and institutional mechanisms, the approaches underestimated the difficulty of achieving change compared with the relative ease of reproducing status quo power relations (Cooper 1994: 7). A further implication of the oversight of state institutions was the neglect of the linkages between state bodies, for example that the influence that the central government exerted over the local government (Cooper 1994: 7; O'Connor, Orloff and Shaver 1999: 11). Poststructural feminism could also be argued to lack specificity. The state was treated as a terrain of struggle without much thought being given to how the state differed from other such terrains (Cooper 1994: 7).

The most persistent counter-argument was directed against poststructuralism's deconstruction of women's subjectivity and identity. It was argued that as soon as women gained strength and power to fight oppression from the subject position of women, postmodern theorists came along and deconstructed the notion of the subject (Walby 1992: 48). Foucault's attack on subjectivity was argued to be so total that it foreclosed any alternative theoretical space in which to conceive non-hegemonic forms of subjectivity (McNay 1992: 12). The notions of 'women' and 'men' were dissolved into shifting, variable social constructs that lacked coherence and stability over time (Walby 1992: 34). This was claimed to prevent women's struggle against oppression. Seyla Benhabib (1995: 29) argued:

> Postmodernism undermines the feminist commitment to women's agency and sense of selfhood, to the reappropriation of women's own history in the name of an emancipated future, and to the exercise of radical social criticism which uncover gender 'in all its endless variety and monotonous similarity'.

Just as women seemed to be gaining a voice in the Western world, postmodernism deconstructed the basis for their action, their common identity.

In addition to the specific criticisms discussed above, all of the approaches fail to engage with debates on globalization, multi-level governance, and institutional change. Thus, it is debatable to what extent the approaches offer tools for studying recent institutional changes such as devolution or the European Union (EU). These were not key issues for liberal or radical feminists who focused upon the neutral and patriarchal states respectively. One can ask whether these new institutions are neutral and patriarchal in similar ways as the states. Do the strategies promoted by these feminist theories, for example integration or autonomy, apply to the new levels of governance as well? Arguably, the approaches do not capture the ways in which discourses, actors and institutions have influence across the levels of governance and state boarders.

Current feminist debates

Most recent feminist debates about gender and the state attempt to address the issue of complex institutional changes taking place at the sub-national, national and international levels, and to evaluate its meaning for feminist debates about the state. In this context, two tendencies that currently inform feminist political and social inquiries can be discerned. On the one hand, an increasing number of scholars argue that the powers of the state have been transformed, and, more specifically, that they have declined. On the other hand, sceptics argue that the state remains important, and that feminists are increasingly engaging with the state. Neither of these approaches pays detailed attention to analytical questions about the state.

The first position surfaces frequently in feminist literatures on globalisation (Jacobs 2000; Kelly *et al.* 2001; Pettman 1996, 1999), multi-level governance (Banaszak, Beckwith and Rucht 2003; Prügl and Meyer 1999), and transnational networks (Keck and Sikkink 1998). It also gains support from the analyses of changing world politics. Transnational prostitution, migration, global policing, international human rights and globalized service economy all take place across, beyond and regardless of state borders. Feminists have been critical about globalization and related trends, and have pointed to their gender-specific consequences. Women in their domestic or reproductive roles have had to compensate for state retreat and for state failure to provide social infrastructure and support (Pettman 1999: 212). In relation to gender and the state – feminist discourses about the state, feminist activism, feminist movements – such conclusions give rise to a concern that women's organizing needs to shift direction away from both its focus and its reliance on the state (Briskin 1999: 29).

Some feminists have confronted this dilemma and argued that the state has reshaped, relocated, and rearticulated its formal powers and policy responsibilities throughout the 1980s and 1990s, and women's movements face a reconfigured state that offers them opportunities for advancing feminist agendas but also threatens feminist successes (Banaszak, Beckwith and Rucht 2003: 3). These scholars suggest that state authority has been *uploaded* to supranational organizations and *downloaded* to substate, provincial or regional governments. A weakening of the power of elected state spheres and a growing reliance on other and partly nonelected state bodies represent *lateral loading* (Banaszak, Beckwith and Rucht 2003: 4–5). As governments have increasingly engaged in lateral loading, women's movements have been presented with a depoliticized and remoter set of state policy-making agencies at the national level (Banaszak, Beckwith and Rucht 2003: 6). Whilst this focus on the transformation of the state is a concern for a number of feminists, there is another significant development in relation to gender and the state. This is the rise in feminist engagements with the state, both scholarly and activist. A number of feminist scholars argue that the state has not lost its centrality in institutionally fixing and resourcing particular discursive categories (O'Connor, Orloff and Shaver 1999: 11). Instead, the state has played an integral role in the restructuring of state social provision throughout the 1990s and the changes cannot be captured without studying the (welfare) state.

Furthermore, recent years have witnessed an increase in state feminism – activities of government structures that are formally charged with furthering women's status and rights – and in the interest of studying this (Mazur 2001; Outshoorn 2004; Stetson 2001; Stetson and Mazur 1995). Here the interest is in the ways in which women's movements have challenged states to deal with women's status and have made states to incorporate women as political actors. Key research questions include how the states respond to feminist demands and what roles state institutions play in advancing the goals of women's movements. (Outshoorn 2004: 1). The state remains a key concept in these debates although some attention is paid to international changes.

Another recent development in feminist political analyses is an interest in gender mainstreaming. Mainstreaming a gender perspective signifies assessing the implications for women and men of any planned action, including legislation, policies or programmes, in all areas and at all levels (Rai 2003, Rees 1998). Gender mainstreaming often gains its impetus from the international levels, such as the EU or the UN, but takes the state and its structures as the location where mainstreaming is implemented. It is thus directed at the state and aims to influence state policies or processes. Furthermore, there has been a diffusion of gender quotas worldwide and nearly all countries in the world have pledged to promote gender-balanced decision-making (Dahlerup 2002; Krook 2004). Campaigns for gender quotas are influenced by international actors and flows of ideas in complex ways (Krook 2004), but also these take the state level as the target of campaigning.

Summing up this trend, Gillian Youngs argues that the state needs to be reclaimed as a political space in feminist theories and practice (2000). Socially and spatially constructed boundaries within and across states, affecting race, class and gender, are depoliticized, if they are not identified as aspects of the dynamics of power relations and struggle (Youngs 2000: 47). Therefore, there is a need to think of the state as a political space within which power struggles continue to take place (Youngs 2000: 46).

The two trends in feminist debates about the state – state transformation and feminists turning to the state – may seem antithetical. However, they share some important features. Scholars focusing upon state transformation (Beckwith, Beckwith and Rucht 2003), state feminism (Mazur 2001; Stetson 2001) and welfare state regimes (O'Connor, Orloff and Shaver 1999) attempt to capture the recent developments through large-scale systematic comparisons of Western states. They seek to be sensitive to national differences and reference the poststructural feminist work on the state as having influenced their approaches. Nonetheless, their emphasis is on generalizations – attempts to define, if not all states, at least the state and feminism in the 'West' or the 'North'. Thus, for example, O'Connor, Orloff and Shaver define their aim as 'to move from institutional frameworks alone towards a larger-scale analysis of the state' (1999: 12). Joyce Outshoorn, in turn, discusses the tenets of 'a theory of state feminism'; the conditions for successful state feminism (2004: 290–1). She recognizes that this project results in a 'loss of detail' and 'runs the risk of eliminating important cultural aspects of the politics in a country' (Outshoorn 2004: 290–1).

One consequence is a paradoxical situation in which these approaches are actually in tension with poststructural feminism despite their acknowledgement of the significance of the poststructural arguments about the differentiated state. The first part of this chapter showed that both Nordic and poststructural feminists have usefully questioned the possibility of universally establishing what the state is. In light of this, I suggest that rather than establishing what the state is, there is a need to search for critical tools to analyse the state. Here one could consider the contributions of the earlier feminist theories of the state in conjunction with the most recent debate about the relevance of the transformed state for feminists.

Nordic and poststructural feminists have established the need to focus both on differences between states and differences within states. Whilst Nordic feminists stressed the need to do comparative research, poststructural feminists highlighted the need to study discursive constructions of the state that differ within and between states. Combining discursive and comparative methods highlights the need to focus on context-specific discourses, institutions and agency rather than abstract theorizing. Contextualizing analyses of the state in this way, challenges the hegemony of the Anglo-American language on states including feminist notions and research (Siim 2000: 9).

In some ways the current debate is informed by the 'in' and 'out' of the state dichotomy, defined in the introduction to this chapter, and therefore one could question the helpfulness of the debate. Nevertheless, the debate is important because it shows that the state cannot be studied in isolation from the diverse institutional changes that are currently taking place and resulting in different multi-level governance frameworks. The consequence for feminist theories about the state is that feminists cannot conceptualize the state in isolation of new institutions and levels of governance. The most recent debates sensitize scholars to the mobility of discourses and institutions between different levels of governance, for example from the EU to the member-states, and the problems related to this.

Conclusion

Both the existence and the need for a feminist theory of the state have been challenged in feminist debates. This chapter has been based on an understanding that we do need critical feminist tools to analyse the state. Initially, much feminist energy was directed into answering questions about the essence of the state: what is the state? Answers ranged from the liberal, patriarchal or capitalist state to the women-friendly or poststructural state. The discussion in the previous section suggested that the question to ask is not one about the essence of the state but how best to analyse the state. The most recent feminist debates on the state, discussed above, clearly show the need for these tools. This chapter has provided one possible way forward and argued for combining the comparative and discursive elements of the previous feminist theories about the state. Feminist comparative discourse analysis sensitizes feminist analyses to the importance of the context. The methodological framework results in an understanding of the impossibility of establishing universally what the state is. It also makes it possible to analyse differences within states: in and between institutions, discourses and actors and to situate states in the changing institutional context.

Further reading

Banaszak, Lee Ann, Beckwith, Karen and Rucht, Dieter (eds) (2003) *Women's Movements Facing the Reconfigured State* (Cambridge: Cambridge University Press).

Bergqvist, Christina *et al.* (eds) (1999) *Equal Democracies: Gender and Politics in the Nordic Countries* (Oslo: Scandinavian University Press).

MacKinnon, Catharine (1989) *Towards a Feminist Theory of the State* (Cambridge, MA: Harvard University Press).

O'Connor, Julia, Orloff, Ann Shola and Shaver, Sheila (1999) *States, Markets, Families: Gender, Liberalism and Social Policy in Australia, Canada, Great Britain and the United States* (Cambridge: Cambridge University Press).

Rai, Shirin and Lievesley, Geraldine (eds) (1996) *Women and the State: International Perspectives* (London: Taylor & Francis).

Randall, Vicky and Waylen, Georgina (eds) (1998) *Gender, Politics and the State* (London: Routledge).

Watson, Sophie (ed.) (1990) *Playing the State* (London: Verso).

Chapter 7

Green Theory

MATTHEW PATERSON, PETER DORAN AND JOHN BARRY

For students of politics, the state has always assumed central importance. However, for many in the Green movements, and the Green theorists articulating their concerns in a more abstract or systematic manner, the importance of the state has often been understated.

In part this is because of the 'personal is political' element in Green politics – with a more all embracing conception of politics than held by many more conventional theories or by many involved in the academic study of politics. Thus one often finds in Green politics an extremely broad understanding of the scope of 'green' politics that encompasses essentially everything one does, from one's choices about consumption, transport, wastes, fertility, and so on. Often these are presented in such broad terms that they can be viewed as 'pre-political', or as simply too big, urgent and important for 'politics' and political activism. This is either presented in the sense that Green politics is about issues of ecological survival which make 'politics' irrelevant, or that the real 'cause' of the 'ecological crisis' is 'beyond politics' and has to do with 'deeper' dynamics of the ecologically destructive consciousness and ignorance of humanity and/or the spiritual malaise of modernity (as in 'deep ecology', e.g. Devall 1988: 160; Naess 1995: 261). Greens thus vacillate between a 'common sense' account of politics as the dirty machinations for state power and thus to be avoided, and one which is an all-encompassing facet of life. Either way, the state doesn't get much serious attention.

In part this neglect is also because of the 'neither left nor right' element in Green movements, which is 'anti-political' and eschews serious discussion of central elements of politics in favour of ideological exhortations concerning the 'common interests of humanity' – humans should be seen not so much as citizens, workers, etc., but as 'plain members' of the 'land community' (Leopold 1949). Greens are thus for the most part instinctive global thinkers, and 'think globally, act locally' has become one of their best-known catchphrases. But this naïve exhortation concerning common global interests has been progressively harder to sustain. In green theory there has thus been a loss of innocence marked by a stepping back from an anarchist rejection of the state. As Grove-White argues (1993), modern environmentalism needs to be seen as having evolved not only as a response to the damaging

135

impacts of specific industrial and social practices, but also, more fundamentally, as a social expression of cultural tensions surrounding the underlying ontologies and epistemologies which have led to such trajectories in modern societies. As a consequence, exploring the role of the state has become more and more important, given the co-evolution of the state system, modernity and geopolitics in securing the practices associated with unsustainable development.

So there has been an undercurrent of attitudes to the state amongst Greens, and occasional articulations by Green theorists, which permit an elaboration of a green theory, or perhaps more precisely a range of green theories of the state. The debate amongst (some) Greens has moreover become more clearly articulated in the last decade, and it is possible to discern a shift in orientation to and mode of analysis of the state by Greens. This chapter attempts to delineate the terrain of this debate. The first part details the sorts of critiques of the state that Greens have engaged in. We then interrogate the claim that this amounts to green theory being an anarchist theory of the state. The third part looks at recent attempts in green theory to go beyond the 'for/against' way of approaching the state and to look at the way the state is being reconstructed, and could be further reconstructed, in response to ecological concerns.

Green critiques of the state

Despite the general neglect of the state in much green theory and practice, yet it is possible to discern therein a number of accounts of the state. They are all more or less united in their highly critical stance, but the nature of this critical account varies widely. When surveying the green literature since the 1960s, broadly four distinct elements in critiques of the state can be discerned. These are:

1. the spatial disjuncture between the territorially-organized state and the spatial characteristics of ecological problems;
2. the predominant mode of rationality in states which is bureaucratic;
3. the nature of the state as a centralizing institution of domination and violence, and which promotes accelerated throughput of resources as a consequence;
4. the way in which the liberal democratic state underwrites a very 'thin' and disempowering version of democratic citizenship and democratic governance.

These critiques entail a proposition that the environmental crises are, in effect, provocations to look anew at the purposes of the state and the state system.

The state and environment: spatial dysfunctions

One of the earliest themes in Green writings concerning the state concerned questions of scale. Two rather distinct orientations can be distinguished here. The earliest contained in the invocation 'small is beautiful' popularized by Fritz Schumacher (1976) and suggests that the central problem is that modern societies have grown too big in scale for their socio-ecological well-being. Much of this was a reaction (of a socially conservative or progressive sort) to 'impersonal bureaucracies', the spatial demands of modern life (commuting, work travel, etc.), and an aesthetic reaction to 'big' architecture, cities, governance systems. But the distinctly ecological dimension is best articulated by Dryzek (1987) and Saurin (1994). The eco-logic is that the larger the scale of human activities, the more remote are those making decisions concerning resource use and the production of pollution from the consequences of those decisions. For Dryzek, the socio-ecological feedback loops need to be short to make for ecologically rational decisions; for Saurin, the distancing involved in modernity/globalization effects a displacement of ecological effects across large scales. In general, in this image, ecological questions are held to be irreducibly local, to do with specific places, ecosystems, and their management. Moreover, Bauman (1989: 25), demonstrates how features of modernization, including distanciation, interrupt our ability to think and behave ethically in the context of globally mediated environmental impacts such as those produced by consumption patterns. For Bauman globalism is synonymous with an ethic of instrumentalism, and the intrinsic asymmetry of global relations between the powerful and the powerless and how for example, the minority world in the West/North is 'always already' harming the majority world in the South.

These processes were, and still are, set in train by a fundamentally political process of reshaping property relations, which is usually called 'enclosure' (*The Ecologist* 1993; Latouche 1993). Enclosure entails a transformation from the management of particular places through varied communal practices towards the modern regime of private property rights. Enclosure ushers in a new political order which disembeds economic activities from their social constraints and reconstructs them in terms of private property rights, monetary exchange systems, legally binding contracts, and of course the state apparatus to enforce them. The 'resources' which were previously resolutely local and particular become through this process abstract and thus available for the global market, with all the distanciating processes noted above. At the same time, 'nature' is linguistically reconstructed as *resources* for *resource management*. (Note the quote marks around the term nature, which indicate its highly contested and problematic place in political discourse, of course particularly problematic for Greens. See Latour 2004 for a useful argument concerning the term.)

Thus, the state has set in train these ecologically problematic processes, and is thus at the centre of these questions concerning scale. The state is the site around which centralized decisions coalesce, and where forms of representation concerning the impacts of ecological degradation are articulated. But when representatives are both themselves physically removed from the sites they represent, and represent a large and diverse population with highly diverging interests (especially regarding particular ecological questions, say a resource extracting activity), then the possibility of responding adequately to the articulation of ecological concerns and interests is remote.

But there is a second spatial metaphor prevalent in Green thinking. This is that 'the Earth is one but the world is not' (WCED 1987: 27). In this discourse, the central contradiction is between the (putatively) global character of ecological questions and the spatial separation of political institutions into territorially organized states. Most starkly put, the logic is for world government (Ophuls 1977); since states are irredeemably oriented around protecting the interests of those within their own territory, they will never be able to pursue environmental co-operation to the extent necessary to avoid ecological collapse. But many more modest arguments for 'transfers of authority' exist, advocating the development of supranational institutions 'with teeth' able to impose solutions to global ecological problems on states. These can be seen in other 'ecoauthoritarian' arguments in the 1970s (Heilbroner 1974), in the arguments of the WCED (1987), in current debates about a 'World Environment Organization' (Low and Gleeson 1998; Newell 2001; Biermann 2000), and the environmental elements to debates about UN reform, most recently in UNEP's attempt to promote new powers for its Governing Council/Global Ministerial Environment Forum in the run up to the World Summit on Sustainable Development in Johannesburg (2002), to debates about multi-level environmental governance (Vogler 2003), of which Eckersley's arguments for a 'multi-tiered' political system is best known within green theory (Eckersley 1992: 144, 175 and 178), to some within the 'global justice' movement (Monbiot 2003).

While both arguments have had their green supporters, the decentralist one has been predominant in green theory and practice. Decentralization is one of the key planks of the *Programme of the German Green Party* (1983), for example, a document widely taken as a key statement of Green principles, and most Green parties around the world similarly advocate decentralization of power away from central states.

Bureaucratic rationalism

A second element in green discourse has been a rejection of predominant forms of rationality in modern societies, which are both themselves prevalent in state operations and which states act to entrench broadly across society. The general form of this is often described as technical or instrumental rationality; its statist form as bureaucratic or administrative rationality. For Scott (1998) European statecraft was devoted to rationalizing and standardizing the complexity and diversity of society into a legible and administratively more convenient form. Certain forms of knowledge and control, notably those associated with the development of modern statecraft, require a narrowing of vision in order to render society and nature susceptible to careful measurement, control and manipulation. This is true today as it was for the early modern European state. As with enclosure, this rationalism was and is in large part to create forms of knowledge which enable market societies to develop, to create the sorts of *people* who can engage efficiently in market operations, and to 'disembed' the market from broader social constraints (Polanyi 1947).

As a consequence, resource managerialism has become the privileged form of state rationality governing environmental questions (Luke 1999). This approach is replete with the language of efficiency, management, and resources. Closely identified with the conservationist ethic established in the United States at the turn of the twentieth century, contemporary resource managerialism turns to experts on ecology to impose corporate needs and public agendas on nature in order to supply the economy and provision society with natural resources held in trust by centralized state authorities. Resource management reflects the character of economics as a 'science of means'. This efficiency-oriented approach focuses on the relationship between means and ends, and it is important to note that the overall quality of the outcome is not considered – only the efficiency of the means matters (Sachs 1999). For Sachs, this 'resource managerialism' has now become a dominant discourse of global institutions and some environmental groups.

Greens offer a critique of instrumental rationality which has many echoes amongst feminist, critical–theoretic (Frankfurt school) and poststructuralist critiques. Specifically, for Greens, the instrumental rationality which emerged as dominant from the scientific revolution onwards, involves a number of moves which engender ecological degradation. First, humanity is separated from the rest of nature, in a dualistic manner where humanity is at the same time made superior (morally and empirically) to 'nature'. Second, facts are made ontologically separate from values. Third, a method of producing knowledge about the world is developed which is purely (purportedly, at least) about producing 'facts'. Fourth, this method is atomistic – it reduces the world to phenomena describable in isolation from the rest of the world. But while the commonplace assertion by scientists that this effects a separation of means and ends, at least for the scientific revolution's 'founding father', Francis Bacon, the purpose behind such knowledge production was clear – to enable more effective human domination of nature (and of women by men; see Merchant 1980).

More generally, it is possible to discern two things here. First, Greens reject claims regarding the 'neutrality' of knowledge, which usually rests on a consequentialist argument that one cannot know in advance the consequences of the production of particular knowledge and thus one must leave scientists free to pursue their intellectual enquiries. Second, Greens assert that even in instrumental rationality, there is still an implicit end involved in the production of knowledge, which is that it rests on a (ethical) separation of humanity from nature, with humans as ends in themselves, and 'nature' reduced to being means to human ends. For Greens, this instrumental rationality (knowledge claims framed by power) is widely held to underpin ecological degradation, both because it ethically fails to generate systems for valuing non-human entities and systems adequately, and because empirically its individualizing method means it fails to identify ecological problems which can only be understood holistically or relationally.

The rationality of the state is a particular form of this instrumental rationality. It similarly (claims to) effect a means/ends, or facts/values, distinction, where the activities and institutions of the state are neutral with respect to ends, they merely supply means to such ends. Critically for green writers (and often drawing on Weber), the institutions evolve to become their own ends. Ecologists have countered instrumental rationality and the administrative mind that is so drawn to calculation, prediction and control. Torgerson (1999:100) recalls that ecology has been called a 'subversive science', deriving its subversive characterization from its ability to orient metaphors that challenge the presumptions of the administrative mind. More recently the emergence of interdisciplinary forms of knowledge, such as ecological economics and 'sustainability science' attempt not just to re-integrate the natural and social sciences, but also explicitly 'repoliticize', 're-ethicize' and ultimately restore democratic standards and accountability to scientific and technological innovation, along the lines that 'risk society' theorists such as Beck advocate. The rise of the corrective 'precautionary principle' is a practical outworking of these debates driven by ecologists.

Domination, violence, accumulation

A third theme in green thought makes stronger claims about the ecological nature of the state, and builds on the two previous points about sovereignty and rationality. This to suggest that, at the very least, historically existing states have engendered environmental degradation as part of their normal operations and internal logic. The two twin, related, elements here are domination/violence, and accumulation. Again, Weber can be invoked here; Spretnak and Capra suggest that it is the features identified by Weber as central to statehood – territoriality and the monopoly of legitimate violence – which are often *the* problem from a green point of view (Spretnak and Capra 1985: 177).

Regarding the state as an instrument of domination, Bookchin is the best known exponent of this view. He suggests (1980; 1982), for example, that the state is the ultimate hierarchical institution which consolidates all other hierarchical institutions. Such institutions of domination simultaneously involve the domination of some humans by others and the domination of non-humans by human societies. More concretely, the political form which states entail is one which sets in train a set of ecologically unsustainable practices. In an argument which has much in common with historical sociologist accounts (Mann 1986; Tilly 1990), Carter thus suggests that the State is part of the dynamic of modern society which has caused the present environmental crisis. He outlines a 'environmentally hazardous dynamic', where '[a] centralized, pseudo-representative, quasi-democratic state stabilizes competitive, inegalitarian economic relations that develop 'non-convivial', environmentally damaging 'hard' technologies whose productivity supports the (nationalistic and militaristic) coercive forces that empower the state' (Carter 1993). State-building is often closely associated with interstate competition, and the military projects involved themselves engender environmental degradation, but also have historically led states to create mechanisms to promote accumulation to provide resources for warfare, and this accumulation, or economic growth, is what at the heart of much of the unsustainable nature of modern societies. The aggressive, militaristic tendencies or capacities of the state are linked to its character as a 'nation-state' and the role of belligerent nationalism is central to a complete understanding of the ideological basis of the capacity of states to mobilize 'their' peoples against 'the enemy' people of other competing nation-states. The construction of economic knowledge has also been informed by this militarist orientation. The whole process of developing a national accounting system in the early twentieth century, and specifically the measure of GDP, was motivated by the need for states to calculate their war-fighting capacity. Equally, much of the rationale for early welfare state benefits was driven by the need to have a healthy population from which to raise an army. Thus the maintenance of 'national identity' and associated traditions, practices and forms of solidarity are part and parcel of the mechanisms the modern nation-state has put in place to secure itself in the eyes of its 'nation'.

Latterly, writers including Rutherford (1999) and Luke (1999) have extended our vocabulary on domination and environmental politics, by drawing on the work of Foucault, notably his work on governmentality. These writers provide the theoretical tools and grammar for writers on environmental politics to explore the links between certain forms of knowledge (e.g. science, technology, economy, security) and subjectivity (e.g. citizen, consumer, worker) associated with modern forms of state power. These forms of power are not always experienced as external sources of domination by a centralized state apparatus; modern forms of power are experienced as a multiple series of localized tactics that touch on every aspect of our lives. Examining the development of a new form of power during the eighteenth and nineteenth centuries, Foucault introduced the term 'biopower' to convey a form of power focused on the fostering of life and the care of populations (Burchell *et al.* 1991). Biopower developed in two distinct and related forms: an 'anatamo-politics' of the human body, focusing on disciplining the body of the individual to increase its utility and manageability through its integration into systems of efficient and economic controls; and a focus on the supervision of the 'species body', or the biopolitics of the population. The operation of biopower has been essential, for example, to bring about the civilization of work and the creation of compliant bodies for industry, as described by Taylor (1985). Foucault noted that the transformation to industrialization and the accompanying production of pliant bodies implicitly raised ecological issues because they disrupted the conventional understandings provided by the classical epistemology for defining human interactions with nature.

Rutherford (1999) has put forward three propositions on how we might frame our understanding of environmental politics and the role of the governmentality. The first is that the concern with ecological problems and the environmental crises can be viewed as a development of what Foucault described as the 'regulatory biopolitics of the population'. The second is that this contemporary biopolitics has given expression to a mode of governmental rationality that is related to the institutionalization of new areas of scientific expertise, which in turn is based on a bio-economic understanding of global systems ecology. Finally, this relatively recent articulation of biopolitics gives rise to new techniques for managing the environment and populations that can be termed 'ecological governmentality'. In our context here, these elements in a Foucauldian approach are best understood as useful ways of understanding the political dynamics of risk society, ecological modernization, and the 'greening of the state', which we discuss below.

Disempowerment and democracy

Whether expressed as the 'emancipatory' critique of the modern liberal state (Eckerlsey 1992) or more directly as the structural inability of liberal democracy to foster participatory forms of governance and citizen empowerment, or the unwillingness of liberal democracy to extend democracy to the spheres of production (as eco-Marxists propose), reproduction (as some eco-feminists argue) and science and technology (Beck), greens find the modern liberal state wanting on democratic as well as ecological grounds.

Representative democracy, based around a competitive party system with periodic elections offers a very 'thin' account of active citizenship, one that is both reduced to the citizen as a bearer of formal legal rights and where the primary relation is between state and citizen and the compliance of the citizen in the ordering processes of the state. As one of us has argued elsewhere (Barry 2005), arguments and analyses of 'Green citizenship' need to be linked to work on developing new Green theories of the state as well as insights into the 'greening of the state' and the characteristics of a 'green state'. Green citizenship is not exclusively attached to the state and also needs to be located within civil society (as Dryzek *et al.* suggest below), as well as organized to enable transnational forms of democracy (Eckersley, 2004) and to be especially cognisant of 'resistance' forms of green citizenship, which, are absolutely central to the creation of 'greener' states.

Greens, in criticizing the liberal state along these lines, have also drawn attention to the ways in which liberal democracy leads to the promotion of the consumer and of consumer values and practices over other interests and forms of identity, including those associated with active citizenship (Barry 1999a; Sagoff 1988). For the eco-authoritarians, the consequence here is that democracy itself has to be sacrificed in the pursuit of sustainability, precisely as democracy is understood to require the pursuit of material affluence for its legitimacy. Ophuls, for example, calls the affluence experienced by western societies over the last two hundred years or so 'abnormal', a material condition which has grounded individual liberty, democracy and stability (1977: 12), and concludes that with the advent of the ecological crisis, interpreted as a return to scarcity, 'the golden age of individualism, liberty and democracy' is all but over.

The eco-authoritarian argument turns on the prioritization of 'survival' and 'security' over ecologically unsustainable and crisis-producing material affluence and the democratic political arrangements that affluence sustains. But it also turns on the assumption that all forms of democracy suffer from the same weaknesses as the liberal kind; namely that they structurally tend to promote individualism, consumerism, etc. But Greens rather argue for a deepening of democracy, for forms of participatory democracy which are not premised on such individualist principles, but rather regard individuals as embedded in communities and in responsibilities both within and beyond those communities (see more below on notions of ecological democracy).

A green anarchism?

The above sets of critiques of the state are common to most Green theorists and practitioners. One question which arises is whether this amounts to Green political theory being a variant of anarchism, arguing for the dismantling of state structures in favour of small scale, self-reliant communities organized politically amongst themselves as direct democracies and between themselves as loose confederations. Best known of these is Bookchin's formulation of 'municipal confederalism' (1992). But this anti-statist position has been consistently criticized from inside and outside green theory. There are a number of elements of this critique (for a longer treatment, see Paterson 2001).

First is a claim that small-scale anarchistic communities would be too parochial and potentially self-interested to provide atmospheres conducive to cross-community co-operation (e.g. Dobson 1990: 101, 124). Part of this argument is therefore that it would be stultifying or oppressive for those within the community, but it also suggests that they would be unconcerned with effects across their borders.

Second is a more general critique which suggests that in rejecting the state Greens reject modernity itself, and that they have a romanticized account of an idyllic past which is both misplaced and utopian (in the pejorative sense).

A third line of criticism of the anarchist conclusions of Carter, Bookchin, and others, is that small-scale self-reliant communities would be unable to deal effectively with those ecological problems which have a global character. The logic of the argument here is usually game-theoretic (Goodin 1992: 156–68). Game theory is a widely used approach coming from economics which analyses the strategic interaction of actors in situations where each relies on the actions of others for the realization of their own goals. On this basis, Goodin argues that small-scale communities would be unable to deal with global environmental problems as there would simply be too many in existence to secure co-operation even if the game structure was a straightforward co-ordination game (where it doesn't matter particularly what actors do as long as they do the same thing – which side of the road to drive on is a paradigm example).

A fourth criticism concerns questions of social justice and economic redistribution. Social justice is widely held to be a key element in Green platforms. Recognizing the reality of increasing socio-economic inequality and poverty, both globally and within societies, the green movement(s) also recognize the limits of existing social policy and state responses to this. But at the same time this involves seeing the state as a necessary (but not sufficient) institution for regulating the corporate-dominated global economy and lessening socio-economic inequality. Many socialists and social democrats would have similar accounts of contemporary injustices. Where the green position is distinctive is in a rejection of the dominant social-democratic view that only by redistributing the fruits of a growing capitalist, competitive economy can inequality, social exclusion and environmental improvement be achieved. In fact the reverse is held to be the case – the fostering of economic growth necessarily entails acceptance of social inequalities. From this point of view, neoliberals and social democrats have more in common than many from either perspective would want to accept – both, if for different reasons, assume growth is the goal of politics. Rather the green path to tackling inequality is premised on redistribution (of existing social wealth) without the commitment to unsustainable and undifferentiated economic growth, alongside a radical shift from money and commodity-based measurements of welfare to a focus on well-being, quality of life and free time. Thus, while accepting the importance of states in redistributive politics, the character of state intervention to secure this is significantly different from conventional views.

Improving the quality of life of individuals and communities requires shifting attention away from income and benefit measurements alone (the fruits of economic growth) towards the non-income (and non-employment) components of quality of life and well-being. As Levett succinctly puts it, 'The key is to target well-being directly, and stop treating economic growth as a proxy for it' (2001: 31).

Overall, our view here is that many of these critiques of green anarchist theory are perhaps at best half right. Certainly, for example, the point that small communities are parochial tends to draw on historical examples that are pre-modern and therefore fail to ask the question of what happens when modern societies self-consciously rescale themselves but retain many other elements of modernity such as universalist ethics. It also misses the fact that nation-states themselves are often strikingly parochial and that the institution of sovereignty, as well as nationalist ideologies, support and entrench such parochialism. There are also flaws with the argument concerning international co-operation, in part because many of the criticisms levelled at green anarchist arguments could similarly be levelled at defenders of the sovereign state.

The strongest is the one focusing on inequality. It is hard to see here how Greens can pursue egalitarian politics without some state-like institutions to enact measures to reduce inequalities of various sorts. But what is clear from the discussion of this, is that in order to mitigate inequalities in the ways that Greens envisage, it is the character of state–economy relations which is key to understanding the possible 'greening' of the state that we discuss below.

Our view is the way to see the weaknesses in the green anarchist critique, is not so much that they are fundamentally flawed, but that they have a weak sense of the historicity of states and statehood, and thus a weak sense of the contradictory nature of the state. In other words, green critics of the state are at the same time right, but tend to operate within an assumption that the state is a static thing – draw on an essentialized Weberian image, rather than a historicized account of the state. As alluded above, if one sees states in terms either of historical sociology, or in Marxian terms of contradictions/regimes of accumulation, etc., then the state becomes not so much a static thing which we have to be for or against, but a complex undergoing continuous contestation, re-formation, and to which new purposes (and contradictions) can be added. In Eckersley's terms, the point is thus not to engage in transcendental critique of the state, but rather immanent critique (2004). An immanent critique is one which focuses on those elements within an existing political order which suggest the possibility of moving towards a fundamentally different order. This thus creates the possibility for Greens of envisaging not so much dismantling the state as greening it.

Greening the state?

Current debates in Green political theory can thus be interpreted as exercises (even where this is not expressly stated) in attempting to think through what the greening of the state might entail. We start here with discrete debates about 'risk society' and 'ecological modernization' before more moving on to broader arguments about the contemporary greening of the state by Dryzek and colleagues, and by Eckersley. There are various sorts of possible interpretations of these debates and the phenomena they analyse; the Green point is to retain critique of what it is about contemporary state forms which is problematic, while recognizing the transformations of states being brought about by ecological reforms, and focus on their potentials.

Risk society and ecological modernization

Environmental politics heralded the onset of 'risk society' (Beck 1992, 1995), a society where contests over the distribution of goods is now joined by deliberation on the distribution of risk. The slow but inexorable emergence of awareness of multiple hazards generated by human industrial and technological endeavour, has begun to disturb long-settled assumptions about the *ends* of politics; and forced a period of accelerated reflexivity and learning at all levels of human activity, both individually and at the level of institutions including the state. We are now more than ever acutely confronted by Foucault's observation (1987) that modernity stands at a threshold where the life of the human species is wagered on its own political strategies. This threshold signals not only the level of present danger but also a challenge to interrogate the dominant (and self-serving) Western narrative that its dominant socio-economic model of development is the only possible model for the world to follow, indeed simply what modernity 'is'.

Out of this learning, provoked by the agency of the environmental movement and others, has arisen a number of discourses on Ecological

Modernization (EM). Again, risk society can be taken as an analysis of the way in which the regulatory mechanisms of contemporary society, which evolved largely during the nineteenth century, fail to deal with the 'mega hazards' of contemporary life. But it can also be taken as an argument that the logic of risk society is the generation of new means of responding to these hazards. Specifically, the attention to risk generates pressure for reflexive mechanisms which are able to articulate popular orientations to risk rather than technocratic ones which redistribute and manage risks.

EM is a key contemporary articulation of how the economy might be, and is being, transformed in an ecological direction. At its core is an assertion, and at times an attempt to demonstrate, the potential compatibility of economic growth and ecological sustainability. But it is also a site of discursive contestation, and an arena in which radical versions may be articulated.

For Hajer, EM is 'basically a modernist and technocratic approach to the environment that suggests that there is a techno-institutional fix for the present problems' (1995: 32). In this mode, there is little fundamental in terms of the transformation of the state involved, and Greens would suggest that many of the basic anti-ecological elements of the state remain in place. In terms of the state, this 'weak' form of EM (Christoff, 1996) consists largely of an accommodation between continental European corporatist traditions and neo-liberal globalization, and its ecological content is effectively a rhetorical assertion of the adding an 'ecological' dimension to policy-making.

But this masks a contestation at the heart of EM discourse. This 'weak' form of EM can be contrasted with 'stronger' forms in which a central element is the extension of democratic decision-making procedures, a more thorough restructuring of the economy, and also with a broader sort of social change which might be called 'reflexive modernization' (Barry 2003; Beck, Lash and Giddens 1994; Christoff 1996). The strong form, entailing as it does the potential for more far-reaching social and economic change and a properly political account of EM processes, entails also a much more thorough restructuring of the state. For example, work by Jänicke, one of the main proponents of EM, casts serious doubt on the delinking of economic growth and environmental protection, i.e. the 'business as usual' approach of weak ecological modernization. In a co-authored work, he and his colleagues conclude that

> active promotion of economic growth needs to be questioned... ecologically-beneficial economic change tends to be neutralised by high growth. Growth rates themselves are an environmental problem. It is apparent that qualitative growth can in the long term only be limited growth, if ecologically negative growth effects are to be compensated by technological and structural change... The industrialised countries will not be able to afford the luxury of high growth rates for much longer.

They will have to become accustomed to solving universal problems not by economic growth, but by political action, as in matters of distribution. (Jänicke *et al.* 2000: 149)

Frequently, strong ecological modernization is held to involve the development of deliberative decision-making procedures, the decentralization of decision-making combined with a range of participative processes (citizens' juries and the like). This reflexive model of EM embraces and envisages transformations which extend into the realms of democracy and the public sphere with a view to breaking the scientistic monopoly on modern knowledge claims.

The green state

In part arising out of ecological modernization and risk society debates, some have recently attempted to formulate theories and analyses of the Green state as a total complex (Barry and Eckersley 2005; Dryzek *et al.* 2003; Eckersley 2004). They do so in a nicely complementary manner. Dryzek *et al.* engage in empirical analyses of four states looking at the ways they are being transformed by responses to environmental questions, while Eckersley asks more normative questions about what a green state might look like and interprets contemporary developments as creating the possibilities for this transformation in more general schematic terms. For both however, contemporary shifts in the ways states operates are suggestive of the possibilities for the development of what both call a 'Green state'.

Dryzek *et al.* focus on four industrialized states – the United States, the United Kingdom, Norway, and Germany. They look at how these states have responded to environmental concerns and what has conditioned the possibilities and constraints on their 'greening'. They use the four cases to suggest a typology of state–civil society relations which shows which sorts of conditions are most propitious for the emergence of Green states. Their typology has two dimensions – whether relations between the state and civil society (and especially the environmental movement) are inclusive or exclusive, and whether such inclusion/exclusion is passive or active. While clearly ideal types, they suggest that the four countries they analyse correspond to the four possible types this generates. Thus the US is passively inclusive, Norway actively inclusive, Germany passively exclusive, and the UK (at least through to the early 1990s) actively exclusive.

They argue on the basis of this typology that the most likely state form for the emergence of strong ecologically modernizing states is the passive–exclusive form exemplified by Germany. This is because the passive–exclusive form enables ideas – both substantive ideas about particular policies, but also broader shifts in culture and values – to filter to the state through popular pressure, but keeps a distinct public sphere outside the state where such ideas can emerge unconstrained, and also makes an element of an oppositional culture possible, enabling diverse strategies by environmental movements. In particular, what it makes potentially possible, is the attachment of the goals of environmental conservation as what they call the economic 'core state imperative' via ecological modernization (2003: 2). As they put it, 'environmentalist interest in pollution control and conservation of material resources can be attached to the economic imperative via the idea of ecological modernization. Demands to protect the intrinsic value of natural systems cannot make this link' (Dryzek *et al.* 2003: 161). However, they are clear that it is only by linking green politics to the legitimation (and not just economic) imperative of the state that more radical and democratic green goals can be articulated and possibly achieved (2003: 193). These findings seem to vindicate advocates of a strong version of ecological modernization, as they underline the symbiotic relationship between an open political culture and capacity for environmental policy innovation.

By contrast, in passively inclusive states like the United States, while this structure did enable much early environmental policy development, and made the US a leader in the field during the 1970s, since environmental movements had relatively easy access to policy-makers, from the 1970s onwards, there was little critical development within the movement. It also meant that other groups similarly had easy access to policy-makers and could in time resist further gains by environmentalists. At the other end, in actively inclusive states like Norway, where the state directly sponsors civil society groups, there is effectively no public sphere outside the state where new ideas can emerge. And in actively exclusive states, such as Britain, there is often a vibrant public sphere, but no channels through which ideas emerging from it can reach the state.

Eckersley provides a broader argument concerning the potential development of Green states. Her intention is specifically to develop an immanent critique, focusing on those elements in actually existing, and emerging, practices of governance which have the potential to be transformed by Greens in the direction of sustainability. Her key points for our purposes are that the two central elements in statehood where transformation will enabling the greening of the state are sovereignty and democracy. Regarding the former, it is shifts in the way that states regard their responsibilities to those beyond their borders which are a condition of possibility of the greening of the state, since the conditions of ecology mean that purely territorially based rule fails to generate policies and practices which deal adequately with its challenges. Regarding democracy, it is a radical reworking of democratic institutions and practices which will make possible the consideration of ecological concerns beyond the state's territorial limits, but will also enable the development of 'strong' ecological modernization strategies. Her overall argument is well expressed in the beginning of her conclusion:

> The anarchic state system, global capitalism, and the administrative state have served in different ways to inhibit the development of greener states and societies. In this book I have shown how three mutually informing counterdevelopments – environmental multilateralism, ecological modernization, and the emergence of green discursive designs – have emerged to moderate, restrain and in some cases transform the anti-ecological dynamics of these deeply embedded structures...This virtuous relationship, however, cannot be deepened without a move from liberal democracy to ecological democracy. (Eckersley 2004: 241)

The term ecological democracy is intended by Eckersley to refer to a form of democracy which differs from liberal democracy in two key respects. First it rejects liberal democracy's presumption of pre-existing autonomous individuals, whose preferences and interests are therefore unquestionable. Second, it is constituted as a 'democracy of the affected' rather than (or more precisely in addition to) a 'democracy of membership'. Thus, the regulative ideal or ambit claim of ecological democracy is that all those potentially affected by ecological risks ought to have some meaningful opportunity to participate, or be represented, in the determination of policies or decisions that may generate risks' (Eckersley 2004: 243). This thus means both that deliberation is a key element in ecological democratic practice (undermining liberal democracy's separation of public and private) and that territoriality is unimportant (as well as species or temporality, although these are not the focus of her analysis) in determining who should get to participate in decisions.

Combined, the analyses of Eckersley and Dryzek *et al.* provide powerful arguments which suggest that the 'green anarchist' position is over-stated; that while there is much which is clearly anti-ecological in contemporary state practice and structures, these should be regarded as historically contingent rather than structurally inherent features of statehood. In sustaining this claim regarding the greening of the state, two elements are key. The first is whether or not states can be treated as having no key features or roles, but simply as evolving complexes of institutions/power which develop specific functions in response to different historical exigencies or pressures. The second is whether different elements in the roles/functions of states are structurally consistent with sustainability/ecological democracy as a role/function.

For Dryzek *et al.*, for example, there is nothing structural about the nature of the state's responsibility for economic growth, say, outside of the historically produced and sedimented nature of that responsibility. Dryzek *et al.* start their account with a 'brief history of the state' (2003: 1–2) which runs through a narrative of state development which is familiar in historical sociology (Manny 1986; Dryzek *etal.* draw explicitly on Skocpol 1979). The first 'core imperative' of states was then to protect its territory from external attack, and contained three elements: 'domestic order, survival and revenue imperatives' (Dyzek *etal.* 2003: 1).

Dryzek *etal.* suggest that the transformations currently underway in response to mobilizations by environmental movements can be interpreted in terms of the development of an ecological function for states. Eckersley's argument similarly depends on a similar narrative regarding the functions of states. Her 'three core challenges' – interstate anarchy, global capitalism, liberal democracy – correspond broadly to the three historically evolved functions of states outlined by Dryzek *etal.* Eckersley's theoretical move, principally developed in her chapter on interstate anarchy (2004: Ch. 2) is in her turn to constructivism (in International Relations) to suggest that the image of international politics as a realm of unremitting competition and hostility between self-regarding sovereign states is only one of a number of possible 'cultures of anarchy' (cf. Goodin 1990; Litfin 1998).

The second question, however, is that even if it is the case that the various functions of states are historically constituted and potentially trans-formable, then are these various functions (potentially) consistent with each other and with an emerging function of sustainability. In other words, how plausible is it to suggest that the functions of the state in pursuing territo-rial security through military power, or economic growth, are consistent with sustainability? Eckersley's response regarding the former is to suggest that they are not consistent, but that militarism is neither a necessary feature of the state, and is in decline because of economic interdependence, and in particular because of democratization. Her response regarding the latter is more evasive. She is rightly critical of weak ecological modernization as it only focuses on technological change and the fostering of 'environmental services and industries' by states (2004: 70–7), and infers that it is economic growth which is the central weakness in this strategy, invoking the standard argument that growth outstrips the efficiency gains technology can effect (2004: 76). Hence the need for 'strong' ecological modernization, which involves the development of discursive/deliberate mechanisms; such mecha-nisms enable a reflection on and decision-making about ends rather than simply means. But in developing this, she has a less than clear answer to the question about the potential compatibility of growth and sustainability:

> On the one hand, the green state would still be dependent on the wealth produced by private capital accumulation, via taxation, its programs and in this sense would still be a capitalist state. On the other, securing private capital accumulation would no longer be the defining feature or primary raison d'être of the state. The state would be more reflective and

market activity would be disciplined, and in some cases curtailed, by social and ecological norms. (Eckersley 2004: 83)

The question arises as to whether the two hands in this sentence can be regarded as compatible with each other; i.e., if the green state is dependent on capital for taxes, and capital is dependent on accumulation for profits (out of which taxes would be paid), then how viable is a strategy of limiting overall accumulation (rather than simply redirecting it, as in weak ecological modernization)? For many state theorists the responsibility of the state for accumulation in capitalist society is more fundamentally structured than this formula by Eckersley suggests (e.g. Jessop 1990; Harvey 1990; Hay 1994; Paterson 2000). This thus takes us back to the historical narrative concerning state functions – an alternative reading is the co-evolution of the capitalist social form (wage-labour, market competition, the primacy of private property) with the political form of the modern state (territoriality/ anarchy, constitutional government, the rule of law) and that the former sets certain conditions of operation for the latter.

Conclusions

We have tried to suggest that Greens should be wary of eco-anarchist views that the state is always and everywhere unreformable and therefore to be bypassed, rejected or otherwise seen not just as part of the problem, but *the* problem. But at the same time, Greens ought to be cautious about endorsing an equally naïve eco-reformist/weak ecological modernization approach which assumes that the state can unproblematically realize green goals. (This sort of debate parallels similar ones in other perspectives committed to radical social change, such as feminism and socialism.) The point is that the state can be a positive force in the transition to a sustainable society, but that this is highly context dependent and fundamentally an issue of political strategy.

One way of responding to this question is to emphasize the strategic nature of greens' orientation towards the state. Doherty for example suggests that, 'The greens have responded to new conditions and issues with a distinctively modern strategy based on accepting the limits of the state in guaranteeing social and political change' (1992: 102). In other words, if Greens would democratize, decentralize and downsize the state (but not in the way in which neo-liberalism conceives of this), then it would be less reliant on capital accumulation and orthodox economic growth.

In this strategic orientation to the state, green states are made by green citizens gathered within civil society (both within and outside the state) forcing states (and the state system internationally) to change. States will not become green by themselves, or at least not in the full sense of 'green' – as we suggest, the most we can expect of endogenous state transformation is some form of 'weak' ecological modernization, as discussed above. In the struggle for more sustainable, just and democratic societies, we need civil disobedience before obedience and more than ever, we need critical citizens and not just law-abiding ones.

In this way considerations of strategy and the potential transformation/s of the state, lead to issues of political economy and the need for greens to focus more explicitly than they have in the past on the political economy of the state within a globalizing capitalist world economy. Here greens have much to learn from Marxist and other forms of critical political economy in the development of their strategies of engagement and disengagement with and from the state and the state system.

An interesting example of the state in green strategy thinking is provided by Alex Begg, who, writing from an activist's perspective and employing Foucauldian and Marxist analyses, describes the existing state as embodying 'power-over' rather than a more emancipatory 'power to'. According to him,

> working at the interface between systems of power is effectively opening up a conduit between the two. You are allowing a flow of energy or resources from one to the other (or more often a combination of both)...Anyone seeking to work for empowerment, equality or social change will have relationships with many bodies shaped and governed by power-over... However, it is not the case that every connection with the dynamics of power-over weakens the process of social change. (Begg 2000: 211)

And as he pragmatically concludes, 'At the end of the day, the question is not whether or not to sup with the devil, but rather whether the spoon is long enough' (Begg 2000: 214).

The real issue for radical social change, according to Begg, is the assessment on a case by case basis of the 'terms of trade' of any 'ethical compromise' one makes between the two systems of power – that is, is the overall impact of the compromise to increase, strengthen the system of 'power to' and/or weaken the system of 'power-over'? This is all the more complex and irredeemably resistant to 'universal' or 'grand theories' and therefore only adequately analysed in terms of an iterative process of specific points of engagement/disengagement – because the practices and institutions of 'power-over' and 'power-to' are not neatly demarcated in the state and capitalist system on the one hand and 'civil society' on the other. Power-over and power to are dispersed throughout and across these spheres.

Cautioning against those in the green movement who would simply seek to 'by-pass' the state, the world of liberal democratic politics, and the market and consumer society, Begg has this to say (2000: 223):

> There is no 'middle way' when one side in the contest is so dominant. There is no way to remain above the grubby worlds of politics and commerce when to abstain from power altogether is to cut oneself off from the means of life. Connections have to be made...It is not about being in the mainstream which gets results, nor about being revolutionary; it is the connection between the two, the ability to have a foot in both camps and your heart in empowerment.

Further reading

Begg, Alex (2000) *Empowering the Earth: Strategies for Social Change* (Totnes: Green Books).

Bookchin, Murray (1980) *Toward an Ecological Society* (Montreal: Black Rose Books).

Dryzek, J., Downes, D., Hunold, C., Schlosberg, D., with Hernes, H. K. (2003) *Green States and Social Movements* (Oxford: Oxford University Press).

Eckersley, Robyn (2004) *The Green State: Rethinking Democracy and Sovereignty* (Cambridge, MA: MIT Press).

Ecologist, The (1993) *Whose Common Future? Reclaiming the Commons* (London: Earthscan).

Sachs, Wolfgang (1999) *Planet Dialectics: Explorations in Environment and Development* (London: Zed Books).

Torgerson, Douglas (1999) *The Promise of Green Politics: Environmentalism and the Public Sphere* (London: Duke University Press).

Chapter 8

Poststructuralism

ALAN FINLAYSON AND JAMES MARTIN

This chapter explores and evaluates poststructuralist approaches to the political theory and analysis of the state. It begins by putting poststructuralism into a very broad philosophical context, relating it to historical changes in Western society and culture and to current trends in political science. We argue that poststructuralism is distinctive in its opposition to analyses that treat politics as derivative of forces that are explicitly or implicitly non-political. Poststructuralists argue that 'the political' is the dimension of social existence in which social relations are constituted and contested and as such a cause and not merely an effect of social phenomena. We regard the state as an *outcome* of political activities as well as a contribution to them and this is because, as we will see, poststructuralism interprets the state not as a 'thing' but as a practice or ensemble of practices. In explicating this view we shall consider, not uncritically, some varieties of poststructuralist theory and analysis: the discourse theory developed by Laclau and Mouffe, critical theories of international relations and Foucauldian approaches to 'governmentality'.

Locating poststructuralism

There is no single version of poststructuralism. It has been adapted to the circumstances and needs of many disciplines including history (Jenkins 1991; White 1987), literary studies and geography (Doel 1999). But, whatever the discipline, poststructuralism responds to problems that have emerged within the characteristic worldview of the scientific, liberal and enlightened West. Foremost among these is heightened uncertainty, a loss of confidence, in the values of the 'Western tradition'; an anxiety that these are not as universally true as was once imagined and that they may not be necessarily good and right for everyone for all time. To help us understand this anxiety we will characterize it philosophically and historically.

Early on in his *Critique of Pure Reason*, Immanuel Kant describes his time – the period of European Enlightenment – as one with a 'ripened power of judgement'. 'Ours', he says, 'is the genuine age of criticism, to which

155

everything must submit', including religion, the law and monarchy. These institutions may try to escape criticism but if they do then they 'cannot lay claim to that unfeigned respect that reason grants only to that which has been able to withstand its free and public examination' (A, xi). In other words, public institutions of varying kinds must justify themselves to human rationality; they cannot rely on tradition, dogma or superstition. Kant's philosophical–political project was to establish and defend the position of reason, to help 'institute a court of justice by which reason may secure its rightful claims...not by mere decrees but according to its own eternal and unchangeable laws' (A, xii). For him, Reason is at the centre of philosophy, morality and public political action. It alone can assess claims to authority and knowledge. This was, and is, a marvellous vision with radical implications. From it came the liberal view that the state must not interfere with individuals but should ensure that each can exercise their public reason, subjecting all institutions to critical scrutiny.

However, poststructuralism questions this enthroning of reason and has thus been accused of irrationality. Critics imagine that in rejecting Kantian Enlightenment, poststructuralism must be hankering for pre-enlightenment superstition. But poststructuralism does not reject Enlightenment: it follows it through. Taking the critical imperative seriously, poststructuralists criticize criticism and use reason against reason, questioning the 'eternal and unchangeable' standpoint from which it claims to derive authority. This is not easy. How can one use reason against itself without falling into unreason or ceasing to be able to think? Yet we must ask if reason is always reasonable and if it is as uniform and unchanging as it can be made to appear. Far from claiming that there is no such thing as reason, poststructuralists argue that there are multiple forms of reason and many rationalities.

For Kant the act of reasoning involved identifying a universal principle to follow. By 'universal' is meant something that applies across specific cases, independently of them. A universal truth is always true and it is true for everyone. The essential Kantian moral maxim tells us to act in line with principles we could reasonably assume to be principles for everyone else. Kant's critics challenge just this claim to universality arguing that any claim regarding universal validity will always be historically and politically specific. This criticism has not just been made philosophically. It has also been made, implicitly but forcefully, by actual historical social movements that have, in practice, challenged the limits of conceptions of reason.

When enlightened states first granted rights to 'the people' they did not grant them to all. The propertyless, the working class, women, ethnic and religious minorities and the peoples of colonized countries were usually excluded. The capacity to reason was not imagined to be found equally in all. The story of modern Europe can be told as one in which the numbers of those deemed capable of reasoning, and deserving of civil and other such rights, have been increased ever further. We might like to imagine that narrative as ending with true universality, embodied in something like the *Universal Declaration of Human Rights*; that each successive extension was implicit from the start; that we have seen, over time, a series of additions to, but not alterations of, our substantive understanding of what rationality is. But each successive adaptation included a critique of the previous state of affairs. Reason was never short of reasons why the poor, female or colonized were not fully rational, could not exercise rights or did not deserve them. Each challenge to the limits of the reasonable raised the possibility that the previous concept of reason had been not merely limited but flawed: that the way in which reason was specified and exercised depended on the exclusion of alternative perspectives.

For instance, the Marxist critique of nineteenth-century liberalism, scathingly expressed in *The Communist Manifesto*, did not reproach it simply for excluding the poor and dispossessed. Marx attacked liberalism for imagining that its way of living, being and thinking was the universal way. In the twentieth century, feminist critiques of patriarchy did not simply demand that women be included in the masculine world of citizenship but exposed the ways in which the exclusion of women was fundamental to social and political structures. To these criticisms were added charges that our way of thinking necessarily excludes non-European perspectives or that it is based on a very particular and increasingly untenable attitude towards the natural world. For such critics traditional reason was seen not as emancipatory but as instrumental and constraining, directed at the attainment of specific goals (see Adorno and Horkehimer 1944[1973]; Held 1980) and as excluding, setting limits to what counts as proper reasoning, regarding other ways of thinking as gibberish to be ignored or suppressed in advance.

However, it is not clear that in Western society such a uniform rationality still holds a position of domination. The traditional division of labour between men and women in the West has not disappeared but it has been altered in many ways; our national cultures are often still imagined to be homogenous or uniform but regional identities are increasingly assertive and the difficult realities of multicultural and transnational societies are becoming apparent. The closed worlds of traditional communities of all kinds (from rural Wales to urban Afghanistan) are connected with and exposed to international networks of communication or trade. The media (satellite television and internet) communicate at such a pace and volume that our conceptions of time and space have changed (Giddens 1991; Beck, Lash and Giddens 1994) and we are surrounded by such a surfeit of images that our mental environment is radically different to that of literate cultures just a century ago (see McLuhan 1964). The pervasive power of commodification unsettles traditional moralities and routines of justification replacing them with the individualised rationalities of market choice. We live amidst discontinuity and disjuncture where the traditional, modern and 'post-modern' commingle and the singular dominance of any particular way of reasoning appears hard to sustain.

In response some have sought to defend or re-found the Kantian vision of reason, making it fit for a pluralized social world, yet worried that without singular Reason and Truth as the guarantee of our choices there will be chaos and moral collapse (e.g. Habermas 1996; Rawls 1973, 1996). Others seem to rejoice in unreason and reject the 'Western' way of being in its entirety, searching for a 'new age' believed to be more natural or spiritual or traditional. But there is another possibility: engaging in a kind of criticism and analysis that does not reject reason but seeks to show and then exceed its historical limits. Such criticism of rationality proceeds by demonstrating how a particular form of reasoning depends on what it excludes, on the limits it sets for itself, and how, in placing some things beyond that limit, it necessarily construes them as anti-rational and undeserving of participation in the 'tribunal' of reason.

Poststructuralism does not try to make reason disappear, but to understand it as multiple in form, limited and partial. Any particular specification of what is to count as rational in a particular context rules things in or out in advance. Poststructuralism tries to make this open to critical consideration. That entails explicating the rationalities that underpin different political institutions and ideologies, theories and practices, movements and moments. In order to understand the state, poststructuralists argue, it is necessary to understand the sort of reasoning that constitutes it and that is constituted by it, that defines the parameters within (and without) which legitimacy can be established.

This sort of conception is at odds with the positivist mainstream of the discipline of political studies. Rational choice theories, for example, often treat individuals as isolated units with more or less fixed preferences that can form the basis of explanatory models. But our approach inquires into the rationality behind choices, the intellectual, deliberative, cultural and ideological processes that go into them. Poststructuralism, then, has links with variations of hermeneutic or interpretive political science. For these there is a fundamental difference between the objects of natural science and those of social science: human beings are conscious, reflective and reflexive creatures living in a world they experience as meaningful because they fill it with symbols and signs, values and meanings. By studying systems of meaning, the interpretivists hope, we may gain insight into the modes or forms of reason particular groups employ.

Interest in meaning and discourse has become increasingly common in political science (Schmidt and Radaelli 2004), public administration (Fox and Miller 1995) and studies of governance (Bevir and Rhodes 2003; Bevir *et al.* 2004) because to understand the interactions of people in government bureaucracies, or politicians negotiating over policies, we have also to understand the cultural worlds they come from, the relations between such worlds and the rationalities by which they are engendered. In politics, just as in Western philosophy more generally, it is now rather difficult to think of governmental or state activity as simply the direct expression of a single political tradition, power or reason. States and governments must be 'reflexive', reassessing their activities in a context of heightened uncertainty, of global political, cultural and economic change (Hay 2002: 197–8). Interpretive political scientists want to help us understand how states are involved in multiple, ongoing relationships, held together by shared (or opposed) values and meanings. Some forms of 'new' institutionalism, for instance, examine the informal norms, values and symbolic forms that shape institutions (see Lowndes 1996: 182; 2002) including the flows of ideas that create institutionalized 'templates' for action. Bevir and Rhodes (2003) emphasize the narratives that political actors (and political scientists) employ when making sense of governance, insisting that actions can only be understood if we also understand the beliefs and values that motivate them and that means examining the 'inherited beliefs and practices' that constitute varying traditions.

Poststructuralism shares much with these approaches. It too examines the frameworks against which actors act. But poststructuralism insists that we cannot establish fixed rules of thought or language, tradition and community that underpin all or some political institutions or groups. Political decisions and actions are not merely expressions of tradition because those traditions and their rules are manifestations of past political victories: a kind of 'sedimented' power. They are systems of meaning that are the object and the mechanism of social control and contestation. For poststructuralists all actions and objects are meaningful but derive their meaning from their relationship to other actions and objects: which is to say from traditions and institutions but also from the ways in which political (or other) actors make use of or activate them. Furthermore, for poststructuralists, the 'actor' does not exist independently of these 'frameworks' or systems of meaning; the 'subject', the being with an identity that acts, is defined by that system and the actions it carries out within or against it (and, as we will see, this may also be the case when the identity in question is that of the state).

For instance, some political scientists wonder why people vote. Voting, it is argued, is an irrational activity since it takes up time and energy disproportionate to the influence a single vote can have. But what meaning does voting have? For the newly enfranchised a vote is part of a much larger expression of liberation and casting it creates and expresses the identity of 'free citizen'. But this does not exhaust the context or possible identities (which may be inexhaustible); there are always other potential meanings for situations, acts and utterances. A vote may be an expression of liberation within one context but, in another, the alienation of power to a distant representative, creating an identity of 'lawful subject'. A vote may be an acclamation, a celebration, an expression of individuality or a duty to the commonweal. Whichever meaning and identity predominates, will depend on overt or covert, present or past, power struggle: an attempt to organize the systems of meaning within which we act. Poststructuralists see this as a fundamentally political activity that far exceeds the narrow realms of parliamentary debating chambers, legal institutions or military headquarters. Individuals do not come together, their aspirations, perceptions and interests already fully formed, but come to have an identity through their position within a broader politicized system of meaning. Thus, many actors and institutions play a role in organizing social systems of meaning that naturalize and legitimate political claims, making the 'rules of the game', how we 'naturally' and 'normally' act seem inevitable and immovable. These are 'discourses' or 'discursive structures' that draw lines of exclusion and inclusion, of what is and is not a legitimate 'move in the game' or an identity that matters, 'drawing...political frontiers between "insiders" and "outsiders"... excluding certain options and structuring relations' (Howarth, Norval and Stavrakakis 2000: 4). In order to act in certain domains understood as political one has to be able to participate in a particular 'language-game' whose rules may shape the sorts of action that can take place. State bureaucracies, for example, are professional domains built around all sorts of professional codes that legitimate and delegitimate certain persons and actions, affording entry to those who have mastered the code while facilitating the exclusion of those who have not. When political actors form preferences, take decisions, prescribe policies and so on, they draw on some set of discursively produced resources that prescribe and shape the outcomes of thought and action. That is to say, they act on the basis of an implicit yet unexamined social theory. Poststructuralists investigate such political discourse in order to perceive something of its structure, rules of performance and institutionalization. But we do not do this in order to uncover an implicit logical structure of propositions which can then be verified or falsified. We do so in order to establish what has been excluded and how, and to try and make something new thinkable. 'Discourses' are open-ended systems, always productive of new possibilities. 'Authorities' of various kinds may seek to control language, meaning and identity within narrow, stable parameters but meaning always exceeds such control. There is not one discursive structure in society as a whole, or even just within the governmental domain, but multiple forms of 'language game' (Wittgenstein 1958) and multiple rationalities that may contradict or clash. The struggle between openness and closure is at the heart of political struggle and it is from this perspective that we may study the phenomenon of the state. We now turn to some different ways in which this has been done.

Laclau and Mouffe: the impossibility of the state

The 'discourse theory' associated with Ernesto Laclau and Chantal Mouffe (1985) represents a significant attempt to take the perspective we have discussed and apply it to political theory and analysis. Laclau and Mouffe conceive of society as a complex ensemble of overlapping, mutually limiting and modifying discursive practices. These discourses are not closed, nor are they organized around or derived from a fixed centre or point of origin. In fact, Laclau and Mouffe argue that society is organized around the *absence* of such a centre. Society, they declare, paradoxically, is 'impossible'. What they mean is that society is never a completed, closed-off, unified entity and it cannot be explained by referring back to some kind of single, controlling principle (1985: 111). Instead of society there is 'the social', which is always in the process of being created through attempts to provide for it an anchor, an incontestable point of reference, that can join together and tie down various elements, specifying what they are and how they relate. Political analysis can therefore examine social formations by examining the ways in which various elements are articulated (combined and recombined) and social identities formed.

For instance, in developed economies, such as the US or the UK, we find the 'articulation' of capitalist production and exchange with liberal individualism and the representative form of democracy. This is not simply a coincidental alignment of three distinct phenomena (a mode of production, an ideology of personhood or identity and a political system). The theory of 'articulation' argues that when combined such phenomena are fundamentally modified. There is no permanent 'essence' to capitalism, individualism or representative democracy. Their articulation creates a distinct form: capitalist liberal democracy. It is important, then, not only to study what we imagine to be 'the things in themselves' but the relations between them. For instance, capitalist production may be articulated with ethnic nationalism and a political structure centred on an authoritarian personality cult: Nazi Fascism. Laclau and Mouffe's discourse analysis is interested in the way such articulations work to produce distinct social formations. It does not see these as naturally or necessarily given forms of society but as the temporary outcome of ongoing political practices and struggles that have sought to define society through combining its elements (including economics, individuals and the political system) in particular ways.

Laclau and Mouffe employ Gramsci's term 'hegemony' to define this process of fixing and associating elements and identities, imposing a dominant meaning on social practices in ways that limit the range of possibilities within a given structure (see Gramsci 1971). Crucially, discourse theory and analysis draws attention to what is suppressed or repressed, excluded or constituted as 'other' or as an enemy, in the attempt to sustain the appearance of unity.

More recently, Laclau has come to understand the process of trying to attain hegemony as one in which a range of subjective identities are related to each other such that they appear to be joined to some kind of universal category (see Laclau 1996). For instance, when President George W. Bush declared 'war on terror', shaped policy on the basis of an 'axis of evil', and sought to constitute a 'coalition of the willing' where 'you are either for us or against us' states were constituted in terms of a very specific set of identities and relationships. On the one side are 'friends' who are for freedom and democracy, and who, despite their differences, are united under these 'universal' categories; on the other the 'enemies' associated with the universal categories of dictatorship and evil. On each side elements are shown to have 'relations of equivalence' all partaking of some more universal element in terms of which they are equivalent. This constitutes a political logic that orders the inter-state field in a particular and limited way and from that stark arrangement demands certain political actions as necessary.

Laclau and Mouffe do not have a theory of the state as a discrete or unified phenomenon. They reject attempts to theorize society from the perspective of one specific 'region' or centre such as the state. As Torfing (1991) indicates, the state should be conceived of as a complex ensemble of various discursively formed rationalities: law, sovereignty, various claims to 'expertise', information and knowledge, forms of, or skills in, communication as well as institutions, departments, bureaucracies, ritualised forms of legitimation, organisations of coercion and control. Political analysis can look at how these are combined and recombined asking what effects they have upon each other. This might enable us to describe, for different states, the varying ways in which the 'centre' is organized. For instance, in some states the systems of law, government and military may be articulated directly with 'the people' whose interests they are held to express. This is a formation we call 'totalitarian' and contrast to the liberal democratic regime in which, increasingly, there is no 'people', only independent individuals who are not directly articulated to the government. Fascist parties seek to articulate the people with government and do so by defining the people in opposition to other kinds of people. Other kinds of state involve an articulation with religion, or God, and the 'people' may be conceived of in religious terms leading to a different series of relations with the law or the military. In the Islamic Republic of Iran, for example, the state is organized according to a principle of divine sovereignty. Society, law, politics and military are articulated under the sign of this one overarching principle of unity.

Laclau and Mouffe's is a macro-level theory concerned to identify and explore certain high-level 'logics' that shape social formations. For them there is no essential unifying element of statehood. The state has an evolving and unpredictable character, its policies, ministries, bureaucracies and personnel are always facing the possibility of conflict and potential disaggregation.

The state, then, is not a single 'institution' or even a number of 'institutions' tied together but, rather, a series of practices, of actions and reactions that draw from 'traditions' and 'habits' but also redraw them – rearticulate them – in every action. For the theory of hegemony, the state is both a site and an outcome of political practices; an ongoing project to 'hegemonize' the plurality of its apparatuses and society itself. Thus the state cannot 'explain' politics since it is an outcome of politics; an assemblage of rationalities that work on and through its structures.

Weakness in the capacity to analyse particular institutions is to be expected from such a general and abstract theory as this. Laclau and Mouffe are concerned to identify general 'logics' rather than make specific pronouncements. They draw attention to the way in which the state is itself politically contested, rather than a definitive precondition of political activity. That said, such 'post-Marxist' theories typically attend to various types of hegemonic activity found within specific fields and take for granted that the nation-state is the terrain of hegemonic struggle (see Nash 2002). It is one thing to use such a theory to examine a specific state and a specific society or social formation. But states also exist in relation to other states. Can a poststructuralist focus on the multiple rationalities that constitute statehood tell us anything about politics at the international level?

Destabilizing state sovereignty

The concept of hegemony has long had significance for the study of international relations where it has been used to describe the way states dominate others in a 'state system'. In such theories the state is taken more or less as a given; as a corporate actor with its own interests and capacities for strategic calculation. Just this idea of a singular, unified 'actor' and its complement, that of a number of such actors contending with each other for power in an essentially anarchic 'international arena', have been questioned by a number of 'critical' theories of international relations. These have examined the very idea of sovereign statehood, exposing its limits and investigating the forms of reasoning presupposed by thinking of the state as a formal unity.

For instance, in his critique of realist and neo-realist literature, Richard Ashley (1988) argues that the discourse of national sovereignty *requires* the concept of international anarchy. Sovereign states with authority over their domestic interiors are taken to be the foundational elements of theories of international politics. The world 'outside' states is imagined as an unregulated, anarchic, space within which a multiplicity of forces compete or co-operate. Anarchy, then, is the 'other' of sovereignty, against which it is defined. This lays the basis for a 'rationality' that constantly asks of the international arena 'How is order possible?'; 'How can order be maintained?'; 'How can policy be co-ordinated'? Rational and self-interested 'state-agents' face an ambiguous, unco-ordinated environment against which they must range. Corresponding theories of the 'balance of power' and the need for its maintenance become the basis for state policies. But the state itself is unquestioned since it is a 'rational presence already there, a sovereign identity that is the self-sufficient source of international history's meaning' (1988: 231). But, he continues, this rigid dichotomy between sovereignty and anarchy creates the very environment it claims to describe (1988: 243). Because sovereignty is taken to be the objective basis of all international politics, ambiguous practices that undermine the notion of the sovereign state as the stable point in an unstable environment, are downgraded and ignored. Non-state actors, agencies that compete with states, even the distinct branches of the state bureaucracy itself, all complicate the idea of unitary actors and may even work against it. The state co-exists alongside trans-national corporations, political movements and NGOs, all of which often transcend and disrupt state boundaries while the migration of populations or refugees problematises state responsibility for citizens. All these things lie beyond the boundaries of unitary sovereignty and bring into question that very concept of bounded statehood. But the rationality built around states' 'sovereign interests' can only be clearly defined if the state's identity can be demarcated between a domestic 'inside' and an international 'outside' (see Walker 1993). As a result international relations are dominated by assumptions about conflict and order that derived from a presumption of rationality rather than from an examination of the possibilities contained within the complex multiplicities of world politics.

Poststructuralist critics, then, take a 'constructivist' approach to international relations. That is to say, they are interested in studying the way concepts and practices of sovereignty or inside/outside distinctions are socially created through, for example, the mutual recognition by other states of national identity, territorial integrity or assumptions concerning trade in capitalist markets (see Biersteker and Weber 1996). In attaching its claim to authority to notions such as national purity or economic success the state continually confronts resistance to its efforts (often as a consequence of its own intervention) which expose the partiality and contingency of its claims. Poststructuralists draw attention to the role of power and exclusion in this process, underlining its *political* nature. As Ashley puts it, the 'figure' of the sovereign state 'is nothing more and nothing less than an arbitrary political representation always in the process of being inscribed within history, through practice, and in the face of all manner of resistant interpretations that must be excluded if the representation is to be counted as a self-evident reality' (1988: 252). This is not meant to suggest that the state does not really exist or is a mere charade; only that its existence as a sovereign entity in an international environment is a kind of myth dependent upon ongoing processes that define and redefine its 'inside' and 'outside' through practices of exclusion that create the very environment within and through which the state is then deemed to act.

Defining the state and 'its' interests is not a matter of inventing 'mere' fictions. Typically it involves very material forms of violence against bodies and identities. Poststructuralist thinkers (among others) draw attention to the 'securitisation' of the international environment through which subjects and identities are constituted in relation to other identities, boundaries and 'threats'. For example, David Campbell (1992) argues that foreign policy should not be understood as the more or less successful expression of a state's given interests and identity but as part of the ongoing attempt to establish that identity and those interests, through the constitution of enemies and dangers against which state action can be ranged and, in the process, defined. This means that the state, as we have seen, requires the anarchy it seeks to eliminate, the enemies against whom it establishes an identity. As Campbell puts it: 'the inability of the state project of security to succeed is the guarantor of the states continued success and impelling identity' (1992: 11–12). In the live televisual spectacle of successful strikes against enemy targets, the state seems to be protecting us yet, simultaneously, we experience a visceral sense of personal insecurity that narrows our ability to see beyond these limits (see Dillon 1996; Edkins 1999). Indeed, identity and violence are often closely related. Campbell (1998) shows how policies in response to ethnic conflict can be damaging because they are shaped by the very same assumptions (that identities are fixed and expressive of a singular political outlook) that they seek to challenge. He argues that we are insufficiently attentive to the contingency and flux of political identity formations and tries to 'deconstruct' the rigid dualisms that underpin the rationalities of foreign policy or conflict resolution. This opens the way for an ethics formed out of the attempt to treat 'the other' not as an opportunity to define ourselves but as a complex, differentiated singularity that cannot be subordinated to a predefined and universal normative law (see Campbell and Shapiro 1999).

This draws attention to the way in which rationalities constitute and define the very space of the international environment in which states are deemed to act. In the study of 'geopolitics', writers such as Gearóid ó Tuathail (1996) and John Agnew (Agnew and Corbridge 1995; Agnew and ó Tuathail 1992) examine the ways in which international space is rendered both meaningful and practically governable through discursive representations. These are embodied in various forms such as maps, public 'common sense', varieties of intellectual reasoning, which contribute to a vision of the international order favourable to certain kinds of action rather than others. The Cold War, for example, involved efforts to envision a dichotomous division of space into broadly homogenous, antagonistic camps, thus obscuring the very real differences between states presumed to be on the same 'side'.

The spatial discourse of 'East *vs* West' validated certain forms of identity and a selective understanding of the purpose and function of other states. It made it possible to imagine the United States as the 'defender' of Western civilization and to interpret events anywhere in the world in terms of that overriding dichotomy (as if the Middle East or South East Asia were merely a theatre for the Cold War). Today, when many things are securitized – from climate and population movements to trade and criminal activities – we can see how each is drawn into the orbit of the overriding security threat of terrorism.

Poststructuralist analyses of state sovereignty expose the arbitrary, shifting boundaries that underscore the supposed stability of the state as a principle and guarantor of order. The rationality of sovereignty places complex decisions and judgements within a stable frame whose unity is presupposed and therefore not open to debate and contestation. In the very moment in which 'it' takes a political decision, the state itself is depoliticized.

Foucault, power and governmentality

So far we have seen how poststructuralists can be understood to 'open up' the state through an examination of the political rationalities that constitute it. By looking at the discursive rationalities that invoke the image of the state as a centre to social life, they have *decentred* the idea of a singular political power. The notion that the state, or indeed sovereignty, should be at the centre of political analysis is made problematic and the very object and method of political analysis destabilised. This is the moment to turn to the work of Michel Foucault.

Foucault polemically challenged political theory and analysis by inveighing against the notion of sovereignty. 'Political theory', he suggested, 'has never ceased to be obsessed with the person of the sovereign' (1980: 121). It is concerned with the single location and origin of power and with secondary questions as to how it may be legitimately exercised, contained and directed. Further, sovereign power is taken to express itself through the setting of limits typically expressed as laws concerning what can't be done. It was just this that Foucault sought to dispute, problematizing the concept of sovereignty in order to open the way to closer examination of the particular and peculiar strategies and practices that comprise contemporary power (see Foucault 1980, 1991). The reduction of power to a state construed as a rational, calculating subject obscures the organizational continuity between state and non-state agencies that work throughout society to administer 'disciplinary' and 'normalizing' techniques of governance. Foucault sought a 'political philosophy that isn't erected around the problem of sovereignty, nor therefore around the problem of law and prohibition' and declared that

'We need to cut off the king's head: in political theory that has still to be done' (Foucault 1980: 121).

From this perspective our object of analysis ceases to be the state and becomes a diverse range of agencies, apparatuses and practices producing varied mechanisms of control and varied forms of knowledge that make areas or aspects of social life available for governmental action. Government works through and out of an ensemble of authorities, knowledges and fields of expertise (medical, academic–intellectual, economic and so on). Conceived as a sovereign authority, the state is a part of a myth of power that characterizes modernity: namely, a repressive instrument emanating from a single, coherent source. Foucault, by contrast, is interested in the operation of power as a positive force dispersed *throughout* society; that is to say, one that does not repress or limit behaviour but creates and encourages certain forms of it. State and government activities are not self-contained but derive from 'a whole series of power networks that invest the body, sexuality, the family, kinship, knowledge, technology and so forth' (Foucault 1980: 122).

In historical studies, Foucault traced the emergence of such networks of power in relation to techniques of control, surveillance and discipline showing how these were adopted within a number of institutional settings in the eighteenth century: prisons, schools, factories, hospitals. These practices made possible new kinds of knowledge about human behaviour leading to the further codification of procedures to monitor and observe subjects, to interview them, to gather information, document and tabulate the results. Such knowledge enabled techniques of moulding behaviour and producing new kinds of person: useful, obedient, and self-monitoring. This form of social control, more subtle than brute force, became increasingly generalized in contemporary society, a 'microphysics of power' in which the human body is the object of knowledges that categorize, problematize, discipline and normalize (Foucault 1977: 24–31).

Subsequently, Foucault drew attention to the exercise of what he called 'bio-power'. In the classical theory of sovereignty a basic power of the sovereign is that over life and death. The sovereign wields the power to decide who shall live and who shall die. Liberal political theory and analysis was concerned precisely with supervising the exercise of that power, regulating the right to restrict, restrain and ultimately to kill. But in the modern era, argues Foucault, governmental power is concerned not only with individuals but with 'the nation' or 'the mass' and 'the people' as a whole, and it has made the conditions of the population (its size, its health, its environment) into objects of policy. No longer is power concerned only with death; it administers to the conditions and processes of life itself. For instance, the study of the ratio of births to deaths helps policies of population management; demography, epidemiology and actuarial inquiry produce knowledge and information making possible intervention into living populations.

Public hygiene becomes an issue of anxiety and its management involves the centralization of power and the development of associated knowledge and applied rationalities. Illness becomes a social and not merely a personal problem, in need of a societal solution, particularly in the case of old age and infirmity. Such sickness requires rationally organized systems of insurance or pensions that the state underwrites. There is also systematic intervention with rational intent into the environment: irrigating, draining and redirecting water flows so as to manage the urban environment with sewage systems or making air quality a policy goal. This creates a relation of state to society or to social action that is not simply repressive or disciplinary. Nor is it easily described in terms of rights. It involves the management of a population and its doings, legitimating and making possible widespread intervention. When population size is an object of policy, intervention into sexual reproduction itself becomes a necessity.

Such activity is not made possible or directed from a single centre of sovereign power. For Foucault it is more like the declaration of a general and permanent state of emergency in society with many agencies, institutions and actors continually developing new techniques and identifying new areas that require examination and intervention. As Foucault put it: 'security mechanisms have to be installed around the random element inherent in a population of living beings so as to optimize a state of life... using overall mechanisms and acting in such a way as to achieve overall states of equilibrium; taking control of life and the biological processes of man-as-species and ensuring that they are not disciplined, but regularized' (2003: 246–7). Such power cannot be referred back to some prior agency that 'wields' it, for its agents are also effects of the practices and knowledges in question (1977: 27–8). Understanding and analysis require examination of the rationalities behind specific interventions; their historical emergence, the reactions they engender and their reformulation.

Foucault's writings on 'governmentality' are thus concerned, not with the disciplinary practices of specific institutions but with techniques for administering whole populations, shaping and guiding the behaviour of subjects who, in modern liberal society, are formally free yet still objects of social policy (see Foucault 1991; Gordon 1991). Individual conduct is not itself the object of policy but, rather, 'the conduct of conduct'; that is, ways of shaping the exercise of freedom. Liberalism, from this perspective, is not just an ideology but also a distinctive 'rationality of government': 'a system of thinking about the nature and practice of government... capable of making some form of that activity thinkable and practicable both to its practitioners and to those upon whom it is practised' (Gordon 1991: 3). Governmental rationalities constitute the objects of government as questions to be solved or failures to be rectified, inviting the formulation of 'programmes' and 'initiatives' which justify the utilization of 'technologies' be they financial measures, legal controls, bargaining procedures, policies of criminalization, efforts to influence diet, exercise and so forth. All are attempts to turn an unruly reality into something amenable to the application of instrumental calculation (Rose and Miller, 1992: 181–7) and government is legitimated in so much as it maintains effectiveness in such domains.

Foucault's work on 'governmentality' has inspired numerous investigations into problematics of government within liberal and neo-liberal discourses (see Burchell *et al.*, 1991; Barry *et al.* 1996; Rose 1999). These have focused on the government of the economy, social policies concerning the family, poverty, the uses of statistics and the nature of welfare and social scientific expertise (see also Rose and Miller 1992; Rose 1996; Rose 1999; Hacking 1991; Donzelot 1980). The technologies employed in these areas, for instance the use of 'experts' in post-war planning, the deployment of incentives to encourage businesses to render themselves more 'competitive', or the recent effort by social democratic states to enhance the role of the 'community' and civil society organizations in delivering welfare, are attempts to alter the behaviour of subjects. The needs and interests, even the physical bodies of citizens (think of housing relocation schemes or hygiene and vaccination programmes) are incorporated within discourses of 'improvement', 'efficiency' and 'care' thereby redefining what those needs, interests and bodies are like. Such technologies and policies do not simply order and command but positively construct types of subject. Such studies demonstrate how the state is one of a number of settings within which the operations of government are exercised. The state does not have a grand function (such as to maintain capitalism or represent the public) to which we can refer back its actions. Rather it grants rationalities 'a temporary institutional durability'. The state, or more particularly the discourses that shape that state, are, as Rose and Miller put it, 'an historically variable linguistic device for conceptualising and articulating ways of ruling' (1992: 177).

The analysis of governmentality highlights the complex and irreducibly plural nature of state practices: indeed, the state begins to look like a variety of porous mini-authorities utilizing knowledge to categorize and shape the subjects that are not alone in the activity of governing. Attention to this complexity has been important in qualifying accounts of the state; both Marxists and feminists have made use of Foucauldian literature to steer away from a purely repressive conception of the state (see Poulantzas 1978; Jessop 1990; Pringle and Watson 1992). The substitution of study of the state for the study of the rationalities contained within it, that may also exceed it, is, we believe, a bold move for political analysis, extending its reach and deepening its scope.

However, invocations of 'the state' or 'government' as though it did represent a unified purpose are frequently made by social and political forces. Despite its organizational diversity, the inviolable symbolic unity of the state is invoked to justify the use of organized force against 'enemies' within and without its boundaries (see Poulantzas 1978: 76–86). At key moments, such as in wartime or during a 'social emergency', the state is invested by certain groups with a unity of purpose that legitimates its distinctive repressive functions and articulates its diverse elements around a relatively coherent project. At such times, the state *does* employ 'repressive' sovereign power in deciding who can live and who shall die. We might need to combine Foucauldian analyses with the study of 'hegemony' and the formation of identities in international space.

Conclusions

We do not, as Hegel did, think that the state is an incarnation of reason. But we do conceive of the state as governing through and by forms of rationality. Poststructuralist approaches to the state do not seek to dismiss the desire for order, simply to collapse reason into a dizzying multiplicity of language games. The world can do that for us. We want only to underline the way in which rationalities are drawn on at the same time as constantly coming up against their limits. These need to be understood in their own right (as dynamic elements of political processes) rather than as expressions of some underlying determining principle.

Poststructuralism does not, of itself, legitimate any specific political orientation. It does however, take a certain attitude towards the world and to the 'the political' as such; to the wider, paradigmatic contexts within which politics (in a narrow sense) are conducted and which are constituted through forms of power and exclusion too often hidden by an exclusive focus on politics as negotiation, bargaining and dialogue. For poststructuralists, the state is positioned somewhat ambiguously towards the political understood in this sense. For it is a site of politics that nevertheless functions by closing down the parameters of the political.

We have seen this, for instance, in arguments about hegemony as well as in views about spatial representation in geopolitics. The state, it is implied, can only secure its management of the wider environment by delimiting politics and subjecting it to forms of reasoning that determine in advance the nature of the 'political game'. Thus the state is both a site of politics and also a source of depoliticization. Whether it be through social and economic policies or action within the international environment, states govern by defining the field in which they can be understood to act, thus making their environment governable by holding off alternative ways of defining the situation. This paradoxical depoliticization, we suggest, is not simply a vice that we put up with in an uncertain world; it is the ineradicable condition of all efforts to impose order on the world and, hence, the very condition of politics itself.

Further reading

Burchell, Graham (ed.) (1991) *The Foucault Effect: Studies in Governmentality* (Chicago: University of Chicago Press).

Edkins, Jenny (1999) *Poststructuralism and International Relations: Bringing the Political Back In* (Boulder, CO: Lynne Rienner).

Finlayson, Alan and Valentine, Jeremy (eds) (2002) *Politics and Poststructuralism* (Edinburgh: Edinburgh University Press).

Howarth, David (2000) *Discourse* (Milton Keynes: Open University Press).

Howarth, David, Norval, Aletta and Stavrakakis, Yannis (2000) *Discourse Theory and Political Analysis: Identities, Hegemonies and Social Change* (Manchester: Manchester University Press).

Rose, Nikolas (1999) *Powers of Freedom* (Cambridge: Cambridge University Press).

Torfing, Jacob (1998) *New Theories of Discourse: Laclau, Mouffe and Zizek* (Oxford: Blackwell).

Walker, R. J. B. (1992) *Inside/Outside: International Relations as Political Theory* (Cambridge: Cambridge University Press).

Chapter 9

Globalization and the State

DAVID MARSH, NICOLA J. SMITH AND NICOLA HOTHI

There appears to be a veritable industry of academic work on globalization, which reflects, in turn, the way in which this term has entered into common currency in the media and even in public discourse. The issue of globalization, and especially the extent to which the process constrains the autonomy of the nation state and makes the pursuit of neo-liberal economic solutions and the marketization of all aspects of life inevitable, is a crucial one for at least two reasons. First, and most important, the issue is crucial for the future of social democracy; if many of the proponents of the globalization thesis are right, then social democracy is doomed. Second, any consideration of the issue throws light on two of the crucial meta-theoretical questions in social science, the relationships between structure and agency and between the material and the ideational. As such, our aim here is to examine, mainly conceptually, but also empirically, the contention that globalization severely restricts the autonomy of the state. Our view is that it is a relationship which is both rarely unpacked and more complicated that most treatments assume.

The globalization debate

Globalization, as a concept, is both highly fashionable and highly contested. Over the past decade, a huge academic literature has developed on the subject. To provide an exhaustive account of this vast and ever-expanding literature is clearly an impossible task. Nevertheless, it is possible to identify five distinct 'schools of thought' within the globalization literature. These are: the hyperglobalist thesis; the sceptical thesis; the complex globalization thesis; the new institutionalist thesis; and the ideational thesis. Here, we outline each of these in turn.

The hyperglobalist thesis

The hyperglobalist thesis is the original and most famous position in the globalization debate. It is associated with a range of highly influential authors such as Robert Reich (1991) and Kenichi Ohmae (1996). For these authors, the world we now live in is dramatically different from twenty or thirty years ago. Whereas nation-states once dominated the global economic map, the world is now 'borderless' in character. This is particularly so in economic terms. Heightened flows of goods, capital, labour and information are believed to move effortlessly across national borders. For example, inflows of foreign direct investment (i.e. investment by firms in other countries) have risen dramatically in recent years (from $59 billion in 1982 to $651 billion in 2002) (UNCTAD 2003). These developments are believed to have 'shrunk' the world, so that it is a much smaller place in terms of geographical distance. For example, it is possible to send an email across the world in seconds or travel across the world physically in just a few hours. This means that investors can transfer vast amounts of money to other countries by simply clicking on a mouse. Indeed, for O'Brien (1992), we have witnessed the 'end of geography'.

For the hyperglobalists, this has profound implications for the role of nation-states (see for instance Gray 1998; Greider 1997; Ohmae 1996). The movement of goods, capital and labour across national borders is believed to undermine the role of national governance. For example, in a 'borderless world', companies can simply pick and choose where to invest, since they are no longer constrained by geography. Since companies are primarily interested in profits, they will be attracted to low-cost locations. This places pressure on governments to keep taxation costs as low as possible, so that firms are not tempted to move elsewhere, taking jobs and money with them. In turn, this has massive social and political implications. If governments face pressure to reduce taxation, this severely reduces their ability to fund 'public goods' such as health and education. Globalization is therefore associated with the growth of a truly free market. Governments should not try to interfere in the economy because the market will always win out. Indeed, Ohmae (1996) argues that globalization has led to the 'end of the nation-state'.

The sceptical thesis

Whilst the hyperglobalist thesis is extremely influential, it has been challenged by a number of sceptical theorists such as Hirst and Thompson (1999), Rugman (2000), Wade (1996) and Zysman (1994). For these authors, the world today is not so different from what it was like even a century ago. In some respects – such as levels of trade and investment – the world economy is actually *less* open and integrated than it was before the First World War. The sceptics also question claims that the world today is 'borderless'. As Hirst and Thompson (1999) note, flows of trade and investment are far from 'global'. Rather, they are highly concentrated within the 'triad' of North America, Europe and Japan. In contrast, the developing countries receive only a minimal share of investment and trade. They estimate that two-thirds of the world's population received just 16 per cent of foreign direct investment in the early 1990s. Nor can capital move effortlessly across national borders, as the extreme globalizers assume. In fact, if a company has invested a great deal of time and money in a particular location (for example, through training staff), the cost of 'exit' is considerable – indeed, it can be greater than paying higher taxes. Rather than being truly 'global', most firms continue to operate from a distinct home base (Wade 1996).

Thus, for the sceptics, the world economy is far from being globalized. Rather, it remains: 'an open international economy that is still fundamentally characterized by exchange between relatively distinct national economies and in which many outcomes, such as the competitive performance of firms and sectors, are substantially determined by processes occurring at the national level' (Hirst and Thompson 1999: 7). Claims that the nation-state is in decline are thus 'at best, premature and, at worst, ill founded' (Gertler 1992: 48). Indeed, the sceptics point to the *growth* of government in the post-war period. For example, the share of government expenditures in GDP averaged 47 per cent in the mid-1990s, compared to just 21 per cent before the Second World War (Rodrik 1997: 49). For the sceptical authors, then, globalization has not laid waste the nation-state, for governments can and do continue to play an important role in the economy.

The complex globalization thesis

However, for authors such as Held, *et al.* (1999) and Dicken (2003), we should conceptualize globalization rather differently. Rather than seeing globalization as an end-state (i.e. something that has *already* happened), they argue that we should see it as a *process* (i.e. something is happen*ing*). Whilst trade and investment flows are far from global (in that they are concentrated within the 'triad'), the rise of regional trading blocs is itself part of a wider process of globalization (see, for instance, Breslin and Higgott 2000). For example, countries wishing to join the European Union (EU) must adopt liberalizing measures, in turn opening up their economies to the world as a whole.

For these authors, then, the world today *is* different from what it was like a century ago. Whilst the *level* of integration is similar, the *nature* of integration is not. This is because it is much deeper, including not only the trade of goods and services between countries, but also the production of goods and services in other countries. For example, three-quarters of Ford cars used to be made in the US, but now less than one quarter are made there. Indeed, the name 'Mondeo' means 'world car'. However, this does not mean that the world is now 'borderless'. Rather, authors such as Dicken (2003) emphasize the considerable unevenness of the world economic map, with each activity being 'grounded' in a specific location. Yet, this is in itself seen as part and parcel of the globalization process, which entails: 'a reconfiguration of power at all levels and the production of new spaces' (Bernard 2000: 153).

In this sense, the complex globalization theorists argue that the world *is* undergoing a fundamental transformation. However, this is quite different from that envisaged by the hyperglobalist theorists, not least because it is not primarily economic. Rather, authors such as Held *et al.* (1999) point to a wide variety of changes, politically, socially and culturally. For example, Robertson (1992) argues that we have seen a rise in 'global consciousness' – the sense that we are all part of a wider community. Thus, globalization is a highly complex (set of) process(es) rather than an end-state – the world may not be global*ized*, but it is global*izing*.

For the complex globalization theorists, this has important implications for the role of nation-states. Whilst they reject claims that globalization has laid waste the nation-state, they do believe that it has changed their role (Cerny 1997; Giddens 1999; Scholte 2000). As Dicken (2003) writes: 'the position of the state is being redefined in the context of a polycentric political-economic system in which national boundaries are more permeable than in the past'. State power is seen to have shifted not only upwards (to international organizations and movements) and downwards (for example to local pressure groups) but also sideways to market actors (such as multinational corporations). This shift in power from states to markets is believed to have heightened competitiveness between nations, so that governments must increasingly give priority to the need to compete in economic terms rather than to social issues such as the distribution of wealth (Cerny 1997). As evidence of this, complex globalization theorists point to a variety of neo-liberal (or market-oriented) measures such as privatization within and outside Europe. Nor is government spending as generous as the sceptical theorists imply. As Rhodes (1997) contends, increased welfare spending can largely be explained in terms of such factors as demographic pressure and low economic growth. Once these factors are accounted for, a process of welfare retrenchment *is* in fact evident. In this sense, whilst there has been no 'triumph of neo-liberalism', there has nevertheless been a *shift towards* neo-liberalism across the world.

The new institutionalist thesis

While the complex thesis has proved phenomenally influential in the globalization literature, another position to achieve considerable prominence is that of the self-titled 'new institutionalists'. As this name suggests, authors such as Hall and Soskice (2001), Garrett (1998), Weiss (2003) and Scharpf

(2000) aim to 'bring institutions back in' to the study of globalization and, indeed, capitalism more generally. While nations may experience common pressures, they argue, the existence of different institutional and cultural environments means that they respond in different ways and achieve different outcomes. In this sense, they argue: 'domestic institutions, depending on their characteristics, can hinder or enable states to respond to new challenges and accomplish new tasks, thus softening, neutralizing, or exaggerating the potentially constraining effects of global markets' (Weiss 2003: 27–8).

Thus, new institutionalists contend that globalization may actually serve to enable nation-states rather than simply constrain them. Indeed, Garrett (1998) argues that it is not *despite*, but *because of*, globalization that social democratic countries have continued to thrive. This is because globalization rewards 'coherent' strategies – whether market liberal or social democratic corporatist – but punishes 'incoherent' regimes. Social democratic corporatist regimes can offer significant benefits to business (such as co-operation between employers and employees and a highly skilled workforce) that provide greater returns on investment than would a low taxation environment. On these grounds, the institutionalists agree wholeheartedly with the sceptics that considerable scope remains for government intervention in economic and social affairs. However, unlike the sceptics, this does not lead them to reject globalization as a 'myth'. Rather, globalization is associated with continuing – and even growing – *divergence* between market liberal and social democratic regimes (Garrett 1998; Hall and Soskice 2001; Weiss 2003). In this sense, globalization is still seen as a crucial driving force for change.

The ideational globalization thesis

Just as the complex globalization theorists have attempted to reclaim the concept of globalization, another group of authors have sought to question (or 'demystify') it (see in particular Hay and Marsh 2000). In so doing, they adopt a rather different approach from the hyperglobalists, sceptics, complex theorists and new institutionalists. In particular, these authors contend that we should not only look at globalization in terms of whether it exists or not. Rather, we should also look at in *ideational* terms (i.e. in terms of the *idea* of globalization, as opposed to its 'material reality'). Their approach reflects a broader shift within the social sciences towards a greater emphasis of the role of ideas in shaping social and political change.

Why then should we look at the role of ideas? Another way of looking at this issue is to ask: do we always have a perfect knowledge of the world in which we live? The answer is clearly 'no'. This means that we have to *interpret* the world – our *ideas* about the world shape our behaviour. Consider, for example, the rise of the Soviet Union. The fact that leaders like Lenin believed in Marxist ideas shaped their actions, *whether or not Marxism was actually true*. In other words, ideas can play an independent causal role in shaping outcomes; ideas can have 'material effects'.

This has important implications for the debate about globalization and the state. For Hay (2000), there has indeed been a policy shift towards neo-liberalism within and outside Europe. However, this does not mean that globalization actually exists, as complex globalization theorists assume. Rather, Hay (2004) agrees with the sceptics that there is little empirical evidence to suggest that the world has been 'globalized'. He finds that European countries have actually been *de*-globalized in recent years in that geographical distance has become more rather than less important in terms of both trade and investment flows. Nevertheless, globalization may play a powerful role in ideational terms. If policy-makers *believe* in globalization, this is likely to shape their approach *whether or not globalization actually exists*. In other words, neo-liberal *ideas* might be creating neo-liberal *policies*. In turn, this might serve to undermine the nation-state. Governments might actually be adopting policies that, in turn, affect their power and sovereignty. For example, in joining European and Monetary Union (EMU), states have signed up to the Stability and Growth Pact, in turn affecting how much they can spend.

In this sense, globalization may be something of a self-fulfilling prophecy. By behaving *as if* it were a reality, policy-makers may actually be *making* it a reality. For Hay, globalization is thus best understood as a (political) consequence rather than as an (economic) cause. This is crucial, for it opens up the potential for change. Conceived as a contingent outcome rather than as an external logic, globalization can ultimately be shaped, or perhaps even resisted altogether. As Hay and Marsh (2000: 14) write, we must 'rediscover the capacity (that the rhetoric of globalization so frequently denies us) of shaping, steering and ultimately transforming the globalized world that we have made and which we must now inhabit'.

This 'ideational' approach is important because of its focus on the role of ideas, although it is not without problems. There is no doubt that the relationship between ideas, material relations and policy outcomes are insufficiently unpacked in the existing literature. As we saw, hyperglobalists argue that globalization leads to policy outcomes in a largely unmediated way. Both sceptics and complex globalization theorists argue that external economic processes are mediated by institutional factors in a given country and it is as mediated that they affect policy outcomes. However, they do not acknowledge the putative independent effect of the discourse(s) of globalization. In contrast, the ideational theorists see the discursive construction of globalization as a, perhaps the, crucial explanatory variable in explaining policy outcomes. As we will discuss below, however, their approach also raises questions about how those ideas relate to the broader economic and political context in which they are constituted. Our argument here is that any full appreciation of the policy options available to, and pursued by, the state needs to consider: the external economic environment in which states are situated; the distinctive ways in which such pressures are mediated by existing institutional and cultural environments (not least at the national level); the discursive construction of those pressures; and, finally, the way in which such discourses are mediated by the broader context in which they are situated. In the following section we will discuss each of these issues in turn.

Unpacking the relationship between economic processes, discourse(s) and policy outcomes

In this section our aim is to examine the relationship between economic process(es), globalization discourse and policy outcomes. Our intention is to show that these relationships are highly complex and, as such, need to be unpacked.

Globalization: the obsession with measurement

We shall spend relatively little space on this issue, although it is the one that has attracted most attention. As we have already indicated, there is considerable controversy about the extent, nature and impact of globalization. In our view, however, this debate generates more heat than light. The sceptics were rightly highly critical of the hyperglobalists. Hirst and Thompson (1999) presented solid empirical evidence that the world is neither 'globalized' nor 'borderless'. However, Held *et al.*'s (1999) book is itself a response to the sceptics; after all the hyperglobalists had already been routed in empirical, if not in discursive, terms. Hay (2004b) sides with Hirst and Thompson, particularly emphasizing regionalization, and uses gravity models to show that trade and investment within Europe have actually become 'de-globalized'.

These issues are certainly important, but they should also not distract us from three main points. First, all countries are much more exposed to international, that is non-domestic, economic pressures than they were previously. This is something that none of the authors discussed above would dispute. Second, all countries are exposed in different ways and to different extents to external economic pressures; so what matters when examining each country is its position rather than the overall 'global' picture. Third, and here Hirst and Thompson, Held *et al.* and Hay would agree, the effect of these changes on policy outcomes is not automatic. In any given country the impact of external economic pressures is shaped partly by the economic and political institutional structures of that country and partly by policy-makers' perceptions of the extent of the country's exposure to international forces and the economic and political structural constraints.

Our major argument here bears reiteration. Let us not become obsessed with arguments about measuring globalization to the extent that we ignore other important issues.

Let us take the intervening variables seriously

It is worth beginning here by restating one of Held *et al.*'s conclusions with which we are sure Hirst and Thompson, Weiss and Hay would concur. External economic pressures (whether 'global', 'international' or 'regional') are

> mediated significantly by state's position in global political, military and economic hierarchies; its domestic economic and political structures; the institutional pattern of domestic politics; and specific government as well as societal strategies for contesting, managing or ameliorating globalizing imperatives.

It is difficult to take issue with this view, partly because it takes a scattergun approach evoking such a wide variety of variables. Certainly, it is a view that needs unpacking. Perhaps the best way to do so is to treat each of its elements separately.

(a) International political, military and economic position

Of course there are (at least) three variables here, although they are obviously related. We shall briefly consider them, focusing on the UK case. We have already dealt in passing with the importance of a state's economic position. However, it seems to us that this issue has been somewhat ignored in the literature which, as we saw, focuses very much on the debate about the aggregate level of globalization/regionalization. Clearly, not all states are inserted into the international economy to the same extent in the same way and these differences are likely to have some effect on states' policy decisions. So, as an example, it is clear that the UK is more integrated into, and thus more likely to be exposed to/affected by, the international economy, than most other European (and indeed OECD) countries. Indeed, A. T. Kearney (2003) figures reveal that, out of 62 countries in 2001, the UK ranked: fourth in terms of total merchandise and services trade; fourth in terms of total FDI inflows and outflows; third in terms of total transfer payments and receipts; second in terms of income payments and receipts; and fourth in terms of total portfolio investment inflows and outflows. Of course, this doesn't mean that its government is inevitably more constrained. However, it is a factor that needs to be considered.

The UK has always been more integrated into the international economy than other countries because of its political and military history. Its imperial, indeed hegemonic, role was particularly strongly reflected in overseas investment (Held *et al.* 1999; Hirst and Thompson 1999). This is not the place to take this argument further, but there is clear path dependency involved here. The UK's past international political and economic orientation in part explains its current high level of integration into the international economy. At the same time, given the key role that financial markets play in the international economy, London's historic role as a financial sector clearly gave it an enormous advantage when financial markets were liberalized in the 1980s. Of course, the UK's world role has declined throughout the last century, but, in the more recent period, its integration into Europe in both economic, and more reluctantly political, terms has increased. The issues involved here are beyond the scope of this paper, but it is important to emphasize one point. Any full understanding of the way in which the internationalization/globalization of economic relations has affected government policy needs to recognise how the changing nature of, in this case, Britain's political/military role has mediated that relationship.

(b) Domestic economic context

The economic structure

The domestic economic situation in a country clearly affects its government's response to international economic pressures. Held *et al.* highlight the economic structure, and that clearly is an important factor. Indeed, Hirst and Thompson (1999) offer an interesting comparison between Sweden and Denmark. They argue that the crisis of the Swedish welfare state has been significantly influenced by the particular structure of the Swedish economy. The economy is strongly export-orientated, with about half of the output of Swedish firms produced abroad, and it is dominated by a few very large Swedish MNCs. At the same time, there are very high levels of public employment. The policy consensus within Swedish society collapsed in the 1980s and in the early 1990s the major employers used their economic position to reject the corporatist bargaining and governance agreements which were an institutional manifestation of this consensus. So, in 1990 the Swedish Employers Federation abandoned central wage bargaining and in 1991 they withdrew from the tripartite institutions of economic governance. As Hirst and Thompson (1999: 169) conclude:

> Sweden's problems are clearly due to a mixture of economic structure, policy errors and conjunctural factors, but the heavy dependence of the economy on large multinational manufacturing exporters, on the

one hand, and public employment on the other, severely limited the options available.

Denmark's experience in the same period, the late 1980s and 1990s, was very different, which itself suggests that any relationship between internationalization and reduced welfare provision is very problematic at best. Economic concentration is much lower in Denmark than in Sweden; numerous small and medium-size firms play a crucial role in the Danish economy. There is no highly centralized corporatist structure, but unemployment benefits are generous and the benefit system is characterized by a high degree of universalism. A combination of this benefit system and an active labour market policy means that the unemployed are not marginalized. In Hirst and Thompson's (1999: 175) view:

> Danish citizens and organized interests seem to have been willing to adapt to crises, making sacrifices in periods of economic difficulty. Undoubtedly, equality and inclusion help to promote such solidaristic and public-minded behaviour: citizens and organized interests have a high degree of influence in the political process and a reasonable expectation that of fairness in the behaviour of governments and other political actors.

Of course, this raises the issue we will discuss next; the domestic political context. However, in Hirst and Thompson's view the structure of the Danish economy, together with the structure of the welfare state, the political context and the political culture, have shaped Denmark's response to international economic pressures.

Corporatist structures

In this comparison Hirst and Thompson raise the issue of the role of corporatist structures, which are probably best understood as politico-economic structures. The existence of such structures can clearly mediate the affect of internationalization on policy outcomes. This is evident in another case which Hirst and Thompson briefly examine: the Netherlands. The Netherlands economy is highly internationalized; indeed in terms of trade it is probably the most internationalized economy in the world. However, it has a network of dense corporatist institutions, and, since 1982, a policy of wage moderation which was negotiated, and renegotiated in 1993, with the employers and the unions. Indeed, Hirst and Thompson (1999: 177), citing Visser and Hemerijck's book *A Dutch Miracle*, emphasize that many observers argue that institutionalized wage restraint has been Holland's single most important weapon in responding to international competition. In Hirst and Thompson's view, these corporatist negotiations, together with the consociational nature of the Dutch political structure, have been crucial in allowing Holland to cope with increased international pressure while retaining high welfare expenditure. Similar conclusions have been drawn about Germany and Austria (Ebbinhaus and Hassel 1999; Schmitter and Grote 1997; Vitols and Casper 1997).

Hirst and Thompson (1999: 180–5) also point out that one of the responses to international competitive pressures in Europe has been a move towards, rather than away from, social pacts/corporatist structures. It is true that these developments have been mainly confined to smaller states, for example, Finland, Ireland, Portugal, Norway and Spain. However, the Italian case is also interesting. Here, reform was initiated from the top, but involved co-operation with unions and employers on wage policy, industrial relations and welfare state reform. Much of the pressure for reform was exogenous, coming particularly from the conditions attached to ERM membership. Nevertheless, the move towards concertation was also affected by the state of domestic public finances, the structure of the Italian pension system and the collapse of the old political system in 1992. The result was: the abolition of the *scala mobile* (which involved 100 per cent indexation of wages to inflation) and the institution of a wage freeze in 1992; the establishment of a new framework of incomes policy and collective bargaining in 1993; and a new accord on pensions, approved by a referendum in 1995. The point again is that the relationship between globalization, corporatist structures and policy outcomes is not a simple one.

There are two separate but related points here; the first concerns the existence, or otherwise, of corporatist structures; the second concerns their role; and the third concerns their effect. Increased international competition, may lead to the creation of, or continued reliance on, corporatist structures as in the cases briefly examined above. On the other hand, a government may respond to such pressures by withdrawing from involvement in discussions over prices and incomes, as was the case in the UK after 1979. Which strategy a particular government pursues is likely to be affected by the domestic economic and political context.

Of course, even when a government has created, or continued to use existing, corporatist structures, this does not mean that those structures performed the same function in the 1980s and 1990s as they had in the 1960s and 1970s. So, Martin Rhodes (1997) argues that the competitive corporatism of the 1980s and 1990s was designed to enhance international competitiveness, rather than sharing the egalitarian and redistributive goals of old corporatism. In his view, the exchange relationship involve in contemporary corporatism is crucially different because what unions get is not rights and entitlements, but voice and the chance to influence labour market and welfare policy.

In a sense, the crucial question is whether the existence of such corporatist structures effect what governments do. Hirst and Thompson (1999) certainly suggest they do and, in particular, that they help ensure continued higher welfare provision. In a similar vein, in the case of Australia, some observers have argued that the corporatism, associated with the eight Accords agreed between the Australian Council of Trade Unions (ACTU) during its time in office between 1983 and 1996, had an important influence on labour market and industrial policy during that period (Capling and Galligan 1992; Goldfinch 2000; Singleton 1990). Indeed, Capling and Galligan (1992) contend that Australia liberalized its trade regime only after establishing a number of corporatist-style industry plans that were designed to allow the industry to respond more effectively to international competition. The point is that the existence of these Accords, particular in the 1980s, taken together with political/electoral considerations which we discuss below, was an important factor in influencing the way in which pressures of international competitiveness affected policy outcomes.

Prior economic policies

Of course, it is not just the structure of the economy or the existence, or otherwise, of corporatist structures, that has an effect. Even if we don't embrace the full force of Rose's (1990) argument that, in the realms of policy-making and delivery, inheritance is more important than choice, nevertheless, current policies are clearly shaped by past policies. In this way, if we take the UK as an example, the move towards neo-liberal economic policies, and particularly the speed with which the UK embraced both privatization and active labour market policies, owes a great deal to the limited nature of its social democracy in the earlier period. There is a good deal of literature which questions whether the UK ever had Keynesianism, social democracy or a post-war consensus (for a review of this see Kerr 2001). The thrust of this argument is that there was a great deal of continuity in British economic policy pre-war, during the so-called post-war consensus and during Thatcherism. The key policy during all this period was the defence of sterling. Most observers would not agree with the Kerr and Marsh (1999) line that Thatcherism was a embodiment of, as much as a break with, the past. However, most would acknowledge that the UK's social democracy was of a particular and limited kind that made the conversion to neo-liberalism easier than in Europe.

(c) The domestic socio-political context

As we already argued one of the problems with much of the literature on globalization is that it is economistic. It focuses on economic developments and sees them as determining, or strongly constraining, the political decisions of government. However, political and social structures also constrain or facilitate governments.

The political structure

Political structures can clearly act as a constraint on radical change, and so mediate the effect of global economic pressures. Certainly, it is easier to change policy direction in systems characterized by strong executive government. So, Hirst and Thompson (1999: 174) argue:

> Denmark...does not lack the elite voices that have been so successful in transforming countries like the UK and then New Zealand in an anti-welfare direction. What has been missing is political capacity. Most Danish governments have been coalitions without large majorities. Confronted with strong public support for welfare, political parties have hesitated to follow arguments for radical reform.

Indeed, the New Zealand case is particularly interesting here. The Labour government elected in 1984 embarked on a far-reaching programme of economic liberalism. With a secure parliamentary majority, the government was able to push through these changes, despite the fact that it had not campaigned on a programme of economic reform (Goldfinch 2000). However, in 1996 New Zealand introduced a mixed member proportional (MMP) system, after 150 years of majoritarian electoral rules, in large part in order to prevent any future government embarking on such radical new directions without a real mandate or consultation with social interests. It is hard to think that there could be better evidence of the role that political structures can play.

Federal structures can also affect a government's capacity to respond to increased global competition. In federal structures, particularly ones like Australia where strong second chambers represent state interests, central government has to take account of those interests. Indeed, Goldfinch (2000) suggests that Australia's federal structure was an important factor that helps explain the different development, and success, of economic rationalist policies in Australia as compared to New Zealand.

Changes in social and political values

The 1980s and 1990s may have been marked by an increased international-ization of economic competition. However, there has also been a growth in the importance of environmental and gender issues in political terms and of social movements that campaigned on these issues both nationally and internationally. In addition, in countries like Australia, New Zealand and Canada, there has been a rise in the importance of issues surrounding the treatment of indigenous people. Two points are important here. First, these issues affected voters' and governments' behaviour (on their influence in Australia and New Zealand see Goldfinch 2000). Second, the relationship between such issues and increased economic competitiveness is a complicated, and often antagonistic, one. In particular, environmentalists and campaigners for indigenous rights often see TNCs as an important part of the problem. As such, in responding to such issues, for ideological or electoral reasons, governments may be going against the interest of TNCs of international financial markets.

In contrast, Keating (2000) presents a different picture of changing social and political values in Australia in this period. He suggests that increased education and a more open society has lead to increased prosperity for most. At the same time, economic changes have also resulted in less security, a greater scepticism about authority, political disaffection and, perhaps particularly, greater individualism and less willingness to support higher taxes. He argues that government policy is affected by these changes. Australian governments have tried to respond by targeting services, creating more efficient and effective delivery, but not by challenging the electorate on taxes.

It is not our concern here to adjudicate on this debate or to claim Australia as a typical case. Rather, we want to emphasize two points. First, it is crucial to put the economic changes in the context of other social changes and not, by definition, to privilege them. Second, and this follows, it is also important to examine how economic change, economic values, social change and social and political values relate. Third, and this returns us to the main theme of this piece, one certainly can't read off policy consequences, or present and future policy trajectories merely from a knowledge of increasing international competition (see, for instance, Kelly 1992).

Electoral constraints

Political parties exist, in large part, to try to win power. As such, the behaviour of governments is invariably influenced by their desire to be re-elected. Obviously, the economic performance of government has a crucial effect on their re-election chances; although, as we shall argue below, the discursive construction of that economic performance, and how it is perceived by the electorate, may also be particularly important. However, other factors, like those discussed in the last section also affect voting behaviour and government's judgements of which policies will win or lose votes. In addition, governments may have particular links, structural, historical or ideological with particular interest that affect their policy decisions. In this vein, the Australian example is again revealing. While the Hawke and Keating governments pursued economic rationalist policies, driven in large part by international economic competitiveness pressures, they were also faced with other social developments that had electoral resonance and operated in a political context in which their historic links with the trade union movement were important.

(d) Discourses

The final issue to be addressed is the role of discourses in shaping political outcomes. For Hay (2004b), the real power of globalization lies not in its material 'reality' but in its discursive construction. In particular, he argues that: the extent of globalization is contestable (here of course his position shares much with Hirst and Thompson); the link between welfare expenditure and international competitiveness is complex, so that there is a strong argument that welfare spending can lead to greater, not less, competitiveness; and there are contested discourses of globalization and the mix between those discourses differs across time and space. With Rosamond, Hay also outlines several conditions under which ideas about globalization are used instead of European integration, and vice versa. For example, they argue that globalization is more likely to be invoked where European integration is unpopular and uncontested, where the government cannot claim to be influential in the process of integration, where the approach to integration has traditionally been arms-length, and where globalization is conceived positively (Hay and Rosamond 2002).

While Hay plausibly suggests *that* ideas about globalization play an important role in shaping political outcomes, his work also raises important questions (which Hay himself acknowledges) about how such discourses relate to the broader economic, political and cultural context in which they are situated. For, any full understanding of globalization needs to explore: the actual economic processes which constrain states; the discursive construction of those constraints; and the way in such discourses are, in turn, shaped by the context in which they are constituted. To cite Heffernan (2002: 749), ideas 'have to work with, rather than against, the grain of social, political and economic interests, within and without the state, and in line with the demands of the economy'. This means exploring not only the dominant discourses used by political elites but also the wider context in which these discourses are situated. As Blyth (1997: 238) notes: 'The elite game may tell us how the ideas get from the blackboard to the party, but not how or why certain ideas come to be accepted over others.' So, if ideas are to be treated seriously, then we need to consider the reasons *why* particular discourses (in this case, of globalization) have come to dominate.

Let us again use the UK as a case. As we have seen, the actual extent of globalization is limited, although the UK is more exposed to external economic pressures than other OECD countries. However, the Labour government argues very strongly that globalization means that there is no alternative but to pursue neo-liberal policies (Watson and Hay 2003; Hay and Smith 2005). So, the government is constrained not by the 'reality' of globalization, but by the dominant discourse of/about globalization.

All of this raises the obvious question: *why* does the Labour government pursue neo-liberal policies if the economic pressures to do so are much less pressing than some argue? If we work the various implications to this question through, then we see that the relationship(s) between realit(ies) and discourse(s) is very complex.

One might argue that New Labour simply do not know the truth. There may be some validity to this argument. As Hay (2002) rightly notes, actors do not possess perfect information about the context in which they find themselves but instead have to interpret that context – and their interpretations may be wrong. Yet, ideas must also have some resonance with people's experiences if they are to be adopted (Marsh 1999). As we have noted, many countries are indeed more exposed to international pressures than they were previously. The concept of globalization may therefore be powerful precisely because it *seems* to capture 'real' processes. As Walsh (2000: 485) writes: 'ideas reduce uncertainty about how the social world operates by providing decision makers with simplified models of reality'. Of course this reality may be grossly distorted. However, the key point here is that New Labour's discourse of globalization has not simply emerged from thin air, but instead relates, at least in part, to 'real' economic processes.

One might also posit that New Labour has pursued neo-liberal policies because they think that they are the best, using the globalization argument as a useful one to buttress their view. Here, of course, globalization becomes an opportunity, rather than a constraint (in the same way that, Europe can act as an opportunity, not just a constraint, especially for the Conservatives). In particular, New Labour uses the globalization argument to suggest they have no alternative but to pursue neo-liberal economic policies, so they are not to blame for any cuts in welfare or increases in inequality. This has certainly been a useful tool for New Labour in reducing the extent and effectiveness of 'Old Labour' attacks on economic policy.

But, even if we take this line, it leads immediately to another question: why might New Labour think neo-liberal policies were the best? Here we might look at the role of the external economic context (Britain's exposure to international markets is greater than elsewhere in Europe). In contrast, one might suggest that New Labour's policy preferences are driven by political, especially electoral, considerations. So, they may pursue these policies to create an image of governing economic competence within an electoral and party institutional setting. That argument opens up other interesting lines: if governments are largely driven by winning elections, and if elections are decided around the issue of governing economic competence, then the crucial concern is what shapes images of governing economic competence? This takes us back to 'real' economic performance and how that is, in turn, discursively constructed.

This relates to a further point, for discourses are not just mediated by material factors but also by existing discourses. Ideas about globalization may appeal, in part, because they are a means to re-articulate existing discourses, and particularly that of neo-liberalism. As Hirst and Thompson (Hirst and Thompson 1999: 262) argue, the rhetoric of globalization was a godsend for the Right, providing a new argument in favour of de-regulation, free trade and public sector cutbacks 'after the disastrous failure of the monetarist and individualist policy experiments of the 1980s'.

In turn, ideas must also resonate with broader social and cultural discourses if they are to be successful. In Ireland, for example, ideas about globalization have fed into existing discourses of national identity (Smith 2005). Since the 1960s, Irish nationalism has: 'proceeded from an assumption that the primary objective was to reap the benefits from full economic participation in the world economy' (Breen, Hannan *et al.* 1990: 38). Globalization has been presented as a means through which Ireland could become an equal on the international stage, both economically and politically. As one Irish politician declared, globalization means: 'we are all great powers now' (O'Donnell 1997).

By this token, however, existing discourses do not necessarily facilitate particular ideas but can also constrain them. In Australia, for example, the dominant discourse of globalization has been challenged by appeals to existing anti-immigration sentiment, articulated in terms of 'One Nation'. This discursive struggle is occurring within the context of broader social and political changes, such as the challenging of white settler culture and the championing of aboriginal rights. As Johnson (2000: 146) writes: 'Issues of gender, sexuality, race and ethnicity are challenging older power relations and conceptions of liberal citizenship ... Key economic issues include the changing relationships between state and economy in Australian discourse associated with the development of neo-liberal ideology'. This contestation may be a worldwide phenomenon – highlighted by the truly international nature of the anti-globalization movement. Indeed, even in countries where globalization discourse has come to dominate it is contested. In Ireland, for example, the electorate's rejection of the Nice Treaty on EU enlargement was seen, in part, to reflect anti-globalization sentiment and a growing sense of discontent with the dominant policy paradigm (*Irish Times*, 9 June 2001). Once again, this highlights the highly complex and contingent way in which globalization discourse is used.

Conclusion

The aim of this chapter has been twofold: first, to outline the various positions in the globalization literature, particularly, in relation to the affect of globalization on the nation state; and, second, to examine in greater detail the complex relationship between economic processes, discourse(s) and policy outcomes. In so doing, we have made three core claims. First, and in contrast to many conventional accounts, we have argued that one cannot read the 'hollowing out' of the state from globalization. This is not only because external economic pressures are crucially mediated within distinctive national contexts but also, as Hay demonstrates, because these economic pressures are by no means 'globalized'. Second – and again in contrast to most conventional accounts, including the complex globalization thesis – we have emphasized the need to take the role of discourses seriously. Whilst external economic factors certainly influence the policy options available to a state, the discursive construction of that context also crucially mediates governments' responses. Third – and this is where we engage with Hay's approach – those discourses do not, however, simply emerge from thin air. Rather, they are crucially mediated by the broader economic, political and cultural context in which they are situated. In this sense, the relationship between the material and the ideational is best seen as dialectical; that is, interactive and iterative. So, the question is not so much whether economic pressures, political factors, ideational factors and so on 'matter', but rather how they might be unpacked in order to investigate the complex way in which they interact within specific contexts. We have attempted to give a flavour of how this might be done through a variety of different examples and country case studies.

Further reading

Dicken, P. (2003) *Global Shift: Reshaping the Global Economic Map in the 21st Century* (London: Sage).

Hay, C. and Marsh, D. (2000) *Demystifying Globalization* (Basingstoke and New York: Macmillan).

Held, D. *et al.* (1999) *Global Transformations: Politics, Economics and Culture* (Cambridge: Polity).

Hirst, P. and Thompson, G. (1999) *Globalization in Question: The International Economy and the Possibilities of Governance* (Cambridge: Polity Press).

Weiss, L. (2003) *States in the Global Economy: Bringing Domestic Institutions Back In* (Cambridge: Cambridge University Press).

Chapter 10

The Transformation of the State

GEORG SØRENSEN

Introduction

A comprehensive debate about state transformation has been under way for some time (see for example Rosenau 1990; Camilleri and Falk 1992; Ohmae 1996; Strange 1996; Held, McGrew, Goldblatt and Perraton 1999; Weiss 1998; Rosecrance 1999). The debate was pushed by economic globalization; many observers were quick to point out that global economic networks changed the economic substance of states in major ways, because they undermined what had previously been predominantly national economies. The debate was also pushed by processes of political co-operation and integration in Europe and the development of governance networks on a global scale. These economic and political processes in turn helped challenge traditional notions of nationhood and citizenship and thus created a new debate about identity and community. All this in turn helped stimulate new reflections on the institution of sovereignty and the future of the sovereign state. Finally, the end of the Cold War as well as 9/11 encouraged new deliberations on the future of war and violent conflict; because of states central role in warfare this debate also concerns the fate of the state.

This chapter seeks to introduce the most important elements of the debate about the transformation of the state and to investigate how the main positions taken are connected to major different theoretical views (see Sørensen 2004 for an in-depth treatment; some of what follows draws on that work). There are three central standpoints in the debate; they are characterized by different views on what is happening to the state (Sørensen 2004; see also Held McGrew, Goldblatt and Perraton 1999). One view can be called the 'retreat of the state' view; it argues that the changes taking place are a serious threat to the power and autonomy of the state. Some even argue that the changes herald an end to the sovereign state as we know it. Another view is the 'state-centric' one; it finds that the state retains its distinctive importance. The changes taking place are not really new; nor are they very different from what has happened earlier; states remain strong, with special powers.

The third view, finally, focuses on state transformation. It argues that both the 'retreat' and the 'state-centric' stance provide insights, but also contain serious shortcomings. The insights concern the fact that whereas states have lost influence and autonomy in some areas, as indicated by the 'retreat' argument, they have also been strengthened in various respects, as emphasized by the 'state-centric' argument. The shortcomings are narrow definitions and lack of comprehensive analysis. Both of these views overly downplay the general process of *change* in sovereign statehood over time, leading to new strength in some areas and new weaknesses in others.

This more comprehensive view can be called transformationalist. Most scholars will probably say that they are transformationalists today, but the devil is in the detail: how much exactly has changed in which major areas and what does that mean for the overall standing of the state? Is it at all possible to generalize about these changes or is every sovereign state so unique that this is out of the question?

This chapter will argue that some general trends can be identified: we know that the old model of a territorially well-defined national state as of the mid-twentieth century doesn't hold up. We are not entirely sure what is taking its place; that is the reason for the popularity of the imprecise 'post-terminology': the state is often claimed to be 'post-national', 'post-industrial', 'post-sovereign', etc. Still, it is possible to tease out some general ideas about what is happening.

The following sections look at the debate about state transformation in major areas: the economy; political changes; community; sovereignty. The various changes in statehood are then drawn together and it is suggested how they can be interpreted in terms of a new ideal type of (postmodern) state. A subsequent section establishes a link between state theory and the major positions in the debate about state transformation. It is shown how different theories about the state are compelled to view the changes taking place in a certain light. The theoretical views are therefore frequently potentially biased in their analysis of what is going on.

Before we begin, it should be noted that this whole debate about the transformation of the state contains a Eurocentric bias: it is concerned with the advanced liberal states in Europe, North America, and East Asia. There is no mentioning of the very weak states in the South, in particular in Sub-Saharan Africa, or of the modernizing states in Asia and Latin America. Because it traces the debate, the present chapter also contains this Eurocentric or 'Westerncentric' bias.

Economic transformation: the effects of globalization

Economic globalization (see also Chapter 9), is about the intensification of all kinds of economic relations across borders: production, distribution, finance, management. No-one denies that economic globalization takes place: the national economies of the world are more inter-connected than ever before. But when it comes to interpretation of these developments, there is less agreement.

Some argue that a global economy is in the making (Dicken 1998). So-called 'shallow integration', which is 'manifested largely through arm's length *trade* in goods and services between independent firms' is being replaced by 'deep integration' meaning that 'larger parts of economic activity became organized primarily by transnational corporations (TNCs). "Deep" integration extends to the level of *production* of goods and services and, in addition, increases visible and invisible trade. Linkages between national economies are therefore increasingly influenced by the cross-border value adding activities within TNCs...and within networks established by TNCs' (UNCTAD 1993: 113). This type of analysis frequently supports the 'retreat of the state view'.

State-centrists, by contrast, argue that economic globalization is not really new. Economic relations between states were very developed already at the eve of World War I; in other words, there is little news in the fact of economic interdependence (Thomson and Krasner 1989).

This debate on the ramifications of economic globalization is not easily settled because the whole process is so comprehensive in scope and content that it is always possible to find some support for both of the views presented here. But there is also room for common ground between the extremes. Most observers on either side would agree that economic globalization is taking place in the following ways:

- internationalization of national economic spaces through growing penetration (inward flows) and extraversion (outward flows);
- formation of regional economic blocs embracing several national economies – including, most notably the formation of various formally organized blocs in the triadic regions of North America, Europe and East Asia – and the development of formal links between these blocs, notably through the Asia–Pacific Economic Co-operation forum, the New Transatlantic Agenda and the Asia–Europe meetings;
- growth of more 'local internationalization' or 'virtual regions' through the development of economic ties between contiguous or non-contiguous local and regional authorities in different national economies – ties that often bypass the level of the national state but may also be sponsored by the latter;
- extension and deepening of multinationalization as multinational companies, transnational banks and international producer services firms move from limited economic activities abroad to more comprehensive and worldwide strategies, sometimes extending to 'global localization'

whereby firms pursue a global strategy based on exploiting and/or adjusting to local differences;

- widening and deepening of international regimes covering economic and economically relevant issues; and
- emergence of globalization proper through the introduction and acceptance of global norms and standards, the adoption of global benchmarking, the development of globally integrated markets together with globally oriented strategies, and 'deracinated' firms with no evident national operational base. (Points quoted from Jessop 2002:115–16)

Economic globalization also has consequences for the relationship between states and markets. 'State-centric' scholars believe that states remain in control of markets; 'retreat' scholars that markets are now much stronger and states correspondingly weaker. But instead of this 'states losing' and 'markets winning' or vice-versa view, we may look at the state/market relationship as one that has always fluctuated and changed due to different political and economic contexts. World War II led to a high level of state involvement in the economy. In Western Europe in particular, a leading role for the state continued after the war in context of Keynesian welfare state policies.

Changes since the 1980s have not meant a reduced, but sooner a changed role for the state. First, the activity of states has moved away from stressing functions of economic management towards stressing procedural-regulatory functions. The creation of a single market in the context of the EU, for example, has involved a huge number of regulatory directives aimed at enabling the free movement of goods, services, capital and people.

Second, political authority is being disaggregated into a diverse array of various government or public agencies, each of which interacts with a wide range of private companies, groups and organizations. Such public policy networks engage both private and public units in order to complement existing market-based or government-based arrangements considered insufficient (Reinicke 2000: 50).

In this way, states and markets are brought closer together. The state is becoming a more polymorphous entity, diffused into complex networks involving a range of other actors. On the one hand, there is a movement away from the 'central role of the official state apparatus in securing state-sponsored economic and social projects' (Jessop 1997: 574). On the other hand, the making of state regulations to a large extent takes place in transgovernmental networks also involving a diverse group of other actors.

In conclusion, states as well as markets have been transformed under conditions of economic globalization. Instead of a reduced role for the state, the role of the state has changed. States operate under different circumstances than before; in some way they are subject to new constraints, but states have also developed new ways of regulating the market. Thus the transformation that has taken place contains elements of states both 'losing' and 'winning'.

Political transformation: towards multi-level governance

Economic globalization and other factors have helped increase the inter-connectedness between states. In other words, states are increasingly influenced by events and decisions made beyond their territorial reach. At the same time, activities undertaken by states progressively more have consequences not merely within their own jurisdictions, but elsewhere as well. The result is an increasing demand for political co-operation across borders (Zürn 1999).

The development of cross-border co-operation takes place in three major ways. First, *interstate* relations expand, especially through cooperation in IGOs. The number of such organizations doubled between 1950 and the mid-1990s. During the same period, many international organizations became of increasing importance for the member states (Held *et al.* 1999: 54). Second, *transgovernmental* relations have grown; increasingly, ministries and other units of government (such as regulatory agencies, courts and executives) are connected with their counterparts in other countries in a dense web of policy networks. According to one observer, 'transgovernmentalism is rapidly becoming the most widespread and effective mode of international governance' (Slaughter 1997: 185).

The third major development is the expansion of *transnational* relations, that is, cross-border relations between individuals, groups and organizations from civil society (non-state actors). The number of INGOs increased from 832 in 1951 to 5,472 by the mid-1990s (Held *et al.* 1999; Zacher 1992). They often form part of the public policy networks mentioned in the previous section.

Many observers find that a significant transformations is taking place. In earlier days, national *governments* ruled within well-defined territorial borders. Today, politics is increasingly taking the shape of international or global *governance*, a term that refers to activities everywhere – local, national, regional, global – involving regulation and control. Governance is thus an international, transgovernmental and transnational activity that includes not only governments or units of government and traditional international organizations, but also non-governmental organizations and other non-state actors.

Some argue that a 'global polity' is emerging (Ougaard and Higgott 2002). The global polity contains two important changes compared to an earlier phase of national government. First, governments are increasingly enmeshed in a complex network of international organizations to which they make a variety of commitments, some of which are of a more binding nature than previously. Second, many non-state actors influence the processes of governance; regulation and control is no longer a sole preserve of states.

Co-operation across borders is frequently not global in scope; it is rather regional. Regional co-operation has developed the most in Europe. The EU contains a significant element of supranational governance, meaning that EU institutions in some areas have the powers to write the rules for member states. The European Court of Justice, the European Commission and the Council of Ministers can make decisions going against single members. Rulings by the European Court take priority over rulings by national courts.

The EU, then, is the clearest example of what could be called multi-level governance: that is, a situation where political power is diffused and decentralised. Instead of a purely or mainly national political regulation, a complex network of supranational, national and subnational regulation has developed. It is a two-way process in the sense that integration at the political level has stimulated integration between societies and vice versa.

There are several other examples of regional co-operation in the world; but the EU is in a class by itself in terms of the intensity and extensity of co-operation. The other regional initiatives are of a more traditional kind, limited to more narrowly defined economic or other policy areas, and without impinging on the sovereignty of their members, defined as their autonomous right to regulate domestic affairs.

How should we interpret the increased importance of multi-level governance? 'Retreat' scholars see it as an indication that states are less powerful and influential than before. State-centrists emphasize that states remain in control. There are two major aspects of this debate. First, 'retreat scholars' tend to emphasize that co-operation is becoming more demanding, containing supranational elements affecting the sovereignty of states. State-centrists maintain that most co-operation continues to be of the traditional type where states remain in the driver's seat and can refuse to be pushed around by international organizations. Second, 'retreat scholars' find that co-operation generally make states weaker because more power is allocated to other actors, including the international organizations. State-centrists, by contrast, find that co-operation contributes to strengthen states. By co-operating states achieve powers of regulation that they would not otherwise have had, in such areas as environmental regulation, currency stability or crime prevention.

It should take only a moment's reflection to appreciate that both state-centric scholars and retreat scholars make valid points. International co-operation offers both new opportunities for regulations well as new constraints on states. Some forms for co-operation are more demanding (and perhaps also rewarding) than others. What we can say on the general level is that states are in a process of transformation that probably makes them stronger in some respects and weaker in other respects. The net result is difficult to calculate in advance; it will vary substantially across states and across issue-areas.

One further aspect of this political transformation should be mentioned. The growing importance of multi-level governance presents new challenges to democracy. Multi-level governance is not based on a distinct constitutional framework; therefore, core decision-makers are not subject to sufficient accountability and control. Decisions are often made behind closed doors, frequently by high-ranking bureaucrats without a clear democratic mandate. Citizens are not adequately informed about salient issues and thus not capable of conducting a public debate about them. There is no obvious *demos* at the international level, that is to say, there is no well-defined political or moral community outside of the independent state. Without such a clearly defined community many aspects of the democratic process become problematic: participation, debate, accountability, transparency, legitimacy.

Yet one can also argue that multi-level governance is good for democracy because it helps bring complex regional and global processes under political control: seen from the individual state this means improving the capacity for regulating the forces that shape people's lives. Furthermore, some scholars believe that the new challenges to democracy can be successfully confronted. Joseph Nye, for example, argues that the democratic legitimacy of multi-level governance can be safeguarded if international institutions are designed in such a way the they 'preserve as much space as possible for domestic political processes to operate' (Nye 2001: 3).

Because multi-level governance is such a complex entity, this debate about democratic pros and cons will surely continue. It is no longer sufficient to merely think about democracy within the framework of the independent state.

The transformation of community

The nation-state is based on two kinds of community: a community of citizenship concerning the relations between citizens and the state (including political, social, and economic rights and obligations); and a community of sentiment, meaning a common language and a common cultural and historical identity based on literature, myths, symbols, music, art, and so on. Are these two kinds of community in transformation and if yes, what is taking their place?

Let us look at the community of citizens first. One major development in this area is that civil and other rights are no longer being granted solely by the sovereign state. At the global level, a set of universal human rights has been defined; in some regional contexts, close co-operation has led to common rights for citizens of different countries.

The most important regional case is the EU. A Union citizenship was established with the Maastricht Treaty of 1992. Citizens of the EU have rights to employment, residence, and social security in all member states. Full political rights is long-term goal; at present citizens can vote and run as candidates in local and European elections.

At the same time, guestworkers come into the EU from non-member states; they do not have citizenship in the host countries, but they still make claims on the social and political system. Yosemin Soysal has studied guestworkers in Germany; they 'participate in the educational system, welfare schemes, and labour markets. They join trade unions, take part in politics through collective bargaining and associational activity, and sometimes vote in local elections. They exercise rights and duties with respect to the host polity and the state' (Soysal 1994: 2). Soysal sees in this a transformation of citizenship towards a 'postnational membership' based on universal human rights rather than on the national rights flowing from shared national citizenship and a national community of sentiment. 'Rights increasingly assume universality, legal uniformity, and abstractness, and are defined at the global level. Identities, in contrast, still express particularity, and are conceived as being territorially bounded' (Soysal 1994: 159).

In other words, the process indicates a break-up between citizenship rights on the one hand and the cultural–historic community of sentiment on the other. In earlier historical processes of nation-state formation, these two elements were woven closely together. One further challenge to the community of citizens concerns what one scholar calls the practice of 'citizenship without moorings' (Rosenau 1997: 282).

The various aspects of globalization, including much improved possibilities for interaction and communication between people on a world scale, provide the means for people to address such global issues in a transnational dialogue between concerned individuals (rather than between defined groups of national citizens). The ability to visibly affect the global agenda and to help change the course of events puts traditional, national political leadership as well as citizen loyalty and support much more into question than earlier. Citizens 'are thus more ready to rethink the collectivities with which they identify and to redefine the balance between their own and society's interest' (Rosenau 1997: 286).

In sum, a number of different forces are at work to transform the coherent 'community of citizens' as it existed in context of the nation-states. What about the emotional attachment to the nation? It is clear that the 'national community of sentiment' must also be expected to change in the new context of more intense transnational relations.

Anthony Giddens argues that self-identity is becoming 'a reflexively organized endeavour' (Giddens 1991: 5). Individuals no longer 'rest content with an identity that is simply handed down, inherited, or built on a traditional status. A person's identity has in large part to be discovered, constructed, actively sustained' (Giddens 1994: 82).

When identity is something that has to be actively created and sustained by individuals, the attachment to the national 'community of sentiment' can no longer be taken for granted. What – if anything – may be complementing or even replacing the attachment to that national community? One possibility is that a collective identity 'above' the nation is emerging. This 'Western civic identity is a consensus around a set of norms and principles, most importantly political democracy, constitutional government, individual rights, private property-based economic systems, and toleration of diversity in non-civic areas of ethnicity and religion' (Deudney and Ikenberry 1999: 193; see also Linklater 1998).

Such a Western civic identity need not replace the national 'community of sentiment'; it may co-exist with it. The question is whether such identities pertain mainly to well-educated elites and less to other groups. Manuel Castells argues that groups exposed to negative effects of globalization and transnational network will tend to take on a *'resistance identity*: generated by those actors that are in positions/conditions devalued and/or stigmatized by the logic of domination, thus building trenches of resistance and survival on the basis of principles different from, or opposed to, those permeating the institutions of society' (Castells 1998: 8). There a regional movements that vie for secession, or at least for a substantial increase in regional autonomy; there are nationalistic movements stressing a very exclusive definition of national identity, and there are local community movements and religious or ethnic movements.

How should these changes be understood in terms of the larger debate about state transformation? 'Retreat' scholars argue that with the transformation of nationhood the state is weakened because the link between the state and its people is being diluted; loyalties are projected in new directions and additional sources of citizenship emerge. State-centric scholars argue that nationhood remains strong both in the 'community of citizens' aspect and the 'community of sentiment' aspects. The bond between state and people has not been severely weakened.

State-centrists have a point. the nation is not under pressure in the sense that national communities are being replaced by other types of community. But that does not mean everything is the same as before. The content of nationhood itself is being transformed to incorporate new aspects. In other words, national identities increasingly contain elements that are supranational and also local. A clear commitment to European co-operation is progressively more a part of the national identities of the people of EU-member states. At the same time, local identities grow stronger. The long run result of these processes remains uncertain. But at the present time, these transformations of community do not appear to weaken the state because they do not severely dilute national identity affiliations.

The transformation of sovereignty

Sovereignty encapsulates the rules that define the locus of political authority and set the context for relations between states. Modern sovereign authority is centralized and rests with the government ruling a population within a defined territory. The institution of sovereignty thus bestows supreme political authority upon the government. When a state possesses sovereignty it has constitutional independence; other entities have no political authority within the state's territory (James 1999).

Constitutional independence is the juridical core of sovereignty. But sovereignty is more than that; it is also a set of rules regulating how sovereign states go about playing the game of sovereignty and how conduct relations with each other. There are two basic regulative rules in the classical game of sovereignty: non-intervention and reciprocity. Non-intervention means that states have a right to choose their own path, to conduct their affairs without outside interference. States are free to decide what they want without meddling from others. Reciprocity means giving and taking for mutual advantage. States make deals with each other as equal partners; there is no preferential treatment or positive discrimination.

Several scholars think that the substance of states has been transformed, not least because of globalization (Scholte 2000; Elkins 1995, Lapidoth 1992). According to them, the state today has fewer opportunities for controlling and regulating what goes on inside its borders. Electronic communication and mass media; global financial flows; cross-border environmental problems; global multinational corporations. All this means that states are in a process of moving beyond sovereignty or into 'the twilight of sovereignty' (Wriston 1992).

Sceptical scholars retort that these developments concern the substance of statehood; they have to do with the state's actual capacity for controlling a variety of crossborder flows and conditions. The sceptics emphasize that the idea of 'twilight of sovereignty' is based on a category mistake. Sovereignty is a legal institution; it comprises constitutional independence and regulative rules. When some scholars argues that sovereignty is ending because the opportunities for state control are being eroded, they are making the category mistake of conflating the issue of state substance with the issue of the legal institution of sovereignty (Jackson 1999).

The sceptical scholars also find that proponents of the 'twilight' idea tend to misrepresent history, because they overstate the actual degree of state control in earlier days. There has never been some golden age in the past, where states could effectively control transborder flows. And states have grown very much stronger over time when it comes to military power and the capacity for control and surveillance of citizens as well as effective tax-collection (Thomson and Krasner 1989).

These remarks focus on the substantial changes in statehood and the consequences for sovereignty; now let us zoom in on sovereignty as a legal institution. Have there been changes in the core content of sovereignty (constitutional independence) or in the regulative rules of sovereignty and if so, what are the results of such changes?

As regards constitutional independence, the vast majority of scholars agree that it remains in place. Sovereignty as constitutional independence is the one dominant principle of political organization in the international system. But when it comes to drawing the implications of that situation, there is no agreement at all. Those sympathetic to the 'twilight' thesis tend to see the persistence of sovereignty as little more than an empty shell disguising the radical changes that have taken place (Camilleri and Falk 1992). The sceptical scholars, by contrast, see in the continued dominance of sovereignty as constitutional independence the sustained viability of the institution of sovereignty. the sovereign state remains the preferred form of political organization; no serious competitor has emerged (Jackson 1999).

Let us turn to the regulative rules of sovereignty. In this area, there is agreement that changes have taken place but, once again, the implications of those changes are interpreted quite differently. Those supporting the 'twilight' thesis find that new patters of authority are emerging which place regulative powers in the hands of non-state actors. In this way, the game of non-intervention that leaves all political authority in the hands of the sovereign state is gradually being replaced by a different game of 'post-sovereignty' (Scholte 2000: 138), where political authority is dispersed among several different actors. The results is that states are under pressure, because they lose their traditional monopoly on political regulation and control.

Sceptics beg to differ. They make two different arguments. First, the emergence of new sources of political authority at the supranational level (such as for example the EU and, in smaller measure, the WTO) is not seen as a loss or even a debilitating constraint on those states that are subjected to it. The new sources of authority are rather seen as a way of complementing or even strengthening the regulative powers of the individual state.

Take the EU. During the past two decades, institutions at the European level have gained considerable influence over areas that were traditionally the prerogatives of national politics: currency, border controls, social policy, and so on. But sceptics maintain that this has happened in ways that have nothing to do with the 'twilight' thesis. States consent to comply with supranational regulation, but they do it in their own best interest because, as a collective, states are themselves the sources of such regulation, and seen from the single state, the new set-up allows for increased influence over fellow states. The single state thus gets new possibilities for controlling events outside its territorial jurisdiction.

The other argument made by sceptics against the 'twilight' thesis is a historical one. It repeats the view presented above: challenges to the sovereign authority of states is nothing new at all. Historically, sovereignty was always contested; in this context, the challenges produced by globalization are neither new nor particularly dangerous in terms of challenging sovereignty.

In sum, the debate about sovereignty in the face of globalization is not so much about change or continuity. Scholars agree that the juridical core of sovereignty – constitutional independence – stays in place. They also agree that some changes are taking place in the actual substance of statehood and in the regulative rules of sovereignty. The real debate is about the appropriate interpretation of these new developments, including the extent to which they deviate or not from earlier historical phases of sovereign statehood. Let me suggest my own view on the implications of the changes recorded here.

The substance of advanced statehood is changing in context of globalization. This is particularly evident in the case of the EU. Instead of distinct national economies, major parts of the economic activity is embedded in cross-border networks. Instead of national polities, there is multi-level governance involving supranational institutions. These developments have spurred changes in the regulative rules of the sovereignty game. Instead of non-intervention, EU member states conduct comprehensive intervention in each other's affairs. That is, they agree to accept rules made by outsiders (fellow members) as the law in their own states, their own jurisdiction. They do so in order to regulate transnational affairs over which the individual state would have little or no control. This could be called 'regulated intervention'.

EU members have also modified the rule of reciprocity. They sometimes give preferential treatment, or *unequal* treatment to members according to special needs. For example, poor regions in the EU get such preferential treatment. Additional economic resources are redistributed to those regions because of their special needs. This could be called 'co-operative reciprocity'.

Some scholars argue that these changes in sovereignty are not merely relevant for the EU; they will increasingly pertain to other states also, spurred by economic globalization and multi-level governance. If this is true, a major change in the institution of sovereignty is under way. That does not mean that we have moved beyond or into the 'twilight' of sovereignty. Sovereignty in the form of constitutional independence remains the globally dominant principle of political organization. But the actual game of sovereignty, as expressed in the regulative rules of the institution, will surely develop and change, not least due to the challenges brought about by globalization.

The connection to theories: interpretations of state transformation

It has already been indicated that there are different interpretations of what is going on as regards state transformation. This debate is not merely about empirical disagreement. Different theoretical traditions lie behind the major positions in the debate about the state. By means of their theoretical approach, they are compelled to view the changes taking place in a certain light.

There are three main ways of looking at states and power; the first is state-centric; it is connected to elitism in political science and the realist tradition in IR (International Relations). The second springs from the pluralist or liberal tradition in political thought; the third, which I shall call the critical view – is linked to theories inspired by IPE (International Political Economy), by neo-Marxism (see Chapter 4) and by historical sociology. The 'state-centric' view is often connected to the realist approach while 'retreat' scholars frequently draw on the liberal tradition. 'Transformation' scholars, finally, typically subscribe to the critical view but there are exceptions and by no means all scholars are easily classified in this way. There is no room here for a comprehensive introduction to theories on the state (for an overview, see Chapters 1–3). I merely want to demonstrate how theories help persuade scholars to take certain views on state transformation.

State-centric analysis as represented by realism (Morgenthau 1966; Waltz 1979; for an overview see Jackson and Sørensen 2003) simply assumes that the international system is a system of sovereign states. States control the means of violence; they set the rules of the game for all other actors, including corporations, individuals and organizations. States jealously guard their freedom and autonomy; for that reason there is no world government and there never will be.

Against this background, it is easy to understand why state-centric realists are sceptical faced with the idea about states in retreat. When the basic assumption is that states set the rules of the game for everybody else, and when the power of states resides especially in arsenals of military force controlled by states that are unitary and coherent actors, then any claim about states being in retreat because of the increasing power of private corporations, or because of the advance of market forces in general, must be met with the highest scepticism. The short answer given by realists is: markets and corporations (and all other non-state actors) develop because states want them to, and, when the crunch comes, when violent conflict looms again (and at some point it always will), states, especially the strongest ones, remain in firm control.

Pluralists or liberals have a different view of states and power. The liberal starting point is the individual citizen; states are not primarily concentrations or instruments of power; they are caretakers of the rule of law and the rights of citizens to life, liberty and property. From the beginning, therefore, individuals and groups in civil society are the central focus for liberals. They argue that transnational relations – that is, relations across border between individuals and groups ('non-state actors') – have become of increasing importance in recent decades. That is one major reason for the 'erosion . . . of state and governmental power' (Rosenau 1993: 274).

The state was never a strong, unitary, coherent and autonomous actor for liberals; it was always a guardian of individuals and groups in civil society and therefore strongly influenced by these 'non-state actors'. In the liberal view, power is distributed among many actors across a vast range of issue areas; and states are increasingly under pressure form the transnational relations conducted by individuals and groups. That is the basis for the 'retreat of the state' view supported by many liberals.

The critical view, finally, recognizes the existence of a system of sovereign states based on territory, population and government. But the critical view emphasizes the co-existence of sovereign states with a global economic system based on capitalism. Proponents of this view are mostly interested in the relationship between politics and economics, and especially in the ability of states to exploit the possibilities for economic and social development in a capitalist world system (e.g. Jessop 2002). A major focus in this context is the relationship between states and markets. The critical view follows Karl Polanyi (1944[1957]) in conceiving of that relationship as a dialectical one. That is to say, states create and regulate markets; but markets, once created, are also sources of power that may constrain states. Realists contend that states are in control of markets; many liberals see markets as a formidable force challenging and constraining states.

The critical view perceives the state – market connection as an evolving relationship of interdependence in which each side needs (and benefits from) the other. At the same time, states and markets are sources of political and economic power and different kinds of balances between them are possible. That leads towards a 'transformation' view where states are neither 'winning' nor 'losing' but where the relative power position of states (and other actors) may change over time and across issues.

None of these different theoretical views are inherently right or wrong. They are different grips on a complex reality; each of them is the starting point for an analysis that throws light on some aspects of that reality and leaves other aspects in the dark. In one sense they are like different games. Each may be useful for certain analytical purposes and less useful for others. Just as we respect that people want to play different games, we must respect the individual merits of each theoretical perspective on its own terms.

At the same time, all three theories have something to say about states and power and how the power of states develops over time. When we want to find out how states are changing and what the consequences are for the power of states relative to others, we must begin with an open theoretical view. We cannot merely assume that states remain in the driver's seat or that individuals and groups from civil society are always in control. We must begin with the open analytical position that states are being transformed in a way which may both increase and reduce their power and influence in the international system. In that specific sense the critical view has an advantage over the two other theories simply because it is more open towards grasping the complex ways in which states are being transformed.

Yet I am not trying to persuade the reader to adopt the critical view and reject the two others. The intention is merely to emphasize how different theoretical starting points compel us to look at the real world in rather different ways.

Let me now summarize the changes in statehood identified above and try to get an overall grip on what is happening to the state.

Changes in statehood

States have always undergone development and change. The modern, territorial nation-state of the mid-twentieth century has been transformed. We cannot be entirely sure about what has taken its place because the changes are still in progress. Major developments are easier to identify in retrospect; the development of the modern state, for example, was under way for many decades, even centuries. We now know, with hindsight, that the modern state came to full maturity by the mid-twentieth century. If we focus on the three major aspects of statehood that have been discussed above – economy, government, and nationhood – the modern state can be seen as an ideal type with some characteristic features (Figure 10.1 below).

Yet as indicated above, the modern state has been transformed. There is no stage where states are 'finally developed'; state transformation is the rule and not the exception. The current process of change has lasted for several decades and is still unfolding. That is why I suggest the label of 'the post-modern state' as a way of summarizing those changes still under way. (The term was used by Robert Cooper in a 1996 article and therefore many attribute it to him; I did, however, suggest the term in a book in 1995, edited with Hans Henrik Holm. See Holm and Sørensen 1995: 203.) As already pointed out, the 'post-'prefix is a way of emphasizing that we are not quite clear on what shape and form the postmodern state will eventually take

Figure 10.1 *The modern and the postmodern state*

	The modern state	The postmodern state
Government	A centralized system of democratic rule, based on a set of administrative, policing and military organizations, sanctioned by a legal order, claiming a monopoly of the legitimate use of force, all within a defined territory.	Multi-level governance in several interlocked arenas overlapping each other. Governance in context of supranational, international, transgovernmental and transnational relations.
Nationhood	A people within a territory making up a community of citizens (with political, social and economic rights) and a community of sentiment based on linguistic, cultural and historical bonds. Nationhood involves a high level of cohesion, binding nation and state together.	Supranational elements in nationhood, both with respect to the 'community of citizens' and the 'community of sentiment'. Collective loyalties increasingly projected away from the state.
Economy	A segregated national economy, self-sustained in the sense that it comprises the main sectors needed for its reproduction. The major part of economic activity takes place at home.	'Deep integration': major part of economic activity is embedded in cross-border networks. The 'national' economy is much less self-sustained than it used to be.

Source: Adapted from Boxes 1.1 and 9.2 in Georg Sørensen, *The Transformation of the State* (2004), by permission of Palgrave Macmillan.

but, at the same time, we are quite certain that it is different from the modern state. The reader should be warned that the label 'postmodern' is being used in several different ways by scholars, some of which do not at all correspond to the way it is used here. The ideal type of the modern and the postmodern state are set forth in the figure below.

The postmodern state is an attempt to portray major trends of state transformation among the advanced countries in the OECD-world. It should be reiterated that the postmodern state is an ideal type. It thus attempts to draw out and clarify major trends in the real world, but it is not an accurate picture of the real world. Actual states will conform to the ideal type in different degrees. Some will argue that the ideal type is too Eurocentric in a narrow sense; it really only pertains to EU-Europe while countries such as Japan or the United States are not really as postmodern as the EU-members.

There is some truth in the claim; the most demanding forms of multi-level governance, for example, are most developed in context of EU-co-operation. But it would be misleading to claim that the notion of postmodern statehood is only relevant for Europe. Take a closer look at the United States. In terms of the general level of integration the US is high on the list. The annual Globalization Index measures four aspects: (a) political engagement: memberships in international organizations, UN Security Council missions in which each country participates, and foreign embassies that each country host; (b) technology: number of internet users, internet hosts, and secure servers; (c) personal contact: international travel and tourism, international telephone traffic, and cross-border transfers; (d) economic integration: trade, foreign direct investment and portfolio capital flows; and income payments and receipts. On that index, the United States holds place no. 11, in front of such countries as Germany, Spain, New Zealand, and France.

In the economic sphere, the change from 'shallow' integration to 'deep' integration in the case of the US is documented by the high levels of intrafirm trade (i.e. trade among transnational corporations and their affiliated); this trade amounted to 47 per cent of the US total value of imports in 2001 and 32 per cent of the value of exports (*Foreign Policy* 2003). As regards nationhood, there was always a universalist element in US national identity; one might even say that the 'Western civic identity' identified above originates in the United States. The idea of a 'citizenship without moorings' is also highly relevant for the US.

That leaves the level of politics or government. The United States surely participates in the development of relations across borders, including inter-state, transgovernmental and transnational relations (Slaughter 2004). At the same time, US unilateralism has been pronounced in the response to 9/11 and other unilateral moves (e.g. withdrawal from the Kyoto agreement, rejection of the Biological Weapons Protocol, refusal to ratify the International Criminal Court treaty and the Comprehensive Test Ban Treaty). Some see in this a turn towards a unilateral order based on unrestrained US power.

But this interpretation overstates the changes mentioned here. They must instead be put in context of the more fundamental goals of US foreign policy. These goals reflect the basic values of domestic civil society in the United States: open market economies; liberal democracy; civil and political liberties. As regards the fundamentals of promoting liberal political and economic values, US policies have been in harmony with the concerns of the consolidated democracies in Europe. In this light, the deviations in unilateral direction recorded above appear less serious than they are often interpreted in the current debate.

Furthermore, even if a neoconservative political faction is currently very influential in the US, several observers emphasize that even with her great military power, the US 'cannot go it alone' in a complex, and increasingly integrated world (Nye 2002). Nye argues that if unilateralists 'try to elevate unilateralism from an occasional temporary tactic to a full-fledged strategy, they are likely to fail for three reasons: (1) the intrinsically multi-lateral nature of a number of important transnational issues in a global age, (2) the costly effects on our soft power, and (3) the changing nature of sover-eignty' (Nye 2002: 163). Soft power is the 'ability to structure a situation so that other nations develop preferences or define their interests in ways consistent with one's own nation' (Nye 1990: 91).

The struggle against mass-murder terrorism will require networks of 'co-operating government agencies' (Nye 2003: 65) as much as it will require unilateral military action. And even when it comes to such military action itself, there continues to be sharp in-built constraints to the US utilization of her preponderant power (Posen 2003).

In sum, the claim is that the current processes of state transformation among the advanced countries can be understood as an ongoing shift from modern to postmodern statehood. These types of statehood are ideal types and real world states may conform more or less to them. But they are relevant for the larger group of advanced OECD-countries rather than merely for EU-Europe.

Conclusion: new debates in the wake of state transformation

The transformation from modern towards postmodern statehood may not seem very dramatic. But it does have wide-ranging consequences in several important areas, some of which have already been hinted at above. Democracy no longer unfolds merely within the context of the sovereign state. Therefore, the three basic questions about democracy demands new answers. The questions are: (1) Who are the people? (2) In what sense should the people rule? (3) How far should popular rule extend? (cf. Heywood 1997: 66).

The institution of sovereignty is changing as well. Multi-level governance is quite the opposite of non-intervention; it is rather systematic intervention in national affairs by international or supranational institutions. What it means to be sovereign is very different under conditions of multi-level governance compared with traditional conditions of national government. Furthermore, the 'domestic' affairs and the 'international' context of any one country can no longer easily be separated. But frequently both the discipline of IR and the discipline of comparative politics continue as if nothing has happened.

Traditional notions of state power are challenged as well. Because war between postmodern states is out of the question, it would appear that military power is losing significance whereas non-material, intangible sources of power including soft power are of increasing importance. At the same time, the aftermath of 9/11 has demonstrated the continued relevance of military power. What is state power under conditions of postmodern statehood and who has it?

In sum, the transformation of statehood presents scholars with a large new menu of analytical and substantial challenges. The traditional approaches need to be further developed in order to confront the new situation. There are many big questions that call for better answers than scholars (and policy-makers) have been able to come up with so far. The issue of state transformation and its consequences will be high on our analytical agenda for a very long time.

Further reading

Dicken, P. (2003) *Global Shift. Reshaping the Global Economic Map in the 21st Century* (London: Sage).

Held, D., McGrew, A., Goldblatt, D. and Perraton, J. (1999) *Global Transformations: Politics, Economics and Culture* (Cambridge: Cambridge University Press).

Jessop, B. (2002) *The Future of the Capitalist State* (Cambridge: Polity Press).

Political Studies, 47:3 (1999). Special Issue on Sovereignty with a wide-ranging coverage of that important institution.

Sørensen, G. (2004) *The Transformation of the State: Beyond the Myth of Retreat* (London: Palgrave Macmillan).

Weiss, L. (1998) *The Myth of the Powerless State: Governing the Economy in a Global Era* (Cambridge: Polity Press).

Chapter 11

Governance, Government and the State

B. GUY PETERS AND JON PIERRE

Governance is shorthand for the pursuit of collective interests and the steering and coordination of society. During the 1990s, new or emerging models of governance have become debated among social scientists and practitioners alike as a combined result of budgetary cutbacks, the 'hollowing out' of the state, the development towards an enabling or regulatory state, a growing interest among politicians to forge partnerships with strategic societal actors, and a 'multi-layering' of political authority. Together, these developments have raised questions about the ability of the state to be at the centre of governance. What is changing, in short, is the role of government in governance, and this change has brought with it complex questions concerning democratic input and accountability.

The recent debate on the role of the state in providing governance has featured growing doubts concerning the extent still can effectively play this role. Globalization theorists and 'hollow-state' observers alike seem to argue that governance is a process increasingly dominated by other actors than the state and its institutions. This chapter will argue that a more rewarding perspective on these issues is to conceive of recent changes within and outside the state in terms of a transformation of the state and its relationship to actors in its external environment. Theories of governance help us understand the historical trajectory of these developments and the current role of the state in the advanced Western democracies.

One of the fundamental tasks for any society is to govern itself. For most of the past three centuries or more we have associated that task with the state, and its monopoly of legitimate force within a territory. The term 'Westphalian state' is commonly used, denoting the inception of this type of governance structure at the termination of the Thirty Years' War in Europe. In other parts of the world, e.g. China and Japan, analogous state structures had grown independently of this concept. The dominant pattern of governing has been hierarchical, with governments deciding – through democratic means or not – what laws and policies would be adopted and then proceeding to attempt to implement those rules. Especially in democratic systems societal actors may be involved in this process, on both the input and output sides, but government remained the final arbiter of law and policy.

The state has been experiencing challenges to its traditional role in governance coming from outside the society (globalization) and from within the society itself in the form of networks and other social actors seeking greater autonomy. In this paper we will be taking the currently unpopular view that, although governance has indeed changed, the state continues to play a major, if not the major, role in governing. Further we will argue that especially in democratic states we should value governance through institutions that are broadly, if imperfectly, accountable to the public as opposed to more narrowly conceived patterns of sectoral governance.

Understanding the so-called shift from government to governance

> Current use does not treat governance as a synonym for government. Rather governance signifies a change in the meaning of government, referring to a *new* process of governing; or a *changed* condition of ordered rule; or the *new* method by which society is governed. (Rhodes 1996:652–3; italics in original)

Well, yes and no. Rhodes' oft-cited argument that governance, the 'new governance', as it were, refers to fundamental changes in governing was instrumental in triggering widespread interest in governance as a phenomenon. Rhodes believed that the change in the style of governing in the United Kingdom during the 1980s meant the emergence of a distinctly new governing process summarized as 'governing without government'. Public–private partnerships, market-based administrative reform and the rolling back of the state coupled with the deregulation of markets were all seen as elements of a large-scale transformation of the ways in which the modern state – the 'hollow state' – governed society.

In this 'hollow state' the formal institutions of government have been largely replaced by the capacity of social actors such as networks and markets to govern. To the extent that it is important government is there to legitimate the actions of the social actors and to provide representative democracy, while the 'real' democracy is expressed through the involvement of individuals and groups in networks. Thatcherism clearly represented a new era in British politics and society, and that pattern has persisted, and in some ways been expanded by the Blair government.

All of that having been said, however, it also seems clear that some of the conclusions Rhodes drew from these changes were ethnocentric or exaggerated, or possibly both. First of all, while the emergence of institutionalized forms of concerted action between public and private actors was a novelty to the British political milieu, it was certainly a familiar phenomenon both in (the rest of) Europe (Katzenstein 1984; Kraemer 1964) and even in the United States (see, for example, Beauregard 1988). Corporatism is perhaps the most obvious example of such public–private co-operation but there exist a wide variety of other forms of either ad hoc or more continuous and institutionalized forms of public–private exchanges at all levels of the political system. Thus, what struck Rhodes as new and original in Britain is part of the political history in many other parts of the world. This is not to denigrate his work, merely to suggest that the novelty of the phenomenon is called into question when applied to a cross-national comparison. Even so, however, the British developments over the past couple of decades have been more profound and have had bigger ramifications on the political system than in most other parts of the world with the exception of the Antipodes.

Second, and more important in terms of theory development, what is changing is not a process of governing from government to governance but the role of government in governance. It is, of course, not the case that contemporary British governance takes place without government; rather, what has changed is the centrality of government in governance and the *modus operandi* of government within that new model of governance. As soon as we conceptualize the developments Rhodes uses to illustrate his argument in that fashion, we can more easily ascertain what is new and what is not. Also, we will be in a better position to apply governance theory in comparative research. And, finally, by doing so we have also escaped the trap of singling out one national context – a case which arguably displays one of the more extreme transformations in these respects – as a norm or a yardstick with which we assess similar developments in other institutional and political contexts.

So exactly what is happening in terms of changes in governance? The next section of the chapter discusses some general patterns in contemporary governance change. Following that, we will briefly discuss how these changes have affected the state. The next section of the chapter looks more at the resilience of institutions and how institutions adapt to changes in their environment.

Emerging models of governance

In a different context (Pierre and Peters 2004) the present authors have elaborated a typology of governance model which aims at distinguishing between different such models along various key dimensions of governance, such as actors, processes and outcomes. One of the overarching problems in designing sustainable governance is how to weigh the significance of institutions, as carriers of collective interests and objectives, against the autonomy of societal actors and markets.

On one end of the spectrum we see institutions powerful and resourceful enough to do basically what they see fit – either in terms of their own interests or in terms of what they believe to be in the interests of society – in any given situation (see Table 11.1). This model of governance ensures that collective goals are imposed on society but runs the risk of choking markets and civil society. This model of governance is also likely to make ill-informed decisions; the degree of institutional self-sufficiency which is typical to this type of governance provides few incentives for institutions to engage in dialogue with key actors in its external environment. The other end of the spectrum sees governance as a process shaped by inter-organizational networks at the level of the policy sector, pretty much the way Rhodes (1996) describes 'the new governance'. Here, collective objectives are obstructed by coalitions of sectoral actors and interests. While this model of governance might be said to be sufficiently in touch with society to make good choices, those choice will not reflect the collective preferences of the polity but rather those of a very small segment of society.

Between those two stark alternatives are a variety of forms of governing that relate state and society in different ways, but find a means of balancing the roles of those two broad segments of political and social life. For example, the pluralist (liberal) model of governing retains the public sector as the dominant actor, picking and choosing among alternative representatives of

Table 11.1   *Models of governance*

Model	Characteristics
Etatiste	Dominant role for state institutions. Limited involvement and feedback from society.
Liberal	Involvement of limited number of societal actors, selected carefully by state institutions. Pluralist, with government choosing the legitimate actors.
State-centric	State remains dominant actor, but societal actors have some autonomous sources of legitimacy, and some claims for involvement, corporatist bargaining being a prime example.
'Dutch'	Networks become central, if not dominant, participants, but state retains capacity to make autonomous decisions and and 'steer from a distance'.
Governace without government	Networks and markets are dominant actors. State legitimates the actions of these societal actors

civil society, but yet allowing that civil society some influence over policy. Likewise, a state-centric conception of governing, exemplified by corporatist models (Wiarda, 1996), permits societal actors even greater involvement, but at the price of co-optation into the governance activities of the state. Finally, the 'Dutch' model (Kooiman, 2004) uses networks for a significant portion of governance activity, but government still retains the capacity to 'steer at a distance'.

Given these complex trade-offs between different aspects of governance, it is perhaps little surprise that much of contemporary design of governance appears to be a process of trial and error. One example is the current wave of regional institutional reform across Europe where objectives related to economic development and EU-compatibility are weighed against collective input, democratic debate and accountability. The result, according to one observer, is that few countries, if any, have been able to present a reform which seems to work (Newman, 2000). Another example of problematic governance design can be found in the field of administrative reform. Many countries seem to experience a hangover from the aggressive market-based reforms implemented during the 1980s and 1990s and are now exploring alternative strategies to strengthen the role of political institutions and actors. The Antipodes, for example, were leaders in the market-based reforms of new public management (NPM) but now are finding ways to reassert a stronger governance role for the public sector.

At the same time, it should also be noted that although many of the currently emerging forms of governance display some form of institutionalized exchange between state and society, the object of reform does not seem to be to look back in time at the models of governance that were typical to many countries prior to Thatcher, NPM and deregulated financial markets. Instead, there are signs that the pendulum movement is slowly beginning to swing back towards governance models that accord political institutions a more central role. In the Scandinavian countries, it appears as if the fascination with decentralized government is slowly fading and that processes of subtle forms of recentralization are on their way. In Sweden, for example, several major government commissions are examining carefully both the decentralized local government system and the deconcentrated system of public administration.

If anything, it seems clear from the current debate in many countries that institutions are much more capable of adapting than most observers have hitherto believed them to be. We will return to that issue later in this chapter. The state that remains in the face of the numerous changes in governance is still a powerful actor. There may have been some hollowing out, but when assessed more carefully we can now see that the 'shell' that remains retains much of its real power. While it is difficult to deny that there is now a powerful international marketplace that affects the capacity to make autonomous economic policy decisions, that market is itself, however, negotiated rather than autonomous, and governments remain the major negotiators in fora such as the WTO, the IMF, and within numerous other international regimes.

Likewise, at the domestic level, clearing some of the baggage of the hierarchical state may produce even more capacity to govern. This enhancement in governance capacity is manifested simply because the power is not used on every minor detail of policy but instead is used to shape the directions of policy and the basic goals for governing. As described in several places the State now 'enables' as much as it 'directs', but it can still make the choice of what things to enable and what things not to support. That selectivity then becomes a means of husbanding resources, choosing those battles that must be fought, and making strategic choices about governance. Thus, the enabling state can also become the strategic state.

The resilience of institutions

States are more than simply an aggregation of institutions, but those institutions do a great deal to define a state, and to shape its capacity for governance (see Painter and Pierre 2004). If there is a well-developed and well-functioning set of institutions then the states blessed with those institutions are likely to be able to cope with increased strength and diversity of pressures coming from both the domestic and international environments. Conversely, in failing states, such as those found in much of Africa or the Caucasus, the institutions are present in form but not in function, so that these states are largely at the mercy of the external forces that impinge upon them. Thus, it may not be so much the state *per se* that has been failing in governance but certain forms of the state operating in certain conditions.

Joel Migdal (1988) has pointed out the importance of different types of matches and mismatches between the relative strengths of states and their societies. The interactions between the state and the environment become more complex when the international market becomes a player also, so that strong states may be able to mediate between their societies and the international environment, while weaker states may be at the mercy of both external forces. In some instances states can use the power of external economic actors – the World Trade Organization or the European Central bank – to overcome the power of entrenched social interests, or perhaps even forge coalitions with powerful domestic actors (environmental NGOs perhaps) against external actors (see Pauly and Grande, 2005). One of the clearest examples is the current fiscal probity of Italian and Irish governments in response to their membership in the EMS, after decades of huge deficits. The fundamental point is that states are not at the mercy of non-state actors and can govern. They may not always govern alone, but they can govern.

We have argued elsewhere (Peters 2002; Peters and Pierre forthcoming; Pierre and Peters 2000), and will continue to argue here, that the most appropriate place at which to begin an analysis of governance is the state, rather than beginning with the external actors – social or economic. This is in part an analytic stance, but it is also a theoretical position. Analytically, beginning with the state enables us to see when deviations from this *a priori* expectation may have occurred, and hence identify the points at which either international economic or domestic social forces may have intervened. Theoretically, we will be arguing that despite the important changes that many scholars of governance (Rhodes 1997; Tihonen 2004) have identified (and in some cases perhaps exaggerated) a great deal of the governance action in most societies, occurs through state organs.

What do state institutions do for governance?

Having said that the state and its institutions are central elements for an understanding of governance, how do we conceptualize that process actually functioning? Given that we have defined governance as a process of steering the economy and society, and have identified four key elements involved in that steering, we can more readily identify the manner in which the formal (and informal) institutions of the state influence that steering process. The central element of this analysis is that we are defining steering, and hence governance, as a goal-directed activity, with the need to establish collective goals and develop the means of reaching those goals. In a democratic context those societal goals would have to be identified by some more or less inclusive process, and attaining the goals would have to be accomplished through a process that recognizes individual rights and due process, but any method of governance will require goal setting and implementation. As Buchanan and Tullock (1962) argued, the general *ex ante* agreement on majority rule in most societies, once enshrined in formal rules, is a powerful means of ensuring legitimacy of decisions.

The most important thing about state institutions for the governance process is that they provide an agreed upon mechanism for establishing priorities, and for making choices among competing priorities. Social and political actors have any number of goals that they would like to see the society pursue, and to use the authority and financial resources of the state to make possible. However, given that resources are finite, there is a need to prioritize those goals. The political process, usually through a legislature of some sort, provides the means for making decisions that have the force of law. Whether by majority rule or other voting rules within these institutions provide a means of making the difficult choices required.

A second requirement for effective governance in the reconciliation of goals and programmes that, even with legislative choices, may be conflicting or at a minimum inconsistent. Governments adopt any number of laws and with the mobilization of different coalitions for different purposes with in governments there is no guarantee of consistency. Therefore, some means of co-ordination and clarification of the policies adopted by government will be required (see, for example, Scharpf 1996) for good governance. Although less formalized means have some potential (Bardach 1998), the general means of producing policy co-ordination is through institutions such as cabinets and central agencies.

A third component of governing is implementation, or the actual steering of economy and society. Implementation conventionally has been considered the province of the public bureaucracy, although increasingly it utilizes non-governmental actors and the instruments of 'new governance' (Salamon 2002), but even those instruments tend to function in the 'shadow of hierarchy' and to be backed by the possibility of using authority. Further, the macro-institutional structure of a country tends to have significant influence over implementation, given the importance of federalism, or other structures of sub-national government, for the implementation of programmes from the central government.

Finally, in order to be able to steer effectively one needs to understand the consequences of previous decisions, and hence feedback and accountability are important to governance. in any society the feedback element is crucial, to provide for on-going correction and change of policy, but for democratic governments the accountability element included in this stage is also important. The public bureaucracy, and its agents when programmes are not implemented directly by public employees, must be held to account for their actions so that citizens can have some assurance that their rights are being respected, and that public money is being used appropriately. Thus, the feedback component of governance involves both policy change and scrutiny of the actions of individuals responsible. This aspect of governance also involves a number of institutional players, ranging from legislatures to specialized oversight and accountability organizations (Hood *et al.* 2004). Arguably, although some private sector 'watchdogs' can be useful, the ultimate responsibility for accountability must reside with public institutions.

Having described the role of existing public sector institutions in the process of governance, it is important to understand the role of these institutions in other than those descriptive terms. The inherited, and persisting, institutional structures of states are crucial first for the legitimation of the policy choices made by government. In a more globalized and inter-dependent world national governments may have to respond to a number of external forces, but policy choices may still need to be legitimated through some rather conventional mechanisms. Likewise, in a world of governance in which networks of private sector actors are crucial to the formation and especially the implementation of public policy, the interactions of those social partners with government are important for the success of government, but cannot replace the legal mandates of states and governments. Thus, the actions of networks will in most circumstances be carried on within a context of state power, power that can be withdrawn if deemed necessary.

As well as conveying legitimacy, some of the institutions of the public sector are peculiarly well suited for performing certain governance activities. In particular, the institutions of the public sector have been designed to resolve conflicts, while neither markets nor networks are designed to do so. Markets tend to assume away conflicts, or assume that the most powerful economic actors will (and should) win. Networks are generally assumed to be co-operative and non-competitive, but if a network surrounding a policy area is inclusive and has within it a range of socio-economic interests it may well find collaborative solutions to problems impossible, having no *ex ante* method for legitimately deciding between winners and losers. Political institutions were designed under an assumption of conflict, often intense conflict, and their constitutive rules provide the means of providing a solution.

Further, although the critics of contemporary government would certainly not agree, conventional institutions of government do a reasonably good job of channelling the demands from the society into the processes of decision-making. Advocates of deliberative government (Dryzek 2003), communitarianism (Selznick 2002), referenda (but see Budge 1996) and networks argue that these conventional institutions privilege certain types of interests and exclude others. Although there is some logic to that position, there are several other points that should be made. First, the conventional political institutions establish *ex ante* rules for inclusion and have developed structures that channel and aggregate interests, so that the manner of inclusion is known in advance. Further, these structures are widely diverse and can provide a number of avenues for participation. For example, the public bureaucracy increasingly is a major, if not the major, locus of participation for social interests.

We should also point out that the proposed alternatives to the instruments of interest intermediation are perhaps no more inclusive than are the more conventional institutions. For example, although discursive democracy is meant to be inclusive, its reliance on advocacy and discourse advantages the more articulate, especially members of the middle class. Likewise, networks tend to involve the social actors that are immediately concerned with the policy area, but the broader society has little or no ability to exert any influence, even if they may be affected by the policy choices, if for no other reason than they are taxpayers. Thus, the advocates of other forms of governance can point to significant problems in producing better outcomes through presumably more open and democratic means of public involvement.

Institutions and political change

A focus on the institutions may appear to express an excessive concern with the persistence of patterns of governing. The path dependence that has been central to the study of public policy from an institutionalist perspective can also apply to the institutions themselves, so that many vestigial institutions may remain in contemporary governments. Once created, both institutions and the policies they make tend to persist unless there is a strong political force that can produce change. Even as governments are responding more to characteristics in their socio-economic environment, however, they are making those responses in the context of an institutional structure that may have been inherited from decades, if not centuries, before. Institutional, especially historical institutional, analysis tends to focus on the persistence of those institutions, but that should not obscure the fact that there has been institutional change, and that institutions can be adaptive. Still, change may often be in the form of a 'punctuated equilibrium' rather than steady adaptation to changing circumstances, given the capacity of institutions to protect themselves from external pressues.

The state is not as entrenched and inflexible as critics might like to have us believe. One of the standard justifications for the view of governance that stresses networks and other less formal means of action is that the state is bureaucratic, ossified, and non-responsive. Certainly governments at times do appear to correspond to those unflattering descriptions, but the political system has demonstrated that it can also be responsive and reformist. That is true both for the reform of policies being delivered by the state, and for the state itself (Bouckaert and Pollitt, 2004). Three particular forms of adaptation on the part of the state should be noted here, as reflecting their capacity to cope with changing circumstances.

One of the most important patterns of change in contemporary states has been their capacity to cope with blended, or dual, sovereignty, and to find means of continuing to act as state entities even in the face of merger into larger state-like unions – the European Union as the obvious example – or complex transnational regimes such as that managed by the World Trade Organization, or perhaps even more significantly the International Criminal Court. While state institutions persist, they share control over important sections of their policy regimens with other actors, but most have been able to do so with minimum difficulty. Thus, even in areas that have been 'defining functions' of states (Rose 1974) adaptation has been possible, and state-driven (if no longer exclusive) governance persists.

A second important change in the governance patterns of contemporary states has been in the selection of instruments used to achiever their policy purposes. At one level, rather than relying on command and control instruments as in the past governments are now utilizing 'softer' instruments to achieve their policy goals. For example, social programmes increasingly are implemented through co-operative arrangements with partners in the not-for-profit sector that reduce the costs for government but perhaps more importantly reduce the perceived intrusiveness of the programmes. One of the best examples of the use of 'soft law' of this type is in the European Union, with its use of the 'open method of co-ordination' (Radealli 2003) as a means of achieving European social and employment goals. At a second level, governments have shifted from direct provision of some types of benefits to regulators of private provision, so that again the same services may be delivered but in a less intrusive, and less costly, manner.

Finally, states have changed structurally, and have decentralized and deconcentrated significantly. Part of the administrative logic of the new public management has been to empower managers of autonomous and quasi-autonomous public organizations to make more of their own decisions about policy and management, and to reduce hierarchical control over these managers and their organizations. This administrative policy has been adopted in the pursuit of greater efficiency in the public sector but it may have other policy and political consequences as well. In particular, this structural change may have opened up government for greater influence from social actors, while limiting the capacity of political leaders to control government. Those changes have, however, resulted in programmes in some governments to return to the centre and to attempt to find ways of imposing more central policy priorities on government as a whole (see Peters 2004).

These three types of change are all important, and they have altered some aspects of governance, but they by no means amount to an incapacity of the contemporary state to govern, and to govern effectively. Indeed, to the extent that one of the changes may have been having that effect the state has acted to reassert its influence, and reversed the reform, at least in part. Therefore, the sense of a state structure that is not sufficiently nimble to match environmental change does not appear supported by the evidence. If we were to examine policy changes at even more of a micro-level, e.g. specific types of taxation, we can also find that states have responded to meet the challenges posed by economic change, and have been able to maintain their streams of revenue despite those challenges.

Summary

The state and its institutions have been changing, but they remain viable actors in making and implementing policy, and in governance taken more generally. Indeed, the state to a great extent retains its central position in selecting and legitimating policy goals, although it may do so in a more co-operative and less intrusive manner than in the past. The international environment can impact the range of possible actions for states, although certainly some more that others, and governments are increasingly involved with social partners in the selection and execution of laws, but the formal institutions do retain substantial importance. Indeed, in many ways the most remarkable feature of contemporary governance is not so much what has changed but what has remained the same.

Governance, the state and political power

To this point we have been painting a picture of the transformation of the hierarchical and autonomous state that had been the centrepiece of the Westphalian State system in international politics, and also the centre of the mixed-economy, welfare state in domestic politics. That model of governing was very convenient for those at the centre of the institutional apparatus. They could make decisions and expect them to be executed with minimal direct involvement of other actors. While the implementation literature made it clear to academics that these systems for making and executing policy did not necessarily function as smoothly as the models might have one believe, they did function, and during the post-World War II period helped produce an era of substantial economic growth and growing equality of opportunity, in the Western democracies at least. Although this form of governance was successful for a substantial period of time, overloads of demands and fiscal problems generated significant problems. Society also changed and demanded greater participation. Thus, both on the political right and the political left there were demands for change, and indeed some substantial change. As noted above, some of these changes involved altering forms of service delivery in order to enhance the efficiency of the public sector. Other changes involved debureaucratization and involving social actors in decisions. We could enumerate a number of changes of both sorts, but the fundamental point is that the linear, autonomous conception of governing had been replaced by far more complex arrangements for making and delivering policy.

The complexity that is inherent in contemporary patterns of governance does not, however, imply that governments have lost their power in governing. What it does mean is that the state is exercising that power in different ways. For example, as partnerships and other means of linking the public and private sectors become more prevalent, the state's power is exercised through bargaining and linking their resouces with those of the private sector. In many ways these arrangements may actually enhance public power. First, although government may want the resources brought to the table by private sector actors, government may bring a more central resource, namely legitimacy for engaging in action in the name of the public. Governments at time squander that resource, but it remains a major asset.

In addition, the public sector can, if it is coordinated and can pursue coherent policy goals, provide a central direction to more diverse and diffuse actors in the private sector. One of the most important criteria for governance is the need to create a set of common goals for the society, and that goal setting function is most likely to occur in government, as opposed to the numerous and diverse groups pressing their demands on the public sector. Therefore, a common set of goals may be more effective in governing than the more complex and perhaps confused set coming from society. The 'central mind of government', in Dror's (2001) terms, and with that the opportunity to govern strategically, can be a decided advantage in governing.

Following from the above point, conflict resolution is a central activity for government and for governing. There are any number of policy views held by members of society, most of which contain some elements of the public interest as well as the more selective interests of the advocates. The difficulty in governing therefore is selecting among this array of worthy policy proposals. The institutions in the public sector have the mechanisms for doing this, whether through voting in legislative bodies, or more technocratic forms of decision-making in the bureaucracy, or even legal decision-making in the courts. Networks do not have such forms of conflict resolution that are agreed *ex ante*. Bargaining does provide a means of resolving some conflicts, but generally not those in which there are direct conflicts among groups. Thus, any movement toward 'governance without government' complicates conflict resolution, but government may have to come back in the end to cope with fundamental disagreements.

One of the luxuries that the development of networks and the involvement of the private sector in governance affords government is that its own involvement in governance can be selective and instrumental. That is, government can now govern with a lighter hand, and can use those instruments of 'new governance' (see Salamon 2002) that may be less obtrusive. So long as the decisions made by networks remain within the bounds acceptable to existing law and the general policy values of the government there may be no reason to squander scarce political capital and intervene. But we should not forget that those instruments still depend upon the power and legitimate authority of the public sector for much of their effectiveness, and that most of the goal-setting will still be done through the public sector.

Conclusion

In summary, the rumours of the death of the state are exaggerated. We would certainly not want to deny that governing has changed, and that international, and especially societal, actors are important players. That having been said, for many countries they have been significant components of governance for decades if not centuries. Further, the international dimension of governance may have increased, but may serve as much as a locus and arena for state action as it does a real constraint on governing – at least for the affluent industrial countries.

Therefore, we would advocate some caution when considering many of the contemporary discussions of governance. They need to be considered in light of a complex history of governing and government. They also need ot be considered in light of the complexity of contemporary governance processes and structures. Governing still involves choosing and therefore advantages structures that have the capacity to produce more coherent and strategic decisions. Despite the numerous critiques of government, it may still be more capable of providing a coherent picture of the future of society than can any other institution, and is more capable of resolving the inherent conflicts among sectors of society that will be required to pursue that vision.

Further reading

Jreisat, J. S. (2002) *Governance and Developing Countries* (Leiden: Brill).

Kjaer, A. M. (2004) *Governance* (Cambridge: Polity).

Kooiman, J. (2004) *Governing as Governance* (London: Sage).

Nye, J. S. and Donahue, J. D. (2000) *Governance in a Globalizing World* (Washington, DC: The Brookings Institution).

Pierre, J. and Peters, B. G. (2000) *Goverance, Politics and the State* (Basingstoke and New York: Palgrave Macmillan).

www.worldbank.org/wbi/governance

Chapter 12

Public/Private: The Boundaries of the State

MATTHEW FLINDERS

As previous chapters have demonstrated, 'the state' is an elusive and contested concept. Understanding its nature, trajectory and role has not been helped by the fact that the conceptual lenses that have historically been employed to study the state have employed a fairly narrow institutional focus. This restricted view of the state topography, with its emphasis on departments of state at the national level and elected government at the regional/state/provincial level, has created the impression of a fairly homogenous, fixed and stable entity. The opposite is true. In fact the boundaries of the state are far from clear, either by nature, role or direction. Internationally, the last quarter of the twentieth century witnessed significant changes in the structure and governance of the state, a change imbued with the belief that public services or functions need not necessarily be delivered or conducted by purely public institutions. The central argument of this chapter is therefore that the state consists of a highly heterogeneous network of organizations and that controlling, steering and scrutinizing this increasingly diverse flotilla of organizations and partnerships, many of which enjoy significant levels of autonomy from elected politicians and legislatures, remains the primary challenge of modern governance.

The modern state could not function without delegation. The growth in the responsibilities of the modern state have a demanded a structural capacity than can only be fulfilled through widespread delegation. The delegation of responsibilities to quasi-autonomous 'para-statal' actors operating on the boundaries of the state arguably empowers governments to address a wide range of social issues simultaneously without having to be involved with the minutiae of day-to-day socio-political interactions. Historically as embryonic state bureaucracies developed in the nineteenth century it was common to delegate tasks to independent boards or commissions or enter into contracts with private sector companies for the provision of certain services. France, Germany and the USA, for example, each have a long and diverse history of using public–private partnerships, or '3Ps' as they are known in Canada and North America, within their respective state structures (Osborne

2000). Despite concerns about accountability and institutional complexity the overall trend throughout the twentieth century, with intermittent ebbs and flows, is one of growth in the number and role of delegated public bodies and a concomitant blurring of the public/private distinction.

In recent decades, however, the scale and extent of delegated governance has increased markedly to an unprecedented level as part of a global trend towards the creation of agencies, arm's-length bodies and 3Ps (the latter defined as long-term purchase of service contracts between the state and for-profit private sector bodies). The centrifugal pressures of new public management have led to a rapid increase in the number of these 'hybrid' bodies and a concomitant blurring of the public–private distinction in a great number of countries (see Pollitt and Talbot 2004; Ghobadian *et al.* 2004; Hodge and Greve 2005). Although variations in the pace of reform or in relation to the specific form of delegated governance employed will be found when comparing different countries the trends, issues and themes highlighted below will, to a greater or lesser extent, be found in the United States, mainland Europe, Australasia and in an increasing number of developing countries, like in Jamaica (Osei 2004; Talbot 2004), and 'transitional' states, like Latvia (see Pollitt 2004).

An historical perspective usefully exposes the inter-relationship between responsibilities, capacity, delegation and the boundaries of the state in the context of previous attempts to either retreat or advance its role (for a discussion see Gill 2003). Neo-liberal attempts to 'rollback' the boundaries of the state in a number of advanced liberal democracies in response to a perceived crisis during the 1970s have arguably led not to a reduction in the role, budget or powers of the state but to a redefinition, transformation or change in the structure of the state. There has been a change in governing frameworks from hierarchical bureaucracies to complex networks and markets: a shift from govern*ment* to govern*ance* in which the extent of delegated responsibilities and the role of private contractors has increased. Para-statals and P3s represent instruments for meeting the obligations of the state and offer an infra-structural capacity for coping with crises and public demands (see Cohn 2005).

This growth in delegated governance has not always been welcomed. For much of the twentieth century research and literature on the topic of delegated governance – 'fringe bodies, quangos and all that' (Chester 1979) – was permeated with an implicit and frequently explicit normative bias against the role and use of these bodies. Since the mid-1990s a more balanced strand of literature has evolved in the UK, mainland Europe and the United States that has sought to encourage a more reflective analysis, which recognizes the problems associated with traditional forms of government *in addition* to the challenges raised by quasi-autonomous public bodies and 3Ps. This includes the work of Flinders and Smith (1998), van Thiel (2001), OECD (2002), Koppell (2003), Flinders (2004) and Pollitt and Talbot (2004). In different ways each of these books has sought to unravel simplistic assumptions about the structure and nature of the state while also generating new ideas and perspectives through theoretically informed research.

The aim of this chapter is to introduce the reader to the sphere of delegated governance (arm's-length public bodies and public–private partnerships) and highlight a number of related themes and issues, the intention being to shed light on the innate complexity of modern governance and encourage an expansive and sophisticated approach to how 'the state' is empirically and conceptually understood. For example, the increasing blurring of the boundaries of the state raises questions about the capacity of core executives and the steering of complex networks. From a conceptual point of view the increasing institutional hybridity poses questions about the legitimacy and accountability of the state, particularly in light of the fact that traditional understandings and procedures in relation to these concepts have historically been wedded to a state structure that to some extent no longer exists. The blurring of the public–private boundary also raises questions about the 'public sphere' and the degree to which certain societal dimensions or capacities should be protected or insulated from private interests.

The focus of this chapter is therefore on the outer fringes or boundaries of the state, (the 'grey zone' as it is known in Denmark), where the public–private distinction becomes opaque and the established frameworks for ensuring legitimacy, accountability and control become less clear. This chapter is divided into three sections. The first section seeks to dissect and tease apart the institutional structure of the contemporary state in order to demonstrate the great organizational heterogeneity that exists. The second section explores three themes (accountability, complexity and depoliticization) at both the conceptual and empirical level surrounding the existence of this dense tier of delegated governance. The final section seeks to provoke further interest in the study of delegated governance through the elaboration of a number of critical issues for the future. The next section reviews the topography and scale of delegated governance.

The topography of the state

This section seeks to dissect the anatomy of the state in order to demonstrate the vast range of hybrid and para-statal organizations that currently exist at the national level. Understanding this dense administrative terrain is important for a number of reasons but not least because a review of this kind will illuminate and explain the definitional debates that have tended to dominate this field and have to some extent concealed more important debates regarding the trajectory, structure and role of the state. Moreover outlining the range of organizational forms that currently exist may also add weight to the views of those who see the Westminster model (the dominant conceptual lens in countries including Australia, New Zealand, Canada and the UK), with its emphasis on departments each headed by a minister, as somewhat outdated, misleading and over-simplistic. While departments of state clearly continue to exist they form a shrinking section of an increasingly diverse administrative sphere.

Providing a map, or at least a sketch, of the topography of the contemporary state facilitates understanding in relation to ideas about degrees of autonomy. It is clear that some forms of delegated governance are designed and intended to have more autonomy than other forms. Hived-in agencies (meaning they are still formally part of their parent department) are intended to have less autonomy than hived-out bodies. While it is possible to map out this spectrum of autonomy it is much harder to ascertain why certain functions have been designated to certain organizational forms. It is equally difficult to understand why certain tasks are viewed by politicians and officials as suitable for delegation whereas other apparently similar tasks are not. Another challenge relates to appreciating the difference between theoretical and actual organizational autonomy. It would be naïve to automatically assume that an organization actually enjoys the practical autonomy its status is assumed to provide. Experiences in a host of countries suggest that politicians are frequently reluctant to cede control and will often seek to develop informal control mechanisms.

Clearly the degree of flexibility enjoyed by politicians in terms of delegating state functions to quasi-autonomous bodies or 3Ps also varies from country to country and is conditioned by a blend of constitutional, legal, cultural and historical factors. Taken together these factors create a path-dependency that may either facilitate or frustrate the process of delegating tasks to new tools or forms of governance. The freedom of members of the executive in the US and The Netherlands is restricted to some extent by the constitutional powers granted to their respective legislatures in relation to creating, merging or abolishing delegated public bodies. In the UK, by contrast, members of the executive enjoy great flexibility in relation to the structure of the state. However the impact of country-specific limitations on delegation and varying national pathways towards the increased use of 3Ps has to some extent been ameliorated by a broader shift in governing mentality; a shift that has generally accepted the logic of delegation and led to a general trend towards what Pollitt and Talbot (2004) refer to as 'unbundling' government.

The structure of the modern state at the national level can be viewed as a series of concentric circles or ripples on a pond with departments of state at the centre and a number of organizational forms, each enjoying a greater degree of autonomy as they radiate out from the centre. Figure 12.1 provides an overview of the structure of the British state at the national level as of March 2005 by way of example.

Figure 12.1 *Delegated governance and PPPs: an overview*

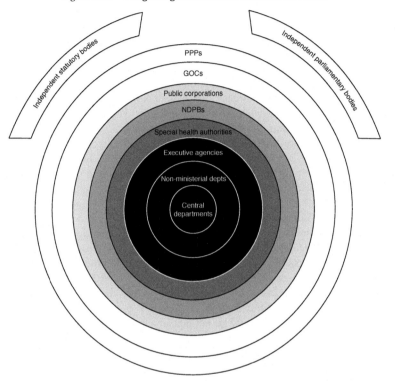

The most striking feature of this figure is the simple variety of organizations that exist beyond the twenty or so ministerial departments of state. This includes no less than 26 non-ministerial departments, 11 public corporations, 127 executive agencies, 17 national special health authorities, 439 advisory non-departmental public bodies (NDPBs), 36 tribunal NDPBs, over 200 executive NDPBs and 147 independent monitoring boards. On the very edge of the state exist a number of government-owned companies and 3Ps. In Britain the government has entered into more than 550 private finance initiative projects, a distinct form of P3, with a total capital value of 35 billion pounds. These projects include 34 hospitals and 119 other health projects, 239 refurbished schools, 23 transport projects, 34 police and fire stations, 13 prisons and secure training centres, 12 waste and water installations and a variety of other projects involving defence, leisure, tourism, culture, housing and IT.

Figure 12.1 also includes two organizational forms that are distinct and separate from the spectrum of autonomy. Independent statutory bodies generally cover professional regulatory bodies (such as the General Medical

Council and Law Society). These bodies have certain regulatory roles and are usually founded in statute but they receive no public monies and are viewed as being completely distinct from the governmental framework. However, this does not prevent a government from considering amending the founding legislation where professional self-regulation is viewed as being problematic. The second disconnected organizational form on Figure 12.1 refers to independent parliamentary bodies, for example the Electoral Commission and the Church Commissioners, that are formally independent of political influence but are funded by and directly accountable to Parliament rather than to a government department.

The UK is by no means unique in having such a disaggregated administrative landscape (see Modeen and Rosas 1988). Canada, the United States, France, Germany, The Netherlands, New Zealand, Spain, Sweden and Australia, to mention but a few, have similarly complex delegated state structures (see Table 12.1). The state in New Zealand, for example, includes around 3,000 organizations but fewer than 50 of these are departments of state, the remainder being a complex tier of quasi-autonomous Crown entities. The sheer scale of delegated governance in terms of resources, role and personnel is surprising; especially when viewed against the relative dearth of academic research in the field. Research by the OECD in 2002 found that it was by no means uncommon for more staff to be employed in what they described as 'distributed public governance' organizations than traditional departments of state. The implicit and increasing heterogeneity of modern state structures relates directly to the shift from govern*ment* to govern*ance* that was examined by Pierre and Peters in the previous chapter. It is not that the mechanisms of governance have replaced the traditional institutions of government but that the latter now exists in and operates through an increasingly dense web or network of organizations each of which enjoys a significant degree of day-to-day autonomy from elected politicians.

Analysing the existence and evolution of delegated governance within various state structures not only point to country specific variations in form and extent but also a number of evolutionary similarities or areas of convergence. First, since the mid-1980s wave after wave of reform has attempted to delegate as many functions as possible along the spectrum of autonomy from the centre outwards. Consequently the role of central departments has changed from administering public policy to co-ordinating the web of organizations, each of which enjoy different degrees of autonomy, to which implementation has now been delegated.

A second evolutionary pattern borne out through comparative research is that the process of delegating roles and responsibilities to para-statal bodies or P3s has not been undertaken in a systematic or logical manner

Table 12.1 *A comparative review: examples of delegated or 'para-statal' bodies*

Country	Quasi-autonomous bodies (examples)
France	Public establishments (*éstablissements publics Nationaux*)
	Independent administrative authorities (*autorités administratives indépendantes*)
Germany	Federal agencies (*unmittelbare Bundesverwaltung*)
	Indirect federal administration (*mitelbare Bundesverwaltung*)
	Private law entities (*Bundesverwaltung in Privatrechtsform*)
The Netherlands	Independent adminstrative bodies (*zelfstandige bestuursorganen, ZBOs*)
	Agencies (*agentschappen*)
Sweden	Boards and agencies
Denmark	Special public agencies
	State-owned companies
	Self-governing institutions
	Private companies with contracts for public services.
Spain	Autonomous bodies (*organismos autonomos*)
	Public enitities (*entitades publicas empresariales, EPE*)
	Public bodies (*organismos publicos*)
Italy	Public establishments (*enti pubblici*)
	Independent administrative authorities (*autorite adminstrative indepdendente*)
	Agencies (*agenzie*)
United States	Independent agencies
	Independent regulatory commissions
	Government-owned enterprises/corporations
	Hybrid bodies
Japan	Independent administrative institutions (dokuritsu-gyoseihojn)
Thailand	Autonomous public organizations (*ongkarn mahachon*)
New Zealand	Crown entities
	Semi-autonomous bodies
Canada	Special operating agencies
	Legislated service agencies
	Departmental agencies

(see OECD 2002). The delegation of tasks has largely been bereft of any coherent legal framework or even a broad statement of principles. Functions have largely been delegated on an ad hoc basis, which explains why the fringes of the state tend to be messy, confused and devoid of any underpinning rationale or logic. An awareness that delegated governance is a systemic issue in advanced liberal democracies, and of the democratic and public policy implications of this fact, has really only developed in recent years.

A third general area of convergence would appear to be a trend away from delegating tasks to quasi-autonomous public bodies towards establishing P3s with the private sector, such as the private finance initiative in the UK or the privately financed projects in Australia. In some countries, such as the UK, this process has been stimulated by the fact that there are very few areas of state responsibility that have not already been delegated. However, there is a wider shift towards utilizing P3s as an innovative way to deliver certain services in partnership *with but not directly by* the state. Thereby constructing a 'middle-way' state system somewhere between corporatist models of traditional social democrats and the minimal state pro-privatization ideal of neo-liberals. This delegation of responsibilities to bodies or partnerships on the fringe of the state is not necessarily aimed at achieving a smaller state or reducing public services but it is an explicit recognition that the modern state may not be the best manager of public services and that other structures may deliver improved levels of service. It is also linked to the issue of capacity as governments are increasingly seeking to buy in capacity from the private sector to complement or improve that offered by traditional state structures.

This shift in statecraft has been nurtured and promoted by major international financial institutions, including the World Bank, International Monetary Fund and the European Bank for Reconstruction and Development (Jones 1999). Consequently, 3Ps are an increasingly significant aspect of state structures around the world. Indeed, Bovaird (2004a) notes how 3Ps are now written into legislation in many countries (e.g. urban policy legislation in the UK and US, industrial policies in France and economic development practices in Italy and the Netherlands). However, with the possible exception of Ireland, the concept and use of 3Ps has been hotly contested in most countries. Some politicians have voiced concerns about the further diminution of direct political control, trade unions have frequently interpreted 3Ps as 'privatization by stealth' and public interest groups have criticized state reforms that are based upon the introduction of the profit motive. Despite these concerns and criticisms Bovaird (2004b) suggests that 3Ps have evolved from 'contested concepts to prevalent practice'.

A fourth trend indicates a common pattern of 3P development. State systems commonly begin by experimenting with construction or low-salience partnerships (road building, waste collection, etc.) which then begins an incremental process through which further areas of state activity are gradually opened up to 3Ps (care for the elderly, education provision, clinical medicine, welfare-to-work programmes, prison management, etc.). Cross-comparative research also reveals that a common underlying reason for delegating function to the boundaries of the state – constraints on spending resources combined with a public reluctance to pay higher taxes. In this context the efficiency gains suggested (but rarely delivered) by either delegating functions to independent public bodies or entering into 3Ps become attractive.

A final trend to be found across the world relates to organizational drift. It is common for functions to 'drift' along this spectrum of autonomy from the centre to the periphery and relatively rare, but not unknown, for a function to be drawn back in towards the department. The Forensic Science Service (FSS) in the UK is a good example of organizational 'drift'. It used to be part of a central department (the Home Office) until it became an executive agency in 1991, a trading fund in 1999, and in 2005 the government announced its intention to establish the FSS as a government-owned company as a step towards establishing the service as a 3P at some point in the future. Not only do organizations evolve and frequently 'drift' but certain organizational forms of delegated governance frequently spawn sub-species which themselves enjoy further autonomy. The creation of 3Ps, for example, will frequently lead to the creation of a new independent body to oversee and regulate the relationship between the commissioning public sector authority and the private sector partner. For example, in the UK a new independent body called the Office of the Public Private Partnership Arbiter will determine disputes arising from the thirty-year 3Ps for the maintenance, renewal and upgrade of parts of the London underground tube train system. In the US 3Ps for highway construction or renewal commonly involve the creation of a semi-independent quasi-governmental entity, separate from local, state or federal government, with various degrees of increased responsibility for project development and finance (see Lockwood 1990). It is therefore possible to trace the development of a complex web of independent organizations, each of which enjoys an indirect relationship with elected politicians, each enjoying differing degrees of autonomy which further strain traditional forms of co-ordination and accountability. Appreciating the existence and impact of this multi-level aspect may add further weight to those proponents of the multi-level governance (MLG) approach as a more realistic and nuanced organizing perspective for the study of modern governing processes (for a discussion see Bache and Flinders 2004).

Indeed it is critical to appreciate that the boundaries of the state operate not only horizontally but also vertically in that delegated organizational forms exist at the sub-national, supra-national and global levels. For example, a number of arm's-length agencies exist within the evolving architecture of what could be interpreted as a European state project (see Table 12.2).

Beyond the supra-national tier exist a number of independent global actors such as the World Bank, International Monetary Fund, International Atomic Energy Agency, International Council of Arbitration for Sport, World Anti-Doping Agency and the World Intellectual Property Organization. The delegation of tasks to quasi-autonomous actors at the supranational

Table 12.2   *European quasi-autonomous agencies and independent financial institutions*

Founding basis	Agencies
EC Treaty	European Environment Agency
	European Agency for Reconstruction
	European Maritime Safety Agency
	European Food Safety Authority
	European Aviation Safety Agency
	European Railway Agency
	European Network and Information Security Agency
	Community Plant Variety Office
	Translation Centre for Bodies of the European Union
	European Agency for Safety and Health at Work
	Office for Harmonisation in the Internal Market
	European Medicines Agency
	European Monitoring Centre for Drugs and Drug Addiction
	European Training Foundation
	European Foundation for the Improvement of Working and Living Conditions
	European Monitoring Centre on Racism and Xenophobia
	European Centre for the Development of Vocational Training
Euratom Treaty	Euratom Supply Agency
Second and Third Pillars	European Union Institute for Security Studies
	European Police Office-Europol
	European Union Satellite Centre
	EuroJust
	European Agency for the Management of the External Borders
Autonomous financial institutions	European Central Bank
	European Investment Bank

and global level creates a clear link with recent research on the evolving structures and processes of MLG both within and between states. Organizations that operate on the boundaries of nation states must increasingly report to and operate within an external environment dictated to some extent by similarly independent organizations at the supranational level.

For example, European regulatory agencies in particular fulfil an increasingly important role in relation to global governance by providing a clear institutional locus through which to establish links with other supranational and global bodies. The European Medicines Agency (EMA) fulfils a dual-purpose role. Firstly, it fulfils a *downward* regulatory and co-ordinating role in relation to a network of 42 competent independent regulatory authorities at the national level (Medicines and Healthcare Products Regulatory Agency in the UK., National Institute for Medicine and Pharmacy in Portugal, Irish Medicines Board, etc.). Secondly, the EMA performs an *upwards* co-ordinating and harmonization role through its relationship with other supranational and global actors in this policy field (notably the Food and Drug Administration in the US and the World Health Organization). A similar network can be identified in the sphere of banking and finance where the European Central Bank and the European Investment Bank, operating through the European System of Central Banks, fulfil a similar two-way governance function; a *downward* co-ordinating and regulatory role in relation to national independent central banks and an *upwards* role in relation to global financial actors including the World Bank, International Monetary Fund and the OECD.

It is therefore possible to identify emergent structures of MLG that exist and operate at one-remove from governmental structures. The outcome of political and managerial reforms, particularly during the later decades of the twentieth century, has led to the creation of complex matrices in which functions have been redistributed both vertically and horizontally. Consequently, the reality of contemporary state structures is that they are highly fluid and heterogeneous networks consisting of a dense or 'thick' layer of organizations to which specific responsibilities have been delegated towards the outer fringes. As a result the boundaries of the state have become increasingly opaque, jurisdictional boundaries have become increasingly enmeshed and overlapping and the boundary between the public and private sectors is becoming increasingly blurred. Although these delegated public bodies and 3Ps play a central and largely positive role in modern governance their existence does create a number of challenges (both administrative and democratic). These challenges will be the topic of the next section.

The state: complexity, accountability and depoliticization

Arm's-length bodies and 3Ps have been increasingly utilized as a tool of governance within state projects because theoretically they offer a range of benefits over traditional governmental structures or procurement methods. Advocates of 3Ps suggest that inviting private sector partners to design, build and in some cases even manage public facilities can deliver increased levels of efficiency while transferring risk onto the private sector partner. The decision to delegate tasks away from central state departments to parastatal bodies is based on assumptions regarding managerial flexibility, efficiency, esoteric expertise, legitimacy and the capacity to construct inclusive board structures that bring together a range of stakeholders (see Flinders

2006). Many of these positive characteristics are *assumed* rather than *proven*. This section focuses on three core issues that form major challenges or issues for those interested in understanding the contemporary state: complexity, accountability and depoliticization.

Complexity

The unintended consequence of delegation away from large multi-purpose ministerial departments to generally single-purpose arm's-length agencies and the increasing involvement of private actors can often be a decline in strategic capacity, especially where institutions enjoy a legally entrenched autonomy. Clearly the co-ordination of a wide variety of organizations and actors is a complex task as national executives must attempt to strengthen its levers of control whilst working through an increased number of bureaucratic linkages and across a fragmented structure. In this context Downs' (1967) laws of bureaucracy (imperfect control, lessening control, diminishing control and counter control) are pertinent. Put simply, the greater number of organizations involved in a network, the greater the number of potential veto-points and therefore the harder it will become for politicians to steer the system towards desired policy objectives. Clearly the growth in the number of independent bodies and P3s within state systems over recent decades has markedly increased the number of linkages in the chain of delegation.

However, as the OECD's 2002 analysis of 'distributed public governance' in nine countries discovered, the trend towards delegation was not matched with any systematic reflection or analysis on the consequences of this process for control and co-ordination. As Head of the British Civil Service in 1999 Sir Richard Wilson pondered on exactly this point and concluded, 'I would not claim that the manner in which we implemented all these reforms over the years was a model to emulate. There was not enough overall vision or strategic planning.' The growth in the number of linkages, and potentially the number of constriction points, is particularly problematic in policy sectors that demand an integrated approach or do not lend themselves to traditionally recognized functional distinctions. Issues such as mental health, homelessness and drugs awareness demand a high degree of inter-organizational collaboration in order to achieve effective outcomes. An institutional and cultural defect of 'unbundling' the state into predominantly single-purpose public bodies and 3Ps may well be 'tunnel vision' in which actors focus on achieving their targets, thereby undermining the incentives for multi-agency co-operation.

As a result elected politicians must devise ways to steer increasingly complex networks whilst upholding the operational independence of the organizations concerned. Contemporary projects concerning 'joined-up' or 'holistic' governance represent an attempt to devise new mechanisms or tools to steer dense organizational webs. Wright and Hayward (2000) analysed how the core executives of France, Germany, The Netherlands, Italy, Austria and Spain have sought to increase their steering capacity. Their conclusion noted (2000: 31):

> there was a persistent and increasing need to co-ordinate – not only in the six countries we investigated. It is a characteristic of advanced industrial societies. Core executives everywhere are locked into a plurality of inter-dependent forms of co-ordinative exchange, mixing both processes of unilateral adjustment and interactive modalities of co-ordination, of hierarchy and network.

A range of procedural and institutional reforms can be implemented with the aim of increasing strategic capacity and integration (shared budgets, merged structures, joint interface arrangements, cross-departmental public service agreements, etc.). Paradoxically, a tool frequently used to increase the steering capacity of the centre is to create a new independent regulatory agency to oversee a complex network of actors in a specific policy sector where problems have demonstrated the need for greater integration. In Britain this has been clearly seen in relation to food safety, media regulation and the railway system. The Food Standards Agency, Office of the Communications Regulator and the Strategic Railway Authority are all para-statal bodies created under the Labour government since 1997 to assume responsibility for specific policy sectors in which fragmentation is thought to have led to a range of concerns.

The issue of steering increasingly complex webs or networks of organizations, which often operate at and across different levels of govern*ment* and govern*ance*, is a central challenge for politicians. In essence, state structures appear to be evolving in a manner that Rosenau (2004) has termed 'fragmegration'. This relates to the creation of an increasingly fragmented state structure (i.e. more single-purpose delegated agencies, 3Ps, etc.) while at the same time attempting to foster greater integration (via notions of 'joined-up' and 'holistic' government) within the overall system. Increased complexity, however, is not just a challenge in terms of steering and co-ordination but it may also be problematic in terms of flexibility.

This flexibility dimension is particularly pronounced in relation to 3Ps, as many contracts are for between 15 and 30 years, sometimes longer, and this raises questions about the constrictions contractual obligations may place on either future governments that do not share the previous government's policy goals, or simply if circumstances change. The existence of a legally binding contract means that when a 3P contract needs to be renegotiated by a department of state the private sector contractor is in a very powerful position – achieving policy change may well involve lengthy and costly contract renegotiation. There is also the fact that many forms of 3Ps mean that new governments will inherit significant financial obligations. This raises the possibility that the policy flexibility of future governments vis-à-vis state structures may well be substantially constrained by the need to service significant contractual repayments entered into by previous governments. This issue is likely to become increasingly important as the proportion of total investment made up by 3Ps escalates – 'more and more of the budget will be committed, leaving less and less to the discretion of the public agencies and reducing flexibility' (Pollock *et al.* 2001: 14).

The flexibility and complexity dimensions relate to what appears to be the underlining theme of this chapter – state capacity. The shifting boundaries of the state are leading not just to institutional fragmentation in terms of structures but also in terms of knowledge. The delegation of tasks to para-statals or P3s is designed to deliver increased *institutional* capacity and yet this process risks undermining the *intellectual* capacity of the state in terms of its institutional history and epistemic potential as the delegation of tasks risks 'de-skilling' the state in certain areas and fields, thereby creating information asymmetries that weaken its bargaining position and reducing its holistic knowledge base. The issue of intellectual capacity and knowledge is not only an issue for core departments but also for external actors who may wish to hold delegated bodies and partnerships to account. The delegation of tasks to para-statals and P3s establishes a complex network of inter-dependency; when problems occur within this network or tensions occur regarding expected standards or operating norms achieving accountability and responsibility for these issues can be problematic, this will be the topic of the next sub-section.

Accountability

Delegated public bodies and P3s are the topic of an extensive literature concerning the accountability frameworks surrounding them. It is arguably fair to suggest that these bodies are viewed at best as democratically suspicious and, at worst, democratically illegitimate. However, debates surrounding the accountability of delegated organizational forms have tended to adopt a rather rosy view of the practical utility of traditional accountability frameworks towards the latter end of the twentieth century. Moreover, in terms of legitimacy there has been a failure to acknowledge that 'electoral' legitimacy is just one form of a complex concept and that other forms (expertise, experience, objectivity, professionalism) should not be derided. Moreover, falling turnouts in general elections across Europe, indications of low public trust in politics and multiple examples of political scandal do not engender faith in 'traditional' models. It is therefore important to locate statements regarding the accountability of delegated public bodies and 3Ps within a context that acknowledges the practical (in)adequacy, rather than the theoretical operation, of traditional modes of behaviour. In some cases the creation of 3Ps or independent bodies may actually lead to improved levels of accountability, new and innovative forms of downwards accountability and provide new democratic arenas in which members of the public can participate.

However, in terms of the traditional (upwards) approach to accountability through departments to ministers and then to a legislature it is clear that the delegation of tasks to organizations that have been explicitly created with a high degree of autonomy from mainstream departments is problematic. An organizational relationship has been adopted in which the direct link between minister and elements of the state bureaucracy has been severed. The creation of a quasi-autonomous relationship between ministers and delegated public bodies creates a 'buffer zone' through which ministers can on occasion seek to abdicate responsibility and 'blame shift' (see Hood 2002). The potential for shifting blame can to some extent be ameliorated through effective parliamentary scrutiny procedures. However, a central theme running throughout the country reports of the OECD's (2002) inquiry into 'distributed public governance' is the failure of parliamentary scrutiny mechanisms adequately to develop in a manner that allows them effectively to oversee their respective state structures. In Britain the House of Commons' select committees have long lamented their failure to oversee the vast majority of autonomous bodies while the French parliament is known as 'the great outsider' in relation to playing a role in the creation or oversight of delegated bodies.

In some ways the accountability of the delegated public bodies that operate at the boundaries of state structures is ensured, albeit in an awkward manner, by the fact that these organizations operate under the auspices of a parent department. There is generally a named secretary of state who can be called to account to the legislature about a particular concern or incident surrounding one of these organizations. In Westminster democracies in particular, such as Canada, New Zealand, Australia and the UK, the capacity for blame-shifting is bounded by the convention of individual ministerial responsibility, which provides a constitutional 'back-stop' in the form of a minister. If an issue becomes politically salient in the eyes of the public or MPs they will still look to ministers to provide an account or accept responsibility, irrespective of whether the policy is the responsibility of a state-owned company, an independent regulator or a quasi-autonomous agency.

However, for 3Ps a range of factors further complicates the issue of accountability; as the Institute for Public Policy Research (IPPR) has recognized (2004: 4) 'Public–Private Partnerships, like many forms of contracting for public services, disrupt traditional accountability structures.' This issue is particularly significant in light of the fact that there have been several high profile problems, scandals and failures with 3Ps. For example, in the Netherlands auditors have revealed that 3Ps for large-city transport projects have been far more expensive than conventional procurement, in New Zealand the 'Armstrong Affair' during 2002 put P3s at the centre of a national debate concerning ethics, integrity and the public interest, in the US costs for waste treatment partnerships have spiralled far beyond original estimates leading to project cancellation, in Demark the local authority of Farum became embroiled in a disastrous financial scandal concerning the 3Ps it had entered, in Nova Scotia a P3 for thirty new schools collapsed leaving the province with long-term liabilities and a total project cost 32 million dollars above conventional procurement methods, in the UK multi-million pound 3Ps for government information technology systems have been plagued by failure.

Each of these incidents has illuminated the problem of achieving clarity of accountability within complex webs. These concerns are especially problematic if the public body responsible for managing the relationship with a private partner is not the same body that negotiated the contract in the first place. A change in political control at the local or national level may create a critical tension if the incoming government does not share the values and import enshrined in the partnership contract. This is likely to lead to confused accountability, possibly the emergence of blame-games between stakeholders within the partnership. However, while the introduction of partnerships may increasingly demonstrate the fault lines that have existed for a number of decades in the spheres of accountability it is also possible to suggest that some 3Ps may offer new forms of accountability and a degree of democratic potential. The IPPR (2002, 213) note:

> partnerships create new challenges for public accountability. Devolving authority over decision-making and public expenditure to non-elected partnerships creates the need for new and robust forms of accountability. Community engagement can help to address the potential legitimacy deficit of some PPPs...as hybrid forms of public service organization become more common, so the need for hybrid models of accountability will grow.

In Britain, for example, the Department of Health (2002) has vigorously claimed that establishment of a number of hospitals as public interest companies with an increased level of independent and autonomy from Whitehall will create 'a new form of social ownership where health services are owned by and accountable to local people rather than to central government'. In terms of financial accountability some forms of 3Ps clearly build in a number of long-term and explicit safeguards relating to quality of service that can deliver a level of public accountability that could not be delivered under conventional public procurement methods. Many contracts build in deductions for poor performance and reserve powers that allow ministers to take immediate control over the operation of services in certain circumstances. However, there is a question over whether the financial penalties applying to companies involved in P3s are adequate. Politicians have frequently been reluctant to apply their contractual rights in relation to financial penalties, and even termination, due to a fear of discouraging the private sector from entering future 3Ps. And yet this reluctance undermines the fundamental logic and benefits of entering into 3Ps in the first place.

Although there would appear to be an imbalance between the rewards for success and penalties for failure, there are many different types and models of accountability. It may be that some forms of delegated governance are best legitimated not through the traditional model that focuses on either local councillors or ministers. This would take the form of new models of democracy involving the creation of new elected or indirectly elected forums. Some independent public bodies reserve positions on their board for members of the public, their role being to represent the public's interest rather than a particular sectional group. Many independent public bodies are well aware of a wider perception that they are not adequately accountable and have gone to great lengths to design and implement new and innovative accountability arenas and information flows (open meetings, user surveys, web-based consultations, etc.). Places on the management boards of some P3s can also be reserved for members of the public with individuals being selected by local elections, as is the case with some Public Interest Companies in the U.K. It may well be therefore that the boundaries of the state may offer valuable new civic governance arrangements in which members of the public can be reconnected to the public realm, no matter what type of institution delivers the service.

But two serious challenges confront those who advocate the construction of pluralistic accountability structures in relation to delegated governance. Firstly, from a conceptual position, reconciling the creation of 'fuzzy' or 'multicentric' accountability structures that reflect the increasingly diverse and fragmented state with a clear and effective bond of accountability between the governors and the governed is difficult. The great quality of the convention of individual ministerial responsibility, for example, *was* its clarity and focus. Therefore, promoting a pluralistic perspective also risks making the overall system weaker, vacuous and more complex. Secondly, from an empirical position the current framework for the use of 3Ps tends not to ensure transparency and openness in relation to the information that is required if the democratic potential of these forms of governance is to be realized. In many countries there are reduced powers for external audit to examine the use of public monies within 3Ps compared with the audit environment for most public bodies. In addition, freedom of information legislation rarely empowers interested parties to access even the most basic information, a 'commercial confidentiality' exemption often being unnecessarily over-used in order to prevent the release of information (for a case study see the research of Auerbach *et al.* 2003 in Canada). Ironically, it is exactly this release of information that may demonstrate value for money, silence critics and help to foster public trust. A more robust and comprehensive framework for the release of information on 3Ps would help to foster confidence and thereby encourage members of the public to get involved with what may potentially become new democratic arenas.

However, the creation of new democratic arenas does raise questions surrounding those who will participate in them and how new state structures may be able to encourage the politically estranged to get involved and prevent a small group of unrepresentative community activists wielding too much power. With a general trend towards falling electoral turnouts at the national and local level there is little evidence of an appetite for greater electoral engagement from the public. Many para-statals have experienced great difficulty in trying to recruit 'public members' for their boards. The rhetoric of progressive governance, social ownership and direct accountability assumes that the public want to be involved in the running of new governance structures but there is little evidence for this assumption. For example, in the UK the boards of the first wave of hospitals with independent foundation trust hospitals were elected during 2004 on the basis of a derisory electoral turnout – the board in one case being elected by well-under 1 per cent of those eligible to vote (see Klein 2004).

A core belief of the 'progressive governance' enthusiasts across Europe is that it is necessary to redefine the structure and culture of state bureaucracies in order to increase efficiency, standards and choice while protecting the public sector ethos. As part of this agenda many governments have sought to challenge the traditional public–private distinction and develop a 'third way' in which the positive attributes of both the private and public sectors can be combined. The theoretical capacity of arm's-length bodies and 3Ps to offer independence and control while at the same time marrying the public and private sectors make them a particularly attractive governance mechanism. The result of which has been a marked shift in the nature and contours of the state. A key reason for this shift relates to a belief in possibility and benefits of 'depoliticization' as a central tool of statecraft. This has clear implications for complexity and accountability as well as broader understandings of the concept of the state. This will be the topic of the next sub-section.

Depoliticization

Although the concept of depoliticization has existed as an important theme in international politics, development studies, and political theory for some time, in recent years it has become a significant issue for scholars interested in governance and the state (Burnham 2001). Within the same period depoliticization has been proposed by think tanks and pressure groups as a solution to both public policy and constitutional challenges. The European Policy Forum (2000) has described the 'depoliticization of many government decisions' as 'one of the most promising developments' since the Second World War while in the UK the Labour government has stated:

> What governs our approach is a clear desire to place power where it should be: increasingly not with politicians, but with those best fitted in different ways to deploy it. Interest rates are not set by politicians in the Treasury but by the Bank of England. Minimum wages are not determined in the DTI, but by the Low Pay Commission. Membership of the House of Lords will be determined not in Downing Street but in an independent Appointments Commission. This depoliticizing of key decision-making is a vital element in bringing power closer to the people. (Falconer 2003)

Depoliticization refers to an attempt to sever political connections, or as Burnham (2001: 128) defines it: 'the process of placing at one remove the political character of decision-making'. Buller and Flinders (2005) have sought to distinguish between different types of depoliticization tactics and have outlined three distinct yet inter-dependent forms (see Table 12.3).

Each of these depoliticization techniques raises fundamental questions about the nature, role, capacity and structure of modern states. Moreover, the techniques should not be viewed in isolation; it is common for a range of depoliticization measures to be employed within the same policy sphere in a complementary manner.

More broadly, the logic of depoliticization appears to have been accepted not only within the governing mentality of the political elite of many nation

Table 12.3   *Depoliticization tactics*

Depoliticization tactic	Form	Example
Institutional	Principal–agent relationship created between minister and 'independent' agency.	Food Standards Agency
Rule-based	The adoption of explicit rules into the decision-making process.	Exchange Rate Mechanism
Preference-shaping	The espousal of a rhetorical position that seeks to portray certain issues as beyond the control of national politicians.	Globalization

states but also within the minds of the public. As Lord Dahrendorf noted in his afterword to '*Disaffected Democracies*' (Pharr and Putnam 2000: 312):

> Ostensibly non-political institutions are more acceptable to many citizens than explicitly political ones. There is consequently much support for independent central banks...At the same time there is little resistance to the creation of ever more 'quangos' or organizations that look non-governmental while in fact serving governmental functions.

Arguably the most common form of depoliticization is institutional and involves the creation of para-statal bodies to which specific policy, decision-making or regulatory powers are delegated. The theoretical rationale is that politicians are rational self-interested utility maximizers, who may adopt irrational policies for short-term political gains, the mere potential of which is said to undermine both policy credibility and the commitment of private actors. However, the adoption of such a theoretical position to legitimate the transfer of functions to insulated bodies largely beyond the scope of parliamentary politics arguably needs to be substantiated with empirical evidence to legitimize the democratic costs of such a reform. The link between delegation and superior economic outcomes has been strongly critiqued, Pollitt (2004: 331) notes:

> Neither in the UK nor in the Netherlands, nor apparently in any other country has there been any scientific study that shows that the conversion from a division of a ministry to an autonomous agency or quangos consistently produces enhancements in efficiency or effectiveness.

The creation of para-statals can arguably only be justified in exceptional circumstances, as the democratic implications are far-reaching. As Shapiro (1997: 289) notes, 'The creation of such an "apolitical" independent agency is rather like constitutionally guaranteeing rights. It is the announcement by the demos that it does not trust itself and wishes to put certain policy questions beyond its own reach.' There is also a clear link between depoliticization and complexity and accountability. The current vogue towards depoliticization has contributed to the creation of an increasingly complex state structure. Moreover, in terms of accountability it is possible to suggest that depoliticization is a strategy that can be used to abdicate political responsibility for making highly emotive value-based judgements in policy sectors that are devoid of historical precedent or societal accord. The danger is that a disconnection between the state and politics may occur through the delegation of responsibilities and the rhetorical veneer of depoliticization. It is in this vein that Poggi (1990: 192) has warned against 'the neutralization of democratic politics and its replacement by bureaucratic politics... invisible politics' and Mouffe (2000) has similarly noted the existence of a 'democratic paradox' stemming from a belief that reducing the role of elected politicians can enhance the legitimacy of the decision-making process. On the contrary, Mouffe argues that depoliticization may augment public confusion about where responsibility lies and how to play a role in the policy-making process and that visible arenas of political contestation are a vital element of a modern and healthy democracy without which the public may withdraw, disaffected, from politics and adopt less constructive forms of expression.

There are also a number of practical issues that deserve brief comment. First, although politicians may claim an organization operates beyond direct political control it would be naïve to assume the organization has been depoliticized or that influence cannot operate via a number of informal channels. The international comparative research of the COBRA network based at the Catholic University of Leuven into autonomy and control in the public sector has discovered a frequent discrepancy between the autonomy some delegated organizations are supposed to enjoy in theory compared to their actual autonomy. This 'rhetoric–reality gap' has been evident in relation to a number of theoretically depoliticized organisations. For example, the British Broadcasting Corporation was established as a public corporation on the basis that there was a need to insulate the organization from political influence and manipulation. However, the memoirs of the former Director General, Greg Dyke, highlight the extent of informal pressure placed on the corporation during 2003 and 2004 by the Prime Minister's Director of Communications and other officials (see Dyke 2004).

The issue of informal political control and influence exposes a deeper and more fundamental problem with the notion of depoliticization vis-à-vis the state – an issue is made no less political by delegating responsibility for that area of policy to an appointed arm's-length body. While politicians may seek to insulate certain issues from the political domain, it is unlikely that the wider public of that polity will accept that a certain issue is no longer 'political' – decisions about interest rates, human cloning or the safety of food remain intensely political decisions. Depoliticization is, therefore, something of a misnomer for a process that might more accurately be referred to as arena-shifting: the politics remains but the decision-making arena changes.

The degree of true 'depoliticization' is also questionable at the empirical as well as conceptual level; not only do 'depoliticized' bodies operate within a narrow and prescriptive policy framework set by ministers but their members are also generally appointed and funded by ministers. Concerns about depoliticization and the increasing delegation of responsibilities to arm's-length bodies and 3Ps are essentially debates about the (re)distribution of power within evolving state projects: delegation is a synonym for the transfer of power. Majone (2002: 322) notes, 'the debate about the delegation of powers is really a debate about the fundamental political organization of the polity, rather than merely an issue of political and administrative efficiency'. These wider issues of the role, structure and responsibilities of evolving state projects and particularly in relation to organizations on the fringe or periphery, will be the topic of the next and concluding section.

Shifting sands: the boundaries of the state

Delegated public bodies and 3Ps have arguably become an essential and integral part of the modern state. It is for this reason that the aim of this chapter has been to introduce the reader to the sphere of delegated governance and highlight a number of related themes and issues, the intention being to shed light on the innate complexity of modern governance and encourage an expansive and sophisticated approach to how the state is empirically and conceptually understood. Indeed, without detailed refinement and further precision 'the state' is arguably an unhelpful and misleading concept in that it suggests a stability and homogeneity that simply does not exist. Moreover the contemporary magnitude of delegated governance and the opening-up of more and more areas of state activity to 3Ps are exposing many of the ambiguities and flawed assumptions of traditional state theories as well as posing new questions about the complexities of modern (multi-level) governance, the trade-off between certain state-related concepts and whether there are certain core responsibilities that must remain state functions. It is these broader questions arising from the existence of delegated governance mechanisms that this concluding section considers.

The work of Hooghe and Marks (2003) on multi-level governance (MLG) and the 'unravelling' of state projects provide a valuable framework for conceptualizing recent trends and challenges. They identify two types of MLG. Type I MLG echoes federalist thought, conceiving the dispersion of authority as being restricted to a 'limited number of non-overlapping jurisdictional boundaries at a limited number of levels'. In this view, authority is relatively stable and analysis is focused on individual levels of government rather than specific policies. Type II MLG provides a vision of governance that is 'a complex, fluid, patchwork of innumerable, overlapping jurisdictions'. Here, governance locates around particular functions, and jurisdictions tend to be flexible as demands for governance change. The value of this simple framework is that it identifies the emergence of single-purpose public bodies with varying degrees of day-to-day autonomy as existing alongside but not in place of traditional governmental frameworks. The 'multi-level' dimension also puts emphasis on the fact that, as noted above, delegated public bodies at the national level increasingly operate within a context structured and defined to some extent by autonomous actors at the supra-national and global level. As Hix (1998: 54) notes:

The EU is transforming politics and government at the European and national levels into a system of multi-level, non-hierachichal, deliberative and apolitical governance via a complex web of public/private networks and quasi-autonomous agencies.

Reflecting on the notion of MLG also feeds into the related debate regarding state capacity – or what has been termed the 'hollowing out' of the state (Rhodes 1994; Milward and Provan 2000). The creation of delegated public bodies and 3Ps operating at one remove from the state executives may be cited as further evidence of the diminution of the power of the state. Conversely, the creation of new strategic autonomous bodies could be interpreted as an attempt at 'filling in' or empowering state capacity. The inference is that any analyses of delegated governance mechanisms must be located within an appreciation of broader debates concerning the transfer and location of power and the implications this may have for governing capacities.

These debates frequently hinge on perceived or actual trade-offs between certain state-related concepts that are commonly presented as zero-sum games in which an increase on one dimension leads to a direct and equal reduction on the other – for example, accountability versus efficiency, independence versus control, public service ethos versus private sector values, or simply 'public' versus 'private' – when in fact these concepts are far too diverse and multi-directional to be understood in such simplistic and normative terms. Any understanding of 'the state' and associated concepts needs to begin from a more reflective and nuanced position that accepts the inherent complexity of modern governance. Independence and control may well be complementary (positive-sum) rather than conflictual (zero-sum) in certain political and governance environments. Imposing certain accountability frameworks may well increase the efficiency of an organization, but these may not be traditional upward-focused scrutiny channels but citizen-focused downward scrutiny mechanisms. Likewise the delegation of key executive or regulatory functions to arm's-length bodies does not necessarily mean that the centre has 'lost' control but simply that there has been a change of relationship which may well mean that the principal has greater strategic control over the agent than they previously enjoyed.

It is also critical to appreciate that the shifting boundaries of the state and the increasingly blurred distinction between the public and private sectors is creating a fervent debate concerning the limits of delegation and whether certain core state functions exist. Fundamental questions are being asked about the limits of the state, the future role of the private sector and whether certain cultural norms or principles – the public service ethos – that to some extent formed a binding glue amongst state employees, thereby possibly protecting certain values (integrity, due process, fairness, probity, loyalty, etc.), has been eroded and whether this matters. Leitch and Motion (2003) suggest that a potential consequence of the blurring of the demarcation between the public and private sectors is the opening of a 'legitimacy gap'. This gap is thought to occur when there is a perceptible difference between the expectations that are held by the public about the way an organization or partnership should behave and behaviour in practice. The problems surrounding the experience of several 3Ps (for example, the 2002 'Armstrong Affair' in New Zealand) have particularly focused on a difference in values or public morality especially in relation to the legitimate and acceptable role of the private sector in the decision-making processes of a democracy.

Understanding the role and extent of delegated governance not only, therefore, generates empirical questions about where 'the state' begins and ends, its institutional make-up and evolutionary developmental phases but it also provokes figurative and symbolic debates about the limits of the state, the public sphere and the fundamental nature of certain tasks or processes that may arguably need to be insulated for various reasons from the vagaries of the market and the profit motive. In essence, the state is a rapidly evolving organism within which a severe tension exists between the centrifugal pressures of management reform and the centripetal logic of political control. At the root of this tension lays a fundamental dilemma facing modern states; a dilemma regarding public expectations vis-à-vis the state and the capacity of political actors to control or suppress public expectations within a political marketplace. Higher public expectations and public resistance to paying higher taxes combined with factors such as longer-life expectancy are pressuring governments across the world into experimenting with innovative tools of governance in an attempt to maximize efficiency within the public sector. This drive to 'get more bang from each buck' is increasingly based upon delegating responsibilities away from the core state and entering into 3Ps. As a result the relationship between state structures and democratic frameworks are becoming more opaque and this risk of disconnectedness becomes more pressing.

Indeed, the theme of disconnection unites the issues of complexity, accountability and depoliticization discussed above. The delegation of tasks beyond direct political control via para-statal organizations and P3s has never been successfully accommodated within the democratic framework of representative democracy. It may well be, therefore, that the increasingly inter-dependent polity and complex state structures necessitate alternative understandings regarding the nature and feasibility of democracy and the relationship between individuals and the state. It is reconciling the manner in which the state is evolving within a clear and coherent democratic structure that is a central challenge for contemporary theorists of both democracy and the state.

Further reading

Flinders, Matthew (2006) *Walking Without Order: Delegated Governance and the British State* (Oxford: Oxford University Press).

Gill, G. (2003) *The Nature and Development of the Modern State* (London: Palgrave).

Hodge, G. and Greve, C. (2005) *The Challenge of Public–Private Partnerships* (Cheltenham, Glos.: Edward Elgar).

Koppell, J. *The Politics of Quasi-Government* (Cambridge: Cambridge University Press, 2003).

Poggi, G. (1990) *The State: Its Nature, Development and Prospects* (Cambridge: Polity Press).

Pollitt, C. and Talbot, C. (2004) *Unbundled Government: A Critical Analysis of the Global Trend to Agencies, Quangos and Contractualization* (London: Routledge).

Conclusion

MICHAEL LISTER AND DAVID MARSH

This book has surveyed a great deal of work on the state and reflects the views of a variety of different authors. As such, it is impossible to offer a simple conclusion that reflects all that diversity. Rather, we shall focus on two questions which, explicitly or implicitly, engage many of the contributors and return to some of the key themes raised in the Introduction. To what extent have theories of the state changed over the past few decades? Has the importance of the state, more specifically the nation state, declined in that period?

Changing theories of the state: has there been a convergence?

As noted in the preface to this volume, in part this book developed out of the section on power and the state in the first edition of Marsh and Stoker's *Theory and Methods in Political Science* (1995). Many felt that, while that section had merits, it covered too narrow a range of state theory and failed to examine applied work on the state. At the same time, one of the arguments in that section which attracted some comment was Marsh's contention (1995: Ch. 14) that there had been some convergence between the three theories covered, Marxism, elitism and pluralism. Here, we want to re-examine that argument in the light of the chapters in this book, addressing the question: to what extent does the argument about convergence hold in the light of the broader range of theories considered here?

Marsh's argument was that some convergence had occurred, although there remained key differences, particularly between pluralism and the other two theories. More specifically, he claimed that there were six key aspects of that convergence: an increased focus on the structural basis of privilege; a greater role for agency; the identification of limited number of bases of structured inequality; a growing statism; an emphasis on contingency; and a move to ascribe primacy to politics. Here, on the basis of the discussion in this book, we focus on five slightly different areas where our contributors offer some evidence of convergence: an emphasis on contingency; an acceptance that power is concentrated; an emphasis on the role of both structure and agency; a 'cultural turn'; and an increased focus on the state and its

248

institutions. Our aim is to identify both the extent of the convergence and the differences that remain.

Contingency: is a theory of the state possible?

To an extent, contingency seems a key feature of most of the theoretical positions analysed here. Most obviously, contingency is at the core of both pluralism and poststructuralism, although not in quite the same way. Pluralism sees power as diffuse, with no interest winning consistently across time and space. So, the government doesn't forward the interest of one class, gender or, indeed, interest group and, thus, the outcome of any policy decision is contingent. In contrast, poststructuralists operate with a much more radical notion of contingency. In their view, which in ontological terms is anti-foundationalist, there is no fixed 'reality' that exists independent of our understanding it. At the same time, the meanings we attach to institutions and practices are contingent and constructed within discourses. As such, they are also contested. Consequently, a general theory of the state which can be applied across time and space and which is thus extra-discursive is impossible.

Although most other theories do not go as far as to embrace such an anti-foundationalist position, few, if any, theorists would now argue that it is possible to develop a general theory of the state. Of course, pluralism never had a theory of the state. Pluralists certainly argued that power was not concentrated, but the exact nature of the distribution of influence in a particular society was an empirical question and the distribution would change over time. Similarly, as Evans indicates, it has often been argued that modern elitism is better viewed as an empirical refutation of pluralism, rather than a theory of the state. In contrast, historically, Marxism offered a clear theory of the state, along with a theory of history. However, most modern Marxists no longer adhere to a materialist theory of history or, as Hay shows, think that either a general Marxist theory of the state or even a theory of the capitalist state is possible. Rather, modern Marxist theorists like Jessop (1990) see Marxism as providing a set of concepts that can be used to examine particular states.

So, any idea that it is possible to develop a general theory of the state is now widely dismissed, although for different reasons from within different positions. Pluralism was never interested in a theory of the state and, while classical elitism had such aspirations, modern elitism is rooted in an empirical critique of pluralism. Marxism has changed most in this respect, with modern Marxists rejecting economism and determinism and embracing contingency and indeterminacy. Most fundamentally, poststructuralism is based on contingency, instability and conflict; so the state is a complex and contested series of sites where different discourses interrelate and compete. As such, no one theory of this terrain is possible.

A concentration of power: but how much?

The view that all positions now see power as, at least to some extent, concentrated seems confirmed by this broader survey of state theory, although, inevitably, with major qualifications as far as pluralism is concerned. Of course, elitism and Marxism always emphasized that power was concentrated. In addition, of the additional approaches considered in this volume, both feminism and green theory would see power as concentrated; to feminists patriarchy ensures that men exercise power, while, to most green theorists, the state and dominant economic interests combine to ensure the exploitation of the environment in their interest.

Even contemporary pluralism acknowledges that some groups are more powerful than others. Smith emphasizes this point arguing that as classical pluralism developed into neo-pluralism authors like Lowi (1969), McConnell (1966) and, particularly, Lindblom (1982) recognized that some groups, especially business, have a privileged position in liberal capitalist systems; that is that they have more power/influence. In addition, they accepted, implicitly if not always explicitly, that this position is, at least in part, structural. So, to Lindblom for example, governments need co-operation from business in order to ensure the economic growth on which they are dependent for re-election. Similarly, other groups may have a privileged position in relation to particular policy areas; for example, farmers' groups in relation to agricultural policy or doctors' professional bodies in health policy. Again, the position of these groups is in large part structural, with government depending on them for the effective delivery of policy. Of course, pluralists are not concerned mainly, let alone exclusively, with such structural power. Rather, their emphasis is still on interest group activity and the role that the interaction between these groups and government plays in the evolution of policy; a point we return to in the next section.

However, there remains one way in which pluralism differs from all the other state theories considered here. Of all the theories discussed in this book, probably only some strands of elitism would not accept a normative commitment to a political system in which power is diffuse or, at least, in which the concentration of power is limited (it is an interesting observation that, while almost all state theorists think power is very concentrated, few defend that concentration) but only pluralists argue that this is the case empirically. Most pluralists may have accepted the idea that certain groups occupy a structurally privileged position, but, in their view, this does not mean that power is concentrated. Instead, they argue that no one group dominates across both time and space. So, business may have a privileged position in relation to economic policy-making, broadly defined, at present, but it does not have influence in other policy spheres and its influence in the economic sphere has, and will continue to, ebb and flow over time.

As such, the idea that some groups have more power because of their privileged structural position has permeated pluralist thought, but it remains a much more important aspect of elitism, Marxism and most feminism, than of pluralism. In addition, poststructuralism sees plurality as axiomatic, viewing power as dispersed throughout society, thus, as Finlayson and Martin argue, destabilizing the idea of a singular political power. In this way, it seems to share much with pluralism, but this seeming similarity is illusory. Poststructuralists do not see power, as pluralists would, as diffuse in the sense that it is shared among various groups within society. Rather, in their view, at any one time a dominant discourse may lead to some groups in society being privileged. However, such privilege is always contested and unstable.

Structure and agency: towards a dialectical approach

Marsh (1995) argued that, to an extent, pluralism has increasingly acknowledged the role of structures and structured privileged. He also suggested that, in contrast, Marxism has moved away from its structuralist roots to acknowledge an increased role for agency. Smith's chapter in this volume confirms this analysis of pluralism, while emphasizing that pluralism's focus is upon political structures; hence, the interest in policy networks and iron triangles. Hay's chapter on Marxism charts the move away from economism and determinism and makes clear that this move leaves space for the role of agents and sees outcomes from the process as contingent – a point discussed above.

The key point here is that it is now widely acknowledged that any analysis of state/civil society relations has to recognize the role of structures *and* agents. Of the positions considered here, only poststructuralism would probably dissent from this view, given that, to them, the distinction between structures and agents is of little utility as it make no sense to talk of structures, and indeed agents, outside of a discourse. At the same time, there are still clear differences in the way that the other theoretical positions considered here view the structure/agency problem. So, pluralists still tend to privilege agency, as does public choice theory. However, it is increasingly common to see the relationship between structure and agency as dialectical; that is interactive and iterative. In this view, structures may constrain or facilitate agents, but agents interpret structures and, in acting, change them. This type of conceptualization is common in modern Marxism, in Weberian-inspired elitism and in historical and discursive institutionalism. We return to this issue in the second section of this conclusion.

The cultural turn: emphasizing the role of the ideational

The whole of social science has been influenced but what is often called the 'cultural turn'. In this collection that 'turn' is most evident in the chapters by Schmidt and Finlayson and Martin. As we emphasized, in broad terms poststructuralism operates from within an anti-foundationalist ontological position that rejects the notion that there is any real world independent of discourse. So, the 'real' is socially or culturally constructed; 'reality' is complex and irreducibly plural. Of course, this means, as we saw above, that poststructuralism, and other anti-foundationalist positions, have a very different conception of the state and of power than most of the other positions. However, the crucial point here is that this approach has had an important influence on other positions, in particular in emphasizing the need to take the role of culture and the ideational more seriously.

This influence is particularly evident in the new-institutionalist literature examine by Schmidt. Certainly, sociological, historical and, especially, discursive institutionalism have acknowledged the causal role of ideas and culture in explaining the form and actions of the state. In addition, the cultural turn has also played a crucial role within feminism, in many ways being at the core of third-wave feminism, and in much modern Marxism.

At the same time, of course, green political practice is based in large part on the view that ideas, green ideas, can subvert the material 'reality' involved in capitalist exploitation of the environment. In a rather different vein, pluralism has always allowed space for the role of ideas, seeing the political process as analogous to the market, with interest groups promoting ideas and policies competing for influence over government.

So, there is a general recognition of the role of the ideational realm in contemporary state theory. However, while poststructuralism prioritizes discourse, and views any distinction between the material and the ideational as meaningless (both are constructed in and through discourse), most Marxists see the relationship between the material and the ideational realms as dialectical. So, the ideational realm helps construct an understanding of the material world and through that construction changes it, while the material world affects the resonance, that is the effectiveness, of those ideational constructs. Again, this is an issue we return to in the next section.

Statism and institutionalism: is there more focus on the state?

In one sense, this book is based on the view that the state remains important and this is an issue that we return to in the next section. Actually, among the positions considered here, there are somewhat contradictory views on the role and importance of the state. So, in different ways, Marxism and pluralism have, more recently, paid more attention to the independent role of the state. In Marxism, as Hay shows, the move away from economism led to a focus on the relative autonomy of the capitalist state; indeed, in more recent times, both Jessop and Block have argued that the state can be completely autonomous from the ruling, capitalist, class. Of course most pluralists, tend to talk of the government rather than the state. Nevertheless, some like Nordlinger (1981) see modern pluralism as characterized by conflict between sections of government and their interest groups (for example, a Ministry of Agriculture and farmers' groups) and other sections of government and their interest groups (for example, a Ministry of Health and doctors' groups) over an area of policy (in this case perhaps diet and health). Pluralism is again retained, because no one interest wins consistently across time and space.

Of course, in some ways the rise of new institutionalism best reflects the renewed interest in the state. As Schmidt shows, while there are significant differences between the types of new institutionalism, all the types see the state and its institutions as a crucial focus of study, although not necessarily as the power centre.

In contrast, other theoretical positions are less focused on the state, or in the case of public choice theory see the role of the state as largely malign. Once again, it is poststructuralism that most challenges other ideas about the role of the state. As Finlayson and Martin argue, to the poststructuralist most other approaches treat power as a tool possessed and exercised by the state (although perhaps exercised in the interests of particular sections of society; capitalists, men etc.). However, to the poststructuralists power is a process, not a tool. It is dispersed throughout society and enshrined in state institutions and practices. These practices are complex and plural; they do not simply reflect or promote one set of interests, but neither is there pluralism. As such, the state is complex and needs to be disaggregated into various institutions and practices. It is a site, or a series of sites, in which competing discourses are played out. Consequently, it is characterized by change, instability and conflict. Overall, from this perspective, plurality is the key feature of both power and the state. In this position, the state and its institutions and practices may be an important focus of study, but it doesn't exercise power and isn't necessarily even one of the main loci of power.

At the same time, other positions also question the necessary primacy of the state as a locus of power or a focus of study. This is clearly reflected in the move towards talking of governance, rather than government, which is seen in much modern elitism and pluralism and among some new institutionalists. The argument here is that the state has been hollowed out, upwards, in the UK by power shifting to the EU, sideways, by the growth of executive agencies and private–public partnerships, and downwards, by devolution and the growth of powerful policy networks. In this view, contemporary societal developments, often characterized as a move from a modern towards a postmodern society – e.g. globalization; increasingly complex social identities and the growing importance of social divisions based on consumption, rather than production, locations, as well as the decline of the nation state – all mean that analyses and explanations which focus on the state are misguided.

Overall, while there has been a renewed interest in the state in Marxism, pluralism and new institutionalism, such a focus has been challenged by other positions. Here again, the answer may be that we need to reject the dualism, which leads to a privileging of either the state or civil society. Rather, the focus should be very directly on the relationship *between* the state and civil society, not on privileging either.

The role of the state: challenges and responses

In this section we return to the question raised in the Introduction, about the continuing relevance of the state, before considering what issues need to provide the focus of a more sophisticated view on the role of the state.

The state still matters: but it may no longer do the things it did

In this section we turn to the issue of the role that the state plays in contemporary society. Many have argued that the nation state has been hollowed out by a series of related processes. As we indicated earlier, in this volume we have concentrated on four processes that many see as related: globalization; a shift from a modern to a postmodern state; a move from government to governance; and the decline of the public sector, with a concomitant increase in role played by the private sector in governance. Here, we shall argue, following the lead of our contributors, that, to the extent that such processes have been occurring, they do not mean that the role of the state has declined in any simplistic way. Rather, the role of the state has changed, so that we need a more subtle and complex analysis of the contemporary state, something that this volume begins to provide.

Clearly, this volume identifies changes within economic, political and social processes which have affected the state. David Marsh and Nicki Smith and Nicky Hothi analyse the ways in which changes, perceived and actual, in the global economy, probably more accurately characterized as internationalisation than globalization, have impacted upon the autonomy and sovereignty of the state. Similarly, George Sørensen identifies a change from a modern to a postmodern state. The modern state was based upon a community of people with linguistic, cultural and historical bonds, and as such a common identity, a national government, which was centralized, if democratic, and a primarily domestic economy. In contrast, in the post-modern state government is more differentiated and multi-level, identities are more complex, with both subnational (often ethnic) and supranational elements (European identity or Islamic identity), and the economic system is increasingly international. At the same time, Guy Peters and Jon Pierre discuss the putative move from government to governance, marked by a move towards a multi-level governance based on networks, rather than hierarchy or markets (a distinction we discuss at more length below). Finally, Matthew Flinders focuses on the expansion of delegated governance, where state control and accountability are weakened and the role of the private sector increased.

The key point here however, is that, while each of these contributions acknowledges that the processes they identify have, to an extent, changed the role of the state, none see this as necessarily indicating a decline in the state's role. Rather, they argue that any view that the importance and centrality of the state is being eroded is simplistic. So, while globalization, whether seen in material or ideational terms, may have transformed the context in which the state operates, it has not rendered it less important, because the state remains a crucial actor in these globalizing processes. Similarly, while postmodern states, if such they be, may have lost some direct control over policy formulation and implementation, they retain crucial legitimating and co-ordinating roles. Consequently, modern governance involves the state in more complex relationships with other governmental and societal actors, but it doesn't inevitably reduce its role or its power. Crucially then, the relationship between state and societal, or public and private, actors should not be conceived in zero-sum terms, with one 'side' exercising power at the expense of the other.

Another way of approaching these issues is to invoke the distinction between networks, hierarchies and markets as modes of governance (Williamson 1985; Thompson *et al.* 1991). Hierarchy as a mode of govern-ance involves close links (a strong coupling) between the public and the private sphere, with centralized control exercised by government. In contrast, the market involves a more heterogeneous mode of governance in which there is no structural coupling, with outcomes the result of market interactions between public and private actors without the state performing any co-ordinating role. For many, given that hierarchical modes of govern-ance increasingly seem outdated and that there is growing dissatisfaction with market-led solutions, networks are seen as an increasingly attractive, and increasingly common, mode of governance (Thompson 2003). Here, the state still has a key role, it still exerts power, but it does so less directly in the context of, and to an extent through, networks, in which actors have shared interests (it is a positive-sum game) and develop interdependent relationships based on reciprocity, trust and solidarity (Lowndes and Skelcher 1998). Three points are important here. First, as Thompson suggests, it is misguided to see these modes of governance as necessarily mutually exclusive, rather networks may coexist with hierarchies and markets. Second, to the extent that networks are becoming the dominant mode of governance, then the role of the state remains vital as it provides a crucial co-ordinating and legitimating role. Third, of the three modes of governance only markets involve a more limited role for the state and we would argue that, in a political system like the UK, markets are relatively less important as a mode of governance with hierarchy probably still being the dominant mode, even if networks are becoming more important (on this see Marsh, Richards and Smith 2001).

What would a more sophisticated conceptualization of the state look like?

Here, we focus on three important issues: the move from coercion to consent as the key underpinning of rule; the continuing active role of the state; and the changing nature of legitimacy.

From coercion to consent

Our argument here is that the stress in much literature on the state on its control over legitimate coercion is misguided in a period where rule depends much more heavily on consent than it did. At the same time however, the state still plays a very active role in the creation of this consent.

In our view, while the role of the state may be changing, such change does not translate straightforwardly into decline or diminishment. Indeed, it may be the case that, as modes of governance are changing, what is occurring is not a weakening in the power of the state but a change in the ways in which it exerts that power. The discussion of the distinction between hierarchies, markets and networks above suggests we may see this in terms of a shift from the state exerting power through coercion, to state acting as a co-ordinator or facilitator. This marks a departure from a Weberian, or neo-Weberian conception of the state which defines the state in terms of a dedicated personnel enjoying a monopoly of legitimate force. Certainly, historically, states, or state actors, exercised centralized power which was, in the last instance, backed by their legitimate monopoly control over coercive power – of course, to many theorists, particularly Marxists and elitists, the actions of these actors forwarded particular interests within society. Consequently, initially at least, hierarchy as a mode of governance rested, to a large extent, on this control. Obviously, while the nation state still, in most senses, enjoys that monopoly, it is much less important, and certainly much less obvious. Modern rule is based more on consent, than on coercion; although, of course, some would argue that such consent is manufactured or 'false'. To put it another way, the legitimacy of the increasingly complex contemporary state, in which networks play a more important role, depends on the state acting as a co-ordinator or facilitator. As such, we need a broader conception of the state which moves beyond the Weberian definition and reflects both that many actors, many of them non-state actors, are involved in modern governance and that the role of the state is now a different one, with more emphasis on the co-ordination of an increasingly complex mode of governance and less on its monopoly control over legitimate coercion.

Of course, these types of argument should not be pushed too far. The state has not become one actor amongst many. There are a number of reasons for continuing to afford the state a special position in analyses of social, economic and political processes. The fact that the state seems to make greater use of non-state actors should not obscure the fact that it is the decision of the state as to which areas to involve non-state actors in delivery, implementation or design of policy. There may be perceived pressures for non-state solutions to certain areas or issues, but it remains the decision of state actors whether to use public institutions or to make use of private sector resources. Such decisions are, and are likely to remain, contentious political decisions, reflecting different sets of ideas.

The active role of the state

In terms of arguments that the autonomy of the state is increasingly constrained by external economic factors, the picture is a little more complex. Our view would be that, whilst there are changes to the global economic system occurring, states do not simply respond to these changes. Rather, as some authors in this collection have argued, the reaction of states to changes in the economy, in terms of policy responses and institutional reconfiguration, is heavily mediated by the ideas which state actors hold about the environment in which they exist. As such, the process of globalization, we would contend, does not mandate a singular response from the state. The particular ways in which the state responds to these pressures is heavily mediated through an ideational filter. So, whilst some states may undertake actions which seem to erode their power and authority, this is their decision, not a response to some structured necessity. Indeed, although there is a large literature on state convergence (see Hay 2000; Garrett 1998), few would argue that the specific ways in which states adapt to economic changes are the result of structural imperatives. States are under pressure to change and adapt, and always have been. However, the specific ways in which the state responds to these challenges still predominantly reflects decisions made by state actors.

A curious feature of the debates about the hollowing out of the state is that it seems to be a process without agents. The state, we are told, is losing power and authority upwards to supranational institutions, sideways to the private sphere and downwards to increased demands for localism and devolved government. Yet, these changes are apparently occurring without anybody doing anything. Globalization is frequently appealed to as an external (structural) constraint. State inefficiency inexorably leads to greater involvement of the private sphere and the diversity of modern nation states requires an ever greater devolution of power and decision making to the periphery. However, these are not processes without agents. As has briefly been discussed above, the changes associated with globalization are taken by states, on the basis of particular understandings of what is occurring, and crucially, different states take different decisions on such matters.

The discussion of globalization by Marsh, Smith and Hothi clearly confirms this point. Much of the literature on globalization treats it as a process that acts as a structural constraint upon the state. However, the state has been a key actor in creating and sustaining the process. So, states have consistently followed policies, notably the liberalization of tariffs, markets and finance, which have facilitated the processes of globalization. Most importantly, Marsh, Smith and Hothi suggest that, in doing so, the UK New Labour government may be using the threat of globalization and the associated logic of no alternative (that is, the argument that globalization means there is no alternative but to pursue neo-liberal economic policies) as a means of party control, suppressing support for traditional social democratic policies. To the extent that this is true, globalization is used to facilitate the pursuit of policies New Labour wants to pursue; it is not a constraint.

It is clear then that the decisions taken by states which seem to weaken their power and influence can have favourable and useful consequences. For example, the decision by the Labour government in Britain to grant independence to the Bank of England as soon as it came to power in 1997 seemed to have divested the state of a number of what were hitherto seen as crucial instruments of economic management, thus reducing its autonomy. However, it could be argued that this empowered the state, at least in political terms. The state is now no longer responsible for fiscal policy and hence cannot be blamed for it, but it can, as the Labour government has done, bask in the glow of successful fiscal policy, claiming to preside over unparalleled economic stability and prosperity. It is also perfectly possible to see the new localism in the UK, where the central state sets targets which local services are expected to deliver on, and which is sometimes seen as an aspect of the hollowing out of the state, in precisely the same terms. Local government has more responsibility and takes the criticism if central government policies are not effectively delivered. Certainly, in our view it is too simplistic to see the state as a victim of structural processes which reduce its power. The state, as calculating agent is heavily implicated in these processes, sometimes for deeply political reasons.

It is also crucial to emphasize that different states are more or less constrained by global pressures. For example, a developing country may well have limited room for manoeuvre if an IMF loan is made dependent on economic liberalization. In contrast, the United States finds it easy to resist international pressure to sign up to the Kyoto climate agreement. As such, the decline in the autonomy of the state is differentially experienced and, consequently, we may not be witnessing a decline of the state *per se*, but, rather, a widening of the asymmetries of power between states.

The state and problems of legitimacy

As mentioned above, the state may choose to delegate the delivery of policy, or sometimes both design and delivery, but it is the state which legitimates it. The private sector cannot legitimately claim to represent the public good; it is only under the auspices of state delegation that such a claim can be made. Under this argument, it is the state that represents the people. Of course, many would argue that this claim is too simplistic. Legitimacy is a complex concept. The legitimacy of a monarch came from God. When this idea was increasingly criticized, theorists argued that legitimacy came from the people; that is the people are sovereign and they elect their representatives. The state has legitimacy because it is representative of the people.

However, this conception of legitimacy might be seen to be problematic for two reasons. Firstly, there has been a significant decline in political participation in many countries. As fewer and fewer people are involved in the selection of their representatives, the legitimacy of the state and the government may increasingly be called into question. Some may argue that a lack of political participation indicates the politics of contentment; that it is not real disaffection with the government and the state that produces declining political participation, but rather satisfaction, and as such that there is no threat to the legitimacy of the state. However, as Piven and Cloward succinctly phrase it, 'no one has satisfactorily explained why "the politics of happiness" is so consistently concentrated amongst the least well off' (Piven and Cloward 1989: 13).

The second point is a separate, if related, one. In many states there is some debate about who is a citizen and so definitions of the 'people' are contested. Here, we return to the issue of identity and notions of national identity are far from unproblematic. Increasingly, in most advanced states there are large numbers of residents, from foreign workers to illegal asylum seekers, who are not citizens. At the same time, there are even more people, first or second generation immigrants, who are citizens, but are regarded by many of the host population as failing to assimilate, or integrate. From the other perspective, many from ethnic, cultural and religious minorities often feel they are treated as 'second class' citizens and are not, in effect, represented by the state. Of course, the key point here is that modern states are now multi-ethnic, multi-cultural and have citizens drawn from various religious faiths, some very strongly held. Consequently, in contemporary states people have complex identities, reflected in the emergence of new terms which people use to self-identify; for example British Asian or British Muslim. Such complexities clearly make governance more difficult and, if such complexities are not addressed and resolved, then the legitimacy of the state may come into question. All this means that work on the state needs to pay particular attentions to the connection between the state and national, ethnic and religious identities.

Of course, these arguments should not be pushed too far. In most advanced democratic states, more people vote than abstain. At the same time, whilst the multicultural nature of modern states places pressures on the state to recognize and reflect that diversity, few members of minority groups reject the authority of the state. As such, while there are pressures upon the state, it has no real rival. Indeed, supranational political bodies, such as the EU are blighted by far greater legitimacy problems than nation states (see Schmidt 2004; Majone 1998). Consequently, whilst the state may face legitimacy challenges, it is at present, and for the foreseeable future, the body most equipped to deal with them.

Future directions

In the course of putting this book together, we have become conscious of other issues that could be usefully covered in future editions of this book, notably the relationship between the state, nation, nationalism and ethnicity; and the relationship between the state and international organizations.

In terms of the relationship between nationalism, ethnicity and the state, the issue becomes one of questioning the status of the concept of nation state. The idea of the nation state refers to a form of identification and belonging which subsumes local affiliations and is associated with the process of modernization (Gellner 1983). Yet, it is suggested in some quarters that processes such as globalization have weakened the ethnic and cultural bonds that underpin a nation and, hence, the notion of a nation state. If states are no longer national states, what underpins them and binds them together? The role, therefore, that nationalism and nations play in developments in contemporary states is an intriguing one. Some authors have argued that nations do not have mythical continuities with ancient communities. A distinction is drawn between ethnic groups, which have notions of kinship and a shared sense of history and culture, and nations, which are seen to be rational political organizations which may draw upon ethnic symbols for decorative purposes (Breuilly 1996; Hobsbawm 1990). How we conceive of nations, nationalism and ethnicity and their relationship to the state has significant implications for how we seek to analyse and understand the changes and challenges to which the state is subject.

Many of the preceeding chapters made reference to the arguments that the state is in decline, and contended that this was too simplistic and the developments should be seen as changes, with gains in state power and autonomy in some areas matched by declines elsewhere. There was, though, an acknowledgement of the increasing role played by international organizations, be they part of a putative global civil society, transnational business groups, international bodies such as the UN, IMF and WTO. It might be legitimately argued that this volume may have analysed in greater detail the relationship between such organizations and the state. We would argue that, while international organizations may be growing in importance, it is the state which, at present remains dominant. Of course, it could be argued that such a view reflects the fact we live and work within Western states and that the relationship between international organizations and developing states is a rather different one. Certainly, these remain areas for future exploration.

Bibliography

Abdelal, Rawi, Blyth, Mark and Parsons, Craig (2005) *Constructivist Political Economy* (Princeton: Princeton University Press).

Abrams, P. A. (1988) 'Notes on the Difficulty of Studying the State', *Journal of Historical Sociology*, 1(1): 58–89.

Acker, Joan (1989) 'The Problem with Patriarchy', *Sociology* 23(2): 235–40.

Acker, Joan (1992) 'Gendering Organizational Theory', in Albert J. Mills and Peta Tancred (eds), *Gendering Organizational Analysis* (Newbury Park, London and New Delhi: Sage).

Adler, E. and Haas, P. (1992) 'Conclusion: Epistemic Communities, World Order, and the Creation of a Reflective Research Programme', in P. Haas (ed.), *Knowledge, Power and International Policy Co-ordination*, special issue of *International Organization*.

Adorno, T. W. and Horkheimer, M. (1944/1973) *Dialectic of Enlightenment* (London, Allen Lane).

Afshar, Haleh (ed.) (1996) *Women and Politics in the Third World* (London: Routledge).

Aglietta, M. (1979) *A Theory of Capitalist Regulation* (London: New Left Books).

Agnew, John and Ó Tuathail, Gearóid (1992) 'Geopolitics and discourse: practical geopolitical reasoning in American foreign policy', *Political Geography*, 11: 190–204.

Agnew, John and Corbridge, Stuart (1995) *Mastering Space: Hegemony, Territory and International Political Economy* (London: Routledge).

Allen, J. (1990) 'Does Feminism Need a Theory of the State?', in S. Watson (ed.), *Playing the State: Australian Feminist Interventions* (London: Verso).

Almond, G. A. and Powell, G. B. (1966) *Comparative Politics Today: A World View* (London and New York: HarperCollins).

Almond, Gabriel (1966) 'Political Theory and Political Science', *American Political Science Review*, 60:(4).

Althusser, L. (1969) *For Marx* (London: Allen Lane).

Althusser, L. (1974) *Essays in Self-Criticism* (London: New Left Books).

Altvater, E. (1973) 'Notes on Some Problems of State Interventionalism', *Kapitalistate*, 1: 97–108; 2: 76–83.

Alvarez, Sonia E. (1990) *Engendering Democracy in Brazil: Women's Movements in Transition Politics* (Princeton, NJ: Princeton University Press).

Amos, Valerie and Parmar, Pratibha (1984) 'Challenging Imperial Feminism', *Feminist Review*, 17: 3–19.

Anttonen, Anneli (1994) 'Hyvinvointivaltion naisystävälliset kasvot', in Anneli Anttonen, Lea Henriksson and Ritva Nätkin (eds), *Naisten hyvinvointivaltio* (Tampere: Vastapaino).

Arrow, K. and Debreu, G. (1954), 'Existence of an Equilibrium for a Competitive Economy', *Econometrica*, 22: 265–90.

Ashley, Richard K. (1988) 'Untying the Sovereign State: A Double Reading of the Anarchy Problematique', *Millennium*, 17(2): 227–62.

Auerbach, L., Donner, A., Peters, D., Townson, M. and Yalnizyan, A. (2003) *Finding Hospital Infrastructure: Why P3s Don't Work, and What Will* (Ottawa: CCPA).

Avineri, S. (1968) *The Social and Political Thought of Karl Marx* (Cambridge: Cambridge University Press).

Axelrod, Robert (1984) *The Evolution of Cooperation* (New York: Basic Books).

Bache, I. and Flinders, M. (2004) *Multi-level Governance* (Oxford: Oxford University Press).

Bachrach, P. and Baratz, M. (1962) 'Two Faces of Power', *American Political Science Review*, 56: 947–52.

Banaszak, Lee Ann, Beckwith, Karen and Rucht, Dieter (2003) 'When Power Relocates: Interactive Changes in Women's Movements and States', in *idem* (eds), *Women's Movements Facing the Reconfigured State* (Cambridge: Cambridge University Press).

Banuri, Tariq and Spanger-Siegfried, Erika (2000) 'UNEP and Civil Society: Recommendations for a Coherent Framework of Engagement', paper prepared for UNEP by the Stockholm Environment Institute, Boston Centre and Tellus Institute.

Bardach, E. (1998) *Getting Agencies to Work Together* (Washington, DC: The Brookings Institution).

Barrett, Michèle (1980) *Women's Oppression Today: Problems in Marxist Feminist Analysis* (London: Verso).

Barrett, Michèle and McIntosh, Mary (1985) 'Ethnocentrism and Socialist–Feminist Theory', *Feminist Review*, 20: 22–47.

Barrett, Michèle and Phillips, Anne (eds) (1992) *Destabilizing Theory* (Cambridge: Polity Press).

Barrow, C. W. (1993) *Critical Theories of the State: Marxist, Neo-Marxist, Post-Marxist* (Madiscon: University of Wisconsin Press).

Barry, Andrew *et al.* (eds) (1996) *Foucault and Political Reason: Liberalism, Neo-Liberalism and Rationalities of Government* (London, UCL Press).

Barry, J. and Doherty, B. (2001) 'The Greens and Social Policy: Movements, Politics and Practice?', *Social Policy and Administration*, 35(5): 587–607.

Barry, John (1999a) *Rethinking Green Politics: Nature, Virtue and Progress* (London: Sage).

Barry, John (1999b) *Environment and Social Theory* (London: Routledge).

Barry, John (2003) 'Ecological Modernization', in J. Proops and E. Page (eds), *Environmental Thought* (Chelterham, Glos.: Edward Elgar).

Barry, John (2005) 'Resistance is Fertile: From Environmental to Sustainability Citizenship', in D. Bell and A. Dobson (eds), *Environmental Citizenship: Getting from Here to There?* (Cambridge, MA: MIT Press).

Barry, John and Eckersley, Robyn (eds) (2005) *The Global Ecological Crisis and the Nation-State* (Cambridge, MA: MIT Press).

Bates, R., Grief, A. Levi, M., Rosenthal J.-L. and Weingast, B. (1998) *Analytic Narratives* (Princeton, NJ: Princeton University Press).

Bates, Robert (1987) 'Contra Contractarianism: Some Reflections on the New Institutionalism', *Politics and Society*, 16: 387–401.

Bauman, Zygmunt (1989) *Modernity and the Holocaust* (Cambridge, Polity Press).

Beck, Ulrich (1992) *Risk Society: Toward a New Modernity* (Cambridge: Polity Press).

Beck, Ulrich (1995) *Ecological Politics in an Age of Risk* (Cambridge: Polity Press).

Beck, Ulrich, Lash, Scott and Giddens, Anthony (1994) *Reflexive Modernization*, (Cambridge: Polity Press).

Begg, Alex (2000) *Empowering the Earth: Strategies for Social Change* (Totnes: Green Books).

Bell, S. (2004) *Australia's Money Mandarins: The Reserve Bank and the Politics of Money* (Cambridge: Cambridge University Press).

Benhabib, Seyla (1995) 'Feminism and Postmodernism: An Uneasy Alliance', in Seyla Benhabib *et al.* (eds) *Feminist Contentions* (London: Routledge).

Benson, J. K. (1982) 'A Framework for Policy Analysis', in D. Rodgers, D. Whitton *et al.* (eds), *Intergovernmental Coordination* (Ames: Iowa State University Press).

Bentley, A. (1967) *The Process of Government* (Chicago, Chicago University Press).

Berg, A. van den (1988) *The Immanent Utopia: From Marxism on the State to the State of Marxism* (Princeton, NJ: Princeton University Press).

Berg, A. van den (1988) *The Immanent Utopia: From Marxism on the State to the State of Marxism.* (Princeton, NJ: Princeton University Press).

Berger, Thomas U. (1998) *Cultures of Antimilitarism: National Security in Germany and Japan* (Baltimore: Johns Hopkins University Press).

Bergqvist, Christina *et al.* (eds) (1999) *Equal Democracies: Gender and Politics in the Nordic Countries* (Oslo: Scandinavian University Press).

Berman, Sheri (1998) *The Social Democratic Moment: Ideas and Politics in the Making of Interwar Europe* (Cambridge: Harvard University Press).

Betramsen, R. B., Frolund, J. P., and Torfing, J. (1991) *State, Economy and Society* (London: Unwin Hyman).

Bevir, Mark and Rhodes, R. A. W (2003) *Interpreting British Governance* (London: Routledge).

Bevir, Mark, Dowding, Keith, Finlayson, Alan, Hay, Colin and Rhodes, Rod (2004) 'The Interpretive Approach in Political Science: A Symposium', *British Journal of Politics and International Relations*, 6(2): 129–64.

Biermann, Frank (2000) 'The Case for a World Environment Organization', *Environment*, 42(9): 22–31.

Biersteker, T. J. and Weber, Cynthia (eds) (1996) *State Sovereignty as Social Construct* (Cambridge: Cambridge University Press).

Birch, A. (1993) *The Concepts and Theories of Modern Democracy* (London: Routledge).

Block, F. (1987a) 'The Ruling Class Does Not Rule: Notes on the Marxist Theory of the State', in *Idem, Revising State Theory: Essays in Politics and Postindustrialism.* (Philadelphia: Temple University Press).

Block, F. (1987b) 'Beyond Relative Autonomy: State Managers as Historical Subjects', in *Idem, Revising State Theory: Essays in Politics and Postindustrialism* (Philadelphia: Temple University Press).

Block, F. (1990) *Revising State Theory: Essays in Politics and Postindustrialism* (Philadelphia: Temple University Press).

Blyth, M. (1997) '"Any More Bright Ideas?" The Ideational Turn in Comparative Political Economy', *Comparative Politics*, 29(2): 229–50.

Blyth, M. (2002) *Great Transformations: Economic Ideas and Institutional Change in the Twentieth Century* (New York: Cambridge University Press).

Blyth, M. (2003) 'Structures do not Come with an Instruction Sheet: Interests, Ideas, and Progress in Political Science', *Perspectives on Politics*, 1(4): 695–706.

Bonefeld, W. (1993) 'Crisis of Theory: Bob Jessop's Theory of Capitalist Reproduction', *Capital & Class*, 50: 25–48.

Bookchin, Murray (1980) *Toward an Ecological Society* (Montreal: Black Rose Books).

Bookchin, Murray (1982) *The Ecology of Freedom: The Emergence and Dissolution of Hierarchy* (Palo Alto, CA: Cheshire Books).

Bookchin, Murray (1992), 'Libertarian Municipalism', *Society and Nature*, 1(1): 93–104.

Borchorst, Anette and Siim, Birte (1987) 'Women and the Advanced Welfare State – A New Kind of Patriarchal Power', in Ann Showstack Sassoon (ed.), *Women and the State: The Shifting Boundaries of Public and Private* (London: Hutchinson).

Borchorst, Anette and Siim, Birte (2002) 'The Women-friendly Welfare States Revisited', *NORA: Nordic Journal of Women's Studies*, 10(2): 90–8.

Bottomore, T. (1973) 'Ruling Elite or Ruling Class', in J. Urry and J. Wakeford (eds), *Power in Britain* (London: Heinemann).

Bottomore, T. (1993) *Elites and Society* (London: Routledge).

Bouckaert, G. and Pollitt, C. (2004) *Public Management Reform: A Comparative Analysis*, 2nd edn (Oxford: Oxford University Press).

Bovaird, T. (2004a) 'Public–Private Partnerships in Western Europe and the US', in A. Ghobadian, N. O'Regan, D. Gallear and H. Viney (2004) *Public–Private Partnerships* (Basingstoke and New York: Palgrave Macmillan).

Bovaird, T. (2004b) 'Public–Private Partnerships: From Contested Concepts to Prevalent Practice', *International Review of Administrative Sciences*, 70(2): 199–215.

Breen, R., Hannan, D. *et al.* (1990) *Understanding Contemporary Ireland: State, Class and Development in the Republic of Ireland* (Dublin: Gill & Macmillan).

Brennan, G. and Lomasky, L. (1993) *Democracy and Decision* (Cambridge: Cambridge University Press).

Breslin, S. and Higgott, R. (2000) 'Studying Regions: Learning from the Old, Constructing the New', *New Political Economy*, 5(3): 333–53.

Breuilly, J. (1996) 'Approaches to Nationalism', in G. Balakrishnan, *Mapping the Nation* (London: Verso).

Briskin, Linda (1999) 'Mapping Women's Organizing in Sweden and Canada: Some Thematic Considerations', in Linda Briskin and Mona Eliasson (eds), *Women's Organizing and Public Policy in Canada and Sweden* (Montreal and Kingston: McGill-Queen's University Press).

Briskin, Linda and Eliasson, Mona (1999) 'Preface: Collaboration and Comparison', in *idem* (eds), *Women's Organizing and Public Policy in Canada and Sweden* (Montreal and Kingston: McGill-Queen's University Press).

Brown, W. (1992) 'Finding the Man in the State', *Feminist Studies*, 18(1): 7–34.

Brown, Wendy (1995) *States of Injury: Power and Freedom in Late Modernity* (Princeton: Princeton University Press).

Bryson, V. (1992) *Feminist Political Theory* (Basingstoke and New York: Palgrave Macmillan).

Buchanan, J. (1984) 'Politics without Romance', in J. Buchanan and R. Tollison (eds), *The Theory of Public Choice II* (Ann Arbor: University of Michigan Press).

Buchanan, J. (1988) 'Market Failure and Political Failure', *Cato Journal*, 8: 1–13.

Buchanan, J. and Wagner, R. (1977) *Democracy in Deficit* (New York: Basic Books).

Buchanan, J. and Wagner, R. (1978) *The Consequences of Mr Keynes* (London: IEA).

Buchanan, J. M. and G. Tullock (1962) *The Calculus of Consent* (Ann Arbor: University of Michigan Press).

Budge, I. (1996) *The New Challenge of Direct Democracy* (Cambridge: Polity Press).

Bukharin, N. I. (1921 [1926]) *Historical Materialism: A System of Sociology* (London: Allen & Unwin).

Buller, J. (1999) 'A Critical Appraisal of the Statecraft Interpretation', *Public Administration*, 77(4): 691–712.

Buller, J. (2000) *National Statecraft and European Integration* (London: Pinter).

Buller, J. and Flinders, M. (2005) 'Democracy, Depoliticization and Arena-Shifting', paper given at the SCANCOR 'Autonomization of the State' Conference, 1April 2005, Stanford University, USA.

Bulpitt, J. (1986a) 'The Discipline of the New Democracy: Mrs Thatcher's Domestic Statecraft', *Political Studies*, 34: 19–39.

Bulpitt, J. (1986b) 'Continuity, Autonomy and Peripheralization: the Anatomy of the Centre's Statecraft in England', in Z. Layton-Henry and P. Rich (eds), *Race, Government and Politics in Britain* (Basingstroke and New York: Palgrave Macmillan).

Bulpitt, J. (1995) 'Historical Politics: Macro, In-Time, Governing Regime Analysis', in J. Lovenduski and J. Stanyer (eds), *Contemporary Political Studies 1995* Volume 2, Exeter: PSA).

Burchell, Gordon, Gordon, Colin and Miller, Peter (eds) (1991) *The Foucault Effect: Studies in Governmentality* (Chicago: University of Chicago Press).

Burnham, J. (1943) *The Managerial Revolution* (London: Putnam).

Burnham, P. (2001) 'New Labour and the Politics of Depoliticization', *British Journal of Politics and International Relations*, 3(2): 127–49.

Cameron, D. R. (1978) 'The Expansion of the Public Economy: A Comparative Analysis', *American Political Science Review*, 72(4), 1243–61.

Camilleri, J. A. and Falk, J. (1992) *The End of Sovereignty?* (Aldershot: Edward Elgar).

Campbell, David (1992) *Writing Security: United States Foreign Policy and the Politics of Identity* (Manchester University Press: Manchester).

Campbell, David (1998) *National Deconstruction: Violence Identity and Justice in Bosnia* (University of Minnesota Press: Minneapolis).

Campbell, David and Shapiro Michael (1999) *Moral Spaces: Rethinking Ethics and World Politics* (Minneapolis: Minnesota University Press).

Campbell, J. L. (2001) 'Institutional Analysis and the Role of Ideas in Political Economy', in J. L. Campbell and O. K. Pedersen (eds), *The Second Movement* in *Institutional Analysis* (Princeton, NJ: Princeton University Press).

Campbell, J. L. and Pedersen, O. K. (eds) (2001) *The Second Movement* in *Institutional Analysis* (Princeton, NJ: Princeton University Press).

Campbell, John L. (2004) *Institutional Change and Globalization* (Princeton, NJ: Princeton University Press).

Campbell, John L. and Pedersen, Ove (2001) *The Rise of NeoLiberalism and Institutional Analysis* (Princeton, NJ: Princeton University Press).

Capling, A. and Galligan, B. (1992) *Beyond the Protective State: The Political Economy of Australia's Manufacturing Industry* (Cambridge: Cambridge University Press).

Carnoy, M. (1984) *The State and Political Theory* (Princeton, NJ: Princeton University Press).

Carter, Alan (1993) 'Towards a Green Political Theory', in Andrew Dobson and Paul Lucardie (eds) (1993) *The Politics of Nature: Explorations in Green Political Theory* (London: Routledge).

Castells, M. (1998) *The Power of Identity* (Oxford: Blackwell).

Cerny, P. G. (1997) 'Paradoxes of the Competition State: The Dynamics of Political Globalization', *Government and Opposition*, 32(2), 251–74.

Cerny, P. G. (2000) 'Political Globalization and the Competition state' in R. Stubbs and G. R. D. Underhill (eds), *Political Economy and the Changing Global Order* (Ontario: Oxford University Press).

Chappell, Louise (2000) 'Interacting with the State', in *International Feminist Journal of Politics*, 2(2): 244–75.

Checkel, Jeffrey (1998) 'The Constructivist Turn in International Relations Theory', *World Politics*, 50: 324–48.

Chester, D. N. (1979) 'Fringe Bodies, Quangos and All That', *Public Administration*, 57.(1) pp 51–54

Chondroleou, G. (2002) *Policy Networks in Comparative Perspective: Media Policy Networks and Regulation Policy in Britain and Greece*, PhD: York University, UK.

Christensen, Ann-Dorte and Siim, Birte (2001) *Køn, Demokrati og Modernitet* (Copenhagen: Hans Reitzel).

Christoff, P. (1996) 'Ecological Modernisation, Ecological Modernities', *Environmental Politics*, 5(3): 476–500.

Cockett, R. (1995) *Thinking the Unthinkable : Think-Tanks and the Economic Counter-Revolution, 1931–1983* (London: Fontana).

Cohn, D. (2005) 'The Public–Private "Fetish": Moving beyond the Rhetoric', *Revue Gouvernance*, 1(2): 2–15.

Colletti, L. (1972) *From Rousseau to Lenin: Studies in Ideology and Society* (New York: Monthly Review Press).

Colletti, L. (1975) 'Introduction', in L. Colletti (ed.) *Karl Marx: Early Writings* (London: Pelican).

Collier, D. and Collier, R. (1991) *Shaping the Political Arena* (Princeton, NJ: Princeton University Press).

Conca, K. (1994) 'Untying the Ecology–Sovereignty Debate', *Millennium*, 23(3): 701–11.

Connell, R. W. (1987) *Gender and Power* (Cambridge: Polity Press).

Connell, R. W. (1990) 'The State, Gender and Sexual Politics: Theory and Appraisal', *Theory and Society*, 19: 507–44.

Coole, D. (1988) *Women in Political Theory* (Brighton, Sussex: Wheatsheaf Books).

Cooper, D. (1994) *Sexing the City* (London: Rivers Oram Press).

Cooper, D. (1995) *Power in Struggle: Feminism, Sexuality and the State* (Buckingham: Open University Press).

Cooper, D. (1998) *Governing out of Order: Space, Law and the Politics of Belonging* (London and New York: Rivers Oram Press).

Cooper, R. (1996) *The Post-Modern State and World Order* (London: Demos).

Cox, R. (2000) 'Political Economy and World Order: Problems of Power and Knowledge at the Turn of the Millennium', in R. Stubbs and G. R. D. Underhill (eds), *Political Economy and the Changing Global Order*, 2nd edn (Ontario: Oxford University Press).

Crone, P. (1989) *Pre-Industrial Societies* (Oxford: Blackwell).

Dahl, R. (1958) 'A Critique of the Ruling Elite Model', *American Political Science Review*, 52(2): 463–9.

Dahl, R. (1961a) *Who Governs?* (New Haven: Yale University Press).

Dahl, R. (1961b) 'The Behavioral Approach in Political Science: Epitaph for a Monument to a Successful Protest', *American Political Science Review*, 55(4): 763–72.

Dahl, R. (1963) *Pluralist Democracy in the United States: Conflict and Consent* (Chicago: Rand McNally).

Dahl, R. (1969) 'The Behavioral Approach in Political Science', in Heinz Eulau (ed.), *Behaviorism in Political Science* (New York: Atherton).

Dahlerup, D. (1987) 'Confusing Concepts, Confusing Reality: A Theoretical Discussion of the Patriarchal State', in Anne Showstack Sassoon (ed.), *Women and the State* (London: Routledge).

Dahlerup, D. (2002) 'Using Quotas to Increase Women's Political Representation', in Azza Karam (ed.), *Women in Parliament: Beyond Numbers*, 2nd edn (Stockholm: International IDEA).

Dahrendorf, R. (1959) *Class and Class Conflict in Industrial Society* (Stanford: Stanford University Press).

Dale, J. and Foster, Peggy (1986) *Feminists and State Welfare* (London: Routledge & Kegan Paul).

Daly, M. and Lewis, J. (1998) 'Introduction: Conceptualising Social Care in the Context of Welfare State Restructuring', in Jane Lewis (ed.), *Gender, Social Care and Welfare State Restructuring in Europe* (Aldershot: Ashgate).

Davies, J. S. (2001) *Partnerships and Regimes: The Politics of Urban Regeneration in the UK* (Aldershot: Ashgate).

DeFilippis, J. (2001) 'The Myth of Social Capital in Community Development', *Housing Policy Debate*, 12: 781–805.

Delphy, C. and Leonard, D. (1992) *Familiar Exploitation: A New Analysis of Marriage in Contemporary Western Society* (Cambridge: Polity Press).

Deudney, D. and G. J. Ikenberry (1999) 'The Nature and Sources of Liberal International Order', *Review of International Studies*, 25(2): 179–96.

Devall, B. (1988) *Simple in Means, Rich in Ends: Practising Deep Ecology* (Salt Lake, Utah: Gibbs Smith).

Dicken, P. (1998) *Global Shift: Transforming the World Economy* (London: Paul Chapman).

Dicken, P. (2003) *Global Shift: Reshaping the Global Economic Map in the 21st Century* (London: Sage).

Dillon, M. (1996) *Politics of Security: Towards a Political Philosophy of Continental Thought* (London: Routledge).

DiMaggio, P. and Powell, W. (1983) 'The Iron Cage Revisited: Institutional Isomorphism and Collective Rationality in Organizational Fields', *American Sociological Review*, 48: 147–60.

DiMaggio, P. J. and Powell, W. W. (1991) 'Introduction', in *idem, The New Institutionalism in Organizational Analysis* (Chicago: University of Chicago Press).

Dobbin, F. (1994) *Forging Industrial Policy* (Cambridge: Cambridge University Press).

Dobson, A. (1990) *Green Political Thought* (London: Unwin Hyman).

Doel, M. (1999) *Poststructuralist Geographies: the Diabolical Art of Spatial Science* (Edinburgh, Edinburgh University Press).

Domhoff, G. W. (1967) *Who Rules America?* (Englewood Cliffs, NJ: Prentice-Hall).

Domhoff, G. W. (1970) *The Higher Circles: the Governing Class in America* (New York: Random House).

Domhoff, G. W. (1979) *The Powers That Be: Processes of Ruling Class Domination in America* (New York: Vintage Books).

Domhoff, G. W. (1980) *Power Structure Research* (Beverly Hills, CA: Sage).

Domhoff, G. W. (1987) *Who Rules America?* (Englewood Cliffs, NJ: Prentice-Hall).

Domhoff, G. W. (1990) *The Power Elite and the State* (New York: Aldine de Gruyter).

Donzelot, J. (1980) *The Policing of Families* (London Hutchinson).

Dore, E. and Molyneux, M. (2000) (eds) *Hidden Stories of Gender and the State in Latin America* (Durham, NC and London: Duke University Press).

Dowding, K. (1995) *The Civil Service* (London: Routledge).

Dowding, K. (2001) 'There Must Be An End to Confusion: Policy Networks, Intellectual Fatigue, and the Need for Political Science Methods Courses in British Universities', *Political Studies*, 49(1): 89–105.

Dowding, Keith (2001) 'There Must Be End to Confusion: Policy Networks, Intellectual Fatigue, and the Need for Political Science Methods Courses in British Universities', *Political Studies*, 49: 89–105.

Downs, A. (1957) *An Economic Theory of Democracy* (New York: Harper & Row).

Downs, A. (1967) *Inside Bureaucracy* (Boston: Little, Brown).

Draper, H. (1977) *Karl Marx's Theory of Revolution*. Volume 1: *State and Bureaucracy* (New York: Monthly Review Press).

Dror, Y. (2001) *The Capacity to Govern* (London: Frank Cass).

Dryzek, J. (1987) *Rational Ecology: Environment and Political Economy* (Oxford: Basil Blackwell).

Dryzek, J. (1996) 'Political Inclusion and the Dynamics of Democratization', *American Political Science Review*, 90: 475–87.

Dryzek, J. (2000) *Deliberative Democracy and Beyond: Liberals, Critics, Contestations* (Oxford: Oxford University Press).

Dryzek, J. (2000) *Deliberative Democracy and Beyond* (Oxford: Oxford University Press).

Dryzek, J., Downes, D., Hunold, C., Schlosberg, D., with Hernes, H. K. (2003) *Green States and Social Movements* (Oxford: Oxford University Press).

Dunleavy, P. (1991) *Democracy, Bureaucracy and Public Choice: Economic Explanations in Political Science* (London: Harvester Wheatsheaf).

Dunleavy, P. and O'Leary, B. (1987) *Theories of the State: The Politics of Liberal Democracy* (Basingstoke: Palgrave Macmillan).

Dyke, G. (2004) *Inside Story* (London: HarperCollins).

Easton, D. (1953) *The Political System* (New York: Harper).

Easton, D. (1967) *A Framework for Political Analysis* (Englewood Cliffs, NJ: Prentice-Hall).

Ebbinhaus, B. and Hassel, A. (1999) 'The role of tripartite concertation in the reform of the welfare state', in *State Intervention and Industrial Relations at the End of the 1990s* (Brussels: ETUI).

Eckersley, R. (1992) *Environmentalism and Political Theory: Towards an Ecocentric Approach* (London: UCL Press).

Eckersley, R. (2004) *The Green State: Rethinking Democracy and Sovereignty*, Cambridge MA: MIT Press.

Edkins, J. (1999) *Poststructuralism and International Relations: Bringing the Political Back In* (Boulder, CO: Lynne Rienner).

Eisenstein, H. (1991) 'Speaking for Women? Voices from the Australian Femocrat Experiment', in *Australian Feminist Studies*, 14: 29–42.

Eisenstein, H. (1996) *Inside Agitators: Australian Femocrats and the State* (Philadelphia: Temple University Press).

Eisenstein, Z. (1979) 'Developing a Theory of Capitalist Patriarchy and Socialist Feminism', in *idem* (ed.), *Capitalist Patriarchy and the Case for Socialist Feminism* (New York and London: Monthly Review Press).

Eisenstein, Z. (1984) *Feminism and Sexual Equality: Crisis in Liberal America* (New York: Monthly Review Press).

Eisenstein, Z. (1986) *The Radical Future of Liberal Feminism* (Boston: Northeastern University Press).

Elkin, S. (1986) 'Regulation and Regime: A Comparative Analysis', *Journal of Public Policy*, 6(1): 49–72.

Elkins, D. J. (1995) *Beyond Sovereignty: Territorial and Political Economy in the Twenty-First Century* (Toronto: University of Toronto Press).

Elshtain, J. B. (1981) *Public Man, Private Woman: Women in Social and Political Thought* (Oxford: Martin Robertson).

Elster, J. (1986), 'Introduction', in *idem* (ed.), *Rational Choice* (Oxford: Blackwell).

Elster, J. (1989), *The Cement of Society* (Cambridge: Cambridge University Press).

Elster, J. and Hylland, A. (eds) (1986) *Foundations of Social Choice Theory* (Cambridge: Cambridge University Press).

Engels, F. (1844 [1975]) 'Outline of a Critique of Political Economy', in K. Marx and Engels, F. *Collected Works*, Vol. 3 (London: Lawrence & Wishart).

Engels, F. (1878 [1947]) *Anti-Dühring* (Moscow: Progress Publishers).

Engels, F. (1884 [1978]) *The Origin of the Family, Private Property and the State* (Peking: Foreign Language Press).

Enloe, C. (1990) *Bananas, Beaches and Bases: Making Feminist Sense of International Politics* (Berkeley, CA: University of California Press).

European Policy Forum (2000) *Making Decisions in Britain* (London : European Policy Forum).

Evans, M. (2001) 'Understanding Dialectics in Policy Network Analysis', *Political Studies*, 49(3): 542–50.

Evans, P. B., Rueschemeyer, D. and Skocpol, T. (eds) (1985) *Bringing the State Back In* (Cambridge: Cambridge University Press).

Falconer, Lord 'Department for Constitutional Affairs: Justice, Rights and Democracy', speech to the Institute for Public Policy Research, London, 3 December 2003. See also Lord Falconer. Constitutional Reform Speech, University College London, 8 December 2003.

Femia, J. V. (1981) *Gramsci's Political Thought: Hegemony, Consciousness, and the Revolutionary Process* (Oxford: Clarendon Press).

Ferguson, Kathy (1984) *The Feminist Case Against Bureaucracy* (Philadelphia: Temple University Press).

Finegold, K. and Skocpol, T. (1995) 'Marxist Approaches to Politics and the State', in *idem, State and Party in America's New Deal* (Madison: University of Wisconsin Press).

Finer, S. (1966) *Anonymous Empire* (London: Pall Mall).

Finnemore, M. (1996a) 'Norms, Culture, and World Politics: Insights from Sociology's Institutionalism', *International Organization*, 50(2): 325–47.

Finnemore, M. (1996b) 'Constructing Norms of Humanitarian Intervention', in Peter Katzenstein (ed.), *The Cultural of National Security* (Ithaca: Cornell University Press).

Finnemore, M. and Sikkink, K. (1998) 'International Norm Dynamics and Political Change', *International Organization*, 52: 887–917.

Fiore, G. (1970) *Antonio Gramsci: Life of a Revolutionary* (London: New Left Books).

Fligstein, N. (1990) *The Transformation of Corporate Control* (Cambridge, MA: Harvard University Press).

Fligstein, N. and Mara-Drita, I. (1996) 'How to Make a Market: Reflections on the Attempt to Create a Single Market in the European Union', *American Journal of Sociology*, 102: 1–32.

Flinders, M. (2004) 'Distributed Public Governance in Britain', *Public Administration*, 82(4): 883–909.

Flinders, M. (2005) 'The Politics of Public–Private Partnerships', *British Journal of Politics and International Relations*, 7(2): 543–67.

Flinders, M. (2006) *Walking Without Order: Delegated Governance and the British State* (Oxford : Oxford University Press).

Follett, M. P. (1918) *The New State* (New York: Longmans, Green).

Foreign Policy (2004) 'Globalization Index 2003' (A. T. Kearney), *Foreign Policy*, March/April.

Foucault, M. (1977) *Discipline and Punish* (Harmondsworth, Penguin).

Foucault, M. (1980) 'Truth and Power', in Colin Gordon (ed.), *Power/Knowledge: Selected Interviews and Other Writings 1972–1977* (London, Harvester Wheatsheaf).

Foucault, M. (1987) *The History of Sexuality*, Part I: *An Introduction* (Harmondsworth: Penguin).

Foucault, M. (1991) 'Governmentality', in Graham Burchell *et al.* (eds), *The Foucault Effect: Studies in Governmentality* (Hemel Hempstead: Harvester Wheatsheaf).

Foucault, M. (2003) *Society Must Be Defended* (Harmondsworth: Penguin).

Fox, C. J. and Miller, H. T. (1995) *Postmodern Public Administration* (London: Sage).

Fraser, N. (1995) 'False Antitheses: A Response to Seyla Benhabib and Judith Butler', in Seyla Benhabib *et al.* (eds), *Feminist Contentions: A Philosophical Exchange* (London: Routledge).

Fraser, N. (1997) *Justice Interrupts: Critical Reflections in the 'Post-Socialist' Condition* (Routledge: London).

Friedan, B. (1962) *The Feminine Mystique* (New York: Dell).

Friedman, M. and Schwartz, A. (1963) *A Monetary History of the United States, 1867–1960*, (Princeton: Princeton University Press).

Gais, T. L., Peterson, M. A. and Walker, J. L. (1984) 'Interest Groups, Iron Triangles and Representative Institutions in American National Government', *British Journal of Political Studies*, 14: 161–85.

Galbraith, J. K. (1963) *American Capitalism* (Harmondsworth: Penguin).

Gamble, A. (2000) *Politics and Fate* (Cambridge: Polity Press).

Garrett, G. (1998) *Partisan Politics in the Global Economy* (Cambridge: Cambridge University Press).

Gellner, E. (1983) *Nations and Nationalism* (Blackwell: Oxford).

Gertler, M. (1992) 'Flexibility Revisited: Districts, Nation-States, and the Forces of Production', *Transactions of the Institute of British Geographers*, 17:259–78.

Ghobadian, A., O'Regan, N. Gallear, D. and Viney, H. (2004) *Public–Private Partnerships* (Basingstoke: Palgrave Macmillan).

Giddens, A. (1984) *The Constitution of Society* (Cambridge: Polity Press).

Giddens, A. (1991a) *The Consequences of Modernity* (Cambridge, Polity Press).

Giddens, A. (1991b) *Modernity and Self-Identity: Self and Society in the Late Modern Age* (Stanford: Stanford University Press).

Giddens, A. (1994) *Beyond Left and Right: The Future of Radical Politics* (Stanford: Stanford University Press).

Giddens, A. (1999) *Runaway World: The Reith Lectures Revisited*, Lecture 1.

Gill, G. (2003) *The Nature and Development of the Modern State*' (Basingstoke and New York: Palgrave Macmillan).

Gold, D. A. *et al.* (1975a) 'Recent Developments in Marxist Theories of the Capitalist State: Part I', *Monthly Review*, 27(5): 29–43.

Gold, D. A. *et al.* (1975b) 'Recent Developments in Marxist Theories of the Capitalist State: Part II', *Monthly Review*, 27 (6): 36–51.

Goldfinch, S. (2000) *Remaking New Zealand and Australian Economic Policy: Ideas, Institutions and Policy Communities* (Wellington: Victoria University Press).

Goldsmith, E. (1991) *The Way: 87 Principles for an Ecological World* (London: Rider).

Goldstein, J. (1993) *Ideas, Interests, and American Trade Policy* (Ithaca, NY: Cornell University Press).

Goldstein, J. and Keohane, R. (1993) *Ideas and Foreign Policy: Beliefs, Institutions and Political Change* (Ithaca: Cornell University Press).

Goodin, R. (1992) *Green Political Theory* (Cambridge: Polity Press).

Goodin, R. E. (1990) 'International Ethics and the Environmental Crisis', *Ethics and International Affairs*, 4: 90–105.

Gordon, C. (1991) 'Governmental Rationality: An Introduction', in Graham Burchell *et al.* (eds), *The Foucault Effect: Studies in Governmentality* (Hemel Hempstead: Harvester Wheatsheaf).

Gordon, D. M. (1988) 'The Global Economy: New Edifice or Crumbling Foundations?' *New Left Review*, 168: 24–64.

Gourevitch, P. A. (1986) *Politics in Hard Times: Comparative Responses to International Economic Crises* (Ithaca, NY: Cornell University Press).

Gramsci, Antonio (1971) *Selections from the Prison Notebooks*, ed., Quentin Hoare and Geoffrey Nowell-Smith, (London: Lawrence & Wishart).

Gray, J. (1998) *False Dawn: The Delusions of Global Capitalism* (London: Granta).

Green, D. and Shapiro, I. (1994) *Pathologies of Rational Choice Theory* (New Haven: Yale University Press).

Greider, W. (1997) *One World, Ready or Not* (New York: Simon & Schuster).

Greve, C., Flinders, M. and Van Thiel, S. (1999) 'Quangos – What's In a Name? Defining Quangos from a Comparative Perspective', *Governance*, 12(2): 129–47.

Grofman, B. (1995) 'Introduction', in *idem* (ed.), *Information, Participation and Choice: An Economic Theory of Democracy in Perspective* (Michigan: University of Michigan Press).

Grove-White, R. (1993) 'Environmentalism: A New Moral Discourse for Technological Society', in Kay Milton (ed.), *Environmentalism: The View from Anthropology* (London: Routledge).

Gutsman, W. (1963) *The British Political Elite* (London: MacGibbon & Kee).

Gwinnett, B. (1998) 'Policing Prostitution: Gender the State and Community Politics', in Vicky Randall and Georgina Waylen (eds), *Gender, Politics and the State* (London: Routledge).

Haas, E. (1990) *When Knowledge is Power: Three Models of Change in International Organizations* (Berkeley: University of California Press).

Haas, P. (ed.) (1992) 'Knowledge, Power and International Policy Coordination', special issue of *International Organization*.

Haas, P. M. (1992) 'Introduction: Epistemic Communities and International Policy Coordination'. *International Organization*, 46: 1–35.

Habermas, J. (1975) *Legitimation Crisis* (London: Heinemann).

Habermas, J. (1996) *Between Facts and Norms: Contributions to a Discourse Theory of Law and Democracy* (Cambridge, MA: MIT Press).

Hacking, I. (1991) 'How Should We Do the History of Statistics?', in Graham Burchell *et al.* (eds), *The Foucault Effect: Studies in Governmentality* (Hemel Hempstead: Harvester Wheatsheaf).

Hajer, M. (1995) *The Politics of Environmental Discourse: Ecological Modernisation and the Policy Process* (Oxford: Clarendon Press).

Hall, J. A. and G. J. Ikenberry (1989) *The State* (Buckingham: Open University Press).

Hall, P. (1986) *Governing the Economy: The Politics of State Intervention in Britain and France* (New York: Oxford University Press).

Hall, P. (1989) 'Conclusion', in *idem* (ed.), *The Political Power of Economic Ideas: Keynesianism across Nations* (Princeton: Princeton University Press).

Hall, P. (1993) 'Policy Paradigms, Social Learning and the State: The Case of Economic Policy-Making in Britain', *Comparative Politics*, 25: 275–96.

Hall, P. A. and Taylor, R. C. R. (1996) 'Political Science and the Three New Institutionalisms', *Political Studies*, 44(4): 936–57.

Hall, P. and Soskice, D. (2001) 'Introduction', in *idem* (eds), *Varieties of Capitalism: The Institutional Foundations of Comparative Advantage* (Oxford: Oxford University Press).

Hall, P. and Taylor, R. (1996) 'Political Science and the Three New Institutionalisms', *Political Studies*, 44: 936–57.

Hall, S. and Jacques, M. (1983) *The Politics of Thatcherism* (London: Lawrence & Wishart).

Harding, S. (1981) 'What is the Real Material Base of Patriarchy and Capital?', in Lydia Sargent (ed.), *Women and Revolution: The Unhappy Marriage of Marxism and Feminism* (London: Pluto Press).

Hartmann, H. (1981) 'The Unhappy Marriage of Marxism and Feminism: Towards a more Progressive Union', in Lydia Sargent (ed.) *Women and Revolution: The Unhappy Marriage of Marxism and Feminism* (London: Pluto Press).

Harvey, D. (1990) *The Condition of Postmodernity* (Oxford: Blackwell).

Hay, C. (1994a) 'Environmental Security and State Legitimacy', in M. O' Connor (ed.), *Is Capitalism Sustainable? Political Economy and the Politics of Ecology* (New York: Guilford Press).

Hay, C. (1994b) 'Werner in Wunderland: Bob Jessop's Strategic–Relational Approach', in F. Sebäi & C. Vercellone (eds.), *École de la Régulation et Critique de La Raison Économique* (Paris: L'Harmattan).

Hay, C. (1996a) *Re-Stating Social and Political Change* (Buckingham: Open University Press).

Hay, C. (1996b) 'Narrating Crisis: The Discursive Construction of the Winter of Discontent', *Sociology*, 30 (2), 253–77.

Hay, C. (2000) 'Contemporary Capitalism, Globalization, Regionalization and the Persistence of National Variation', *Review of International Studies*, 26: 509–31.

Hay, C. (2001) 'The "Crisis" of Keynesianism and the Rise of NeoLiberalism in Britain: An Ideational Institutionalist Approach', in John L. Campbell and Ove Pedersen (eds), *The Rise of NeoLiberalism and Institutional Analysis* (Princeton: Princeton University Press).

Hay, C. (2002) *Political Analysis* (Basingstoke and New York: Palgrave Macmillan).

Hay, C. (2004a) 'Re-Stating Politics, Re-Politicizing the State: Neoliberalism, Economic Imperatives and the Rise of the Competition State', *Political Quarterly*, 75 special issue pp 38–50.

Hay, C. (2004b) 'Common trajectories, variable paces, divergent outcomes? Models of European capitalism under conditions of complex economic interdependence', *Review of International Political Economy*, 11(2): 231–62.

Hay, C. (2004c) 'The Normalising Role of Rationalist Assumptions in the Institutional Embedding of Neo-Liberalism', *Economy and Society*, 33(4): 500–27.

Hay, C. (2006) 'Constructivist Institutionalism', in R. A. W. Rhodes, Sarah Binder and Bert Rockman (eds), *The Oxford Handbook of Political Institutions* (Oxford: Oxford University Press).

Hay, C. and Marsh, D. (2000) *Demystifying Globalization* (London: Macmillan).

Hay, C. and Rosamond, B. (2002) 'Globalisation, European Integration and the Discursive Construction of Economic Imperatives', *Journal of European Public Policy*, 9(2): 147–67.

Hay, C. and Wincott, D. (1998) 'Structure, Agency and Historical Institutionalism', *Political Studies*, 46(5): 951–7.

Hayek, F. (1978) *Law, Legislation and Liberty* (London: Routledge).

Heclo, H. (1978) 'Issue Networks and the Executive Establishment', in King, A. (ed.), *The New American Political System* (Washington, DC: American Enterprise Institute).

Heffernan, R. (2002) '"The possible as the art of politics": understanding consensus politics', *Political Studies*, 50(4): 742–60.

Heilbroner, Robert (1974) *An Inquiry into the Human Prospect* (New York: Harper & Row).

Held, D., A. McGrew, D. Goldblatt, J. Perraton (1999) *Global Transformations: Politics, Economics and Culture* (Cambridge: Cambridge University Press).

Held, David (1980) *Introduction to Critical Theory: Horkheimer to Habermas* (London: Hutchinson).

Hernes, H. M. (1987) *Welfare State and Woman Power* (Oslo: Norwegian University Press).

Hernes, H. M. (1988a) 'Scandinavian Citizenship', *Acta Sociologica* 31(3): 199–215.

Hernes, H. M. (1988b) 'Women and the Welfare State: the Transition from Private to Public Dependence', in Anne Showstack Sassoon (ed.), *Women and the State* (London: Routledge).

Hewitt, C. J. (1974) 'Elites and the Distribution of Power in British Society', in Giddens, A. and Stanworth, P. (eds), *Elites and Power in British Society* (Cambridge: Cambridge University Press).

Heywood, A. (1997) *Politics* (Basingstoke and New York: Palgrave Macmillan).

Higgott, R. (1996) 'Beyond Embedded Liberalism: Governing the International Trade Regime in an Era of Economic Nationalism', in P. Gummett (ed.), *Globalisation and Public Policy* (Cheltenham: Edward Elgar).

Hindmoor, A. (2004) *The Construction of Political Space: New Labour at the Centre* (Oxford: Oxford University Press).

Hirsch, J. (1978) 'The State Apparatus and Social Reproduction: Elements of a Theory of the Bourgeois State', in J. Holloway and S. Picciotto (eds), *State and Capital: A Marxist Debate* (London: Arnold).

Hirst, P. (1994) *Associative Democracy* (Cambridge: Polity Press).

Hirst, P. and Thompson, G. (1999) *Globalisation in Question: The International Economy and the Possibilities of Governance* (Cambridge: Polity Press).

Hix, S. (1998) 'The Study of the EU II', *Journal of European Public Policy*, 5(1): 38–65.

Hobbes, T. (1951[1968]) *Leviathan*, ed. C. Macpherson (Harmondsworth: Penguin).

Hobsbawm, E. J. (1990) *Nations and Nationalism Since 1780* (Cambridge: Cambridge University Press).

Hodge, G. and Greve, C. (2005) *The Challenge of Public–Private Partnerships* (Cheltenham: Edward Elgar).

Holm, H.-H. and Sørensen, G. (1995) 'International Relations Theory in a World of Variation', in H.-H. Holm and G. Sørensen (eds), *Whose World Order? Uneven Globalization and the End of the Cold War* (Boulder, CO: Westview).

Hood, C. (2002) 'The Risk Game and the Blame Game', *Government and Opposition*, 37(1): 15–37.

Hood, C. Rothstein, H. and Baldwin, R. (2004) *The Government of Risk* (Oxford: Oxford University Press).

Hooghe, L. and Marks, G. (2003) 'Unravelling the Central State, But How?', *American Political Science Review*, 97(2): 233–43.

Howarth, David, Norval, Aletta J. and Stavrakakis, Yannis (eds) (2000) *Discourse Theory and Political Analysis: Identities, Hegemonies and Social Change* (Manchester: Manchester University Press).

Immergut, E. (1998) 'The Theoretical Core of the New Institutionalism', *Politics and Society*, 26:1: 5–34.

Immergut, Ellen (1992) *Health Politics: Interests and Institutions in Western Europe* (New York: Cambridge University Press).

Immergut, Ellen (1998) 'The Theoretical Core of the New Institutionalism', *Politics and Society*, 26(1): 5–34.

Ingaro, B. and Israel, G. (1990) *The Invisible Hand: Economic Equilibrium in the History of Science* (Cambridge, MA: MIT Press).

IPPR (2002) *Building Better Partnerships* (London: IPPR).

IPPR (2004) *Opening It Up: Accountability and Partnerships* (London: IPPR).

Jänicke, M. (1990) *State Failure: The Impotence of Politics in Industrial Society.* Cambridge: Polity.

Jänicke, M., Mönch, H. and Binder, M. (2000) 'Structural change and environmental policy', in Stephen Young (ed.), *The Emergence of Ecological Modernisation: Integrating the Environment and the Economy?* (London: Routledge).

Jackson, R. (1999) 'Sovereignty in World Politics: A Glance at the Conceptual and Historical Landscape', *Political Studies*, 47(3): 431–57.

Jackson, R. and G. Sørensen (2003) *Introduction to International Relations* (Oxford: Oxford University Press).

Jacobs, S. (2000) 'Globalisation, States and Women's Agency: Possibilities and Pitfalls', in Susie Jacobs, Ruth Jacobson and Jen Marchbank (eds), *States of Conflict: Gender, Violence and Resistance* (London and New York: Zed Books).

Jacobsen, J. K. (1995) 'Much Ado about Ideas: The Cognitive Factor in Economic Policy', *World Politics*, 47: 283–310.

Jacobsen, K. (2001) 'Political Scientists Have Turned Guerrillas', *The Guardian*, 3 April: 14.

James, A. (1999) 'The Practice of Sovereign Statehood in Contemporary International Society', Special Issue of *Political Studies*, 47:3: 457–74.

Jaquette, Jane S. (2003) 'Feminism and the Challenges of the "Post-Cold War" World', *International Journal of Feminist Politics*, 5(3): 331–54.

Jenkins, K. (1991) *Re-thinking History* (London: Routledge).

Jessop, B. (1977) 'Recent Theories of the Capitalist State', *Cambridge Journal of Economics*, 1(4), 353–72.

Jessop, B. (1978) 'Marx and Engels on the State', in S. Hibbin *et al.* (eds), *Politics, Ideology and the State* (London: Lawrence & Wishart).

Jessop, B. (1982) *The Capitalist State* (Oxford: Martin Robertson).

Jessop, B. (1985) *Nicos Poulantzas: Marxist Theory and Political Strategy* (Basingstoke and New York: Palgrave Macmillan).

Jessop, B. (1990) *State Theory: Putting Capitalist States in Their Place* (Cambridge: Polity Press).

Jessop, B. (1997). 'Capitalism and its Future: Remarks on Regulation, Government and Governance', *Review of International Political Economy*, 4:3: 561–81.

Jessop, B. (2002) *The Future of the Capitalist State* (Cambridge: Polity Press).

Jobert, B. (1992) 'Représentations Sociales, Controverses et Débats dans la Conduite des Politiques Publiques', *Revue Française de Science Politique*, 42: 219–34.

Jones, R. (1999) 'The European Union as a Promoter of Public–Private Partnerships', *International Journal of Public–Private Partnerships*, 1(3): 289–305.

Jordan, A. and Richardson, J. (1982) 'The Policy Process in Britain', in J. Richardson (ed.), *Policy Styles in Western Europe* (London: Allen & Unwin).

Jordan, A. G. (1981) 'Iron Triangles, Wooly Corporatisms and Elastic Nets: Images of the Policy Process' *Journal of Public Policy*, 1: 95–123.

Jordan, A. G. and Richardson, J. (1987a) *Government and Pressure Groups in Britain* (Oxford: Clarendon Press).

Jordan, A. G. and Richardson, J. (1987b) *British Politics and the Policy Process* (London: Unwin Hyman).

Jordan, G. (1990) 'The Pluralism of Pluralism: An Anti-Theory', *Political Studies*, 38(2): 286–301.

Jreisat, J. S. (2002) *Governance and Developing Countries* (Leiden: Brill).

Kadushin, C. (1974) *The American Intellectual Elite* (Boston: Little, Brown).

Katzenstein, P. (ed.) (1978) *Between Power and Plenty* (Madison, WI: University of Wisconsin Press).

Katzenstein, P. J. (1985), *Corporatism and Change* (Ithaca, NY: Cornell University Press).

Katzenstein, P. J. (ed.) (1996a) *The Culture of National Security: Norms and Identity in World Politics* (New York: Columbia University Press).

Katzenstein, P. J. (1996b) *Cultural Norms and National Security: Policy and Military in Postwar Japan* (Ithaca: Cornell University Press).

Kearney A. T. (2003) *Globalisation Index* (Foreign Policy).

Keating, M. (2000) 'The pressures for change', in M. Keating and G. Davis, *The Future of Governance* (Sydney: Allen & Unwin).

Keck, M. E. and Sikkink, K. (1998) *Activists Beyond Borders: Advocacy Networks in International Politics* (Ithaca: Cornell University Press).

Kelly, P. (1992) *The End of Certainty* (Sydney: Allen & Unwin).

Kelly, R. M., Bayes, J. H., Hawkesworth, M. E. and Brigitte Young (eds) (2001) *Gender, Globalisation and Democratization* (Oxford: Rowman & Littlefield).

Kelso, W. A. (1978) *American Democratic Theory: Pluralism and its Critics* (Westport, Conn.: Greenwood Press).

Keohane, R. and Nye, J. (1977) *Power and Interdependence* (Boston: Little, Brown).

Kerr, P. (1999) 'The Postwar Consensus: A Woozle that Wasn't?' in D. Marsh, J. Buller, C. Hay *et al.*, *Post-war British Politics in Perspective* (Cambridge: Polity Press).

Kerr, P. and D. Marsh (1999) 'Explaining Thatcherism: Towards a Multidimensional Approach', in D. Marsh, J. Buller, C. Hay *et al.*, *Post-war British Politics in Perspective* (Cambridge: Polity Press).

Keynes, J. M. (1936) *The General Theory of Employment, Interest and Money* (Basingstoke: Palgrave Macmillan).

Kimber, R. (1993) 'Interest Groups and the Fallacy of the Liberal Fallacy', in J. Richardson (ed.), *Pressure Groups* (Oxford: Oxford University Press).

King, D. (1987) *The New Right* (Basingstoke: Palgrave Macmillan).

King, D. (1999) *In the Name of Liberalism: Illiberal Social Policy in the United States and Britain* (Oxford: Oxford University Press).

Kirkpatrick, Evron (1971) 'The Impact of the Behavioral Approach on Traditional Political Science', in Howard Ball and James A. Lauth, Jr (eds), *Changing Perspectives in Contemporary Political Analysis* (Englewood Cliffs, NJ: Prentice-Hall).

Kjaer, A. M. (2004) *Governance* (Cambridge: Polity Press).

Klein, R. (2004) 'The First Wave of NHS Foundation Trusts', *British Medical Journal*, 328: 1332.

Kooiman, J. (2004) *Governing as Governance* (London: Sage).

Koppell, J. (2003) *The Politics of Quasi-Government* (Cambridge: Cambridge University Press).

Kraemer, P. E. (1968) *The Societal State* (Amsterdam: Kobra).

Krasner, S. (1980) *Defending the National Interest* (Princeton: Princeton University Press).

Krasner, S. (1988) 'Sovereignty: An Institutional Perspective', *Comparative Political Studies*, 21: 66–94.

Krasner, S. (ed.) (1937) *International Regimes* (Ithaca, NY: Cornell University Press).

Kreisky, E. (1995) 'Der Staat ohne Geschlecht? Ansätze feministischer Staatskritik und feministischer Staatserklärung', in Eva Kreisky and Birgit Sauer (eds), *Feministische Standpunkte in der Politikwissenschaft: Eine Einführung* (Frankfurt am Main: Campus).

Kristol, I. (1983) *Reflections of a Neoconservative: Looking Back, Looking Ahead* (New York: Basic Books).

Krook, M. L. (2004) *Politicizing Representation: Campaigns for Candidate Gender Quotas Worldwide*, PhD thesis, Columbia University.

Kuhn, A. and Wolpe, A. M. (eds) (1978) *Feminism and Materialism: Women and the Modes of Production* (London: Routledge & Kegan Paul).

Kymlicka, W. (2001) 'Western Political Theory and Ethnic Relations in Eastern Europe', in W. Kymlicka and M. Opalski (eds), *Can Liberal Pluralism be Exported?* (Oxford: Oxford University Press).

Laborde, C. (2000) *Pluralist Thought and the State in Britain and France, 1900–25* (Basingstoke and New York: Palgrave Macmillan).

Laclau, E. (1975) 'The Specificity of the Political', *Economy & Society*, 4(1): 87–110, reprinted in *idem* (1977) *Politics and Ideology in Marxist Theory: Capitalism, Fascism, Populism* (London: New Left Books).

Laclau, Ernesto (1996) *Emancipation(s)* (London and New York: Verso).

Laclau, Ernesto and Mouffe, Chantal (1985) *Hegemony and Socialist Strategy: Towards a Radical Democratic Politics* (London, Verso).

Lapidoth, R. (1992) 'Sovereignty in Transition', *Journal of International Affairs*, 45, (2): 325–46.

Laski, H. J. (1989) 'The Foundations of Sovereignty and Other Essays', in P. Hirst (ed.) *The Pluralist Theory of the State* (London: Routledge).

Latouche, S. (1993) *In the Wake of the Affluent Society: An Exploration of Post-Development* (London: Zed Books).

Latour, B. (2004) *Politics of Nature* (Cambridge, MA: Harvard University Press).

Laumann, E. (1976) *Networks of Collective Action: A Perspective on Community Influence Systems* (New York: Academic).

Laumann, E. and Pappi, F. (1973) 'New Directions in the Study of Community Elites', *American Sociological Review*, 38: 212–29.

Laumann, E. *et al.* (1977) 'Community-elite Influence Structures: Extension of a Network Approach', *American Journal of Sociology*, 83: 594–631.

Lawson, T. (1997) *Economics and Reality* (London: Routledge).

Lefebvre, H. (1972) *The Sociology of Marx* (Harmondsworth: Penguin).

Leigh, D. and Vulliamy, E. (1997) *Sleaze: The Corruption of Parliament* (London: Fourth Estate).

Leitch, S. and Motion, J. (2003) 'Public–Private Partnerships: Consultation, Co-operation and Collusion', *Journal of Public Affairs*, 3 (3): 273–8.

Lenin, V. I. (1917 [1968]) *The State and Revolution*, in V. I. Lenin, *Selected Works* (Moscow: Progress Publishers).

Leopold, Aldo (1949) *A Sand County Almanac* (Oxford: Oxford University Press).

Levett, R. (2001) 'What Quality, Whose Lives?' *Green Futures*, 28 (May/June): 28–30.

Levi, M. (1989) *Of Rule and Revenue* (Berkeley, CA: University of California Press).

Lindblom, C. (1977) *Politics and Markets* (New York: Basic Books).

Lindblom, C. (1982) 'Another State of Mind', *American Political Science Review*, 76(1): 9–21.

Lindvert, J. (2002) 'A World Apart: Swedish and Australian Gender Equality Policy', *NORA* 2(10): 99–107.

Linklater, A. (1998) *The Transformation of Political Community* (Cambridge: Polity Press).

Lister, R. (1997) *Citizenship: Feminist Perspectives* (Basingstoke and New York: Palgrave Macmillan).

Litfin, K. (ed.) (1998) *The Greening of Sovereignty* (Cambridge, MA: MIT Press).

Lockwood, D. (1964) 'Social Integration and System Integration', in G. K. Zolschan and W. Hirsch (eds), *Explorations in Social Change* (London: Routledge & Kegan Paul).

Lockwood, S. (1990) *Public–Private Partnerships in US Highway Finance* (London: PTRC).

Low, N. and Gleeson, B. (1998) *Justice, Society and Nature: An Exploration of Political Ecology* (London: Routledge).

Lowi, T. (1969) *The End of Liberalism* (New York: Norton).

Lowndes, V. (1996) 'Varieties of New Institutionalism: A Critical Appraisal', *Public Administration*, 74: 181–97.

Lowndes, V. (2002) 'Institutionalism', in David Marsh and Gerry Stoker (eds), *Theory and Methods in Political Science* (Basingstoke and New York: Palgrave Macmillan).

Lowndes, V. and Skelcher, C. (1998) 'The Dynamics of Multi-organisational Partnerships: An Analysis of Changing Modes of Governance', *Public Administration*, 76(2): 313–33.

Luke, T. (1999) *Capitalism, Democracy, and Ecology: Departing from Marx* (Illinois: University of Illinois Press).

Lukes, S. (1974) *Power: A Radical View* (Basingstoke and New York: Palgrave Macmillan).

Lustick, I. (1997) 'The Disciplines of Political Science: Studying the Culture of Rational Choice as a case, in point', *Political Science and Politics* 30(2): 175–9.

M. Laver (1997) *Private Desires, Political Action* (London: Sage).

Machiavelli, N. (1513/1988) *The Prince*, trans. Q. Skinner and R. Price (Cambridge: Cambridge University Press).

MacKinnon, C. A. (1982) 'Feminism, Marxism, Method and the State: An Agenda for Theory', *Signs*, 7(3): 515–44.

MacKinnon, C. A. (1983) 'Feminism, Marxism, Method and the State: Toward Feminist Jurisprudence', *Signs*, 8(4): 645–58.

MacKinnon, C. A. (1985) *Toward a Feminist Theory of the State* (Cambridge, MA: Harvard University Press).

MacKinnon, C. A. (1987) 'Feminism, Marxism, Method and the State', in Sandra Harding (ed.), *Feminism and Methodology* (Milton Keynes: Open University Press).

MacKinnon, C. A. (1989) *Towards a Feminist Theory of the State* (Cambridge, MA: Harvard University Press).

Mahon, R. (1991) 'From "Bringing" to "Putting": The State in Late Twentieth-Century Social Thought', *Canadian Journal of Sociology*, 16(2), 119–44.

Majone, G. (1998) 'Europe's Democratic Deficit'. *European Law Journal*, 4(1): 5–28.

Majone, G. (2002) 'The European Commission: The Limits of Centralization and the Perils of Parliamentarization', *Governance*, 15(3): 375–92.

Mann, Michael (1986) *The Sources of Social Power, Vol. I* (Cambridge: Cambridge University Press).

Mann, Michael (1988) *States, War and Capitalism* (New York: Basil Blackwell).

Mansbridge, J. (ed.) (1990) *Beyond Self-Interest* (Chicago: University of Chicago Press).

March, J. G. and Olsen, J. P. (1984) 'The New Institutionalism: Organizational Factors in Political Life', *American Political Science Review*, 78: 734–49.

March, J. G. and Olsen, J. P. (1989) *Rediscovering Institutions: The Organizational Basis of Politics* (New York: Free Press).

Marsh, D. (1995) 'The Convergence between Theories of the State', in D. Marsh and G. Stoker (eds) *Theory and Methods of Political Science* (Basingstoke and New York: Palgrave Macmillan).

Marsh, D. (1999) 'Explaining Change in the Post-war Period', in *idem* (ed.), *Post-war British Politics in Perspective* (Cambridge: Polity Press).

Marsh, D. (2002) 'Pluralism and the Study of British Politics: It is Always the Happy Hour for Men with Money, Knowledge and Power', in C. Hay (ed.), *British Politics Today* (Cambridge: Polity Press).

Marsh, D. (ed.) (1998) *Comparing Policy Networks* (Milton Keynes: Open University Press).

Marsh, D. and Rhodes, R. A. W. (eds) (1992) *Policy Networks in British Government* (Oxford: Clarendon Press).

Marsh, D. and Smith, M. (2000) 'Understanding Policy Networks: Towards a Dialectical Approach', *Political Studies*, 48: 4–21.

Marsh, D. and Stoker G. (eds) (1995) *Theory and Methods in Political Science* (Basingstoke and New York: Palgrave Macmillan).

Marsh, D. and Stoker, G. (eds) (2002) *Theory and Methods in Political Science*, 2nd edn (Basingstoke and New York: Palgrave Macmillan).

Marsh, D., Richards, D. and Smith, M. (2001) *Changing Patterns of Governance within the UK* (Basingstoke and New York: Palgrave Macmillan).

Marsh, D., Richards, D. and Smith, M. J. (2003) 'Unequal Plurality: Towards an Asymmetric Power Model of British Government', *Government and Opposition*, 38: 306–32.

Martin, L. (2000) *Democratic Commitments* (Princeton: Princeton University Press).

Marx, K. (1843a [1975]) *Critique of Hegel's Doctine of the State*, in L. Colletti (ed.), *Karl Marx: Early Writings* (London: Pelican).

Marx, K. (1843b [1975]) 'On the Jewish Question', in L. Colletti (ed.), *Karl Marx: Early Writings* (London: Pelican).

Marx, K. (1844 [1975]) 'Introduction to a Contribution to a Critique of Hegel's Philosophy of Law', in L. Colletti (ed.), *Karl Marx: Early Writings* (London: Pelican).

Marx, K. (1850 [1978]) *The Class Stuggles in France: 1845 to 1850*, in K. Marx and F. Engels, *Collected Works*, Vol. 10 (London: Lawrence & Wishart).

Marx, K. (1852 [1979]) *The Eighteenth Brumaire of Louis Bonaparte*, in K. Marx and F. Engels, *Collected Works*, Vol. 11 (London: Lawrence & Wishart).

Marx, K. (1859 [1987]) 'Preface to a Contribution to a Critique of Political Economy', in K. Marx and F. Engels, *Collected Works*, Vol. 29 (London: Lawrence & Wishart).

Marx, K. (1871 [1986]) *The Civil War in France*, in K. Marx and F. Engels, *Collected Works*, Vol. 22 (London: Lawrence & Wishart).

Marx, K. and Engels, F. (1845/6 [1964] *The German Ideology* (Moscow: Progress Publishers).

Marx, K. and Engels, F. (1848 [1967]) *The Communist Manifesto* (London: Pelican).

Mazur, A. (ed.) (2001) *State Feminism, Women's Movements and Job Training: Making Democracies Work in the Global Economy* (New York and London: Routledge).

McClure, K. (1992) 'On the Subject of Rights: Pluralism, Plurality and Political Identity', in C. Mouffe (ed.), *Dimensions of Radical Democracy* (London: Verso).

McConnell, G. (1953) *The Decline of American Democracy* (New York: Atheneum).

McConnell, G. (1966) *Private Power and American Democracy* (New York: Alfred A. Knopf).

McCubbins, M. D. and Sullivan, T. (1987) *Congress: Structure and Policy* (Cambridge and New York: Cambridge University Press).

McFarland, A. (2004) *Neopluralism: The Evolution of Political Process Theory* (Kansas: University Press of Kansas).

McIntosh, M. (1978) 'The State and the Oppression of Women', in A. Kuhn and A. Wolpe (eds), *Feminism and Materialism: Women and Modes of Production* (London: Routledge & Kegan Paul).

McLennan, G. (1989) *Marxism, Pluralism and Beyond* (Cambridge: Polity Press).

McLuhan, Marshall (1964) *Understanding Media: The Extensions of Man* (London: Routledge & Kegan Paul).

McNamara, K. (1998) *The Currency of Ideas: Monetary Politics in the European Union* (Ithaca, NY: Cornell University Press).

McNay, L. (1992) *Foucault and Feminism: Power, Gender and the Self* (Cambridge: Polity Press).

McNay, L. (1999) 'Subject, Psyche and Agency: The Work of Judith Butler', in *Theory, Culture and Society*, 16(2): 175–93.

Merchant, C. (1980) *The Death of Nature: Women, Ecology and the Scientific Revolution* (San Francisco: Harper & Row).

Merelman R. (2003) *Pluralism at Yale* (Wisconsin: University of Wisconsin Press).

Meyer, John W. and Rowan, Brian (1977) 'Institutionalized Organizations: formal Structure as Myth and Ceremony', *American Journal of Sociology*, 83: 340–63.

Michels, R. (1911 [1962]) *Political Parties* (New York: Free Press).

Middlemas, K. (1979) *Politics in Industrial Society* (London: André Deutsch).

Migdal, J. (1988) *Strong Societies and Weak States* (Princeton: Princeton University Press).

Miliband, R. (1965) 'Marx and the State', *Socialist Register 1965*: 278–96.

Miliband, R. (1969) *The State in Capitalist Society: An Analysis of the Western System of Power* (London: Weidenfeld & Nicolson).

Miliband, R. (1970) 'The Capitalist State – Reply to Poulantzas', *New Left Review*, 59: 53–60, reprinted in R. Blackburn (ed.) (1972) *Ideology in Social Science* (London: Fontana).

Miliband, R. (1973) 'Poulantzas and the Capitalist State', *New Left Review*, 82: 83–92.

Miliband, R. (1977) *Marxism and Politics* (Oxford: Oxford University Press).

Miliband, R. (1994) *Socialism for a Sceptical Age* (London: Verso).

Millett, K. (1970) *Sexual Politics* (Gardencity: Doubleday).

Mills, C. W. (1956) *The Power Elite* (New York: Oxford University Press).

Milward, H. and Provan, K. (2000) 'Governing the Hollow State', *Journal of Public Administration Research and Theory*, 10(2): 359–79.

Mintz, B. and Schwartz, M. (1985) *The Power Structure of American Business* (Chicago: University of Chicago Press).

Modeen, T. and Rosas, A. (1988) *Indirect Public Administration in Fourteen Countries* (Helsinki: Abo Academy Press).

Moe, T. (2003) 'Power and Political Institutions', paper read at conference on Crafting and Operating Institutions, Yale University (New Haven, CT, April 11–13).

Mol, A. (1996) 'Ecological Modernisation and Institutional Reflexivity: Environmental Reform in the Late Modern Age', *Environmental Politics*, 5(2): 302–23.

Mol, A. (2001) *Globalization and Environmental Reform: The Ecological Modernization of the Global Economy* (Cambridge, MA: MIT Press).

Molyneux, M. (1979) 'Beyond the Domestic Labour Debate', *New Left Review*, 116: 3–27.

Monbiot, G. (2004), *The Age of Consent: A Manifesto for a New World Order* (New York: The New Press).

Moore, G. (1979) 'The Structure of a National Elite Network', *American Sociological Review*, 44 (October): 673–92.

Moravcsik, A. (1998) *The Choice for Europe: Social Purpose and State Power from Messina to Maastricht* (Ithaca, NY: Cornell University Press).

Morgenthau, H. (1966). *Politics Among Nations: The Struggle for Power and Peace* (New York: Alfred Knopf).

Mosca, G. (1896 [1939]) *The Ruling Class* (New York: McGraw Hill).

Mouffe, C. (2000) *The Democratic Paradox* (London: Verso).

Mouzelis, N. (1991) *Back to Sociological Theory: The Construction of Social Orders* (Basingstoke and New York: Palgrave Macmillan).

Mouzelis, N. (1995) *Sociological Theory: What Went Wrong?* (London: Routledge).

Mueller, D. (1993) 'The Future of Public Choice', *Public Choice*, 77: 145–50.

Mueller, D. (2003), *Public Choice III* (Cambridge: Cambridge University Press).

Mueller, D. and Murrell, P. (1986), 'Interest Groups Size and the Size of Government', *Public Choice*, 48: 125–45.

Muller, P. (1995) 'Les Politiques publiques comme construction d'un rapport au monde', in Alain Faure, Gielles Pollet and Philippe Warin (eds), *La Construction du sens dans les politiques publiques: Débats autour de la notion de référentiel* (Paris: L'Harmattan).

Mutz, D. C., Sniderman, P. M. and Brody, R. (eds.) (1996) *Political Persuasion and Attitude Change* (Ann Arbor: University of Michigan Press).

Naess, A. (1995) 'Deep Ecology and Lifestyle', in G. Sessions (ed.), *Deep Ecology for the 21st Century* (Boston and London: Shambala Press).

Nash, K. (2002) 'Thinking Political Sociology: Beyond the Limits of Post-Marxism', *History of the Human Sciences*, 15(4): 97–114.

Newell, P. (2001) 'New Environmental Architectures and the Search for Effectiveness', *Global Environmental Politics* 1(1): 35–44.

Newman, P. (2000) 'Changing Patterns of Regional Governance in the EU', *Urban Studies* 37:895–909.

Nichols, D. (1975) *Three Varieties of Pluralism* (Basingstoke: Palgrave Macmillan).

Nichols, D. (1994) *The Pluralist State*, 2nd edn (Basingstoke and New York: Palgrave Macmillan).

Niskanen, W. (1971) *Bureaucracy and Representative Government* (Chicago: Aldine).

Niskanen, W. (1994) *Bureaucracy and Public Economics* (Aldershot: Edward Elgar).

Nordlinger, E. A. (1981) *On the Autonomy of the Democratic State* (Cambridge, MA: Harvard University Press).

North, Douglass C. (1990) *Institutions, Institutional Change, and Economic Performance* (Cambridge: Cambridge University Press).

Nye, J. S. (1990) *Bound to Lead: The Changing Nature of American Power* (New York: Basic Books).

Nye, J. S. (2002) *The Paradox of American Power* (Oxford: Oxford University Press).

Nye, J. S. (2003) 'US Power and Strategy After Iraq', *Foreign Affairs*, 82(4): 60–73.

Nye, J. S. and Donahue, J. D. (2000) *Governance in a Globalizing World* (Washington, DC: The Brookings Institution).

Nye, J. S. Jr (2001) 'Globalization's Democratic Deficit', *Foreign Affairs*, 80(4): 2–6.

O'Brien, R. (1992) *Global Financial Integration: The End of Geography* (New York: Council on Foreign Relations Press).

O'Connor, J., Orloff, A. S. and Shaver, S. (1999) *States, Markets, Families: Gender, Liberalism and Social Policy in Australia, Canada, Great Britain and the United States* (Cambridge: Cambridge University Press).

O'Donnell, L. (1997) 'Opening address by the Minister of State at the Department of Foreign Affairs with Special Responsibility for Overseas Aid and Human Rights', paper presented to 19th Annual Conference, Royal Irish Academy, 20 November 1997.

OECD (2002) *Distributed Public Governance: Agencies, Authorities and other Autonomous Bodies* (London: OECD).

Offe, C. (1973) *Political Power and Social Classes* (London: New Left Books).

Offe, C. (1974) 'Structural Problems of the Capitalist State: Class Rule and the Political System. On the Selectiveness of Political Institutions', in K. von Beyme (ed.), *German Political Studies* (Beverly Hills, CA: Sage).

Offe, C. (1975) 'The Theory of the Capitalist State and the Problem of Policy Formation', in L. Lindberg *et al.* (eds), *Stress and Contradiction in Modern Capitalism* (Lexington, MA: D.C. Heath).

Offe, C. (1975) *Classes in Contemporary Capitalism* (London: New Left Books).

Offe, C. (1976) 'The Capitalist State: A Reply to Miliband and Laclau', *New Left Review*, 95: 63–83.

Offe, C. (1978) *State, Power, Socialism* (London: New Left Books).

Offe, C. (1984) *Contradictions of the Welfare State* (London: Hutchinson).

Ohmae, K. (1996). *The End of the Nation State: The Rise of Regional Economics* (London: HarperCollins).

Okin, S. M. (1989) *Justice, Gender, and the Family* (New York: Basic Books).

Olsen, M. and Marger, M. (1993) *Power in Modern Societies* (Oxford: Westview Press).

Olson, M. (1971) *The Logic of Collective Action* (Cambridge, MA: Harvard University Press).

O'Neill, J. (1993) *Ecology, Policy and Politics: Human Well-Being and the Natural World* (London: Routledge).

Ophuls, W. (1977) *Ecology and the Politics of Scarcity* (San Francisco: Freeman).

Osborne, S. (2000) *Public–Private Partnerships: Theory and Practice in International Perspective* (London: Routledge).

Osei, P. (2004) 'Public–Private Partnerships in Service Delivery in Developing Countries', in A. Ghobadian, N. O'Regan, D. Gallear and H. Viney (2004) *Public–Private Partnerships* (Basingstoke: Palgrave Macmillan).

Ostrom, E. (1982) 'Beyond Positivism', in *idem, Strategies of Political Inquiry* (Beverly Hills: Sage).

Ostrom, E. (1990) *Governing the Commons* (New York: Cambridge).

Ó Tuathail, G. (1996) *Critical Geopolitics: The Politics of Writing Global Space* (London, Routledge).

Ougaard, M. and Higgott, R. (2002) 'Introduction', in *idem* (eds), *Towards a Global Polity* (London: Routledge).

Outshoorn, Joyce (2004) 'Introduction: Prostitution, Women's Movements and Democratic Politics', in *idem* (ed.), *The Politics of Prostitution: Women's Movements, Democratic States and the Globalisation of Sex Commerce* (Cambridge: Cambridge University Press).

Painter, M. and Pierre, J. (eds) (2004) *Challenges to Policy Capacity* (Basingstoke and New York: Palgrave Macmillan).

Palmer, P. (1983) 'White Women/Black Women: The Dualism of Female Identity and Experience in the United States', *Feminist Studies*, 9(1).

Pareto, V. (1935) *The Mind and Society* (London: Cape).

Pareto, V. (1966) *Sociological Writings* (London: Pall Mall).

Paterson, M. (2000) *Understanding Global Environmental Politics: Domination, Accumulation, Resistance.* (Basingstoke and New York: Palgrave Macmillan).

Paterson, M. (2001) 'Green Politics', in Scott Burchill *et al., Theories of International Relations* (London: Palgrave).

Paul, E., Miller, F. and Paul, J. (eds) (1997) *Self-Interest* (Cambridge: Cambridge University Press).

Pauly, L. and Grande, E. (forthcoming) *Complex Sovereignty* (Toronto: University of Toronto Press).

Peters, B. G. (2002) 'The Future of Governance: Bringing the State Back In – Again', in J. Moon and B. Stone (eds), *Power and Freedom in Modern Politics* (Perth: University of Western Australia Press).

Peters, B. G. (2004) 'Back to the Centre: Rebuilding the State', *Political Quarterly*, 75, special issue: 130–40.

Pettman, J. J. (1996) 'An International Political Economy of Sex?' in E. Kofman and G. Youngs (eds), *Globalization: Theory and Practice* (London: Pinter).

Pettman, J. J. (1999) 'Globalization and the Gendered Politics of Citizenship', in Nira Yuval-Davis and Pnina Werbner (eds), *Women, Citizenship and Difference* (London and New York: Zed Books).

Phillips, Anne (1998) 'Introduction', in *idem* (ed.), *Feminism and Politics* (Oxford: Oxford University Press).

Pierce, R. (2004) 'Clemenson Revisited – the Rise and Fall of the Great English Landowner?' *Policy Studies*, 25(4): 1–17.

Pierre, J. (2000) 'Introduction: Understanding Governance', in *idem*. (ed.), *Debating Governance* (Oxford: Oxford University Press).

Pierre, J. and Peters, B. G. (2000) *Governance, Politics and the State* (Basingstoke and New York: Palgrave Macmillan).

Pierre, J. and Peters, B. G. (2004) *Governing Complex Societies* (Basingstoke and New York: Palgrave Macmillan).

Pierson, C. (1996) *The Modern State* (London: Routledge).

Pierson, Paul (1994) *Dismantling the Welfare State?* (Cambridge: Cambridge University Press).

Pierson, Paul (2004) *Politics in Time: History, Institutions, and Social Analysis* (Princeton: Princeton University Press).

Piven, F. F. and Cloward, R. A. (1989) *Why Americans Don't Vote* (New York: Pantheon).

Poggi, G. (1990) *The State: Its Nature, Development and Prospects* (Cambridge : Polity Press).

Polanyi, K. (1944 [1957]). *The Great Transformation: The Political and Economic Origins of Our Time* (Boston: Beacon Books).

Pollack, Mark (1997) 'Delegation, Agency, and Agenda Setting in the European Community', *International Organization*, 51(1): 99–134.

Pollitt, C. (2004) 'Castles Built on Sand? Agencies in Latvia', in C. Pollitt and C. Talbot (eds), *Unbundled Government: A Critical Analysis of the Global Trend to Agencies, Quangos and Contractualisation* (London: Routledge).

Pollitt, C. and Talbot, C. (2004) *Unbundled Government: A Critical Analysis of the Global Trend to Agencies, Quangos and Contractualisation* (London: Routledge).

Pollock, A. Shaoul, J., Rowland, D. and Player, S. (2001) *Public Services and the Private Sector* (London: Catalyst).

Polsby, N. (1960) 'How to Study Community Power: the Pluralists Alternative', *Journal of Politics*, 22: 474–84.

Polsby, N. (1963) *Community Power and Democratic Theory* (New Haven, CT: Yale University Press).

Polsby, N. (1980) *Community Power and Political Theory* (New Haven, CT: Yale University Press).

Posen, B. R. (2003) 'Command of the Commons. The Military Foundation of US Hegemony', *International Security*, 28(1): 5–46.

Poulantzas, N. (1969) 'The Problems of the Capitalist State', *New Left Review*, 58: 67–78; reprinted in R. Blackburn (ed.) (1972) *Ideology in Social Science* (London: Fontana).

Poulantzas, N. (1976) 'The Capitalist State: A Reply to Miliband and Laclau', *New Left Review*, 95: 63–83.

Poulantzas, Nicos (1978) *State, Power, Socialism* (London: New Left Books).

Pressman, J. L. and Wildavsky, A. (1976) *Implementation* (Berkeley: University of California Press).

Pringle, R. and Watson, S. (1990) 'Fathers, Brothers, Mates: The Fraternal State in Australia', in Sophie Watson (ed.), *Playing the State* (London: Verso).

Pringle, R. and Watson, S. (1992) '"Women's Interests" and the Post-Structuralist State', in Michele Barrett and Anne Phillips (eds), *Destabilizing Theory* (Cambridge: Polity Press).

Programme of the German Green Party (1983) (London: Heretic).

Prügl, Elisabeth and Meyer, Mary K. (1999) 'Gender Politics in Global Governance', in *idem* (eds), *Gender Politics in Global Governance* (Lanham, Md: Rowman & Littlefield).

Przeworski, A. (1991) *Democracy and the Market* (Cambridge: Cambridge University Press).

Przeworski, A. and Teune, H. (1970) *The Logic of Comparative Social Inquiry.* (New York: Wiley).

Putnam, R. (1993) 'The Prosperous Community: Social Capital and Public Life', *The American Prospect*, Spring: 35–42.

Raab, C. (2001) 'Understanding Policy Networks: A Comment on Marsh and Smith', *Political Studies*, 49: 551–6.

Raaum, N. (1995) 'The Political Representation of Women: A Bird's Eye View', in Lauri Karvonen and Per Selle (eds), *Women in Nordic Politics* (Aldershot, Hants: Dartmouth Publishing Company).

Radealli, C. (2003) *The Open Method of Coordination: A New Governance Architecture for the European Union* (Stockholm: Swedish Institute for European Policy Studies).

Rai, S. (1996) 'Women and the State in the Third World: Some Issues for Debate', in Shirin Rai and Geraldine Lievesley (eds), *Women and the State: International Perspectives* (London: Taylor & Francis).

Rai, S. (2003) 'Institutional Mechanisms for the Advancement of Women: Mainstreaming Gender, Democratising the State?' in Shirin Rai (ed.), *Mainstreaming Gender: Democratising the State? Institutional Mechanisms for the Advancement of Women* (Manchester: Manchester University Press).

Rai, S. and Lievesley, G. (eds) (1996) *Women and the State: International Perspectives* (London: Taylor & Francis).

Randall, V. (1998) 'Gender and Power: Women Engage the State', in Vicky Randall and Georgina Waylen (eds), *Gender, Politics and the State* (London: Routledge).

Randall, V. (2002) 'Feminism', in David Marsh and Gerry Stoker (eds), *Theories and Methods in Political Science*, 2nd edn (Basingstoke and New York: Palgrave Macmillan).

Ratner, S. and Altman, J.(1964) *John Dewey and Arthur F. Bentley: A Philosophical Correspondence* (New Brunswick: Rutgers University Press).

Rawls, J. (1973) *A Theory of Justice* (Oxford: Clarendon Press).

Rawls, J. (1996) *Political Liberalism* (New York: Columbia University Press).

Rawnsley, A. (1998), *Servants of the People* (Harmondsworth: Penguin).

Rees, Teresa (1998) *Mainstreaming Equality in the European Union* (London: Routledge).

Reich, R. B. (1991) *The Work of Nations: Preparing Ourselves for 21st-Century Capitalism* (New York: Knopf).

Rein, M. and Schön, D. A. (1991). 'Frame-Reflective Policy Discourse', in P. Wagner *et al.* (eds), *Social Sciences, Modern States, National Experiences, and Theoretical Crossroads* (Cambridge: Cambridge University Press).

Reinicke, W. H. (2000) 'The Other World-wide Web: Global Public Policy Networks', *Foreign Policy*, 117: 44–57.

Rhodes, M. (1997) 'The Welfare State: Internal Challenges, External Constraints', in M. Rhodes, P. Heywood and V. Wright (ed.), *Developments in West European Politics* (Basingstoke and New York: Palgrave Macmillan).

Rhodes, R. (1994), 'The Hollowing Out of the State', *Political Quarterly*, 65: 138–51.

Rhodes, R. (1997) *Understanding Governance* (Milton Keynes: Open University Press).

Rhodes, R. A. W. (1996) 'The New Governance: Governing Without Governance', *Political Sudies*, 44, 652–67.

Rhodes, R. A. W. and Weller, P. (1999) *The Changing World of Top Officials: Mandarins or Valets?* (Oxford: Oxford University Press).

Richardson, J. and Jordan, A. (1979) *Governing under Pressure* (Oxford: Martin Robertson).

Riker, W. (1980) 'Implications from the disequilibrium of majority rule for the study of institutions', *American Political Science Review*, 75: 432–47.

Riker, W. (1982) *Liberalism Against Populism* (San Francisco: Freeman).

Riker, W. and Ordeshook, P. (1968) 'A Theory of the Calculus of Voting', *American Political Science Review*, 62: 25–42.

Rima, I. (1996) *Development of Economic Analysis* (London: Routledge).

Ripley, R. and Franklin, G. (1984) *Congress, the Bureaucracy and Public Policy* (Homewood, IL.: Dorsey).

Risse, T. (2001) 'Who Are We? A Europeanization of National Identities?' in Maria Green Cowles, James Caporaso and Thomas Risse (eds), *Europeanization and Domestic Change*. (Ithaca, NY: Cornell University Press).

Robertson, R. (1992) *Globalisation: Social Theory and Global Culture* (London: Sage).

Rodrik, D. (1997) *Has Globalization Gone Too Far?* (Washington, DC: Institute of International Economics).

Rogoff, K. (1985) 'The Optimal Degree of Commitment to an Intermediate Target', *Quarterly Journal of Economics*, 100: 1169–90.

Rosamond, B. (2002) 'Imaging the European Economy: "Competitiveness" and the Social Construction of "Europe" as an Economic Space, *New Political Economy*, 7(2): 157–77.

Rose, N. (1996) 'Governing "Advanced" Liberal Democracies', in Andrew Barry *et al.* (eds), *Foucault and Political Reason: Liberalism, Neo-Liberalism and Rationalities of Government* (London: UCL Press).

Rose, N. (1999) *Powers of Freedom: Reframing Political Thought*, Cambridge, Cambridge University Press.

Rose, N. and Miller, P. (1992), 'Political Power beyond the State: Problematics of Government', *British Journal of Sociology*, 43(2): 172–205.

Rose, R. (1974) *The Problem of Party Government* (Basingstoke: Palgrave Macmillan).

Rose, R. (1990) 'Inheritance Before Choice in Public Policy', *Journal of Theoretical Politics*, 2(3): 263–91.

Rosecrance, R. (1999) *The Rise of the Virtual State* (New York: Basic Books).

Rosenau, J. (2004) 'Huge Demand, Over-Supply: Governance in an Emerging Epoch', in Bache, I. and Flinders, M. (eds), *Multi-Level Governance* (Oxford: Oxford University Press).

Rosenau, J. N. (1990) *Turbulence in World Politics: A Theory of Change and Continuity* (Princeton: Princeton University Press).

Rosenau, J. N. (1992) 'Governance, Order and Change in World Politics', in J. Rosenau and E. O. Czempiel (eds), *Governance with Government* (Cambridge: Cambridge University Press).

Rosenau, J. N. (1993) 'Citizenship in a changing global order', in J. N. Rosenau and E.-O. Czempiel (eds), *Governance without Government: Order and Change in World Politics* (Cambridge: Cambridge University Press).

Rosenau, J. N. (1997) *Along the Domestic–Foreign Frontier: Exploring Governance in a Turbulent World* (Cambridge: Cambridge University Press).

Rosenberg, A. (1995) *The Philosophy of Social Science* (Boulder, CO: Westview Press).

Routlege, P. (1998) *Gordon Brown* (London: Simon & Schuster).

Rowley, C. and Tullock, G. (1988) 'Introduction', in Rowley, C., Tollison, R. and Tullock, G. (eds), *The Political Economy of Rent Seeking* (Boston: Kluwer Academic).

Ruggie, J. (1998) 'What Makes the World Hang Together? Neo-Utilitarianism and the Social Constructivist Challenge', *International Organization*, 52(4): 855–85.

Rugman, A. (2000) *The End of Globalisation* (London: Random House).

Rutherford, P. (1999) 'The Entry of Life into History', in Eric Darier (ed.), *Discourses of the Environment* (Oxford: Blackwell).

Sabatier, P. and Jenkins-Smith, H. C. (eds) (1993) *Policy Change and Learning: An Advocacy Coalition Approach* (Boulder, CO: Westview).

Sachs, W. (1999) *Planet Dialectics: Explorations in Environment and Development* (London: Zed Books).

Sagoff, M. (1988) *The Economy of the Earth,: Philosophy, Law and the Environment* (Cambridge: Cambridge University Press).

Sahlins, M. (1974) *Stone Age Economics* (London: Tavistock).

Salamon, L. M. (2002) Introduction, in *idem*, (ed.), *Handbook of Policy Instruments* (New York: Oxford University Press).

Sampson, A. (1962) *The Anatomy of Britain* (London: Hodder & Stoughton).

Sampson, A. (1965) *The Anatomy of Britain Today* (London: Hodder & Stoughton).

Sampson, A. (1971) *The New Anatomy of Britain* (London: Hodder & Stoughton).

Sampson, A. (1982) *The Changing Anatomy of Britain* (London: Hodder & Stoughton).

Sanderson, J. (1963) 'Marx and Engels on the State', *Western Political Quarterly*, December 16(4): 946–55.

Sandler, T. (2001) *Economic Concepts for the Social Sciences* (Cambridge: Cambridge University Press).

Sargent, Lydia (1981) 'New Left Women and Men: The Honeymoon is Over', in *idem* (ed.), *Women and Revolution: The Unhappy Marriage of Marxism and Feminism* (London: Pluto Press).

Saurin, J. (1994) 'Global Environmental Degradation, Modernity and Environmental Knowledge', in Caroline Thomas (ed.), *Rio: Unravelling the Consequences* (London: Frank Cass).

Sawer, M. (1990) *Sisters in Suites: Women and Public Policy in Australia* (Sydney: Allen & Unwin).

Sawer, M. (1991) 'Why has the Australian Women's Movement Had More Influence on Government in Australia than Elsewhere?' in Francis Castles (ed.), *Australia Compared* (Sydney: Allen & Unwin).

Scharpf, F. W. (1991) *Crisis and Choice in Social Democracy* (Ithaca, NY: Cornell University Press).

Scharpf, F. W. (1997) *Games Real Actors Play: Actor-Centered Institutionalism in Policy Research* (Boulder, CO: Westview Press).

Scharpf, F. W. (1996) 'Negative and Positive Integration in the Political Economy of European Welfare States', G. Marks, F. W. Scharpf, P. C. Schmitter and W. Streek (eds), *Governance in the European Union* (London: Sage).

Scharpf, F. W. (1999) *Governing in Europe* (Oxford: Oxford University Press).

Scharpf, F. W. (2000) *Governing in Europe* (Oxford: Oxford University Press).

Schattschneider, E. (1935) *Politics, Pressures and the Tariff* (Englewood Cliffs, NJ: Prentice-Hall).

Schmidt, V. A. (2000) 'Values and Discourse in the Politics of Adjustment', in Fritz W. Scharpf and Vivien A. Schmidt (eds), *Welfare and Work in the Open Economy*, Volume I: *From Vulnerability to Competitiveness,* (Oxford: Oxford University Press).

Schmidt, V. A. (2002) *The Futures of European Capitalism* (Oxford: Oxford University Press).

Schmidt, V. A. (2004) 'The European Union: Democratic Legitimacy in a Regional State?', *Journal of Common Market Studies*, 42 (5), 975–97.

Schmidt, V. A. and Radaelli, C. (2004) 'Policy Change and Discourse in Europe: Conceptual and Methodological Issues', *West European Politics*, 27 (2): 183–210.

Schmitter, P. (1985) 'Neo-Corporatism and the State', in W. Grant (ed.), *The Political Economy of Corporatism* (Basingstoke and New York: Palgrave Macmillan).

Schmitter, P. C. and Grote, J. R. (1997) *The Corporate Sisyphus: Past, Present and Future* (Florence: European University Institute).

Scholte, J. A. (2000) *Globalization: A Critical Introduction* (Basingstoke and New York: Palgrave Macmillan).

Schumacher, E. F. (1976) *Small is Beautiful* (London: Sphere).

Scott, J. (1991) *Who Rules Britain?* (Cambridge: Polity Press).

Scott, J. C (1998) *Seeing Like a State: How Certain Schemes to Improve the Human Condition Have Failed* (New Haven and London: Yale University Press).

Self, P. (1993) *Government by the Market* (Basingstoke: Palgrave Macmillan).

Selznick, P. (2002) *The Communitarian Persuasion* (Washington, DC: Woodrow Wilson Center).

Sen, A. (2002) *Rationality and Freedom* (Cambridge, MA: Harvard University Press).

Shapiro, M. (1997) 'The Problems of Independent Agencies in the United States and the European Union', *Journal of European Public Policy*, 4(2): 276–91.

Shennan, J. (1974) *The Origins of the Modern European State, 1450–1725* (London: Hutchinson).

Shepsle, K. (1986) 'Institutional Equilibrium and Equilibrium Institutions', in Herbert F. Weisburg (ed.) *Political Science: The Science of Politics* (New York: Agathon).

Siim, B. (1988) 'Towards a Feminist Rethinking of the Welfare State', in Kathleen Jones and Anna Jónasdóttir (eds), *The Political Interests of Gender* (Oxford: Sage).

Siim, B. (2000) *Gender and Citizenship: Politics and Agency in France, Britain and Denmark* (Cambridge: Cambridge University Press).

Singleton, G. (1990) *The Accord and the Australian Labour Movement* (Melbourne: Melbourne University Press).

Skidelsky, R. (1992) *John Maynard Keynes: The Economist as Saviour* (Basingstoke: Macmillan).

Skinner, Q. (1978) *The Foundations of Modern Political Thought*. Volume 1: *The Renaissance* (Cambridge: Cambridge University Press).

Skinner, Q. (1989) 'The State', in T. Ball *et al.* (eds), *Political Innovation and Conceptual Change* (Cambridge: Cambridge University Press).

Skocpol, T. (1979) *States and Social Revolutions* (Cambridge: Cambridge University Press).

Skowrenek, S. (1995) *The Politics Presidents Make: Leadership from John Adams to George Bush* (Cambridge, MA: Harvard University Press).

Slaughter, A.-M. (1997) 'The Real New World Order', *Foreign Affairs*, 76(5): 183–98.

Slaughter, A.-M. (2004) *A New World Order* (Princeton: Princeton University Press).

Smart, C. (1989) *Feminism and the Power of Law* (London: Routledge).

Smith, A. (1759 [1976]) *The Theory of Moral Sentiments* (Oxford: Clarendon Press).

Smith, A. (1776 [1983]), *The Wealth of Nations* (Oxford: Oxford University Press).

Smith, M. A. (1990) 'Pluralism, Reformed Pluralism and Neo-Pluralism: The Role of Pressure Groups in Policy Making', *Political Studies*, 38: 302–22.

Smith, N. J.-A. (2003) 'Discourses of globalisation and European integration in the Irish Republic', paper presented to UACES Annual Conference, University of Newcastle, 2–4 September 2003.

Smith, N. J.-A. (2005) *Showcasing Globalisation? The Political Economy of the Irish Republic* (Manchester: Manchester University Press).

Somit, A. and Tanenhaus, J. (1982) *The Development of American Political Science from Burgess to Behavioralism* (New York: Irvington).

Sørensen, G. (2004) *The Transformation of the State: Beyond the Myth of Retreat* (Basingstoke and New York: Palgrave Macmillan).

Soysal, Y. N. (1994) *Limits of Citizenship: Migrants and Postnational Membership in Europe* (Chicago: University of Chicago Press).

Spretnak, C. and Capra, F. (1985) *Green Politics: The Global Promise* (London: Paladin).

Squires, J. (2004) 'Politics Beyond Boundaries? A Feminist Perspective', in Adrian Leftwich (ed.), *What is Politics?* (Cambridge: Polity Press).

Stears, M. (2002) *Progressives, Pluralists and the Problems of the State* (Oxford: Oxford University Press).

Steinmo, S. Thelen, K. and Longstreth, F. (eds) (1992) *Structuring Politics: Historical Institutionalism in Comparative Analysis* (Cambridge: Cambridge University Press).

Stephens, G. (1991) 'On the Critique of Rational Choice', *PS: Political Science and Politics*, 24: 429–31.

Stetson, D. (2001) *Abortion Politics, Women's Movements and the Democratic State: A Comparative Study of State Feminism* (Oxford: Oxford University Press).

Stetson, D. and Mazur, A. (1995) 'Introduction', in *idem* (eds) (1995), *Comparative State Feminism* (London: Sage).

Stiglitz, G. (1996) *Whither Socialism?* (Cambridge, MA: MIT Press).

Stiglitz, J. E. (1997) *Economics*, 2nd edn (New York: W. W. Norton & Co).

Stoker, G. and Mossberger, K. (1994), 'Urban Regime Theory in Comparative Perspective', in *Environment and Planning: Government and Policy*, 12: 195–212.

Stone, C. (1989) *Regime Politics: Governing Atlanta 1946–1988* (Lawrence: University Press of Kansas).

Strange, S. (1996) *The Retreat of the State: The Diffusion of Power in the World Economy* (New York: Cambridge University Press).

Stretton, H. and Orchard, L. (1994) *Public Goods, Public Enterprise, Public Choice* (Basingstoke and New York: Palgrave Macmillan).

Sweezy, P. (1942) *The Theory of Capitalist Development* (New York: Monthly Review Press).

Talbot, C. (2004) 'A Radical Departure? Executive Agencies in Jamaica', in C. Pollitt and C. Talbot (eds), *Unbundled Government: A Critical Analysis of the Global Trend to Agencies, Quangos and Contractualisation* (London: Routledge).

Tanzi, V. and Schuknecht, L. (2000) *Public Spending in the Twentieth Century* (Cambridge: Cambridge University Press).

Tarrow, S. (1998) *Power in Movement: Social Movements and Contentious Politics* (Cambridge: Cambridge University Press).

Taylor, C. (1967) 'Neutrality in Political Science', in Alan Ryan (ed.), *The Philosophy of Social Explanation* (London: Oxford University Press).

Taylor, C. (1985) *Philosophy and the Human Sciences* (Cambridge: Cambridge University Press).

Taylor, M. (1987) *The Possibility of Cooperation* (Cambridge: Cambridge University Press).

Thatcher, M. (1993) *The Downing Street Years* (London: HarperCollins).

The Ecologist (1972) *Blueprint for Survival* (Harmondsworth: Penguin).

The Ecologist (1993) *Whose Common Future? Reclaiming the Commons* (London: Earthscan).

Thelen, K. (2003) 'How Institutions Evolve: Insights from Comparative Historical Analysis', in James Mahoney and Dietrich Ruschemeyer (eds), *Comparative Historical Analysis in the Social Sciences* (New York: Cambridge University Press).

Thelen, K. (2004) *How Institutions Evolve: The Political Economy of Skills in Germany, Britain, the United States, and Japan* (New York: Cambridge University Press).

Thelen, K. (1999) 'Historical Institutionalism in Comparative Politics', in *The Annual Review of Political Science* (Palo Alto, CA: Annual Reviews, Inc.).

Thiel, S. van (2001) *Quangos: Trends, Causes, Consequences* (London : Ashgate).

Thompson, G. (2003) *Between Hierarchies and Markets: The Logic and Limits of Network Forms of Organization* (Oxford: Oxford University Press).

Thompson, G., Frances, J., Levacic, R. and Mitchell, J. (eds) (1991) *Markets, Hierarchies and Networks: The Coordination of Social Life* (London: Sage).

Thomson, J. E. and Krasner, S. D. (1989). 'Global Transactions and the Consolidation of Sovereignty', in E.-O. Czempiel and J. N. Rosenau (eds), *Global Changes and*

Theoretical Challenges. Approaches to World Politics for the 1990s (Lexington, MA: Lexington Books).

Tihonen, S. (2004) *From Governing to Governance* (Tampere: University of Tampere Press).

Tilly, C. (ed.) (1975) *The Formation of National States in Western Europe* (Princeton, NJ: Princeton University Press).

Tilly, Charles (1990) *Coercion, Capital and European States, AD 990–1992* (Oxford: Basil Blackwell).

Tollison, R. (1997) 'Rent-Seeking', in D. Mueller (ed.), *Perspectives on Public Choice* (Cambridge: Cambridge University Press).

Torfing, J. (1991) 'A Hegemony Approach to Capitalist Regulation', in R. B. Bertramsen, J. P. F. Thomsen and J. Torfing (eds), *State, Economy and Society* (London: Unwin Hyman).

Torgerson, D. (1999) *The Promise of Green Politics: Environmentalism and the Public Sphere* (London: Duke University Press).

Towns, A. (2002) 'Paradoxes of (In)Equality: Something is Rotten in the Gender Equal State of Sweden', in *Cooperation and Conflict*, 37(2): 157–79.

Truman, D. (1951a) *The Governmental Process* (New York: Alfred A. Knopf).

Truman, D. (1951b) 'The Implications of Political Behavior Research', Social Science Research Council *Items* (December): 37–9.

Tsebelis, G. (2002) *Veto Players: How Political Institutions Work* (Princeton: Princeton University Press).

Tullock, G. (1967) 'The Welfare Costs of Monopolies, Tariffs and Theft', *Western Economic Journal*, 5: 224–32.

Tullock, G. (1976) *The Vote Motive* (London: Institute of Economic Affairs).

Tullock, G. (1989) *The Economics of Special Privilege and Rent Seeking* (Boston: Kluwer Academic).

Tullock, G. (1990) *The Economics of Special Privilege*, in J. Alt and K. Shepsle (eds), *Perspectives on Positive Political Economy* (Cambridge: Cambridge University Press).

UNCTAD (1993) *World Investment Report 1993: Transnational Corporations and Integrated International Production* (New York: United Nations).

Viroli, M. (1992) *From Politics to Reason of State: The Acquisition and Transformation of the Language of Politics, 1250–1600* (Cambridge: Cambridge University Press).

Visser, J. and P. Hemerijk (1999) *A Dutch Miracle* (Amsterdam University Press).

Visvanathan, N., Duggan, L., Nisonoff, L. and Wiegersma, N. (eds) (1997) *The Women, Gender and Development Reader* (London: Zed Books).

Vitols, S. and Casper, S. (1997) 'The German model in the 1990s: problems and prospects', *Industry and Innovation*, 4(1): 1–14.

Vogler, J. (2003) 'Taking Institutions Seriously: How Regime Analysis Can Be Relevant to Multilevel Environmental Governance', *Global Environmental Politics*, 3: (2) 25–39.

Wade, R. (1996) 'Globalisation and its Limits: Reports of the Death of the National Economy are Greatly Exaggerated', in S. Berger and R. P. Dore (eds), *National Diversity and Global Capitalism* (London: Cornell University Press).

Wahl, J. (1925) *Pluralist Philosophies of England and America* (London: Open Court Company).

Wahlke, John C. (1979) 'Pre-Behavioralism in Political Science', *American Political Science Review*, 73: 19.

Wainwright, H. (1993) *Arguments for a New Left* (Oxford: Basil Blackwell).

Walby, S. (1992) 'Post-Post-Modernism? Theorizing Social Complexity' in Michèle Barrett and Anne Phillips (eds), *Destabilizing Theory* (Cambridge: Polity Press).

Walker, J. (1989) 'Introduction: Policy Communities as Global Phenomena', *Governance*, 2:1–4.

Walker, R. B. J. (1993) *Inside/Outside: International Relations as Political Theory* (Cambridge: Cambridge University Press).

Walsh, J. I. (2000) 'When do Ideas Matter? Explaining the Successes and Failures of Thatcherite Ideas', *Comparative Political Studies*, 33(4), 483–516.

Waltz, K. N. (1979) *Theory of International Politics* (Reading, PA: Addison-Wesley).

Walzer, M. (2001) 'Nation States and Immigrant Societies', in W. Kymlicka and M. Opalski (eds), *Can Liberal Pluralism be Exported?* (Oxford: Oxford University Press).

Watson, M. and Hay, C. (2003) 'The Discourse of Globalisation and the Logic of No Alternative: Rendering the Contingent Necessary in the Political Economy of New Labour', *Policy & Politics*, 31(3): 289–305.

Watson, Sophie (1990) 'The State of Play: An Introduction', in *idem* (ed.), *Playing the State* (London: Verso).

Watson, Sophie (1992) 'Femocratic Feminism', in Mike Savage and Anne Witz (eds), *Gender and Bureaucracy* (Oxford: Blackwell).

Waylen, G. (1998) 'Gender, Feminism and the State: an Overview', in Vicky Randall and Georgina Waylen (eds), *Gender, Politics and the State* (London: Routledge).

WCED (1987) *Our Common Future: Report of the World Commission on Environment and Development* (Oxford: Oxford University Press).

Weber, M. (1925/1978) *Economy and Society: An Outline of Interpretative Sociology* (Berkeley, CA: University of California Press).

Weingast, B. (1995) 'A Rational Choice Perspective on the Role of Ideas: Shared Belief Systems, State Sovereignty, and International Cooperation', *Politics and Society*, 23(4) 449–64.

Weingest, B. and Marshall, W. (1988) 'The Industrial Organisation of Congress: or, Why Legislatures, Like Firms, are not Organised as Markets', *Journal of Political Economy*, 96: 132–63.

Weiss, L. (1998) *The Myth of the Powerless State: Governing the Economy in a Global Era* (Cambridge: Polity Press).

Weiss, L. (2003) *States in the Global Economy: Bringing Domestic Institutions Back In* (Cambridge: Cambridge University Press).

Wendt, Alexander (1987) 'The Agent–Structure Problem in International Relations Theory', *International Organization*, 41(3): 335–70.

Wendt, Alexander (1999) *Social Theory of International Relations Theory* (Cambridge: Cambridge University Press).

White, H. (1987) *The Content of the Form: Narrative Discourse and Historical Representation* (Baltimore: Johns Hopkins University Press).

Wiarda, H. J. (1996) *Corporatism and Comparative Politics: The Other Great Ism* (Armonk, NY: M. E. Sharpe).

Williamson, O. (1985) *The Economic Institutions of Capitalism* (New York: Free Press).

Wilson, R. (1999) 'The Civil Service in the New Millennium', speech given at City University, London, 5 May 1999.

Wittgenstein, L. (1958) *Philosophical Investigations* (Oxford, Blackwell).

Wolfe, A. (1974) 'New Directions in the Marxist Theory of Politics', *Politics and Society*, 4(2), 131–60.

Wolfe, A. (1977) *The Limits of Legitimacy: Political Contradictions of Late Capitalism* (New York: Free Press).

Wright, V. and Hayward, J. (2000) 'Governing from the Centre: Policy Co-ordination in Six European Core Executives', in R. A. W. Rhodes (ed.), *Transforming British Government*: Volume 2: *Changing Roles and Relationships* (Basingstoke and New York: Palgrave Macmillan).

Wriston, W. B. (1992) *The Twilight of Sovereignty: How the Information Revolution is Transforming Our World* (New York: Charles Scribner).

www.worldbank.org/wbi/governance

Young, I. M. (1981) 'Beyond the Unhappy Marriage: A Critique of the Dual-Systems Theory', in Lydia Sargent (ed.), *Women and Revolution: The Unhappy Marriage of Marxism and Feminism* (London: Pluto Press).

Youngs, G. (2000) 'Breaking Patriarchal Bonds: Demythologizing the Public–Private', in Marianne Marchand and Anne Sisson Runyan (eds), *Gender and Global Restructuring* (London and New York: Routledge).

Zacher, M. V. (1992) 'The decaying pillars of the Westphalian temple: implications for international order and governance', in J. N. Rosenau and E.-O. Czempiel (eds), *Governance without Government: Order and Change in World Politics* (Cambridge: Cambridge University Press).

Zürn, Michael, (1999) 'The State in this Post National Constellation – Societal Denationalisation and Multilevel Governance', *Arena Working Papers*, WP 99'/35

Zysman, J. (1994) 'How Institutions Create Historically Rooted Trajectories of Growth', *Industrial and Corporate Change*, 3, (1): 243–83.

Author Index

Subject Index